Second Edition

THE TERRORISTS OF
IRAQ

Inside the Strategy and Tactics
of the Iraq Insurgency
2003–2014

Second Edition

THE TERRORISTS OF
IRAQ

Inside the Strategy and Tactics
of the Iraq Insurgency
2003–2014

Malcolm W. Nance

CRC Press
Taylor & Francis Group
Boca Raton London New York

CRC Press is an imprint of the
Taylor & Francis Group, an **informa** business

CRC Press
Taylor & Francis Group
6000 Broken Sound Parkway NW, Suite 300
Boca Raton, FL 33487-2742

Version Date: 20140818

International Standard Book Number-13: 978-1-4987-0689-6 (Hardback)

Library of Congress Cataloging-in-Publication Data

Nance, Malcolm W.
    The terrorists of Iraq : inside the strategy and tactics of the Iraq insurgency 2003-2014 / Malcolm W. Nance. -- 2nd edition.
        pages cm
    Summary: "This highly decorated and highly visible author is revising his first edition of The Terrorists of Iraq in the wake of the most recent turmoil effecting the country. His new edition contains valuable insight to many of the terrorist groups in the region including ISIS, which is being talked about on nearly every news outlet today. The book will continue to draw on the historical analyses, examinations of organizations/weapons/strategy & tactics, and policy recommendations included in the first edition- but, will add valuable insight learned from the most recent crisis and the changes that have occurred in the last 6 years since its publication. "-- Provided by publisher.
    Includes bibliographical references and index.
    ISBN 978-1-4987-0689-6 (hardback)
    1. Iraq--History--2003- 2. Insurgency--Iraq. 3. Terrorism--Iraq. I. Title.

DS79.76.N355 2014
956.7044'3--dc23   2014030285

Visit the Taylor & Francis Web site at
http://www.taylorandfrancis.com

and the CRC Press Web site at
http://www.crcpress.com

Dedicated in Memory
of My Friends Who Gave Their Lives in Iraq

Tracy Hushin
Fabrizio Quattrocchi
Captain Travis Patriquin
Nick Pears
John Dolman

Contents

SECTION II   KNIFE FIGHT IN A PHONE BOOTH— BRINGING ON THE INSURGENCY

Acknowledgments

How did this book come about? It originated with an event that cost four people, including one of the people I dedicated this book to, their lives. In late December 2003, I created four simple rules, and my British, Iraqi, and American security teams needed them to survive the ride from the Baghdad International Airport, also known as BIAP, to the protected Green Zone. At the time it was the single most dangerous road in Iraq—Route IRISH. The rules were:

1. *Never* follow a U.S. Army convoy. If a team sees a convoy leaving the airport, they should stop at the airport gate, wait 20 minutes, and listen for the explosions and gunfire that are sure to come. The harsh reality is that once a convoy is attacked, the next convoy is generally safe.
2. Stagger the convoy with the VIP's vehicle in the left lane and the blocking car with additional bodyguards on the right. The blocking car's position is to take the brunt of the explosions or bullets that almost always come from the Hayy al-Jihad neighborhood to the south side of the road.
3. Minimum speed is 100 mph. Driving in Iraq, there is always safety in speed. Bombs are hard to trigger, and guns are hard to aim when you are moving 7 tons of armored car at 100 mph.
4. No runs to or from the airport at night.

Route IRISH was a killer road. Every advantage was necessary to avoid dying in an insurgent attack. The four lanes, 6 miles of straight protected road, were also known as the Death Drive and VBIED Valley for the route's numerous suicide car bombs and machine gun ambushes. For the first 4 years of the war, it was by far the single most dangerous road in Iraq. The most treacherous section was the 3 miles from the gate of the Green Zone to the gate of the airport. This section was patrolled but not secured by the U.S. Army, and most attacks occurred as civilian traffic was allowed to merge into the route at the Umm Taboulah

Mosque intersection, also known as the Spaghetti Junction, a cloverleaf of on and off ramps leading to Highway 8 and the main boulevards of West Baghdad. It was there that convoys going to and coming from the airport were exposed to the drive-by gun attacks, suicide bombers, and roadside bomb strikes. In real-life terms, it was just 3 minutes of sheer terror. Equally dangerous was the final approach to the airport main gate where nervous American soldiers kill with impunity. Drive a little too fast for their taste, miss the flashlights or hand signals, and you could be given a "terminal warning." Many people have died at this entryway within meters of relative safety, killed by soldiers who should have been their salvation but ended up as their slayers.

One morning in January 2005, a professional four-man personnel security detail (PSD) led by an experienced Kroll security company officer had no idea that when they left the BIAP there was a very slow U.S. Army convoy blocking the road near Spaghetti Junction. The army convoy composed of M-2 Bradley infantry fighting vehicles (IFVs) and armored Humvee jeeps had crept down this last section of the road and was not allowing anyone to pass, friendly or neutral. If forced, the crew in the armored Bradley would use its powerful 25 mm automatic cannon to destroy any vehicle that would try. Too many armor convoys had been hit in the invasion and post-war by suicide car bombs that would drive up at high speed and ram them. To the convoy gunners, everyone was a potential enemy, even Western bodyguard convoys. This policy, though it saved many soldiers' lives, often turned out to have tragic consequences for anyone nearby.

The Kroll team in two armored Toyota Land Cruisers raced down this most dangerous stretch of Route IRISH and closed rapidly on the highway bridge near the mosque. Heavily armored and equipped to stop machine gun bullets and light shrapnel, the SUVs looked like most other Land Cruisers, but were sturdily designed for the attacks that occur frequently in Iraq. In another mile, the two-vehicle convoy would be under the protective cover of the tanks at the Green Zone. Just another mile.

Tracy Hushin, a 36-year-old professional administrator from West Islip, New York, rode in the first armored Land Cruiser. A consummate professional, this Long Islander was the heart of the Bearing Point Corporation in Iraq; she was also a friend of mine. She had gone to the airport to pick up airline tickets so new Iraqi partners to the reconstruction project could fly to Jordan for training. On her return, she met a new British subcontractor to the Bearing Point team and was returning to the safety of the Green Zone, but found herself behind the extremely slow moving U.S. Army armored convoy. A rule for surviving Iraq had been broken and the punishment was death.

In the midst of the slowed traffic was a small sedan hovering behind the American convoy. As the armored SUVs merged into the slower civilian traffic, they were forced to pass this car at a significantly slower speed than was prudent. The occupants in the first Land Cruiser would never know that this little car was a human-guided bomb carrying over 1,000 pounds of high explosives in the four artillery shells that filled the trunk. It was driven by a suicide bomber recruited by Islamic extremists, most likely al-Qaeda in Iraq. He piloted a car custom modified to explode by members of the former regime's intelligence agencies. Nearby in a separate vehicle, an Iraqi insurgent watched the small sedan close on the Western security convoy, and when the suicide bomber was parallel, he pushed a cell phone detonator's CALL button, and the highway was engulfed in flame and steel. The Land Cruiser disintegrated with the car bomb. Tracy Hushin, the two Kroll bodyguards, and the British subcontractor were killed instantly.

We will never know if she saw the suicide bomber, but witnesses say the car bomb or, as the army calls it, a suicide vehicle-borne improvised explosive device (S-VBIED), blew up 1 meter away from the B-7-rated armored SUV. Though the news of Tracy's death devastated me, she was not the first friend I lost in Iraq. The year before, one of my Italian bodyguards, Fabrizio Quatrocchi, was kidnapped in Fallujah. His life was taken by an al-Qaeda terrorist, but he gave his life with such dignity he was awarded the Italian Gold Star—the highest award in Italy. My friend U.S. Army Capt. Travis Patriquin, an outstanding military linguist, Arabist, and contributor to this book, was also among the lost. He was killed in Ramadi in 2007 with a Marine officer while escorting journalists. He was renowned for his in-depth understanding of Arab culture and the tribes of Anbar Province. His efforts were praised from the *New York Times* to *Runner's World* magazine. A friend gave him the highest compliment a soldier could give: "He was good in the woods." It was from recognizing the sacrifice of these friends and those of the Kroll team that made writing this book a personal endeavor—it is written so we can understand the insurgency, and in understanding, we can help save the lives of others.

A formidable research team was assembled to analyze the information that spanned a decade. Chris Sampson, the media researcher at the Terror Asymmetrics Project on Strategy, Tactics, and Radical Ideologies (TAPSTRI) in Hudson, New York, led the way for the inclusion of all the data, media, and maps in the 2014 update. The bulk of the basic research was done by doctoral, graduate, and undergraduate students from the University of Pennsylvania, Macquarie University in Sydney, Australia, and Victoria University at Wellington, New Zealand. Students each contributed to the meticulous detail and depth of knowledge. The University of Pennsylvania research team included Bryan Fields, Laura Gassman,

Christina Alaimo, Elizabeth Ivester, and Josh Soros. Many Iraqis risked their lives over 2 years to collect and confirm much of the information, especially the Iraqi members of our Iraqi security company that operated for 10 years between Mosul, Baghdad, and Basrah. I cannot use their names out of concern for their immediate safety. I also thank the Italian husband and wife bodyguard team of Paulo Simeone and Valeria Castellani. They took the death of our friend and co-worker Fabrizio Quatrocchi harder than all of us.

I also thank many experts in the counterterrorism and security field who assisted me or gave sage advice, including Peter Bergen of CNN; Spencer Ackerman of the *Guardian*; Nir Rosen of the New America Foundation; Dr. Harlan Ullman of the Center for Naval Analysis; my good friend Tim Bowen, director of security at Bearing Point Corporation; Dr. Juan Cole, Warren Marik, and Dr. Ian Wing of the Australian Professional Intelligence Officers Association; Dr. Clive Williams and Dr. Anthony Bergin of the Australia Strategic Policy Institute; Dr. Jim Veitch and Rod Ryan, master sniper and director of Storm Mountain Training Center; Officer Deron Jackson of Washington, D.C., Metropolitan Police; Detective Nick Sabetta of the Connecticut State Police Counterterrorism Division; David P. Mitchell of U.S. Navy's Fleet Naval Air Forces; Nick North and Mark Overton of Naval Special Warfare Command; Rod Cowan, editor of *Security 360* magazine; Corwin Noble of Noble & Associates; Jeff Martini; Omar Hadi of Skylink; Jason Kichen; and the famous Iraqi oil smuggler, Captain Saad.

Many active duty and retired military contributors, mostly Iraq combat veterans, reality-checked the manuscript and facts. Thanks to those members of Advanced Tactical Services "Lightfighter" Tactical Forum (www.lightfighter.net): Chris Farina, Stephen Hilliard, Brad Nelson, Avi Jacobson, Aaron Bender, John Appel, Joe Settles, Frank Ostergaard, Nick Tat, Marc Jensen, Kyle P. Brengel, Bryan Reed, David Quinn, Erick Gelhaus, Eric Graves of Soldier Systems blog, Jason Crosby, Robb Krott, Iakovos D. Petropoulas, Kenneth Melendy, William Durning, and Patrick Kelly. Unnamed members of the military counterinsurgency, contractor, or intelligence community (aka Megaforce) include Clynch, Renee, and her husband, Casket; super spies Brandon and Rgrgordo; super soldiers Basicload, Brando, Dorsai, M4Guru, Rotorstrike, and Major Murphy; the battle-wounded DZhitshard and Brit PSD Argyll; the famous snipers Cyclops and SSGTJAYP; Charles from the French Marines; FROG from SOC.net; and our late brother Travis Patriquin.

My personal thanks go out to Macquarie University's Centre for Policing, Intelligence and Counterterrorism in Sydney, Australia, especially Director Peter Anderson, Sandra Bilson, Marianne Wright, and

Norwegian Ministry of Defense counterterrorism intelligence analyst Stina Backer-Roed. Finally, my deepest thanks go out to Maryse, my wife, who said that the need to understand the insurgency was critical to help bring it to an end. Her patience, expertise, and soothing presence in Iraq brought clarity to this updated edition.

About the Author

Malcolm W. Nance is a counterterrorism and intelligence consultant for the U.S. government's Special Operations, Homeland Security, and Intelligence agencies, with more than 33 years of experience in combatting radical extremism. An honorably retired U.S. Navy Arabic-speaking intelligence collections operator, field interrogator, and Survival, Evasion, Resistance, and Escape specialist, he spent two decades on clandestine antiterrorism and counterterrorism intelligence operations in the Middle East, North Africa, the Balkans, South Asia, and sub-Saharan Africa in direct support of the Special Operations and Intelligence Community. On the morning of 9/11, he eyewitnessed the attack on the Pentagon and became a first responder at the crash site.

A fierce champion of ethics and human rights in intelligence activities, he has trained and advised numerous defense, intelligence, and law enforcement agencies worldwide in understanding and exploiting terrorist strategies, tactics, and ideology to combat the spread of radical extremism. He has authored several books, including *The Terrorist Recognition Handbook: A Practitioner's Manual for Predicting and Identifying Terrorist Activity*; *An End to al-Qaeda: Destroying bin Laden's Jihad and Restoring America's Honor*; and *The Terrorists of Iraq: Inside the Strategy and Tactics of the Iraq Insurgency*.

Mr. Nance has been seen by millions of TV news viewers as a guest policy analyst for CNN, ABC News, FOX News, MSNBC, Al Jazeera, and Al Arabiya, and he has appeared on global interview shows including PBS's *NewsHour*, the BBC's *Hardtalk* and *World Have Your Say*, Australian Broadcasting's *Dateline*, German TV's *ZDF Frontier 21*, and other political talk shows. He has written opinion editorials and has been a source for the *New York Times*, *New York Daily News*, *International Herald Tribune*, *Atlanta Journal-Constitution*, *Washington Post*, *San Diego Union Tribune*, *Times of London*, *Guardian UK*, *Australian*, *Sydney Morning Herald (National)* (Abu Dhabi), and *Daily Telegraph*. He has written articles for distinguished magazines and publications, including *Foreign Policy*, *Security 360*, *Small Wars Journal*,

Counterterrorism, *Special Operations*, and *Counterterrorist*. He regularly speaks at the International Spy Museum in Washington, D.C.

Mr. Nance is a graduate of New York Excelsior University. He is presently executive director of TAPSTRI, the Terror Asymmetrics Project on Strategy, Tactics, and Radical Ideologies in Hudson, New York. He lives and studies between Hudson and Abu Dhabi, UAE.

Introduction

I first arrived in Iraq in late May 2003 to take over security for the largest American nongovernmental organization (NGO) in Iraq. It was a difficult job that ended a few months later when I was recruited to assume a high-level security management position in the Republican Palace of Ambassador L. Paul Bremer's Coalition Provisional Authority. My mission was to keep safe the hundreds of bankers, lawyers, and development experts running the Iraqi Treasury and Central Bank. To accomplish this, I used over 100 British and 250 Iraqi bodyguards as a wall of guns and armor against the insurgents who were hunting them. In late 2003, I established a small team of Iraqis, who worked at great personal risk to cull information on who was attacking military convoys, killing Iraqi civilian employees of the coalition, and destroying reconstruction infrastructure. In the illicit arms markets of Sadr City and Fallujah we recovered captured American weapons and personal effects of soldiers killed, and tried to collect information on specifically who was conducting anti-American attacks. As a former U.S. Navy intelligence operator specializing in the Middle East, I knew that for any of us to survive, my first mission was to study the tactics, techniques, and procedures of the Iraqi insurgents and al-Qaeda terrorists as well as come to understand where their heart for resistance lies. For years, both in and out of Iraq, we would watch, study, plan, and occasionally clash with the insurgents to meet this goal. In 2007 the first edition of *The Terrorists of Iraq* was published.

Like all who go to Iraq with good intentions, the insurgency has taught me very hard personal and political lessons. The most difficult to swallow was that the understanding of the Iraq insurgency from its first days in 2003 was superficial. Even now, in 2014, it is murky, but not by any fault of the historians. The superficiality and lack of interest for in-depth knowledge of the terrorists came from the highest levels of government and a fully compliant news media. The misunderstanding of the nature and capacity of terrorists in Iraq has literally cost more than 200,000 civilians and 4,486 soldiers their lives. The Iraq insurgency is a meat grinder of humanity, but it is a meat grinder powered by political indifference to human life. People are blown apart in suicide bombings, burned alive in their cars, crushed in their beds by fallen homes, and shredded by flying glass and steel each day. For all their brutality, somehow, the means, motives, and methods of the terrorists of Iraq can never seem to be remembered from day to day. Eleven years later, many people seem to have completely forgotten that the meat grinder never stopped.

The September 11, 2001, attacks revealed an American inability to understand that a committed, rational, thinking enemy who is unafraid of death is a nearly implacable foe. It was a horrible failure of imagination. Iraq was invaded because of the same failure. America ignored history, culture, intelligence, and common sense. Many in the world were led to believe that from the first day of the invasion, America was going into Iraq to stop Saddam from giving nuclear, chemical, and biological weapons to al-Qaeda. The world was essentially told that Saddam was bin Laden's sponsor, and that he may have ultimately ordered the attack on America. The statements and assertions were a significant and deliberate deception without any basis in truth or intelligence. It was fabricated from a whole cloth of lies and is now costing Iraq more lives in 2014 than it did in 2003.

Before the U.S.-led invasion of Iraq there were no real formal Iraqi or foreign terrorist groups operating in Iraq. The two exceptions were the Saddam-backed anti-Iranian Mujahideen al-Khalq terrorist group headquartered at Khalis and the extremely small al-Qaeda-inspired Kurdish group Ansar al-Islam based near Halabja in the American-protected "no-fly zone." A decade's analysis of both Saddam's and al-Qaeda's documents captured in the insurgency has verified the assertions of Middle East experts that at the time, al-Qaeda was not present in Saddam Hussein's Iraq, and that they had absolutely no relationship with the tyrannical government. In fact, Saddam viewed al-Qaeda as a mortal threat and wanted them eliminated before they could infect the Iraqi Sunni community. It is true, in the few days before the U.S. invasion, that Iraqi intelligence threw open its doors and allowed the first jihadists in to fight U.S. forces. The U.S. invasion created the jihadist battlefront that is Iraq. By invading an entire people who had never attacked or posed a threat to America or Great Britain, the army presence forced them to fight with every dirty tactic they could find. With their backs to the wall, they chose to let their Arabic-speaking cousins in al-Qaeda join the insurgency as an ally. That was their mistake as well.

Every day for the last 11 years a new tactic would be reported that was more clever and devious than the preceding one. The ultimate result was to let them continue these methods without change to the strategy of the counterinsurgency for 5 years. Even now, as the death toll passes 200,000 or more dead Iraqis, the public, who initially approved of this war—some with heartfelt enthusiasm, most others with skepticism, actually know very little about who is really doing the killing in Iraq. All they know is that *someone* is still killing innocent people at an unacceptable rate and that every attack for more than a decade was attributable to a nebulous entity "al-Qaeda." With this second edition I will once again endeavor to give some clear answers as to who is responsible for performing such carnage, how they do it, why they do it, and what may possibly stop them.

Today Iraq remains embroiled once again in fighting the hardest core of the 5 million Iraqi Sunni who are resisting by aligning themselves with al-Qaeda, now called the Islamic State of Iraq and Syria (ISIS). The border between Syria and Iraq is disappearing as ISIS seizes Iraqi-controlled towns and stokes a Sunni–Shiite sectarian war. The foreign extremists of al-Qaeda are a very small but deadly faction of the 5,000 terrorists who survived the U.S. occupation. The post-war terrorism surge in Iraq, and al-Qaeda's permanent presence there, is a direct result of the U.S. invasion of Iraq and by no other cause.

The 2014 ISIS offensive against the government of Iraq pushed into the outskirts of Baghdad. ISIS is carving out a Sunni-dominated, al-Qaeda-run nation with oil, American weapons, airfields, and a base population to be made into terrorists. All of this stems from the ill-conceived war that has created a perfect storm of anti-American hatred, gained al-Qaeda nearly unlimited advanced weapons, and fashioned a crucible for forging new daring young terrorist leaders in the Middle East. The U.S. invasion created the opportunity for both former Saddam supporters and foreign fighters from al-Qaeda to develop operational terrorism experience as brothers in battle. These terrorists in the field continue to test the mettle of a second generation of fighters—in combat on a scale that could never have been possible without the invasion. Even with a second negotiated settlement of the Sunni insurgency by a new Iraqi government and a strengthening of an internal security apparatus strong enough to defeat the former regime loyalists (FRLs), the Sunni, Shiite, and foreign insurgents may have laid the groundwork for a fully professionalized terrorist safe haven, if not a nation of their own. The Islamic State of Iraq and Syria may far eclipse the Afghan Taliban in ruthlessness, brutality, and tyranny.

George W. Bush and Dick Cheney's Iraq war was a horrific miscalculation. A terrifying blunder that may take decades to fix. Many Islamic extremists and, incomprehensibly, even some fringe American pundits view fighting in Iraq as a positive development. I cannot see how. The potential for this war to create future terrorist groups of far more sophistication and with greater global reach than al-Qaeda, during their best days in Afghanistan, is not only extremely high—it has occurred. If Iraq fails as a nation, inevitably, the reach of the terrorists who fight there will spread to the rest of the Middle East, then Europe, and possibly to

America again. America may be responsible for a weapon-filled, lawless cesspool of terrorism. Political infighting and open public attacks on Islam, and all by the very people who started the Iraq war, are fertilizing the conditions for the terrorists' growth. I do not believe Iraq is yet lost to this fate—there is a way for the Iraqi people to prevail and al-Qaeda to be stopped. First, one must come to know the enemy above all else.

This book is not a political treatise on the Iraq war, though it may occasionally touch on the politics of many operational decisions. As Julius Caesar said before crossing the Rubicon, *Alea Jacta Est*, "the die has been cast." My duty is to once again attempt to provide some clarity and truth on the matter.

The Terrorists of Iraq will help the reader understand who started fighting in the Iraq insurgency, how it has led to the crisis of today, and why. It is a history and analysis of all groups who have demonstrated and used terrorism in Iraq, particularly the former regime loyalists (FRLs) and al-Qaeda in Iraq (AQI). It is also an analysis of how Iraq fits into their Middle East strategy. This book will clearly delineate both political and combat strategies that the enemy saw as critical in forcing the United States and coalition forces to withdraw, and how it will topple the Shiite government that was left behind.

At first the Iraqi insurgency was almost purely fought by the Sunni FRLs, until the awakening to the brutality of al-Qaeda toward their tribes was revealed. After they stopped fighting, al-Qaeda and foreign fighters continued to destabilize the central government. Finally, in 2014, the Sunni population once again sided with AQI/ISIS to take their chances with anyone but the Shiite-dominated government of Nouri al-Maliki. They let ISIS take one third of Iraq with their blessing. Al-Qaeda/ISIS believes that they can carve their terror nation out from the carcass of both Syria and Iraq, to eventually establish a fundamentalist caliphate from Damascus to Baghdad—they will also happily die trying. Most alarming is the casualness with which they operate together as partners. The FRLs operate in cooperation with and directly support any Iraqi Sunni or foreign extremist group that can help them meet their goals.

My book, *The Terrorist Recognition Handbook*, an encyclopedic study of the intelligence indicators of terrorist groups planning or organizing their covert operations, and *An End to al-Qaeda: Destroying bin Laden's Jihad and Restoring America's Honor* contributed greatly to the update of this second edition. This book will illustrate the political, combat, and religious strategy as well as street-level tactics of the insurgents. It will reveal what American, British, and coalition soldiers endured in Iraq on the street every day for 8 years, and what the Iraqi army and people endure now. This book will also reveal how the Iraqis employ very specific terrorist acts at particularly auspicious times to meet their strategic political or propaganda goals during a terror campaign.

Until ISIS seized major parts of Iraq and sought to overthrow the Syrian rebellion, Iraq departed from the Western psyche the day U.S. soldiers departed their bases and left the country for Kuwait. For years, news items described Iraq in terms of coalition soldiers "killed by an explosion" or civilians massacred in "suicide car bomb attack" or a sentry "shot by a sniper." In fact, each type of attack remains vital to the operational strategy of the terrorists in Iraq. For 8 of the last 13 years the terrorists' only strategy was to draw as much American blood as possible. To strike, strike, and restrike until it can take no more of the horror. In a way, it was successful despite the curbing of many of the attacks. The tactics selected by the terrorist insurgents on any given day have a single terminal objective: to kill a government soldier, a perceived collaborator (government workers), or any foreigner to maintain the destabilization of the Shiite majority-based regime. From sniper-initiated ambushes to multiple improvised explosive devices, the terrorists have developed and deployed a wide array of tactics from which to choose and have had ample time to practice them in the field on live human subjects. In fact, specific terrorist tactics have been developed and are used doctrinally by the insurgents in response to mistakes, blunders, and opportunities given to them, usually by errors in our thinking.

There has been an enormous amount of information generated on the war since April 2003, and it has been challenging to catalog it all. In writing this book, no classified information has been used. Every attempt has been made to use independently collected data from an unclassified source. Official reports from the American coalition headquarters, Defense Department press statements, Iraqi and Arab news media transcripts, attributed works of independent journalists, analysis of insurgent communiqués, thousands of hours of watching insurgent video on Zawraa' television, personal interviews with participants in the Iraq war, and my own observations from over 11 years in and out of Iraq make up a significant portion of this work. With the exception of interviews with captured insurgents, there are no anonymous sources of information. The insurgents of ISIS or any other group will not learn anything new from this book; they already know who they are and which tactics, techniques, and procedures are effective. This unbiased analysis of the terrorists and their goals can hopefully limit the killing machine that is the Iraq insurgency and someday bring us a stable partner in the Middle East.

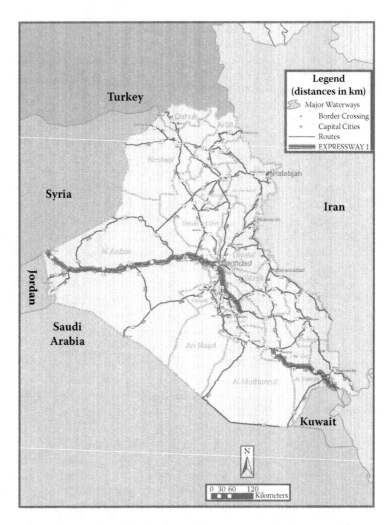

FIGURE 1   Map of Iraq.

Preparation for Insurgency

CHAPTER 1

Who Is Fighting in Iraq?

It is important to know precisely who are the terrorists and insurgents that have been fighting in Iraq. Despite years of analysis of the Iraq insurgency by military analysts, politicians, journalists, and terrorism experts who have offered a wide variety of opinions, theories, and hypotheses, the public remains confused. Where did the terrorists in Iraq come from? How are they organized? Who and what sustains them? How do they operate so effectively? What are they fighting for? Why were they not defeated soundly in the American invasion? What will it take to defeat them?

This confusion is justified, particularly when, after 11 years of fighting, the Iraq branch of al-Qaeda (now called the Islamic State of Iraq and Syria (ISIS)) seized most of northern and western Iraq, threatened an invasion of Baghdad, and erased the Iraq-Syria border—in just 2 weeks. What happened between 2003 and the summer of 2014 to bring us to this point? All of the above questions are linked in the history of the Iraq invasion and hopefully can be answered in the pages that follow.

Terrorists in Iraq have been on a seemingly unstoppable bloodletting since the morning of March 19, 2003, the first day of the American invasion of Iraq. They have been killing soldiers, innocent Iraqis, and citizens from other nations with a brutality and relentlessness never imagined by any group anywhere in the world. The invasion of Iraq by President George W. Bush, Vice President Dick Cheney, Secretary of Defense Donald Rumsfeld, Deputy Secretary of Defense Paul Wolfowitz, and National Security Advisor Condoleezza Rice was supposed to be a short, necessary conflict to remove weapons of mass destruction (WMDs) from Saddam Hussein's control. For more than 6 months they asserted publicly that Saddam Hussein was in league with Osama bin Laden and was planning on giving the WMDs to al-Qaeda. The invasion went forward despite virtually no real evidence and in the face of global opposition. At first it seemed that the traditional ground fight would be a quick one. The Iraqi army was devastated. As Saddam's generals had predicted, the Shiites and Kurds behaved exactly as thought: they abandoned the country to the invaders. During the major combat phase of the war very few of the Iraqi Regular Army's major units had stood up and fought the Americans. With rare exceptions, they disbanded in the face of American combat power, took off their uniforms, and walked home to await the outcome.

The Iraqi resistance was isolated to the cities and casualties were relatively light. After the first 5 weeks of combat President George W. Bush would declare an "end of major combat operations." 139 coalition service members were killed in action. In Washington Iraq was considered a major victory of heavy maneuver forces over what they called dead-enders. However, as the months rolled on the casualties mounted from suicide bomb attacks, snipings, and roadside bombings. Despite growing evidence that by the end of the summer a full-scale guerrilla war was brewing and that terrorists were organizing, Ambassador L. Paul Bremer forbade the use of the word *insurgency* in Baghdad.

Over the next 11 years more than 4,300 additional American soldiers, sailors, airmen, and marines would die at the hands of foreign terrorists and local insurgents in Iraq. Thirty thousand more were wounded or injured in combat. Over the same period, as many as 200,000 Iraqi civilians may have been killed through American, Iraqi, or terrorist actions. Most were innocent victims caught in the cross fire of a war that supposedly had ended in the first 44 days.

Why did the war not end quickly? The simple answer is that Saddam Hussein had 6 months before the invasion to prepare for an insurgency. He did not waste the time foolishly. Even before the first shot was fired Saddam had mastered the moves for a purely Iraqi version of asymmetric warfare—a type of strategic Judo. Years of peacekeeping experience in the Balkans, decades of counterinsurgency and counterrevolutionary war studies, and the written lessons learned from Cuba to the Philippines to Vietnam, El Salvador, and Somalia would be discarded by the Bush Pentagon. Even Israel's disastrous 14-year occupation of Lebanon, where they lost thousands of men to the Hezbollah terrorist group, would not be considered at the decision-making level.

If for some reason the post-9/11 Pentagon seemingly ignored military history, Saddam and his sons Uday and Qusay did not. The Bush administration led themselves to believe that the Iraqi people would never reject the gift of "liberation," nor would they fight back ferociously against an American occupation.

Despite the fresh lessons of Vietnam, when the insurgency came, American commanders often appeared incapable of understanding or responding to an enemy who lived within its own population, enjoyed tremendous support, and thrived on overreaction. In an effort to stop these terrorist attacks, American forces struck at the insurgents, but at the expense of killing and infuriating the local population. As if to punctuate the army's weaknesses, the insurgents struck with near impunity, and like a detached ball of mercury, they spread out at the slightest pressure and were swallowed back in to the community. These simple guerrilla tactics were not only effective in Iraq, but they have proven their worth throughout history by the Viet Cong, Tamil Tigers, Nepali Maoists, Chechen Mujahideen, East Timorese, and Pathet Lao, to name a few. Guerrilla insurgency uses few resources and nearly always has the same effect—it brings about massive retaliation that makes the terrorist more of a hero than a murderer to the occupied people.

It would take 4 years of being hammered by suicide bombers for America to get the message. When General David Petraeus flooded Iraq with additional counterinsurgency trained forces in the 2007 "surge," the terrorists in Iraq had already mastered how to secretly operate where they wanted and how they wanted.

On the other hand, the 2003 invasion of Iraq was a dramatic display of technological brilliance on the part of the American-led coalition. The Americans and British held firepower so awesome that the enemy army literally fled the battlefield once the shooting started. The coalition force was so technologically advanced as to be revolutionary. Victory in conventional combat was never in doubt. The Americans cut through Iraq like a scythe and scattered the Iraqi army to the winds. However, the very same disintegration of the Iraqi army promoted a relatively small loyalist force, the Saddam Fedayeen, to a position where they could test themselves in direct combat with the U.S. forces. Throughout the major combat phase of the invasion it was the Fedayeen that fought the U.S. Army and Marine Corps at the rifle level. The ferocity, determination, and sometimes fearlessness of the Saddam Fedayeen stunned U.S. commanders. As quickly as the Fedayeen appeared on the battlefield to defend Saddam, they disappeared just as fast back in to the population when U.S. tanks entered Firdos Square in Baghdad.

A pressing military question that begs an answer is: Why were the insurgents and foreign terrorists' operations apparently effective despite the enormous manpower and firepower that the United States brought to bear in Iraq? The American forces in Iraq were a most lethal combat force, yet primitive guerrilla-style warfare and rudimentary terrorist tactics of part-time terrorists effectively neutralized the advantage of American high technology. Like the Chechen Muslims and the Tamil Tigers of Sri Lanka, the Iraqi insurgent also planned on harnessing a soldier's deep psychological fear of the local population by dispatching human-guided terror weapons. When terror is carried by individuals longing to die in the face of their heaviest military firepower, it gives the terrorist operative a psychological advantage. To the inexperienced soldier, terrorists are virtually unstoppable and undetectable. Therefore, the soldier shoots, kills, and maims without consideration for the anger this creates within the population.

All in all, the terrorists of Iraq are a breathing, thinking, and evolving guerrilla movement engaged in a ruthless form of primitive combat. They brought the war to the American coalition on their terms, at times of their choosing; now they do the same to the governments of Iraq, Syria, Iran, and by extension, Saudi Arabia, Israel, and the United States.

THE CORNERSTONE OF TERROR: THE EX-BA'ATHIST LOYALISTS

Between 2003 and 2009 the former regime loyalists (FRLs) led by members of the former Saddam Fedayeen units were the principal combat force in the Iraq insurgency. In fact, they provided leadership, guidance, targeteering, and training for the single largest and most capable insurgent group in Iraq at the time: Jaysh al-Mujahideen (aka Jaysh al-Mohammed). In comparison, the other insurgent groups were small terrorist organizations without the in-depth combat capability and intelligence collection capacity of the FRLs. There is ample evidence that the FRLs supplied them with all of the resources they needed when the insurgency bloomed.

In the weeks preceding the invasion the CIA estimated that between 60,000 and 100,000 hard-core regime loyalists out of the 400,000 Iraqi armed forces would fight, and fight hard. This prediction proved true, and many Ba'athists fought the American-led juggernaut. A month later, when the U.S. Marines finally toppled the statue of Saddam in Baghdad's Firdos Square, these FRLs were thought to have been whittled down through combat and desertion to perhaps as few as 5,000. These Iraqis were called dead-enders. The United States saw the fall of Baghdad as an end to the war, but to Saddam's loyalists, it was a sign to transition from traditional combat between large armies to a covert armed resistance movement. This "resistance" movement (called the Muqawamah) would spend an entire generation implementing a unified plan to change Iraqi for better or worse.

The ex-Ba'athist FRLs were composed of Saddam's most ruthless, experienced, and dedicated internal forces: the five major intelligence agencies, the paramilitary Saddam Fedayeen, and remnants of the Special Republican Guard. In particular, the Saddam Fedayeen, a group who surprised American commanders during the invasion with their aggressive and suicidal form of close combat, quickly reorganized, rearmed, and reengaged the coalition forces. While the Americans were present, they would strike at their softest points. They would punish any Iraqi who worked in government or cooperated with the coalition forces. They saw it as critical to wreck any effort to advance the nation toward stability and peace. Initially, the resistance's prospects for success were unlikely to yield fruit, but these true believers persevered for years longer than anyone foresaw, and they may eventually get their wish. The FRLs estimated 20,000 full-time operatives carried out missions that killed 20 times the number of coalition soldiers in the "peace" period than were killed during the initial invasion.

For almost a decade the Iraq insurgency was dominated by groups the U.S. Army called Anti-Iraqi Forces (AIF), former regime loyalists (FRLs), and former regime elements (FREs). The FRLs used plans, money, weapons, and explosives pre-positioned throughout Iraq before the invasion to empower the Sunni fighters and arm foreign terrorists to strike at will. Using suicide bombers, sniper attacks, roadside bombs, and hit-and-run raids, they were a constant threat. During the U.S. occupation former regime loyalists killed on average two U.S. soldiers per day for the 6 years they participated in the insurgency.

American blindness helped the FRLs escape serious scrutiny as well. During the occupation, the misperception in the White House, the media, and the public was that U.S. forces were mainly fighting al-Qaeda. As early as August 2003, after the suicide bomb attack on the United Nations Canal Road headquarters, Abu Musab al-Zarqawi, the leader of al-Qaeda, was being singled out as the greatest threat to Iraq's stability. Considering al-Qaeda's global reputation, there was some justification for the trepidation. However, all the evidence on the ground was that the Iraqi Sunni population as represented by the FRL insurgents was the greater terrorist group. The entire underground ex-Ba'athist regime and its commander, Gen. Izzat Ibrahim al-Douri, were reduced to near-invisible status on the world stage. This served the FRLs very well. The FRLs could perform all of the combat actions they wanted against the Americans and nearly always rely on the fact that many of their attacks would be ascribed to al-Zarqawi's foreign fighters. The FRLs capitalized on this misperception to train, organize, and attack using many of Iraq's Islamic extremist groups as proxies against the coalition.

By 2009 the FRLs and Sunni tribes of Northern and Western Iraq would end their insurgency and cooperate with the Shiite-led government because of al-Qaeda's brutality toward their tribal leaders. However, like any good card shark, they hid a few aces up their sleeve. Even though they formally withdrew from the insurgency, they maintained ties to the remaining groups, al-Qaeda in particular. This came to benefit them because in 2014, after years of being humiliated by Prime Minister Nouri al-Maliki, the FRLs quit the government and facilitated al-Qaeda's ISIS offensive on Iraq and helped seize all Sunni governorates from the government and returned the entire insurgency back to day 1 (Figure 1.1).

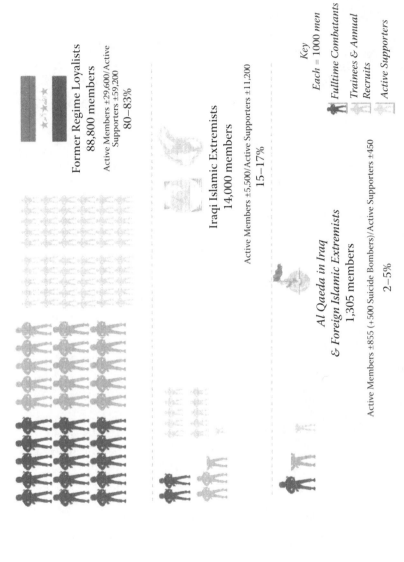

FIGURE 1.1   Manpower estimate of the three wings of the Iraq insurgency (2003–2009).

THE IRAQI RESISTANCE MOVEMENT
AND THE FOREIGN MUJAHIDEEN

Fighting alongside the FRLs was a second wing of the insurgency determined to use terrorist tactics: the Islamic fundamentalist fighters from Iraqi-based groups such as the Ansar al-Sunni, Jaysh al-Islam, and Shiite Mahdi Militia. The Ansar al-Sunnah (AAS) was an amalgam of several Iraqi Sunni extremist groups that operated independently during and after the invasion. Once the occupation began, the Sunni Iraqi terrorists consolidated these small bands into a unified insurgent force. The AAS operated mainly within the north, northwest, and central Iraq. Like the FRLs and foreign extremists, they were dedicated to fighting anyone associated with the American occupation and provided the Sunni community a counterbalance to the Shiite Iraqi-dominated army. The AAS was spearheaded by the former members of the Iraqi-Kurd, al-Qaeda-associated terrorist group Ansar al-Islam (AAI). The Ansar al-Islam was attacked in force during the invasion, but many members slipped away and brought their experience to the AAS. The AAS was the second largest insurgent terrorist group, with manpower estimated to be over 5,000 operatives.

Another branch of anti-American insurgents was the armed Shiite supporters of the young sheik Muqtada al-Sadr. Al-Sadr's Mahdi Militia (Jaysh al-Mahdi (JAM)) was a splinter militia with fringe support within Iraq's Shiite community. For over a year this small minority of young men perceived its own political and religious ambitions crushed by coalition commanders. Unable to gain a foothold under Saddam, local Shiite Islamic extremists found an atmosphere of distrust with the American administration. They believed the Bush administration intended to occupy Iraq and place its own leaders in positions of power. This distrust became explosive when soon after the invasion an expatriate spiritual leader named Abdul Majid al-Khoei attempted to visit the Shrine of Ali in accompaniment with a member of Saddam's former Religious Ministry, Haider Kelidar, and apparently with the blessings of the American administration. Imam al-Khoei and Mr. Kelidar were killed by local Shiite supporters of al-Sadr outside of the Mosque of Ali. The next year, U.S. forces attempted to arrest the young cleric on charges related to this alleged murder. This action, along with the closing of the Sadrist newspaper, led the poor Shiites of southern Iraq and Baghdad to openly take up arms against the coalition in April 2004. Iraqi Shiites who disapproved of the American occupation were inspired by stories of the Lebanese Shiites' victory over the Israeli occupation of southern Lebanon in the 1980s and took on the same task. Within the first year the U.S. Army and Marine Corps found themselves fighting the Mahdi

Militia all across southern and central Iraq. The Mahdi Militia engaged the U.S. Army in bitter combat in Najaf, Karbala, Al Kut, Basrah, and Baghdad, killing dozens of coalition soldiers while losing hundreds of fighters. The JAM disarmed and transformed into a political group, but most militant members merely shifted to another Shiite terror group, the League of the Righteous (Asa'ib Ahl al-Haq (AAH)). The AAH remains the strongest of the Shiite militias, as they are financed, trained, and guided by Iran's special forces, the Iranian Revolutionary Guards Al Quds (Jerusalem) force. Under Iranian tutelage, the two militias may have carried out as many as 6,000 gun and improvised explosive device (IED) attacks on U.S. forces during the occupation.

INTRODUCING AL-QAEDA IN IRAQ (AQI)

The third wing of the insurgency was the al-Qaeda in Mesopotamia (Tanzim Qa'idat al-Jihad fi Bilad al-Rafidayn), or more simply called al-Qaeda in Iraq (note that the U.S. defense intelligence community refers to them as AQI). In 2005 they changed their name to the Islamic Emirate of Iraq (IEI), and then in 2013 to the Islamic State of Iraq and Syria (ISIS) after they joined operations in the Syrian civil war. AQI was led by the Jordanian terrorist Abu Musab al-Zarqawi until his death in 2006 and now falls under the command of Abu Bakr al-Baghdadi, an Iraqi from Samarra.

Let us correct a historical error. Despite years of press bombardment, al-Qaeda did not actually fight during the invasion of Iraq, nor were they present in Saddam's Iraq before it became clear America was determined to attack. Al-Zarqawi and Tawhid Wal-Jihad (TWJ) did enter Iraq a few days before the invasion, but that was to take Saddam's weapons and create safe houses in Fallujah. They knew Saddam would fall, and they waited for this to be complete before attacking the Americans.

AQI started operations in Iraq with a core group of fighters from al-Zarqawi's Jordanian terror group Tawhid Wal-Jihad (TWJ) ("Monotheism and Holy War"). Al-Zarqawi would later merge many of the smaller independent foreign and Iraqi jihadist groups under his TWJ command and fight alongside. AQI did not exist formally until nearly 6 months after the invasion, and not before an intense lobbying effort by al-Zarqawi of Osama bin Laden was successful. In 2004 he swore a Biyan, or allegiance to Osama bin Laden, and was formally given Iraq as a regional affiliate command with the title of Amir al-Mujahideen ("Prince of the Holy Warriors") under the al-Qaeda name. Thus was created al-Qaeda in Iraq. AQI had a disproportionate terror impact in the insurgency. Until the merger of almost all Iraqi and foreign fighters under its banner in 2011, AQI would be one of the smallest terror organizations in Iraq.

Before the invasion of Iraq, Saddam let the doors open for any Arab volunteer who chose to fight the Americans. Many from Syria and Saudi Arabia took this challenge. Knowing the regime's days were numbered, terrorist groups such as the TWJ came in and established open operations in cities such as Fallujah and Ramadi. Politically, the Arab street views this insurgency as a form of comeuppance for American arrogance. Correspondingly, the number of foreign volunteers increased dramatically in 2004 and exploded after the Arab Spring in 2011. Young men are being inspired by the call to Jihad, legitimate or not, from al-Qaeda/ISIS. Recruited from Europe and the Arab nations, particularly Saudi Arabia, AQI finds numerous ready recruits who are infiltrated across the borders to test their mettle against the U.S. Army. Additionally, money was being traded for martyrdom to poor families in Lebanon, Jordan, Algeria, Libya, Morocco, and Sudan who sent their sons to blow up alongside of convoys or at Iraqi police stations. Simply because America invaded Iraq, al-Qaeda now has tens of thousands of potential recruits from which to choose, train, and inspire for future operations against the West. In 2013 the mantel of al-Qaeda's role in the insurgency was fully handed over to its descendant, the Islamic State of Iraq and Syria (ISIS).

These three branches of the insurgency—the FRLs and their nationalist supporters, Iraqi-origin Islamic extremists, both Sunni and Shiite, and foreign Mujahideen extremists—comprise what the American commanders called Anti-Iraqi Forces (AIF). By 2014, many of these Iraqi groups, including the FRLs, seemed to have set aside their philosophical differences and joined al-Qaeda/ISIS in their operations. Few groups have clear goals other than resistance for resistance's sake, and they cooperated solely to derail the political and military objectives of the United States. When that goal was achieved, each wing of the insurgency transformed into covert threats to the future of Iraq as a viable democracy.

Today AQI/ISIS remains a brutal killing machine. Its operatives are believed to be responsible for hundreds of suicide car bombings, killing several thousand Iraqis and foreigners. No matter how the Iraq insurgency continues or devolves, it is clear that al-Qaeda/ISIS has now established a major covert training network in Iraq, has near unlimited ammunition and explosives, and has forged much deeper ties to the other, larger insurgent terrorist groups.

FIGHTING MISPERCEPTIONS

This misperception of who America was fighting was put forward early in 2003 when, during the combat phase of the war, the irregular groups of soldiers defending Iraq were given new caricatures and names almost daily. A few weeks after the end of the war was declared, insurgent attacks were usually in numbers small enough to be dismissed as an unorganized group of dead-enders, so they were called regime death squads, regime terrorists, foreign fighters, and the ubiquitous terrorist forces. Eventually the terrorists' title was changed from the semi-legitimate-sounding Anti-Coalition Forces (ACF) to the more politically friendly Anti-Iraqi Forces (AIF). Coalition soldiers in Iraq were given the insurgent stereotype as a template for their enemy. So they simply concluded that every Iraqi man, woman, and child is a terrorist, will be a terrorist, or can be a terrorist; therefore, they treated the population with disdain and mistrust. Some of these beliefs were based on hard evidence. Iraqi men and women dressed in explosives have blown themselves up at their gates; prepubescent teenage boys have shot soldiers in the head while they bought cold drinks; children's living and dead bodies have been carried up to their checkpoints and rigged to explode, and donkey carts have been used to tow rocket-launching platforms that bombarded their bases. However, the level of disdain and indifference for the Iraqi people shown by the average occupation soldier only made matters much worse.

The insurgent stereotype was not helped by a campaign of positive-sounding denials from U.S. force commanders that there even was an insurgency. In July 2003, some American commanders rejected the idea that there was organized resistance present or forming despite dozens of attacks occurring daily, some synchronized. In an interview after the start of the reconstruction, Lt. Gen. William Wallace, commander of the U.S. V Corps, stated, "There are a number of organized groups that are intent on attacking American soldiers.... We don't believe them to be under a central leadership and we are taking appropriate action to deal with the threat. This is not a resistance movement." In fact, intelligence at the time revealed a clearly well-organized resistance centered in the Sunni regions of northwest Iraq, now known as the Sunni Triangle and organized around the regime's Saddam Fedayeen and intelligence agencies.

By November 2003, as casualties started to mount, military commanders and senior policy makers seemed to blame every group in the world for attacks in Iraq, except the most obvious: the Iraqis who were displaced from power. The administration either failed to recognize or refused to accept the clear intelligence that the Sunni Iraqis were resisting fiercely. By early 2005 this field expedient "bugaboo" strategy created a mindset that practically described the FRLs as a secondary nuisance. The *Washington Post* reported in March 2005 that U.S. commanders seriously considered shifting the bulk of their intelligence and combat operations away from the Ba'athist insurgent threat and elevated the defeat of the foreign fighters to priority number one. This demonstration of Washington's ignorance of the depth, scope, and determination of the FRLs by not clearly identifying them as public enemy number One may have been the single greatest error in the war. Not recognizing the insurgency early enough ended up delaying effective political and military responses. Instead of taking a serious look at the enemy and coming up with a long-term political and military strategy to defeat them, the administration unfortunately took refuge by pointing the blame at the most politically expedient enemy—al-Qaeda. That early scapegoat became a very real enemy.

From the very start, the terrorist insurgents were viewed by Washington not as serious fighters, but through a racist caricature that saw them as bumbling incompetent "Arabs" who just happen to be successful on occasion. This image held sway over the American public for years. The news media did not help in this regard. No matter how competent the Iraqi insurgents revealed themselves to be, they were repeatedly portrayed in the media as a Wile E. Coyote-type cartoon character set up only to be knocked down again and again by the superior American forces—preferably on camera. Images of deaths and bodies of American soldiers were strictly forbidden. This caused a sanitization of the war, which only led to more deaths.

By 2005, this caricature of the insurgent enemy had seeped so deeply into the mindset of the soldiers in the field that U.S. commanders were often at a loss to clearly explain why they seemed so resilient. It created a contradiction that was not easily explained at the time. A simple test was to ask nearly any soldier who and why they are fighting in Iraq, and he or she would have told you that they were hunting al-Qaeda and to avenge the 9/11 attacks. Despite the fact that there was no link between Iraq and the 9/11 attacks, Iraq was placed at the forefront of the war on the al-Qaeda organization, but for the wrong reasons.[1] Later, when U.S. forces withdrew in 2011, many believed that America had vanquished al-Qaeda from the country, when in fact it was only the FRLs who had withdrawn from the insurgency. However, when honestly assessed in proportion to their size, skill, and political impact, the insurgents did exceptionally well against the vastly superior forces they faced in combat.

It is true that the invasion gave thousands of al-Qaeda terrorist recruits a chance to come and try their hand at killing American soldiers in an Arab land. Men who would have rather prayed quietly in their mosques, bought Cheb Khaled rap CDs, or applied for a grant to study engineering in Boston suddenly found an alternative way to validate and bring honor to themselves—they became Mujahideen in Iraq. The title of *Mujihad*, or "Holy Warrior," bestows upon them a greatness and measure of meaning in their lives they could not have achieved before. This desire to die to please their God is highly respected and admired by other, less committed Muslims, both moderate and extremist. They choose to go to Iraq in an effort to defeat us for coming to Iraq. As former CIA officer Michael Scheuer wrote in his book *Imperial Hubris*, by invading Iraq, America gave Osama bin Laden his greatest wish—a land war in the heart of Islamic world.

However, since it has never been adequately explained that 95% of the insurgency was not al-Qaeda, soldiers generally could not understand how bin Laden's followers were in all places at all times and could be so adept at killing. One day the U.S. or Iraqi army could be fighting former Saddam Fedayeen (aka the Army of the Mujahideen), the next it could be the Islamists of Ansar al-Sunnah or the Islamic Army of Iraq, the following it could be attacked by the terrorists of al-Qaeda in Iraq, and on the fourth day it could be all three simultaneously. Add the constant pressure of being in readiness to respond to a spontaneous uprising from the Mahdi Militia or attempts to seize Iraqi territory by the Kurdish Peshmerga, and one can easily understand the level of frustration an occupation force would feel.

Despite the wishful thinking of the coalition, Washington never had a plan for what was known as phase IV of a conflict, the post-war. Only Saddam Hussein, Abu Mussab al-Zarqawi, and the ex-Ba'athists had a definitive strategy for what to do in post-war Iraq. Unlike the Americans, they mobilized the right resources and personnel for the job.

The invasion of Iraq has many facets that all future historians will agree upon. There have been some positive outcomes in the post-invasion period. Iraq was given a chance at forming a secular democracy. It definitively deposed a brutal leader who carried out heinous crimes against his own people. It stopped a regime that had developed and used weapons of mass destruction in the Iran-Iraq war and against the Kurds, and definitively ended a dictatorship that committed aggression against three of its five neighboring countries. The principles of that murderous regime are as dead as Saddam Hussein himself. On the other hand, America chose to engage in a bloody and costly war that it was not prepared to fight. For the Iraqi insurgents the war did not end with President Bush's declaration of "mission accomplished"; it had only just begun. The Saddam Fedayeen and its sister agencies combined to spoil the coalition victory and force a withdrawal. To this end, they came back rearmed, reorganized, and motivated and killed relentlessly for 8 of the last 11 years. In 2014 they quit the "peace" and once again joined forces with al-Qaeda's ISIS. The post-invasion peace, if it could ever be called that, has proven to be a multigenerational sectarian war that continues unabated. If recent history is a guide, Iraq may eventually end up partitioned into three states, including an al-Qaeda-dominated terrorist safe haven, or it will devolve into full-scale civil war, or both.

ENDNOTES

1. National Commission on Terrorist Attacks upon the United States, The 9/11 Commission Report, 2004.

CHAPTER 2

Victory through Defeat
Saddam Plans for Insurgency

REPEATING A VERY BAD HISTORY?

The reasons and logic for the invasion of Iraq will be long discussed and analyzed by historians. Prominent among them, was America right to test the new doctrine of preemptive warfare? This doctrine emphasized using lighter and less manpower-dependent forces than was called for in Gen. Colin Powell's "Powell Doctrine," or war that is only carried out with overwhelming force. Would the forces deployed be enough to secure the peace? Was the decision to invade based on faulty intelligence or political misrepresentation? After a decade, all of these questions seem superfluous in the face of the facts on the ground, but the path to war shaped Saddam's decision to embark on a long, slow bloodletting called al-Muqawamah, or "The Resistance." Before we can understand the reasons for the Iraqis to resist the invasion, a short history lesson is necessary.

Iraq is a nation that was created out of a patchwork of disparate peoples and cultures with borders that suited the creator, not those within them. Iraq's formation was the result of a negotiated division of Ottoman territories after their loss to the Allied powers in WWI. Iraq became an independent state after it was occupied, and then offered by Great Britain to Faisal abn Husayn (King Faisal I). Faisal abn Husayn was an Arab born in the town of Taif in what is present-day Saudi Arabia. Son of Sharif Husayn, Faisal Abn Husayn became allied with the British during WWI while fighting the Ottomans in the Hejaz under the guidance of the notable British Army officer T.E. Lawrence (Lawrence of Arabia).[1] After entering Damascus in 1918, he occupied Transjordan (modern-day Jordan) and Syria until he was selected to be the king of Greater Syria by the Syrian National Conference. However, his disagreements with the French, who occupied Syria, led to his expulsion and exile to England. Fortunately for him, the British were in the process of creating a new state from the lands of Mesopotamia. The British entered Mesopotamia in 1920 under a League of Nations mandate and promptly renamed it the Kingdom of Iraq. An immediate revolt by the Arab and Kurdish population broke out. The entire revolution took the lives of over 2,200 British troops, and 8,450 Iraqi civilians killed or wounded[2] in a religious-based Jihad that took future Prime Minister Winston Churchill 2 years to quell.

Fast-forward to the summer of 2002. The Bush administration entered into discussions with its British allies about solving the problem of the Iraq regime. The British defense and intelligence staff appeared cool to the prospect of going back and reliving the bloody history of their occupation. Recalling the insurrection, modern-day British commanders were undoubtedly reaching back into libraries and universities for classified and unclassified historical studies of the Great Iraqi Arab Revolution. British military graves still populate cemeteries in cities like Basrah, Naseriyah, Baghdad, and Habbaniyah. The Americans were talking officially about preparations for invasion in the spring of 2003. Prime Minister Tony Blair's defense and intelligence staff cautioned against going back and reliving the bloody history of their occupation of Iraq, but the United States was committed to invading. This sentiment is revealed in a July 23, 2002, memo of a meeting of Prime Minster Blair and his senior staff. According to the memo, the United States was ready to effect regime change in Iraq and was requesting assistance. Surprisingly, there was little or no discussion of what to do after Saddam Hussein was removed. In the meeting held at Prime Minister Blair's residence at No. 10 Downing Street, the director of Britain's Secret Intelligence Service, MI-6, Sir Richard Dearlove, reported on his meetings with CIA director George Tenet. His report read:

> There was a perceptible shift in attitude. Military action was now seen as inevitable. Bush wanted to remove Saddam, through military action justified by the conjunction of terrorism and WMD. However, the intelligence and facts were being fixed around the policy. The NSC had no patience with the UN route and no enthusiasm for publishing material on the Iraqi regime's record. There was little discussion in Washington of the aftermath after military action.[3]

The chief of defense staff, Admiral Sir Michael Boyce, reported to the prime minister that British military planners were to brief the British component of the war plan to "CENTCOM (U.S. Central Command) on 1–2 August, Rumsfeld on 3 August and Bush on 4 August." A key component of the war plan would be to soften Iraqi air defense using the legal framework of the United Nations-sponsored no-fly zones. The question was not if the United States was going to war, but when. By the end of September 2002 everyone in the West was sure America was going to war, but what was happening inside of Iraq was less than certain.

UNAMBIGUOUS INDICATORS

By October 2002, Iraq was receiving many unambiguous indicators that war was not only inevitable but imminent. U.S. forces were mobilizing for war and starting to deploy to Kuwait and Qatar. Training of U.S. forces for an invasion was duly reported in the American media, but none of the indicators was more definitive to the Iraqis than the dramatic increase in American air strikes on southern Iraq positions. As the U.S. commanders told the British in July, there had already begun "spikes of activity" to lure Iraq into an engagement. Unknown to Iraq, the American plan called for using the United Nations-sponsored patrols and defensive actions in the northern and southern no-fly zones (NFZs) to start striking critical Iraqi war fighting facilities well in advance of the invasion. As planned, coalition air forces struck high-value surface-to-air missile systems and key Iraqi air defense bunkers and radars even though they were not active. All the Iraqis could do was offer up token resistance with small-caliber anti-aircraft artillery and the occasional surface-to-air missile (SAM) launch. The intent of this secret air offensive was not lost on the Iraqis. Over the 12 years since the first Gulf War, Iraq had become expert in watching anti-air defense suppression flights of the USAF and had a good understanding of their profiles. Iraqi air defense, observing with powerful radars, gave the air defense commanders much of the data they needed to divine that the Americans now had a different game in mind. The hundreds of American air defense suppression flights over southern and northern Iraq, though seemingly random, had distinct activity patterns. Fighter combat air patrols behaved one way and surface-to-air missile battery suppression attacks behaved another. These American aerial attacks on the NFZs were taking a toll on Iraqi air defense and military command and control. Iraqi General Headquarters (GHQ) officers noted that the obvious shift from destroying the odd anti-aircraft gun to the destruction of entire surface-to-air missile communications nodes, command centers, and missile batteries was similar to the pattern in 1991. The last major change in the American operations profile had been seen just before the air strikes on Iraq in 1991 during Operation Desert Storm and in 1998 during Operation Desert Fox. Obviously, the Americans were degrading these nodes for a reason, and that reason was being stated daily to the international media: "regime change." The Americans, taking the risk of transmitting their punch, decided to do as much damage to the Iraqi army and air force command and control before the war started. The Iraqis could only absorb the punches and were fully aware that these strikes would eventually lead to a real contest where nothing less than a knockout blow would be acceptable to the Americans.

THE PREWAR INSURGENCY PLAN

In light of American attacks, the Iraqi GHQ decided to plan for failure. Gen. Izzat Ibrahim al-Douri was a close confidant of Saddam Hussein, a senior member of the elite ruling council, and commander of all Iraqi forces north of Baghdad. One thing was becoming clear to him: Iraq would lose a full-scale invasion by America. With this in mind, he commanded a classified program to prepare for a guerrilla war. This plan may have been known as Project 111.[4] In the event of defeat, he and others who escaped the onslaught would be responsible for logistical and military framework of the post-war insurgency. Along with Saddam, Uday, and Qusay, he would command the insurgent forces, which would use various cover names, such as the "Army of Mohammed" (Jaysh al-Mohammed (JM)) or the "Party of the Return" (Hizb al-Awda), but the real insurgency system would operate under the operational name of the Unified Mujahideen Command. The military wing would be called the Mujahideen Army. According to the interim Iraqi government, Saddam appointed Yasser al-Shab'awi, a former Ba'athist officer, to command the Mujahideen Army.

As early as September 2002, the Iraqi media was broadcasting in its internal propaganda of the preparedness of the Saddam Fedayeen forces to carry out combat in the enemy's rear using commando operations and terrorism. According to U.S. News and World Report magazine, a report issued by the Central Command's Special Operations forces described the prewar preparations of the Iraqi intelligence agencies to train the post-war leadership of the insurgency. According to this report, in September 2002, Saddam ordered between 1,000 and 1,200 select intelligence and Special Operations officers to undergo specialized training at the two Fedayeen training camps in Salman Pak and Bismayah. The selectees were "young and talented" officers from the Iraqi Intelligence Service, the Directorate of Military Intelligence, and the Directorate of General Security. The report went on to say that the officers used a covert name system to identify themselves during training that replaced their real names with numbers. Saddam was "Number One." They were told to "prepare themselves for re-contact following the collapse of the regime."[5] The U.S. Defense Intelligence Agency's Joint Intelligence Task Force would later piece together the involvement of a secret intelligence group in the prewar insurgency plan. The Iraqi Special Security Organization's Special Operations Division, M14-SOD, was tasked by Saddam to prepare a highly specialized, covert program to develop and deploy the components of improvised explosive devices (IEDs) throughout Iraq. This program was called the Challenge Project.[6] The CIA would not find evidence of these preparations until 2004, when its Iraq Survey Group reported on them. The CIA believed M14-SOD and the Challenge Project would become the genesis and knowledge center for the insurgency's covert use of IEDs.

U.S. Army and British forces started major troop deployments to the region in November 2002. Within 90 days, more than 200,000 soldiers, sailors, airmen, and marines would be in Kuwait or en route to the theater. The numbers and the level of mobilization made it clear this was going to be a major invasion. Once this force was ready and armed, there would be no turning back. When the United Nations met on November 8 to vote on Resolution 1441, tensions rose palpably. The resolution, pushed hard by the United States, demanded a tough new weapons inspections regime that warned of "serious consequences." The United States, Britain, and Spain wanted this resolution to clearly authorize military action at the slightest resistance to the inspections. The remaining members of the Security Council were openly skeptical of the Americans' intentions and were wary of starting a conflict. By the end of the month UN weapons inspectors resumed their work in Iraq hunting for indications of new or continuing chemical, biological, and nuclear programs. The inspection regime was the toughest to date, but their work was often characterized by the administration as being completely incapable of actually finding WMDs and hinting that only a military solution could rid Saddam Hussein of the weapons.

While the UN inspected for WMDs, the Iraqis were identifying their weaknesses and making them into strengths. To meet the goals of the Challenge Project, the Iraqis calculated that thousands of tons of weapons would need to be hidden and dispersed, especially artillery shells. The caches would need to be broken down small enough to arm a core squad of 5 men for several months and with enough extras to arm an additional 5 to 15 men. Each cache would also have all of the components to create IEDs, including several dozen heavy-artillery shells, plastic explosives, detonation cord, and mortar rounds. A former Iraqi Intelligence Service officer stated that the intelligence agencies started caching weapons throughout Iraq from August 2002. Evidence of large weapons caching efforts also were reported by U.S. intelligence in January 2003, but may have been mistaken for attempts to hide WMDs instead of preparations for the insurgency.[7] Al-Douri, Qusay and Uday Hussein, and their sublieutenants in the five intelligence services prepared to establish thousands of these weapons caches to be accessed after the war. Resistance would center in the northwestern Iraq region from Baghdad in the center to Mosul in the north and the Jordanian border in the west. This area would become known as the Sunni Triangle. Hussein himself ordered generals to hide weapons systems and sensitive equipment off military bases, in fields, and in homes. Local eyewitnesses in Muthenna and Dhi Qar Province recall observing Special Security agents guarded by Fedayeen burying weapons caches near mosques and in swamps and taking large quantities of weapons home. One Iraqi from Basrah reported large maritime shipping containers were buried west of the city in the desert. When the war started, locals dug them up and found them full of thousands of rifles and rocket-propelled grenade launchers. These thousands of weapons caches would finally convince some U.S. commanders that the war was preplanned. Maj. Gen. Charles H. Swannack Jr., the commanding general of the 82nd Airborne Division, stated, "I believe Saddam Hussein always intended to fight an insurgency should Iraq fall. That's why you see so many of these arms caches out there in significant numbers all over the country. They were planning to go ahead and fight an insurgency."[8]

THE IRAQI WAR PLAN: EMBRACING DEFEAT

By November 2003, the Iraqi general staff assumed that a southern invasion launched out of Kuwait was inevitable. Unless the situation changed dramatically, it became obvious that an American division would also come through Turkey as was being broadcast in media reports. Saddam was said to be confident that the game he had played with the United Nations would work again. However, both of Saddam's sons, Uday, who lead the commando-like Saddam Fedayeen, and Qusay, the commander of the Special Security Organization and its Special Republican Guard, as well as the deputy chief of the armed forces, Lt. Gen. Izzat Ibrahim al-Douri, and the directors of the four other intelligence agencies, perceived that America was not bluffing. They were already taking precautions in case the worst came to pass. Saddam also may have believed privately that America was not going to balk. CIA chief weapons inspector Charles Duelfer's Iraq Survey Group did an assessment of Hussein's activities before the war. He wrote, "Saddam believed that the Iraqi people would not stand to be occupied or conquered by the United States and would resist—leading to an insurgency. Saddam said he expected the war to evolve from traditional warfare to insurgency."[9]

In December 2002, a secret circular went around to the top deputies on the Iraqi National Security Council warning "Iraq will be defeated militarily due to the imbalance of forces," and that Iraqi forces will drag the U.S. military "into Iraqi cities, villages, and the desert and resort to resistance tactics."[10] That same month Saddam held a meeting of the war cabinet concerning war plans. The Minister of Military Industrialization, 'Abd al-Tawab 'Abdallah al-Mullah Huwaysh, told CIA interrogators that Saddam "told his generals to concentrate on their jobs and leave the rest to him, because he had 'something in his hand' (i.e., 'something up his sleeve')."[11] Many believed that it was a secret weapon or weapon of mass destruction, but it is well in line with the efforts he was making to train and prepare the Saddam Fedayeen and other intelligence forces for a post-war insurgency. Director of Iraqi Intelligence Service Gen. Tahir Jalil Habbush al-Tikriti said, "We will be angry if the Americans don't come." According to the CIA's Duelfer Report:

> In Saddam's last three ministers' meetings ... just before the war, he told attendees at least three times "Resist one week, and after that I will take over." ... There are indications that what Saddam actually had in mind was some form of insurgency against the coalition.[12]

Both Saddam and General al-Douri were counting on the Pentagon to be unprepared for a covert guerrilla force trained to conduct commando-style operations in their rear. Knowing that he would have the support of at least 20% of the Iraqi people, al-Douri also knew the distaste the Americans had for long, protracted wars with high casualties. Unlike Saddam, he had no reason to believe that the Americans would not go all the way to Baghdad. The lessons of the British occupation of Iraq in the Great Arab Revolution of 1920 served as his template. With the historical precedence of the Sunni fighting from Mosul and the Shiite rebelling in the south under Imam Shirazi and his son Mirza Muhammad Riza, Iraq had a model for rebellion and resistance. Like its present-day sister, the 1920 British occupation was not popularly received, and a new monarchy was offered to a Saudi, King Faisal, in 1921 by the British. The British had imposed an interim constitution on Iraq and had hand-selected Arab ministers positioned under the direct control of British advisors. Few of the British colonial decisions or public administration methods were popular. In accepting the monarchy, Faisal negotiated an agreement that allowed the British occupation forces to remain in Iraq while also securing eventual independence.[13] When the League of Nations mandate for the occupation ended in 1933, Iraq was granted independence. Crowning this stunning defeat was the fact that the history of instability in Iraq did not end with independence. King Faisal died soon afterward, and the crown passed to his eldest son, Ghazi. An unfortunate car accident killed King Ghazi 6 years later, and he was succeeded by his then infant son, Faisal II. During World War II, a 1941 pro-German coup attempt by one Rashid Ali al-Gaylani led to the reoccupation of Iraq by British forces. Until King Faisal came of age, Iraq was ruled by his uncle, Prince Abdallah, who served as the crown regent until 1953. Like most Middle Eastern monarchies, this one was neither truly popular nor native to the peoples and tribes of the region; it was just accepted as a convenient alternative to the occupation government by British forces. The 1920 revolution is an excellent first example of where history repeats itself. Political leaders in the United States ignored the same warning signs, which had presented themselves so dramatically 80 years earlier—a revolution where virtually every religious and tribal group, led by the Shiite imams of Karbala, fought the British occupation with all they had. Although the source of the resistance would be Sunni, the Shiite would most likely also find the occupation odious, and perhaps a full mirror image of the 1920 revolution could again be induced.

Both Hussein and al-Douri had to have kept in mind the lessons of the American debacle in Vietnam, the Israeli occupation of Lebanon, and the American intervention in Somalia. All of these occupations, or mini-wars, had resulted in superior forces being defeated or humiliated by smaller, more agile forces that were determined to win in the end. Unlike other historic guerrilla wars, the regime planners knew they would not have the support from a strong, friendly ally, but it would need to be a self-sustaining insurgency. The regime would carry out its anti-American activities by seizing and disbursing billions of U.S. dollars of Iraqi treasury money, dispersing thousands of tons of small arms and explosives, and deploying the skilled agents of the secret services to the northwestern desert cities to organize a resistance. These agents would go on to the wild Iraq-Syria border, set up the covert infrastructure of the underground, and create a money and manpower pipeline back into a soon-to-be-occupied Iraq. As early as July 2002, the Ba'ath Party and the Fedayeen had started taking security measures to prepare their members for a long-range insurgency in the American rear. Ba'ath Party documents captured in Operation Iraqi Freedom found that the party "recommended structure for resistance groups fighting coalition forces ... dictates the need for secrecy and directs a transition to covert operations ... organization of cells was to be small and closed in order to prevent penetration by coalition forces (five members) ... members were encouraged to avoid written communication and common party language."[14] The bottom line of Project 111 appears to be that the Americans would win, but they would not be allowed to settle in comfortably.

MOGADISHU ON THE TIGRIS

The Saddam Fedayeen would be the principal weapon to harass and demoralize the American forces. The Hussein brothers would command their forces in both the war and post-invasion as guerrillas fighting in the enemy rear. The older and less stable Qusay relished this mission. A violent movie fanatic, it is said he built his fleet of Toyota and Nissan pickup trucks with heavy machine guns and recoilless rifles mounted on them to create Somali-like "technicals" for the Saddam Fedayeen. This fleet was based on his obsession with the movie *Blackhawk Down*, and Qusay was said to swear to inflict similar damage on the U.S. Army in the exact same way the Somalis did. In fact, he would also use the Fedayeen to train a force of pan-Arab mercenaries to sacrifice their lives in suicide attacks with either car bombs or explosive belts. He ordered hundreds of car bombs to be manufactured and placed in strategic locations with the bombers at hand so they could crash into American forces. Additionally, the Fedayeen trained thousands of Arab students, mercenaries, and terrorists to fight as foot infantry under their command. This force, Qusay reckoned, would make the Americans pay with attacks they could not stop.

But suicide vehicles and commando martyrs would not be enough to sustain the operations tempo. Saddam would also need the cooperation of the Sunni tribes. His years of winning their allegiance with incentives, money, and jobs for their young men would be tested. Some Iraqis believe that Saddam dispatched his director of tribal affairs, Rukan Razuki, to have serious discussions with the tribal chiefs about how the Americans would treat them once the invasion was complete. Razuki explained that expatriate Sunni and Shiite were being prepared by the Americans to take over the control of the government, and that the Americans would ignore and punish the Sunni. Tribal leaders would wait to see how the Americans treated them, but it would not be long before they were convinced that Razuki was right.

TREATED AS LIBERATORS?

As the United States steamed closer to war, a belief in the coming U.S. victory seemed to have given many Washington politicians a heady feeling. The White House publicly pushed an incautious belief that the invasion would be simple, would finance itself, and would be the catalyst to change the face of Middle Eastern politics. The realities of an invasion of Iraq were dismissed in such a way as to have dramatic consequences in the post-war. A few weeks before the start of the war, Vice President Dick Cheney insisted, "I really do believe we will be greeted as liberators."[15]

The vice president was convinced, but now a skeptical American public needed to be made to believe that the war would be fast, easy, and inexpensive. Neoconservative hawks in the administration publicly claimed that U.S. forces would not be seen as invaders. Part of that task fell on the briefings to Congress by Assistant Secretary of Defense Paul Wolfowitz. Secretary Wolfowitz was also a true believer in the rosy assessment of the prospects of a quick and easy war. Like many of the civilian leadership, he ignored or justified warnings from professionals who knew better. When prominent critics popped up, the administration was quick to punish their outspokenness. One such professional was Army Chief of Staff Gen. Eric Shinseki. A lifelong professional, General Shinseki was a soldier's soldier. Before Congress he cut an impressive appearance. In one congressional hearing General Shinseki was asked to give a candid assessment of the manpower needed to secure the war and post-war. Using estimates the Pentagon had formulated, General Shinseki flatly stated that at least 300,000 soldiers would be needed to secure Iraq. Following Shinseki was Deputy Secretary Wolfowitz. Within minutes he publicly rebuked Shinseki and quickly contradicted him. Wolfowitz stated, "I am reasonably certain that they will greet us as liberators, and that will help us to keep requirements down." He went on to explain the expected low cost in capital as the war would be paid for in Iraq oil revenue, and anyone who opposed the occupation would be pointed out by grateful Iraqis. Many American and British politicians echoed this sentiment. Ironically, for citing official U.S. Army calculations based on experience in post-war planning, Shinseki's replacement as chief of staff was announced 1½ years earlier than planned. The general was forced to early retirement from service.

Despite American optimism, the Iraqi people seemed to know that the Saddam regime would not be going away even if the U.S. forces won a resounding victory. The history of the Ba'ath Party was rooted in covert activity aimed at destabilizing a government and killing political enemies. It appears that it was given little consideration by the Pentagon. Having had their brief rebellion abandoned by former President George H.W. Bush in 1991 and subjected to the revenge of Saddam Hussein's terror apparatus, the Shiite community of southern Iraq was particularly skeptical of not only the intentions of the United States, but also its ultimate goals. Organizations like the Saddam Fedayeen, the Special Republican Guard, and the internal security forces existed for the sole purpose of suppressing any dissent and could operate in the underbelly of Iraqi society covertly. Only a clear demonstration of sweeping away all of these forces and their agents from power would suffice in letting the people of Iraq breathe easier, but even that would not be sufficient. Being Iraqi meant understanding the insidious way that the internal security forces had permeated every aspect of Iraqi society. Many Iraqis feared that even after a major war the agents of a regime that did not fall completely could work their way back into the society and kill and intimidate the local populace. It was not hard for Iraqis to imagine that a hard-core group of regime fanatics would resist the U.S. invasion at every step. The fear factor of having these secret forces in the vicinity would temper their enthusiasm for an American occupation.

The U.S. intelligence community was also not so enthusiastic. That there would be resentment against the American forces in Saddam Hussein's Iraq by the deposed Sunnis was not a great leap in intelligence projection. The intelligence community foresaw the power and security vacuum an invasion would create. Any such vacuum would have to be filled by U.S. forces. The CIA warned the White House about the possibility of insurgency and guerrilla warfare numerous times. In January 2003, 2 months before the invasion, the president received two reports from the CIA's National Intelligence Council. These reports were a combined assessment of all sources of intelligence that consolidated the opinions and data from each agency in the intelligence community. According to *USA Today*, one report concluded that an invasion could "increase popular sympathy for terrorist objectives," and another predicted that anti-American insurgency could ensue.[16] The U.S. Army also studied the possibility of insurgency, and the National War College released a study that same month that noted the likelihood of insurgency as well, accurately predicting a revolt.

> Most Iraqis and most other Arabs will probably assume that the United States intervened in Iraq for its own reasons and not to liberate the population. Long-term gratitude is unlikely and suspicion of U.S. motives will increase as the occupation continues. A force initially viewed as liberators can rapidly be relegated to the status of invaders should an unwelcome occupation continue for a prolonged time.... Occupation problems may be especially acute if the United States must implement the bulk of the occupation itself rather than turn these duties over to a postwar international force.... Nevertheless, the United States should not expect that occupation forces will be protected by a bottomless well of gratitude. Most Iraqis will assume that the United States has intervened in their country for its own political purposes and not to liberate them from oppression, an argument that is not terribly difficult to make.[17]

The U.S. Army study also noted, "The longer U.S. presence is maintained, the more likely violent resistance will develop."[18] Again, in February 2003, the CIA warned: "A quick military victory in Iraq will likely be followed by armed resistance from remnants of the Ba'ath Party and Fedayeen Saddam irregulars."[19] These assessments and warnings were not the work of a single individual or analyst, but the compilation of years of experience and data related to occupation of nations by foreign powers. They fell on deaf ears.

Despite Rumsfeld's rejection of the Powell Doctrine, the U.S. Armed Forces were planning to sweep Iraq using overwhelming force and to destroy the Iraqi army in decisive combat. Firepower and skillful maneuver would utterly destroy whatever organized Iraqi force would be fielded until the regime was eliminated and Baghdad occupied. This operation was embodied in the Central Command's war plan called Operational Plan (OPPLAN) 1003. It would eventually be renamed Operation Iraqi Freedom (OIF).

OPPLAN 1003 ensured that the forces aligned against the Iraqis were superior in quality and capable of handling anything that stood in their way. The firepower that would be brought to bear would be nothing less than massive. The coalition had arrayed 466,985 men and women who would be operating and supporting the most technologically advanced army in the world. A total of 231,000 were forward deployed specifically to carry out the invasion. The numerical advantage the Iraqis enjoyed on paper of a 400,000-man active duty army was just that: a paper army.

The bet was that the core of Iraqi forces could be influenced to surrender or walk away from the battlefield as they had done in the first Gulf War. Millions of psychological warfare leaflets encouraging the Iraqis to abandon their positions would be dropped on these forces entreating them to do just that. In the long run, it proved a very effective tactic. Few wanted to fight for Saddam, but the presence of the political cadres backed up by the internal security forces and the vicious Saddam Fedayeen made it almost impossible to defect until the day of the invasion.

The invasion of Iraq would be carried out from four separate lines of approach along three axes using a coalition of predominantly U.S. and British forces. The major push would come from the south. Two forces first spearheaded by the 3rd Infantry Division, the 101st Airborne, the 2nd Brigade Combat Team of the 82nd Airborne Division, and under the command of the V Corps would enter Iraq from the south and head northwest. The 1st Marine Expeditionary Force would penetrate from the south and run directly up the middle through central Iraq. These forces would come to envelop and seize Baghdad from the south, west, and east. Some would bypass Baghdad and clear northern Iraq to Mosul. The 10th Mountain Division and 2nd Calvary would send elements to secure the rear in southern and central Iraq. From the southeast, the British 1st Armored Division would move through Safwan and the Al Faw Peninsula and occupy eastern Iraq north of Al Amarah along the Iranian border. In the west, the American Special Operations forces would seize critical airfields and suspected chemical and biological weapons sites as well as SCUD missile launch sites and await link-up with forces approaching from the south. Australian Special Operations forces would work closely with both British and American commandos. In the north, the 173rd Airborne Infantry would link up with the Special Forces and their Kurd allies, the Kurdish Democratic Party (KDP) and Popular Union of Kurdistan's (PUK) Peshmerga fighters. They would take on the terrorist group Ansar al-Islam and move south to cross the Green Line and seize Kirkuk from the Iraqi military. The 4th Infantry Division, which initially planned to enter Iraq from Turkey in the north, was denied access and was rerouted to enter from Kuwait. The 4th Infantry Division would later take over occupation duties and operate in the Sunni loyalist areas of northwestern Iraq.

The coalition invaded with a much smaller force than the Iraqis, but the invasion was spearheaded by the world's most advanced armored assault force. Numbering approximately 1,000 main battle tanks and 1,000 infantry fighting vehicles to the estimated 2,200 older Iraqi battle tanks and 3,700 vehicles, the coalition had a qualitative advantage over the Iraqi ground forces that would simply drive the Iraqi army off the field in fear of a massacre. The large majority of the Iraqi army would not go near their vehicles, and as predicted, they walked off the battlefield in the face of the invasion. Additionally, the coalition had over 300 attack helicopters and dominated the Iraqi airspace with 1,663 fighter, attack, and support aircraft. The Iraqi army and regime would be savaged throughout the war, and so it would be: Iraq would fall. It was only a matter of how fast.

ENDNOTES

1. T.E. Lawrence, *Seven Pillars of Wisdom*, 2nd ed., Garden City Publishing Co., Garden City, NY, 1938.
2. Scott Peterson, What the British Learned in 1920 by Not Leaving Iraq, *Christian Science Monitor*, March 11, 2004.
3. The Secret Downing Street Memo, *Times*, May 1, 2005, retrieved from http://www.timesonline.co.uk/article/0,,2087-1593607,00.html.
4. Edward T. Pound, Seeds of Chaos, *U.S. News and World Report*, December 20, 2004.
5. Ibid.
6. Thom Shanker, Hussein Agents Are Behind Attacks in Iraq: Pentagon Finds, *New York Times*, April 29, 2004.
7. Comprehensive Report of the Special Advisor to the DCI on Iraq's WMD, http://www.cia.gov/cia/reports/iraq_wmd_2004/chap1.html.
8. Vernon Loeb and Thomas Ricks, Is This Saddam's Counter-Attack? *Washington Post*, November 12, 2003.

9. Study Ties Hussein, Guerrilla Strategy, *Boston Globe*, October 11, 2004, http://www.boston.com/news/nation/washington/articles/2004/10/11/study_ties_hussein_guerrilla_strategy/.

10. Rob Noordland, Tom Masland, and Christopher Dickey, The Insurgents, *Newsweek*, February 7, 2005.

11. Comprehensive Report of the Special Advisor to the DCI on Iraq's WMD, http://www.cia.gov/cia/reports/iraq_wmd_2004.

12. Ibid.

13. Lawrence.

14. Pound.

15. CNN Report: Search for the Smoking Gun, http://www.cnn.com/2003/US/01/10/wbr.smoking.gun/.

16. Prewar Intelligence Predicted Iraqi Insurgency, *USA Today*, October 24, 2004.

17. Conrad C. Crane and W. Andrew Terrill, *Reconstructing Iraq: Insights, Challenges, and Missions for Military Forces in a Post-Conflict Scenario*, U.S. Army War College, February 2003, 56.

18. Ibid.

19. Prewar Intelligence Predicted Iraqi Insurgency, *USA Today*, October 24, 2004.

CHAPTER 3

Crucible of the Insurgency
The Fedayeen Goes to War

By March 2003, the Iraqi armed forces were making preparations for the American invasion. Throughout the country armored and mechanized infantry units started moving from their casernes to date palm groves and graded sand berms called revetments. The Iraqi military command divided their forces into four regional defense sectors. The Northern Defense Sector covered the Turkish and Iranian borders and gave Saddam defense against the U.S.-backed Kurds. The Western Defense Sector covered the borders with Jordan and Syria and protected against the closest approaches from Israel to Iraq. The Central Defense Sector provided a buffer for the defense of Baghdad and was the heart of the regime. In this case, the most important sector, the Southern Defense Sector, defended the Iranian, Kuwaiti, and Saudi Arabian borders. It was from Kuwait and Saudi Arabia that the U.S. attack would come.

Each sector commander was a loyal general under Saddam Hussein who commanded all regular military units, both army and air defense, in that sector. On the other hand, regime units such as the Saddam Fedayeen, the Special Security Service, and Special Republican Guard were under the direct control of Saddam's family, particularly his two sons Uday and Qusay.

It was clear to all in Iraqi society that the Americans were coming. It would be up to the most loyal forces of Saddam Hussein's regime to attempt to stop them. Years of United Nations embargo and a lack of preparedness permeated the army a decade after a devastating loss to the U.S. coalition in the first Gulf War. To the general defense staff the defenders of Iraq would come down to two types of forces that might oppose the Americans: sacrificial forces and loyalist forces. The Iraqi army, navy, and air defense forces would be sacrificed to slow the Americans, while the loyalist forces defended the regime. Despite the propaganda being fed to Saddam Hussein, Iraqi generals knew the army would suffer a rapid defeat by the allied British and American invasion force. The invasion of Iraq was not a question of how well the Iraqi forces could defend, but exactly how fast those who chose to resist the coalition army and marines would collapse or be destroyed. Given that, the senior staff had to make some hard assumptions. In the end, the Iraqis chose a strategy that was simple, proven, and if done right, would be effective: use successive rings of defense around each city from Basrah to Mosul. Each city would defend and hold the Americans down. Hope was placed in the belief that once the Americans broke through, they would meet another ring of defense and wear themselves out.

FIRST LINE OF DEFENSE—THE AIR DEFENSE FORCES

Despite the rhetoric, some forces could never be relied upon to defend Iraq. At the top of the list were the air force and air defense missile forces. At one time a gleaming example of one of the best air forces in the Middle East, by 2003 the Iraqi Air Force (IQAF) was without doubt one of the worst. Gen. Iyad al-Rawi, commander of the air defense forces, promised Saddam vigorous action in the skies over Iraq, but the IQAF was a passing shadow of the aerial juggernaut it became during the Iran-Iraq war and a skeleton of the force decimated during Desert Storm. At the time of the 1991 war it was the sixth largest air force in the world. However, most of the IQAF was lost to a political trick, not aerial combat.

During the first Gulf War, the IQAF was under a merciless systematic bombardment. Saddam managed to secure an agreement with Iraq's former enemy, Iran, to fly the most sophisticated aircraft to Iranian airbases for safekeeping. Iran agreed. So, in the middle of Operation Desert Storm the IQAF fled the country, flying its most advanced aircraft, including the Mirage F-1E and Mig-29 FULCRUM fighter jets, to Iran. The ability of the Iraqis to fly ground strike missions against the American army was likewise in the hands of Iran. Like the other aircraft, they were seized by its neighbor. Thus, more than 100 of Iraq's French-made Mirage F-1EQ5 and F-1EQ6 strike/antishipping aircraft and, most significantly, its Russian-built Su-24 FENCER ground attack aircraft and 33 civil airliners were absorbed into the Iranian air forces. The Iranians were supposed to safeguard the heart of one of the most advanced air forces in the Middle East. After 10 years of war with the Iraqis, the Iranians figured why give them back? The Iranian government quickly came up with a reason to seize them—it simply claimed they had never arrived in Iran and had been shot down by the Americans en route! In an instant Iraq lost its entire fleet of advanced aircraft.

By 2003 the IQAF had a few patched-up Mig-29 fighters and many ancient, poorly maintained Mig-21 FISHBED, Mig-23 FLOGGER, and

Mig-25 FOXBAT fighters. Iraq was left after the first Gulf War with only the ancient, smaller Mig-27 FLOGGER, SU-17 FITTERs, and derelict TU-16 BADGER and TU-22 BLINDER bombers. Almost all would be destroyed on the ground. In the face of an onslaught of American and British fighters, many serviceable IQAF aircraft would be later found buried in the desert sands at airfields in western Iraq instead of sacrificed to the U.S. Air Force. The surface-to-air missile defense forces were in no better shape. The radars and batteries of missiles had been decimated through American air strikes on their positions in the no-fly zones one by one over a 12-year period. The few remaining systems were in such poor condition that many batteries were abandoned by soldiers who fled under relentless pounding from the air. The anti-aircraft artillery (AAA) guns were better off, but any gun larger than the twin-barreled ZSU-23 was an invitation to a quick death from the hundreds of aircraft hunting them. Most AAA guns were eventually used in a direct-fire role against the American ground forces.

SECOND LINE OF DEFENSE—THE IRAQI ARMY

If the Iraqi air forces were a shadow of their heyday, then the Iraqi Regular Army (RA), the second line of defense, was a ghost of what it once was. After a failed Iraqi invasion of Iran in 1981, the Iran-Iraq war turned the small British-trained army into an almost 4-million-man behemoth. For 8 years Iraq used its vast oil wealth to buy some of the world's most advanced tanks, artillery, and missile systems for its soldiers. Victorious in defending Iraq against numerous massive incursions by the Iranian Army, the Iraqi army grew into the Arab powerhouse in the Middle East and the fourth largest army in the world. Compared to its other Middle East counterparts, Iraq had an unstoppable force. However, Saddam's poorly conceived invasion of Kuwait in 1990 brought instant devastation to its best units. The U.S. Air Force savaged it from the air, and the U.S. Army, Marines, and British forces obliterated its most well-trained divisions and brought it to the status of a mere paper army.

By 2003, the 400,000 men arrayed in Iraq's defense were less than reliable. A defanged tiger, the years of UN sanctions and internal witch hunts by Saddam's intelligence agencies gave the conscripted soldiers an attitude ripe for a lackadaisical performance. The RA units included 17 poorly equipped armor and infantry divisions. They would have their combat support infrastructure destroyed before the ground war had begun by a relentless pounding from the U.S. Air Force. Its equipment was equally as bad off. It possessed 1,000 older tanks, mainly T-55s and T-62s (tanks that barely survived the first Gulf War), and a handful of the somewhat more modern but outgunned T-72 tanks. The army also had 1960s generation armored personnel carriers (APCs), all without spare parts or planned maintenance. All of them would offer excellent target practice for the high-technology American M-1A2 Abrams and British Challenger tanks. As in Desert Storm, Iraqi tanks were easy prey for the hundreds of attack aircraft that hunted them. Any tanks or APCs that were caught out in the open were dead meat not only from the U.S. and British Air Force, Navy, and Marine Corps strike aircraft, but also from the U.S. Army's helicopters dedicated to destroying each and every one of them. With all of these strikes against it, the Iraqi Regular Army was primed to surrender at a rate even faster than in 1991.

In the ranks of the RA, the Sunni elite who ran the Ba'athist government were committed to defending Saddam. But 80% of Iraq was not Sunni Arab, but Shiite, Christian, Turkmen, or Sunni Kurd. That meant these ethnic soldiers were most likely not going to get involved in a fight between the Sunni Ba'athists and the Americans. The ethnic minorities—the Kurds, Shiite Arabs, Turkmen, and Armenian Christians—had only but to gain from an American invasion. Entire populations, not just those members in the armed forces, would also be a challenge to the internal security forces. The Shiite service members from southern Iraq, though placed in units along the fortified Kurdish frontier called the Green Line, would not be the best fighters. The rebel Kurdish forces were aligning with the Americans and had already made contact with their CIA and Special Forces partners. The two main Kurdish groups, the Popular Union of Kurdistan (PUK) and the Kurdish Democratic Party (KDP) forces, would strike with the Americans into the Arab-controlled northern Iraq if only to seize the city and oil fields of Kirkuk. A prize to the Kurds, Kirkuk was considered by them to be their natural Kurdish capital. Only Saddam's ruthless ethnic cleansing of the Kurds from Kirkuk and forced immigration of Arabs onto land they claimed foiled their nationalistic aspirations. Now, the Americans would come through the north with some form of special force led by the Kurdish militias. Even Saddam knew the Shiites of southern Iraq would not be so hasty as to openly support the invasion with his Ba'ath Party and Fedayeen supporters in place. The Ba'ath Party and Fedayeen units would be sent to secure the towns, dragoon manpower into the army, and express Saddam's displeasure with traitors. As predicted, once the ground war was launched, the majority of these forces simply did not show up for duty or donned civilian clothing and abandoned their positions to start the long walk home.

THIRD LINE OF DEFENSE—THE REPUBLICAN GUARD

The vanguard of the Iraqi Regular Army, the Republican Guard (RG) forces were no better off despite first pick from the old vehicles, better access to smuggled spare parts, and a modicum of training. The six RG divisions constituted the third layer of defense. The RG was deployed in a semi-integrated defensive ring around the approaches leading to Baghdad. They arrayed themselves in such a way that the U.S. Army and Marine Corps war planners thought it would be the RG divisions that would fight the fiercest and test them in severe combat. Materially they were significantly better than the RA, but to the U.S. and British forces they would be equal to paper targets on a shooting range.

The best chance the Iraqis had was to fight man to man, on foot in the small towns and cities. The Iraqis had the right equipment: billions of rounds of ammunition, AK-47 assault rifles, RPD and PKC machine guns, RPG-7 rocket-propelled grenade (RPG) launchers in the hundreds of thousands, tens of thousands of mortars, and millions of rounds of artillery, land mines, and other explosives that Saddam had produced and stockpiled during the Iran-Iraq war. Iraq's only chance to hurt the Americans was to rely on men being brave enough to rush the American tanks and positions and fight at close quarters with rifles, grenades, and knives. This near-suicidal strategy hoped to stall the Americans advance and bring about many more casualties than they could sustain. This was the only chance of survival for the forces that would be forced to fight through threat of death, the Ba'athist Al Quds army. In the end, they too ran away, and the honor of hard-core close combat was left to the forces Saddam knew would fight—the Saddam Fedayeen, the pan-Arab mercenaries, the foreign terrorists, and the Special Republican Guard.

LAST LINE OF DEFENSE—THE PARAMILITARY IRREGULARS, TERRORISTS, AND SPECIAL REPUBLICAN GUARD

The innermost ring and the last line of defense were left to the irregular paramilitary units of the Saddam Fedayeen, the foreign mercenaries, the emergency forces of the five intelligence agencies, the Al Quds people's defense forces, and the elite Special Republican Guard (SRG). Made up of approximately 26,000 men, the SRG consisted of 14 light infantry battalion-sized elements especially developed to protect the Hussein family in case of a military coup.[1] Like the Praetorian guard of Caesar's Rome, they would be surrounding the critical command centers and centers of political power in Baghdad. Within Baghdad itself were the final layers of protection for Saddam, including the presidential bodyguards, the intelligence apparatus, and top-ranked Ba'athist Party followers. The U.S. Central Command (CENTCOM) war planners believed at the time the SRG was considered the most potent threat inside the last ring of defense, and that once broken, the war would quickly end.

Gen. Izzat Ibrahim al-Douri, commander of the northern Iraq forces and a close confidant of Saddam, would be among the senior commanders to coordinate the arming of the civilian populace to augment the army and RG units. Throughout Iraq a massive arsenal of assault rifles, rockets, mines, and hand grenades was being distributed to nearly every man and woman, particularly in Baghdad and the cities of the Sunni Triangle. Every rifle that could be brought to bear on the Americans would be fielded without regard to the lives of the individual. It was a time that every Iraqi would be expected to sacrifice himself or herself in defense of the nation. Each member of this upper tier of the regime was tied at the hip with the crimes of Hussein and would be sure to fight in some capacity. The regime security apparatus and party members were dispersed across Iraq and organized into small combat teams directed by the Saddam Fedayeen and Ba'ath Party officers. By the beginning of the invasion the loyalist's paramilitary soldiers under arms numbered approximately 97,000 men, and an unknown number of Ba'athists forces would join them. Ba'ath Party members and foreign mercenaries would be counted on to support any areas that the Americans broke through and fill the gaps. Most would simply take those rifles and vanish to await the outcome of the battle and protect their families. Many others went forward through coercion or devotion.

Long before the war necessitated mobilization, Saddam was thinking of a more effective population control mechanism apart from using the Ba'ath Party membership. In February 2001, Saddam ordered the creation of a civilian defense corps called Jaysh Al Quds, or "Jerusalem Army."[2] Organized into 21 "divisions," this army of untrained civilians was a follow-on to the Popular Army, another civil defense force organized during the Iran and Iraq war, disbanded, then reformed again in 1998. It was in fact a mishmash collection of Ba'ath forced "volunteers" and conscripts composed of civilians, party members, and their families armed with empty weapons and given rudimentary military training. One volunteer from each house was required to attend Al Quds training or the family's food ration cards were withheld. It was common for Ba'athists to send poverty-stricken substitutes to the training instead of their own children. The Al Quds was led by former chairman of the Commission on Youth and Sports, the same General al-Rawi who was a chief aid to Uday Hussein. Al-Rawi, like most regime commanders, was skilled in inflating the actual numbers of volunteers to make himself look better and avoid the wrath of the Husseins. He claimed to have fielded what would be a rhetoric-only force of 7 million, while Iraqi news agencies heralded commencement of training 300,000 volunteers to "liberate Jerusalem," or Al Quds in Arabic. Al-Rawi proclaimed that Jerusalem would be liberated from Israel, and that these Iraqis would fight alongside Palestinians in their intifada against Israeli occupation. All of these claims were merely a convenient propaganda smokescreen. The true role of the Al Quds volunteers would be to organize party loyalists to conduct basic gendarmerie and political control duties during any period of civil unrest. The forces were organized in each city and controlled at the neighborhood level from municipal and local Ba'ath Party headquarters and suboffices. At the lowest level, loyalists were assigned to organize the defense of each neighborhood street by street.[3] Now that invasion was upon them, the guns of the Al Quds would be necessary in this war. In December 2002 they were mobilized, armed, and reoriented to a suicidal mission to defend Iraq. Al Quds units were not militarily capable of stopping the U.S. forces, but Saddam and his generals hoped that, under the supervision of the Ba'ath Party political officers and assigned to support the brutal Saddam Fedayeen, they would fill the trenches defending the cities. At best, if forced to fight, they could make the prospect of an easy invasion just a little more costly to the Americans; at worst, they could slow down the American logistics train by forcing them to expend millions of rounds of ammunition killing untrained martyrs. This massing of human targets would be expected to help slow the American advance and hopefully allow the professional soldiers of the RA and Republican Guard as well as the paramilitary Saddam Fedayeen, Arab terrorists, Syrian mercenaries, and other regime forces to strike.

The overwhelming preponderance of the loyalists were from the area known as the Sunni Triangle, which included Ba'athist strongholds in Tikrit, Fallujah, Ramadi, Haditha, Bayji, Sharqat, Baqubah, Dur, Sammarah, Tal Afar, Suwayjah, Iskanderiyah, and Mosul. The loyalties of these people were also beholden to the tribes that benefited greatly under Saddam. In particular, the men from Saddam's Bu-Nasser tribe were among the most loyal and given the jobs that required unyielding loyalty. The paramilitary and intelligence agencies drew their manpower from the triangle, and their entire basis of power rested on the continuing success of Saddam. Saddam Hussein expected all loyalist forces to fanatically defend their cities, provinces, and the capital. The stakes were high; an American victory would mean immediate subjugation of the Sunni population.

The rest of Iraq was under the firm grip of the intelligence and internal security apparatus established by Saddam in each city, in particular the southern Shiite cities of Najaf, Karbala, Hillah, Basrah, Naseriyah, Al Amarah, and the "Saddam City" section of Baghdad. In the north it was a different story—Irbil, Sulaimaniyah, and Dohuk, Zakho, were firmly under the control of the Kurdish KDP and PUK militias and were essentially a free and independent country. Only Kirkuk, a Kurdish city flooded with Saddam-backed Arabs, really remained under Saddam's control after the 1991 Gulf War. The Kurds would surely be coming back for it with the U.S. Army in front of them.

THE SADDAM FEDAYEEN (FIRQAH AL-FIDAYI SADDAM)

The heart of the loyalist resistance was the fearsome Saddam Fedayeen, or "Saddam's Men of Sacrifice." The Fedayeen was a paramilitary organization between 30,000 and 40,000 men designed not only to operate completely above the law, but also to be a law unto itself in Iraq.[4] Created in October 1994 around a corps of 10,000 men, the Fedayeen were a devoted band of shock troops who were organized as a military force capable of ruthlessly putting down any armed rebellion or insurrection, especially in the oppressed Shiite Muslim areas in central and southern Iraq.[5] Initially, the group formed as the "Saddamist Union," a body of active duty soldiers, Republican Guardsmen, and young Ba'athist elite under Qusay Hussein. Originally a form of a loyalist men's club, its members received special privileges, including automatic enrollment in universities, the right to carry weapons, and the peculiar pleasure of being closely aligned with Qusay Hussein. Within the year 15,000 were specially selected to form the core cadre of the Fedayeen Saddam.[6] The Fedayeen started out by curbing private criminal enterprises that were supposed to be government-controlled criminal enterprises. Some forms of regime-sanctioned smuggling had descended into oil and goods privateering by individuals and local tribes. Qusay was tasked to put an end to it. Any outspoken opposition to the Fedayeen was immediately followed by a midnight deployment of its units, who would swiftly and brutally descend on a home, village, or region and do whatever it took to punish the offender. Acting as thugs and enforcers, the Fedayeen were expected to impose swift retribution from the top down. Absolute fear of the black-hooded men was a critical component of their effectiveness.

A more subtle reason for the group's creation was Saddam's need to balance all branches of his government against one another, including those of his own sons; "the Fedayeen was created as a counterweight to the Republican Guard and the [Organization of Special Security], two elite groups that reported to Saddam's youngest son, Qusay."[7] Thus, the Fedayeen Saddam was formed to protect Saddam personally by crushing dissent throughout Iraq and by balancing against mutiny in other security forces. Judith Yaphhe, a former CIA analyst at the National Defense University, describes them as a force dedicated to "regime protection and dirty tricks," as well as operating like a political cadre to put stiffness into the backbones of wavering troops.[8]

The Fedayeen never had an issue with recruitment or manpower. It played on tribal ties and social dissatisfaction in its recruiting; its members were mainly recruited from Hussein's tribe and hometown of Tikrit. The Ba'ath provided many incentives for other young men to join the Fedayeen; the guerrilla fighters received land, extra food rations, and free medical care. The Fedayeen received salaries significantly higher than those of government workers, doctors, and other career fields. The off-the-books perks were legion.

Many members of the Fedayeen started their professional loyalist careers in the Fedayeen feeder group as members of the Ashbal Saddam ("Saddam's Lion Cubs"). The Ashbal was a military organization for children aged 10 to 16 created in 1998 with the task of taking the children of Sunni Party loyalists and sharpening them for work in the Special Security services or recruitment into the Saddam Fedayeen (Figure 3.1).[9] Local Iraqis recall that the Fedayeen also sought out homeless and orphaned boys. Many called themselves the "Sons of Saddam" and loved him for giving them a future and prestige. Along with its fraternal agency, the Iraqi Youth Organization, these young boys were told their missions in a war would be to support the Ba'ath Party through future combat. They were taught the basics of marksmanship, hand-to-hand combat, and games of sniping the enemy and conducting ambush exercises. Iraqi television created propaganda videos showing Saddam Fedayeen officers training children, who beamed with pride as they showed their skills in jumping through fiery hoops and firing the Kalashnikov rifle. Membership in the Fedayeen brought prestige and power that many of these men could not have gained in any other

FIGURE 3.1   Children in Saddam's Lion Cubs (Ashbal Saddam) fire the AK-47 rifle as part of Saddam Fedayeen commando pipeline training.

FIGURE 3.2 Typical insurgent weapons cache prepared and hidden before the 2003 invasion. (From U.S. DoD.)

manner; thus, the Saddam Fedayeen grew from 15,000 party loyalists into a hard corps of 40,000 young commandos fiercely loyal to Saddam and whose livelihood depended upon the continuation of Ba'ath Party power (Figure 3.2).

COMMANDER OF THE SADDAM FEDAYEEN—UDAY HUSSEIN

Uday was born in Baghdad on June 18, 1964, to Saddam's first wife, Sajida. He liked to brag that as a baby he was involved in the politics of the Ba'ath Party, even though the party was still an underground movement at the time of his birth. During the period that Saddam was imprisoned, it was said "Sajida would bring him messages from Bakr [member of the Ba'ath Party], who had been released from prison, that were hidden in baby Uday's clothes, which enabled Saddam to keep abreast of Ba'ath party affairs."[10] Uday was undeniably Saddam's chosen heir in his youth, and he joined the Ba'ath Party at the young age of 12.[11]

Uday was educated at Al Kharkh Al Namouthajiya School in Baghdad, his father's alma mater and the school that his mother ran before her marriage to Saddam. While in school, he became fluent in English and developed a taste for Western culture and technology; at the age of 16, "Uday informed his interviewer that he was good at physics and chemistry and that he wanted to go to the university [MIT] to study nuclear physics."[12] While he never fulfilled his dream of becoming a nuclear scientist, Uday did go on to graduate from the University of Baghdad's College of

Engineering in 1984.[13] That same year Uday married his cousin Saja, the daughter of his uncle Barzan Ibrahim. The union was dissolved after only 6 months, reportedly due to Uday's physical abuse of his wife. No children were produced, leading to rumors of Uday's infertility. It is possible that these rumors fueled Uday's notorious exploitation of women throughout his life as an attempt to disprove the gossip.[14]

Over the years, his reputation developed into one of bloodthirsty ruthlessness equal to that of his father. From his years as a student, he was loud and vulgar in school; girls and compatriot's wives were forced to be his sex slaves, and on a whim he would steal the cars of classmates' families. There are numerous stories of his beating and torturing athletes, kidnapping women, and murdering any who stood in his way. Uday became one of the most hated people in Iraq, for both his extreme violence and his affluent lifestyle in the face of the general poverty of the Iraqi people.[15]

Uday's power base came not only from his position as Saddam's eldest son, but also from the numerous organizations under his control. In 1984, at age 20, Uday assumed the role of director of Iraq's Olympic Committee. This figurehead position allowed Uday to learn the mechanisms of the Iraqi government, including every aspect of corruption, graft, and profit skimming.[16] It also had the secondary effect of placing all sport and youth activities in the country under his direction and control. From this position he laid the seeds of the Saddam Fedayeen. It was later discovered that the Olympic Committee's building housed Uday's personal jail, where he tortured and imprisoned his adversaries. Thus, his position as director of this committee provided Uday with a base of operations for his other political and economic endeavors in Iraq.[17]

Another important position that Uday held was as publisher of *Babel* newspaper. Uday used it as a personal tool. He was able to spread gossip about government officials and others who he wished to see removed from power. To be mentioned negatively in *Babel* was tantamount to a death sentence. Uday also became the owner of Youth TV, a government-run television program providing him with an even wider audience, and thus expanding his influence within the high echelons of government. In 1994, he became head of the Iraqi Journalists Union, effectively placing him at the head of the entire Iraqi media machine. With the power and influence this provided him, Uday developed "profitable enterprises in television, transport, hotels, and food processing."[18] Most importantly, Uday's control over all aspects of Iraqi media provided him with the opportunity to cover up his own illegal actions and shift the blame to innocent victims.[19]

As the most favored son of Saddam, he built an empire of illegal business enterprises; "Uday used violence and intimidation [and the threat of negative media coverage] to extort millions from Iraqi businesses, both legal and illegal."[20] According to Saddam biographer Con Coughlin, Uday was "personally involved in the resale of the humanitarian aid Iraq received from the UN on the black market."[21] Through his illegal business activities, Uday amassed huge amounts of personal wealth that augmented the power already given him by his official positions.[22]

In 1994, Uday was allowed to form the Saddam Fedayeen. Using the Saddam Fedayeen, Uday helped his father eliminate opponents and exert iron-fisted control over Iraq's 25 million people.[23] It also gave him a military power base comparable to that of his younger brother Qusay, who headed the Special Security apparatus in Iraq. Lastly, Uday was elected to a seat in parliament in 2000. It was thought the stature of a political position would placate him and avoid family problems.[24] As Saddam's favorite son, this was highly unlikely.

As Uday worked tirelessly to expand his power within the Ba'ath government, he often felt threatened by those around him; this led to numerous episodes in which Uday personally attacked high-level officials in pursuit of his own interests. In 1988, Uday murdered Kamel Hana Geogeo, Saddam's personal bodyguard and food taster. Geogeo had arranged an affair between Saddam and another woman, who bore Saddam a child, and Uday feared for his inheritance. Uday thus sought out Geogeo at a party and, by some accounts, beat him to death. Other accounts contend that Uday used an electric carving knife to stab and cut Geogeo repeatedly. Regardless of the specific murder weapon, Uday's actions greatly angered his father. He was stripped of his position as head of the Iraqi Olympic Committee, temporarily jailed, and sent into exile in Switzerland. However, his reckless behavior in Switzerland led to his expulsion and he returned to Iraq. After reconciling with his father, Uday was reelected as president of the Olympic Committee and was allowed to resume many of his former activities.[25]

In 1995, Uday disturbed the family peace once again by forcing the resignation of his uncle Watban. Uday published heated criticisms of his performance as head of the Interior Ministry through his media empire. In a drunken rage Uday attacked his uncle, "shooting him in the leg and killing three of his companions while they were attending a private party in Baghdad."[26] While this caused enough trouble on its own in the Hussein circle, it also led to the defection of Hussein and Saddam Kamel to Jordan with their wives, who happened to be Uday's sisters. Kamel was the head of the Military Industrialization Organization, the cover agency for chemical and biological weapons. At the time he was considered the second most powerful man in Iraq. His defection was a boon for Western intelligence as Kamel spoke openly about Saddam's nuclear, biological, and chemical programs under his control. It was Kamel's fear that he would be Uday's next target that led him to run to Jordan, since at that time he held more power in the Ba'ath government than Saddam's oldest son. Saddam was infuriated by this defection, and left it to Uday to find a remedy—a terminal remedy.

Uday lived up to his reputation and decisively resolved the issue. In Saddam's name he lured the Kamel brothers back into Iraq with promises of forgiveness, only to have them immediately killed in a staged gunfight with the Republican Guard and reportedly members of Kamel's own family who feared Saddam. Uday's jealous thirst for power continued to create conflict within the Ba'ath inner circle for the remainder of his life.[27]

Given the widespread hatred of Uday in many Iraqi circles, it is not surprising that there were many assassination attempts on his life. The most serious occurred in December 1996, when eight bullets were fired into Uday from less than 10 feet away. The attack was attributed to a group called al-Nahda, "a group of middle-class Iraqi professionals that had been set up in 1991 to overthrow Saddam."[28] The group of well-educated young people stated they "opposed the dictatorship, opposed the division of Iraq along racial and sectarian lines, and supported democracy."[29] The attackers were never caught, but hundreds to thousands of arrests were made in the search.[30] The assassination attempt led to Saddam's harsh condemnation of the reckless behavior of his family; he criticized Uday especially for attracting such concentrated hatred from the people of Iraq. Uday recovered from the assault, but remained crippled for the rest of his life and was forced to walk with a cane.[31]

Uday found trouble with his father again when day-to-day control of the Fedayeen was stripped from him after reports that he made unauthorized transfers of sophisticated weapons and equipment to his forces, thus upsetting the careful balance of power with his brother Qusay's rival Special Republican Guard. Control was temporarily given to Qusay but was soon returned to Uday. As the threat of an American invasion gathered, Uday was personally involved in the preparations for using the Fedayeen in active combat against the Americans in both the invasion and the post-war. Under his orders, the Fedayeen dragooned men, executed civilians, and took what they needed to prepare for combat.

Uday was served by loyalist deputies. The senior aide to Uday and the operational commander of the Fedayeen was Gen. Iyad Futiyeh al-Rawi. General al-Rawi was Saddam's former chief of staff and a war hero who commanded the Republican Guards during the Iran-Iraq war. Decorated by Saddam 27 times, he was renowned for his combat injury. He received a gunshot wound to the head during a major counteroffensive against Iranian forces near the end of the war, in which he recaptured all of the territory lost to Iran. That forced the Iranians to the bargaining table in 1987. For these acts Saddam awarded him one of Iraq's highest honors, the Qadisiyah Sword. He also held the post of chief of staff of the Al Quds volunteer forces, and worked closely with Uday in commanding the Saddam Fedayeen. Lt. Gen. Muzahim Sa'b

Hassan al-Tikriti was also a former commander of the Fedayeen during the brutal rape-murder spree against Saddam's rival's wives called the anti-prostitution campaign. He later went on to run the Iraqi air defense forces during the invasion period and was subsequently captured by the Americans.

THE PROFESSIONAL TERRORISTS ARRIVE— TAWHID WAL-JIHAD AND AL-QAEDA

Saddam knew that the Al Quds and Ba'ath paramilitary forces would be worthless in some circumstances. If they didn't run, he knew they would not be able to harm the Americans unless they were in the cities where they had a chance. To supplement the Fedayeen and Al Quds forces, he gave the national security team carte blanche to use any form of resistance to the invasion. A weakness of the American military was its palpable fear of terrorist attacks, particularly suicide attacks. If America was going to war on terrorism in Iraq, then naturally they would be wary of encountering terrorists. Saddam chose not to disappoint them. Hussein decided they would be met with a wave of Iraqi and foreign terrorists and hundreds of suicide car bombs. To gain a critical mass of resistance and to invoke a pan-Arab feel of Iraq's defensive jihad, Saddam ordered that any Arab man who wanted to come and fight would be welcomed, armed, and allowed to die as a martyr.

The five Iraqi intelligence organizations, led by the Directorate of General Intelligence, also called for any Arab to come to the aide of Iraq for pay. The U.S. Defense Intelligence Agency estimated 3,000 to 5,000 poor Syrians were recruited by their tribal chiefs or came in need of employment. The Syrians were an almost purely mercenary force. Young men in Damascus, Allepo, Hamah, and those living in the nearby border tribes were paid nearly $1,000 in cash to come to Baghdad, walk into an Al Quds volunteer center, muster into a unit, and fight where the Saddam Fedayeen indicated. The Fedayeen and the Al Quds forces were tasked to train the pan-Arab volunteers from Syria, Palestine, Saudi Arabia, Sudan, Algeria, Jordan, Lebanon, Egypt, and other nations. Many of the volunteers were studying or working in Iraq. Others came just for the battle. The bulk of the volunteer forces went to the Radwaniyah palace complex near Saddam International Airport. Many other Arab volunteers were concentrated in Al Kut, Fallujah, Ramadi, Mahmudiyah, Najaf, and Baghdad. A large contingent of Saudi volunteers was positioned along with the Al Quds and Fedayeen units in Basrah. They had been students at Basrah University but were dragooned or volunteered for the war. The Fedayeen also positioned a large concentration of foreign fighters near their terrorist training camp at Salman Pak southeast of Baghdad. Pentagon military planners justifiably considered them a minor threat compared to the Republican Guard divisions surrounding Baghdad and discounted their war fighting capability. However, they didn't appear to appreciate their potential for post-war terrorism.

Volunteers and mercenaries were not the only foreigners to come. With invasion imminent, the Iraqi Special Security Organization put the word out that any Arab Mujahideen who wanted to fight the Americans were welcome in Iraq. Weapons would be free, targets would be plentiful, and the opportunity for martyrdom would be guaranteed. If the Fedayeen were going to prove a fierce foe, they were a mask for a new and equally deadly threat emerging in Iraq. At the time of Saddam's call for jihad, America's principal terrorist enemy, al-Qaeda, had limited presence in Iraq. Ironically, the Iraqi-Kurd terrorist group Ansar al-Islam (AAI), "Partisans of Islam," operated only in the safety of the American-controlled northern no-fly zone in near Halabjah. Because Hussein's intelligence agencies were so ruthless and effective, Ansar al-Islam could not operate in the mainstream population of Iraq. Al-Qaeda's principal follower, Jordanian Abu Musab al-Zarqawi's group, called Tawhid Wal-Jihad (TWJ), "Monotheism and Holy War," had not been able to operate inside Saddam's Iraq freely despite occasional forays into Baghdad and transiting through Mosul. Hussein detested any challenge to his authority and decided that any Islamic fundamentalist terrorists wanted by America were a threat to him. On July 17, 2002, an all-points bulletin ordered Iraqi internal security to find and arrest al-Zarqawi.[32] But the shoe was on the other foot now. If Hussein was offering entry, non-interference, and unlimited weapons, so be it—it was a partnership of convenience.

With the assistance of Iraqi intelligence's contacts in Syria, al-Qaeda's senior representative in the region, Abu Musab al-Zarqawi, and his TWJ operatives were mobilizing and streaming into Iraq under cover as Arab volunteers. The professional terrorists of al-Qaeda were, in a way, going to assist Iraq. But not in a way Hussein would relish. Contrary to Hussein's desire, al-Qaeda, TWJ, and AAI were looking far past Saddam Hussein and for a different vision of the post-war Iraq. Although they fully intended to fight in combat against the Americans, their real intention was to wait out the defeat of Hussein and start their own jihad against the Americans. To the Mujahideen throughout the Muslim world, the Ba'athist regime was dead and good riddance. They believed that no one who was a true Muslim could resist a pure-hearted call to Islam, no matter what artificial Western name was imposed on them. These Mujahideen saw this as an opportunity to establish a long-term base of operations for al-Qaeda and then to create an Islamic state of Iraq dominated by religiously converted Sunni. Far from the heart of Islam, Afghanistan was never the best place to train and support the

Arab Muslim Mujahideen. In Iraq the Americans were not only giving them an opportunity for an inspirational jihad, but all the resources as well. The invasion of Iraq would be the greatest gift George Bush could give Osama bin Laden. They envisioned a real holy war with heroic men fighting against desperate odds in the heart of historic Islam, just like the first battles of the Prophet Mohammed. Bin Laden knew that by playing a more strategic game than just holding the line in Afghanistan he could gain far more than he bargained for. The American invasion could herald a new day in the evangelism of his Salafist form of Islam. Salafism is a puritanical form of Islam that favors a return to the roots of the first three pure generations of Islam and the companions of the Prophet Mohammed. Bin Laden and al-Qaeda believe in a form of Salafism that can be best described as "neo-Salafism."[33] Anthony Cordesman of the Center for Strategic and International Studies describes it this way: "They see those who do not fit into their definition of piety as apostates. To some, particularly the group led by [Abu Musab] Zarqawi, all other Islamic sects like Shias and even other Sunnis are effectively nonbelievers."[34] It was a gift that even the patient bin Laden could not resist. Al-Qaeda would use Abu Musab al-Zarqawi's TWJ group as its core combat arm and then throughout the occupation inspire others to join the jihad. He quickly backed al-Zarqawi's play but would await tangible results before fully committing.

Al-Qaeda members came into Iraq, under the guise of assistance to Saddam, to establish long-term logistical and jihadist pathways, loot the weapons stockpiles, and inspire tens of thousands of young men to perform jihad against a perceived rape of an Arab country. Additionally, this jihad could gain new lines of revenue that the loss of Afghanistan could not. This invasion was against Islam itself, and the Americans would be sure to conduct themselves in a manner that would enrage every Muslim worldwide. TWJ immediately established themselves along the principal pathways to Jordan and Syria and used Fallujah and Ramadi as their base of operations. Once they arrived they used their position, money, and inspirational speech to collect a vast array of weapons, safe houses, and training sites—all with the blessing of the local Iraqis and the Ba'ath Party.

THE FEDAYEEN BECOME TERRORISTS

The Iraqis were using the prewar period to hone their terrorist combat capabilities as well. The Iraqis had fair expertise in the world of terrorism, but few outside of the Western intelligence and Special Operations communities could imagine the level of intensity and bloodletting planned by the Fedayeen. The Iraqi Special Security Organization (SSO) and the Iraqi Intelligence Service (IIS) were renown for their terrorism camps and had maintained a capability to develop and export advanced improvised explosive devices over the years. For example, in 1991, during Operation Desert Storm, an attempt by an IIS agent on the life of the American ambassador to Indonesia, John Monjo, failed. Working in this Asian country as a foreign expatriate, the IIS agent managed to plant 24 sticks of dynamite in a plant pot outside of the wall of the ambassador's living room. The device was poorly positioned and was found before it exploded. Former FBI Chief of National Security Neil Gallagher reported that before the first Gulf War, Iraq had dispatched 40 two-man teams to conduct attacks worldwide. The few attempts that came off were extremely amateurish. One would-be bomber of the American library in the Philippines was killed carrying a device that prematurely exploded. His partner reported that they were dropped off by the Iraqi consul general and gave investigators the Iraqi diplomat's official business card.[35]

Not all attempts at terrorism were so buffoonish. An extremely sophisticated Iraq intelligence-built car bomb was seized in Kuwait in 1993 in a failed attempt to kill former President George H.W. Bush during his visit to Kuwait. Despite the amateurish use of an untrained bomber coerced by the IIS to deliver and detonate the device, the car bomb was designed as a remotely triggered Toyota Land Cruiser that had between 40 and 50 pounds of RDX plastic explosives. Additionally, 10 other bombs were found in the car for a bombing campaign throughout Kuwait. Eleven Iraqis and three Kuwaitis were tried for the plot.[36] In 1993, President Bill Clinton launched retaliatory air strikes that destroyed the IIS headquarters in Baghdad. The style and components of the Kuwait bombs were consistent with a type of Iraqi-built bombs found in other attempted attacks in the Middle East. The construction and delivery tradecraft represented a capability that just needed sharpening. By 2003 the Iraqi vehicle-borne improvised explosive device (VBIED) would become the global standard for car bombs.

In September 2002, the five Iraqi intelligence agencies started bringing covert and clandestine agents home from overseas assignments. Some were left on station and tasked to perform disruptive terrorist acts overseas if the opportunity presented itself. The head of the Directorate of General Security, Iraq's principal intelligence agency, was Barzan Ibrahim al-Hassan al-Tikriti. In the immediate prewar he sought out to contract or coordinate terrorist suicide bombings in Amman, Jordan, the Philippines, and the United States. Though none came to fruition, the Iraqi intelligence agencies did start combat skills training for fighting in the enemy's rear. Improvised explosive devices, use of rockets and small mortars, as well as suicide car bomb construction were all in the curriculum (Figure 3.3). Once occupied, there would be no time to do

FIGURE 3.3   The Special Security Organization's Ghafiqi Project (M21) taught Saddam Fedayeen and select loyalist officers how to make IEDs from discarded artillery shells, such as this Army of the Mujahideen "super IED" shown in 2004.

this, and hundreds of suicide car bombs would need to be prepared in advance for the defense of Baghdad. Already given access to the best weapons, the intelligence agencies and their emergency forces worked to ensure they would be able to use those skills not only during the invasion, but once the Americans occupied the Sunni Triangle.

INVASION AND S-VBIEDS—INTRODUCTION OF THE SUICIDE CAR BOMB TO IRAQ

The American and British invasion blitzed through Iraq with forces heading to Basrah, suffering delays by the Fedayeen in Naseriyah, Samawah, and massacring jihadist volunteers north of al-Kut. Something new was about to be introduced in the history of Iraq. On the morning of March 21, 2003, Iraqi Army Sergeant Ali Jaafar al-Nomani, dressed as a civilian and driving an explosive-filled taxi cab, drove up to a checkpoint of the 1st Brigade, 3rd Infantry Division, on Highway 9 north of Najaf. The car stopped short of the checkpoint and al-Nomani waved for the four soldiers manning the post to approach and assist him. As they surrounded the vehicle he was asked to open the trunk. He complied gladly, went to the trunk, and activated a detonator. The booby-trapped taxi exploded, killing all four soldiers and the bomber. There had never before been a suicide bomb exploded in Saddam's part of Iraq. The extremist group Ansar al-Islam had attacked the Kurds twice before with suicide bombers weeks prior to the war,[37] but this was a new tactic for Saddam in the defense of Baghdad. Al-Nomani had successfully tested it against the Americans in Najaf courtesy of Iraqi intelligence and the Fedayeen. The U.S. forces had experienced suicidal infantry and crazed civilian foot attacks during the march from Kuwait, but no one had seriously warned that the first of hundreds of S-VBIEDs was headed their way.

Counterterrorism professionals called S-VBIEDs human-guided weapons. This terrorist tool had several advantages. First, it would kill Americans using minimal forces; second, it would covertly deliver precision explosives in areas where regular forces would be quickly killed; and finally, it led to a calculated backlash from the Americans' severe crackdown on vehicles entering coalition lines. The Iraqis knew this would cause civilian casualties, as the Americans became suspicious of any approaching vehicle. This would provide them with a propaganda coup as well. Saddam Hussein later praised Sergeant Nomani's attack and awarded two posthumous medals to the bomber's family. The Americans did not fail on their part. Within 24 hours of the S-VBIED attack a van with Iraqi civilians was fired upon and seven women and children were killed. Outrage at the U.S. forces' rules of engagement against civilians created a firestorm of complaints that further inflamed the already frayed opinions in the Middle East.

On April 2, 2003, elements of the 75th Ranger Regiment seized the Haditha Dam. This mission as reported by the Central Command was to prevent a release of the dam's water by Saddam, which could destroy downriver areas near Karbala. The local Fedayeen and loyalists were clustered in the town of Haditha, just south of the dam. From there the Americans on the dam were bombarded by mortars and some artillery. It was from here that the Haditha Fedayeen dispatched the second suicide bomb attack of the war. On the night of April 3, three men of the U.S. 3rd Battalion of the 75th Ranger Regiment, Capt. Russell Rippletoe, Staff Sgt. Nino Livaudais, and Spc. Ryan Long, stepped out of the dark of their checkpoint to stop an approaching vehicle. As the car drove up the Rangers saw no reason for alarm. Two women were seated inside and appeared unarmed. The vehicle rolled to a stop near the men and a pregnant woman emerged. She started frantically screaming and waving for the three rangers to approach closer. The men moved forward believing the pregnant woman needed assistance. They were walking toward her when the women detonated a bomb hidden inside the vehicle. The blast instantly killed all three rangers and the two women. Within twenty-four hours of the Haditha Dam attack the Iraqi government broadcast a pre-mission videotape of two women, Wadad Jamil Jassem and Nour Qaddour al-Shanbari, the pregnant woman. Al-Shanbari was seen on video standing before an Iraqi flag and swore on the Qu'ran "to defend Iraq ... and take revenge from the enemies of the (Islamic) nation, Americans, imperialists, Zionists, and Arabs who have submitted to the foreigners.... We say to our leader and holy war comrade, the hero commander Saddam Hussein, that you have sisters that you and history will boast about." Saddam Hussein called them heroes of Iraq.

This attack would be praised by Saddam and would inspire a wave of S-VBIED attacks during the 3rd Infantry Division's assault on Baghdad. A week later, the local Fedayeen blew up an oil stabilization plant's pipelines near the Haditha Dam. This fire burned for more than 2 weeks. These infrastructure attacks would come to be another hallmark in economic recovery sabotage. Despite the heavy military presence, this region of Iraq would never be fully stabilized.

By the time U.S. forces approached Baghdad, they had started to see terrorist tactics become an integral part of the planning of the Iraqi regime. When the 3rd Infantry Division arrived in Baghdad, it executed a series of high-speed dashes through the western defenses of the city called thunder runs. The Americans knew what organized forces could generally be engaged around the city, but no one knew for sure what the irregular forces would bring to bear. The American M-1A2 tanks and M-2 Bradley armored fighting vehicles (AFVs) were nearly invulnerable to RPG-7 rocket fire, but they could still be overrun by dozens of enemy soldiers. The Fedayeen had studied American tactics from the beginning of the invasion, and they were well aware that the only way to defeat American armor was to close on it as rapidly as possible and attempt to defeat it in close combat. The battle in Naseriyah convinced the Fedayeen that the Americans were vulnerable in close quarters. The Fedayeen planned on using pickup and civilian vehicles to rapidly close on U.S. forces and then jump out and engage them. These Somali-like "technicals" driven by the Saddam Fedayeen brought ZSU-23 twin anti-aircraft guns directly to bear on the approaching American tank columns. The SRG had Land Rovers with recoilless rifles to quickly move fire support about the city. Though civilian traffic was light, it was present because of the American speed of advance. Startled drivers saw the lumbering Bradley AFVs and M-1 Abrams tanks speed down Baghdad's main western approach and quickly got out of their way. The manic Fedayeen were easier to identify. They would madly drive orange and white taxicabs, small private cars, or machine gun-laden technicals and attempt to close on the American tanks. Packed with men, they would be massacred in a blaze of 25 mm cannon or heavy machine gunfire. During the first of these thunder runs the Americans found more of Saddam's secret weapons waiting. Hundreds of S-VBIEDs were prepared by the covert Special Operations Unit M-14 SOD, the military's Special Unit 999, and the Saddam Fedayeen. These S-VBIEDs would be driven mainly by Syrians. When they died in combat their families would be paid their salary for their martyrdom. As the tanks approached each of the three critical overpasses, the S-VBIEDs would come speeding down ramps and attempt to blow up the tanks and AFVs by ramming them. Most were killed, and many S-VBIEDs failed to detonate once they struck their targets. The ones that did detonate usually exploded after being hosed down by the machine guns and cannons of the 3rd Infantry Division tanks and Bradley AFVs. Despite the relentless wall of rockets, self-propelled guns, and heavy machine guns fired throughout the running gun battle, dozens of RPG rounds slammed into U.S. tanks with little to no effect. Only one M-1 tank was knocked out of the battle by a lucky RPG rocket shot into its engine compartment fired from behind and below. Thinner-skinned vehicles didn't fare so well, as several fuel trucks and ammunition carriers were destroyed by mortar or rocket fire as they attempted to refuel the armored column. Tragedy struck when a large Iraqi ballistic missile struck an American armored brigade's headquarters and decimated its command staff. The Fedayeen and mercenaries fought fiercely but were slaughtered by the hundreds. Major Mike Donovan, commander of the first thunder run, categorized the wave after wave of suicidal resistance as "determined, but stupid."[38]

The bulk of the major combat was fought by Iraqi irregular forces that were not in uniform but street clothes. They consisted of hard-core Saddam Fedayeen, dragooned members of the Ba'ath Party, the scattered remnants of the Republican Guard, the Special Republican Guard, and the internal security and intelligence apparatus. Additionally, foreign-trained terrorists and volunteers joined the Iraqi forces. The foreign fighters made their way into Baghdad and were armed and put on the line to engage as small units. Teams would attempt to sneak up the embankments of overpasses and get high-angle shots on the passing tanks only to be evaporated by tank rounds or heavy machine guns. Others would lay down a fusillade of fire on any and all American forces only to be devastated by the superior firepower. Southeast of Baghdad the U.S. Marines fought a short but pitched battle with the foreigners recruited to man the lines at Salman Pak and quickly overcame all opposition to enter the city. The second of the thunder runs took the 3rd Infantry Division directly into the heart of Baghdad, and they successfully overcame the SRG and Fedayeen to capture the Republican Palace. The Americans had seized the center of Iraq's power. Despite small counterattacks at the fringes, it was apparent to all that the reign of Saddam Hussein was over.

THE FEDAYEEN DISPERSE

It was clear that the Americans and British had seized Iraq in an aggressive and brilliantly executed war. The only fly in the ointment appeared to be the Saddam Fedayeen and their terrorist allies. The British Ministry of Defense report on the lessons of the war stated, "The greater threat to the coalition, particularly to lines of communication and rear areas, was from paramilitary and irregular forces closely associated with the Saddam regime."[39] The success of the Saddam Fedayeen and irregular forces in slowing and harassing a major combat force of more than 150,000 men was unexpected. Like the Vietcong before them, the Iraqi irregular forces led by the Saddam Fedayeen proved that a small, highly agile force, even with poor training, could harass a large force and inflict surprising numbers of casualties. Like some of the intelligence assessments before the war, groupthink occurred again with political decision makers universally downplaying or underestimating the determination of the regime elements to resist the occupation. Although the outcome of the war was never in doubt, the stereotype of the Iraqis based on their poor performance in the 1991 Gulf War predisposed American military planners to believe there was no national pride to sustain resistance or face overwhelming American firepower. However, American forces had never before fought the regime's internal security apparatus or the newly formed Saddam Fedayeen. These paramilitaries combined with amateur terrorists to provide a surprising factor. Gaming these forces out, many commanders saw them as nothing more than police forces or thugs that could be bypassed and who would wither under direct fire. Yet many of these forces, in Basra, Naseriyah, Samawah, and Najaf, would fight ferociously. The Saddam Fedayeen would harass U.S. forces on the route between Naseriyah and Najaf with such frequency that reserve brigades had to be brought into Iraq early to secure the rear supply routes from their attacks. The determination of the Saddam Fedayeen to fight in the south proved surprising to some U.S. forces commanders; the commander of the U.S. V Corps, Lt. Gen. William Wallace, characterized the Saddam Fedayeen this way:

> We had to adjust to his paramilitary, which were more fanatical and more aggressive than we expected (them) to be. The adjustment that we made was to actually fight and have a presence in some of these urban areas that we had not really planned to do. We planned to bypass them. But we found it necessary to establish a presence to stop these paramilitaries from influencing our operations.[40]

The U.S. Army's official study of the invasion of Iraq agreed in this assessment and added:

> More surprising, the Fedayeen and other paramilitary forces proved more of a threat than anyone had expected. While the paramilitaries were always considered part of the enemy's capabilities, the intelligence

and operations communities had never anticipated how ferocious, tenacious and fanatical they would be.[41]

The American forces attacked with brilliance and precision, but relying on the poor intelligence from the Iraqi National Congress and cheerleading from the civilian leadership in the administration, including President Bush himself, it is clear they adopted an unwise and incautious groupthink about what the post-war would bring. With opinions from unpopular Iraqi exiles like Ahmed Chalabi and neoconservative hawks like Richard Pearle and Douglas Feith, the Bush war cabinet, minus perhaps Colin Powell, made the decision with an unshakable ideological belief that the Iraqi people would welcome U.S. forces with flowers and cheers. However, the opinions of the career intelligence officers and professional Middle East diplomats at the State Department warned as early as September 2002 that despite Saddam Hussein's brutal treatment of his people, there was a clear risk of backlash and resentment of being a nation occupied by a foreign force. Saddam Hussein and his generals may have been brutal—they killed many of their own people and turned torture into an art—but they held a key card that the Bush administration discounted: resistance to the occupation.

ENDNOTES

1. On Point—The History of the U.S. Army Invasion of Iraq, U.S. Department of the Army, 2005.
2. Iraq Starts Training Al Quds Volunteers, Agence France Presse, March 1, 2001.
3. Ali Albahrani, Saddam Trains 300,000 Volunteers for Jihad against Israel, *Shia News*, March 25, 2000.
4. Analysis: Who Are the Saddam Fedayeen? United Press International, March 27, 2003.
5. Most Loyal Soldiers in Iraq Belong to Fedayeen Saddam, *Seattle Times*, March 27, 2003.
6. Andrew Cockburn and Patrick Cockburn, *Saddam Hussein, an American Obsession*, Verso, London, 2000, 162.
7. Shadowy Fedayeen Pose a Random, Deadly Threat, *Sacramento Bee*, March 29, 2003.
8. Analysis: Who Are the Saddam Fedayeen? United Press International, March 27, 2003.
9. The Boys Hand-Picked to Be Martyrs for Saddam, *Sunday Mail*, March 30, 2003.
10. Con Coughlin, *Saddam, King of Terror*, Harper Collins Publishers, New York, 2002, 51.

11. Andrew Cockburn and Patrick Cockburn, *Saddam Hussein, an American Obsession*, Verso, London, 2000, 162.
12. Con Coughlin, *Saddam, King of Terror*, Harper Collins Publishers, New York, 2002, 132.
13. Andrew Cockburn and Patrick Cockburn, *Saddam Hussein, an American Obsession*, Verso, London, 2000, 162; Con Coughlin, *Saddam, King of Terror*, Harper Collins Publishers, New York, 2002, 20.
14. Coughlin and Cockburn, Obituary of Qusay Hussein, *Daily Telegraph*, London, July 24, 2003.
15. Coughlin and Cockburn, Violent Portrait: Aide Tells of Uday, *Boston Globe*, April 24, 2003.
16. Con Coughlin, *Saddam, King of Terror*, Harper Collins Publishers, New York, 2002, 20.
17. Coughlin and Cockburn, Obituary of Qusay Hussein, *Daily Telegraph*, London, July 24, 2003.
18. Coughlin and Cockburn, Obituary of Qusay Hussein.
19. Andrew Cockburn and Patrick Cockburn, *Saddam Hussein, an American Obsession*, Verso, London, 2000, 162.
20. Coughlin and Cockburn, Violent Portrait: Aide Tells of Uday, *Boston Globe*, April 24, 2003.
21. Con Coughlin, *Saddam, King of Terror*, Harper Collins Publishers, New York, 2002, 292.
22. Con Coughlin, *Saddam, King of Terror*, Harper Collins Publishers, New York, 2002, 255; Andrew Cockburn and Patrick Cockburn, *Saddam Hussein, an American Obsession*, Verso, London, 2000, 162.
23. Dead Brothers Reveled in Brutality, Ottawa Citizen, July 23, 2003.
24. Uday Is Staging a Comeback, Financial Times, April 1, 2000.
25. Coughlin and Cockburn, Violent Portrait: Aide Tells of Uday, *Boston Globe*, April 24, 2003, 230–235.
26. Con Coughlin, *Saddam, King of Terror*, Harper Collins Publishers, New York, 2002, 299.
27. Con Coughlin, *Saddam, King of Terror*, Harper Collins Publishers, New York, 2002, 20; Andrew Cockburn and Patrick Cockburn, *Saddam Hussein, an American Obsession*, Verso, London, 2000, 162.
28. Con Coughlin, *Saddam, King of Terror*, Harper Collins Publishers, New York, 2002, 306.
29. Con Coughlin, *Saddam, King of Terror*, Harper Collins Publishers, New York, 2002, 255.
30. Ibid.
31. Ibid.

32. Iraq Arrest Warrant for Abu Musab Zarqawi in Arabic, Document ISZG-2004-0199920, U.S. Department of Defense.
33. Malcolm W. Nance, *An End to al-Qaeda: Destroying bin Laden's Jihad and Restoring America's Honor*, St. Martin's Press, New York, 2010, 77.
34. Anthony Cordesman, The Iraqi Insurgency and the Risk of Civil War: Who Are the Players? Working Draft, Center for Strategic and International Studies, March 1, 2006.
35. David E. Kaplan and Kevin Whitelaw, Saddam's Secret Weapon, *U.S. News and World Report*, January 11, 2003.
36. Patterns of Global Terrorism, U.S. Department of State, 1994.
37. Robert J. Bunker and John P. Sullivan, Suicide Bombing in Operation Iraqi Freedom, U.S. Army Land Warfare Papers 24, Institute of Land Warfare, September 2004.
38. Battle for Baghdad, Interview with Major Donovan, Discovery Channel–*New York Times*.
39. Anthony H. Cordesman, *The Iraq War: Strategy, Tactics, and Military Lessons*, Center for Strategic and International Studies Press, Washington, DC, 2003.
40. Ibid.
41. Col. Gregory Fontenot, E.J. Degen, and David Tohn, On Point—The United States Army in Operation Iraqi Freedom, U.S. Naval Institute, Annapolis, MD, 2005.

CHAPTER 4

Victory from the Jaws of Defeat

Launching the Iraq Insurgency

On April 9, 2003 a U.S. Marine Corps combat engineer's tank pulled down the statue of Saddam Hussein in Firdous Square, the symbolic center of Iraq. The Americans had cut through the Regular Army and Republican Guard like a scythe. Defeat had come in just 3 weeks. The Americans had quickly thrust their way into Baghdad and had seized the seat of Iraqi power. Saddam Hussein and the remaining loyal Iraqi high command evacuated to the Sunnah Triangle to watch the nation come under American control. For the Americans this war was over. By the first week of May, U.S. commanders hoped that "mopping up" would be the final order of the day and that the regime elements would acquiesce to democracy building efforts of Ambassador L. Paul Bremer.

By mid-April 2003, elements of the 4th Infantry Division were clearing up the last of the major paramilitary resistance north of Baghdad near Taji and Samarra. Thirty to forty Fedayeen members were engaged by armored forces while resupplying at the Taji airbase. The U.S. Army reported small skirmishes that destroyed 8 Fedayeen technicals and the capture of 30 POWs. From this point forward the bulk of the resistance would be small-scale skirmishes in which the Fedayeen and former regime loyalists engaged coalition forces with small arms or rocket-propelled grenade (RPG) fire.

IMPLEMENTING THE INSURGENCY

Time magazine reporter Joe Klein wrote that a few days after the regime fell, Saddam Hussein met with his top surviving commanders or their representatives to start the insurgency.[1] Pieced together from U.S. Army intelligence reports, Klein reported that Hussein secretly met a representative of Gen. Izzat Ibrahim al-Douri and Muhammed Yunis al-Ahmed, the head of the Directorate of Military Security (DMS), and two other ex-generals. The DMS was the covert internal security branch of the military intelligence forces and had several special operations units under it, including Unit 999. Saddam ordered them to "rebuild your networks."[2] Thus, the insurgency in occupied Iraq started. The Fedayeen, who had never been entirely defeated, were still dispersing to their hometowns and reorganizing for the long resistance. The Americans were not watching the operational movements of the dispersed Fedayeen forces with much interest except in those regions where the forces continued to fight. Some high-profile counterterror operations were being conducted, but they seemed to focus on TV-friendly operations. Of particular note, the arrest of former Palestinian terrorist Mohammad Abbas, also known as Abu Abbas, the mastermind of the maritime hijacking of the *Achille Lauro*, was done with exceptional ease but was hailed as a major counterterrorist arrest.

THE SECOND "1920 REVOLUTION"

Although this was not the first time that an insurgency had been planned and executed in Iraq, the Bush administration seemed determined to ignore history and forge their own reality. In doing so, they seemed to have forgotten that the British already had some experience with an armed insurgency between the Tigris and Euphrates. On the other hand, Saddam was relying on the natural resistance of his people and friendly Arabs to fight an occupation by foreigner armies. Hussein and his senior staff, for all their apparent bravado in public, did plan a guerrilla war designed to inflict continuous casualties on American soldiers well after the end of an active conflict. This hope was not without basis or precedent. The center of gravity for this invasion was the American people's willingness to take casualties. The British knew this firsthand.

Britain's Mesopotamian Expeditionary Force first entered the region now known as Iraq in 1914; Britain was at war with the Ottoman Empire during WWI, and thus was seeking to protect the Allies' regional interests in the Persian Gulf. Iraq did not yet exist as a state; rather, the three independent regions of Basra, Baghdad, and Mosul were autonomous regions within the Ottoman Empire. Though the ruling class consisted of Sunni Muslims, the general population of the area was similar to the demographics of today, with the south 50% Shiite Muslim, the center and northwest 20% Sunni Muslim, the north 20% Kurd, and a small population of Christians, Jews, and Turkmen.

Once WWI ended and the newly created League of Nations declared Iraq to be a mandate under British control, resistance increased rapidly.

The British successfully took control of Baghdad in 1917 and Kirkuk and Mosul in 1918. After the murder of a British officer in 1919, Iraqis formed secret groups to oppose British rule and seek independence. This developed into a mass political movement that uncharacteristically brought about cooperation between traditionally hostile Shiite clerics and Sunni nationalists. The movement called for cooperation in the nationalist cause for independence, and a full-scale armed revolt began in June 1920. As the revolt continued through November, provisional governments were established in various regions, and even the Kurds joined in the conflict. The 1920 resistance abated only when the British agreed to recognize the Arabs' right to an independent state; this in turn ensured British dominance in the region by making the state indebted to Britain for its creation.

Like its present-day sister, the 1920 British occupation was not popularly received. The British had imposed an interim constitution on Iraq and had hand-selected Arab ministers positioned under the direct control of British advisors. Few of the British colonial decisions or public administration methods were popular. The occupation also resulted in the rise of nationalist groups "resenting British cooperation and usurpation of rights and, ultimately, a disturbing pattern of military revolts, political repression, ethnic cleansing, and civil unrest."[3] A new monarchy was offered to a Saudi, King Faisal, in 1921 by the British. In accepting the monarchy, Faisal negotiated an agreement that allowed the British occupation forces to remain in Iraq while also securing eventual independence.[4] When the League of Nations mandate for the occupation ended in 1933, Iraq was granted independence. Crowning this stunning turnabout for the British was the fact that the history of instability in Iraq didn't end with independence. King Faisal died soon afterward and the crown passed to his eldest son, Ghazi. An unfortunate car accident killed King Ghazi 6 years later, and he was succeeded by his then infant son Faisal II. During World War II, a 1941 pro-German coup attempt by one Rashid Ali al-Gaylani led to the reoccupation of Iraq by British forces. Until King Faisal came of age, Iraq was ruled by his uncle, Prince Abdallah, who served as the crown regent until 1953. Like most Middle Eastern monarchies, this one was neither truly popular nor native to the peoples and tribes of the region; it was just accepted as a convenient alternative to the occupation government by British forces. The 1920 revolution is an excellent first example of where history repeats itself and political leaders in the United States ignored the same warning signs that had presented themselves so dramatically 80 years earlier—a revolution where virtually every religious and tribal group, led by the Shiite imams of Karbala, fought the British occupation with all they had.

Although the revolution ended within 5 months, the insurgency became a symbol for both Iraqis and Arabs across the region.[5] Every Iraqi school child learned one lesson in history of the British occupation—resistance was possible. Resistance got results. The only reason the 1920 revolt failed was because the insurgents kept up a high level of attacks and quickly ran out of arms, ammunition, and supplies. Saddam Hussein saw that this would not be the case in the 2003 insurgency. Former Minister of Defense Sultan Hashim Ahmad al-Ta'i told CIA interrogators:

> We knew the goal was to make the Regime fall.... We thought the forces would arrive in Baghdad or outside Baghdad in 20 days or a month. We accepted that the cities on the way would be lost. All commanders knew this and accepted it. Saddam Hussein thought that the people would, of their own accord, take to the streets and fight with light arms, and that this would deter the U.S. forces from entering the cities.[6]

Additionally, as we would see replayed in the American occupation, the support and approval of the occupation government for any Iraqi in power meant that it was doomed to eventual failure. History has shown that other Arab nations fought occupation forces with armed resistance that led to their expulsion. In 1982, Israel invaded Lebanon in an attempt to destroy the Palestinian Liberation Organization and to remove Syrian forces. In the initial days of that invasion, the Lebanese Shiite population of the south, happy to be rid of the Palestinians, celebrated the arrival of the Israeli army. However, Israeli army arrogance toward the poor Shiite population and a complete disregard for civilian casualties created a homegrown resistance. The Shiites exploded with resentment and created, with the help of Iran and Syria, an armed resistance force called Hezbollah, or "Party of God." They announced themselves to the world through a series of suicide car bombings in 1983 that killed hundreds of foreign diplomats and soldiers. Later that year they would attack in earnest using their terrorist arm, the Islamic Jihad Organization, to launch suicide vehicle-borne improvised explosive devices (S-VBIEDs) against the U.S. Marines, the French foreign legion, and Israeli army headquarters in Lebanon nearly simultaneously. Within a year the Israelis would be bogged down in a bloody 18-year occupation of southern Lebanon and created a deeply ingrained Islamic insurgency that used suicide bombers, roadside IEDs, and armed raids to kill more than 2,000 Israeli soldiers, which led to a humiliating withdrawal. As former UN weapons inspector and U.S. Marine Corps intelligence officer Scott Ritter observed, "The 18-year occupation not only failed to defeat the PLO but it also created an Islamic fundamentalist movement that today poses a serious threat to the security of Israel and the Middle East region."[7]

LEADING THE RESISTANCE—LT. GEN.
IZZAT IBRAHIM AL-DOURI

Number six on a list of the most wanted men in Iraq, Lt. Gen. Izzat Ibrahim al-Douri (Figure 4.1) was born July 1, 1942, in the small town of Ad Dwar, near Tikrit. The son of a poor ice vendor, Izzat received no formal education, but was able to ally himself with Saddam Hussein at a young age. This stemmed from the fact that Izzat hailed from the same clan area as Saddam, but had no independent power base of his own; thus, he posed no threat to the future president and was able to gain power through unwavering loyalty to Saddam. Their relationship was further solidified by a brief marriage between al-Douri 's daughter and Saddam's oldest son, Uday.[8]

Alongside Saddam, al-Douri became involved with the Ba'ath Party at a young age. He supported the party during its underground years in the 1960s and was one of the chief engineers of the 1968 coup d'état, which brought the Ba'ath to power. Al-Douri held many important positions: vice chairman of the Revolutionary Command Council (RCC), commander of the northern region, deputy secretary general of the Ba'ath Party regional command, and deputy commander of the IQAF. During the 1970s, he also served as Minister of both Agriculture and the Interior.

As vice chairman of the Revolutionary Command Council, al-Douri played an integral part in the planning and execution of Iraq's wars against Iran and Kuwait and participated in the brutal repression of

FIGURE 4.1   General Izzat Ibrahim al-Douri, first leader of the former regime loyalist insurgency.

tribal uprisings following the first Gulf War. In a search for anti-Saddam rebels during this time, he assisted in the draining of the marshes (where rebels were hiding), completely destroying the Marsh Arabs' way of life. Additionally, al-Douri was held responsible for the genocidal Anfal campaigns waged against tribes in the north, in which chemical weapons were used on the city of Halabja, killing more than 5,000 Kurds.[9]

In Hawija, al-Douri took land from the Kurds and reallocated it to Sunni Arabs, rewarding them for their support of the regime. Al-Douri also built support for the Ba'athist regime among Sunni Islamists. In 1992, Saddam started a subtle but clear strategy of co-opting Islam in Iraq. Saddam wanted to win the influence of Islamists after the first Gulf War. Saddam saw that he was losing the nationalist base of the Ba'ath Party and went on a campaign to establish an Islamic tribal base within the government. The Special Security Organization in particular had its Ba'athist nationalist base quietly replaced with loyalist Islamists.[10] During the Return to Faith Campaign (al-Hamlah al-Imaniyyah) in 1993, al-Douri, a practitioner of the mystic Sufi form of Sunni Islam, allowed Sunni mosques more freedom in their religious practices. He co-chaired a conference on the role of faith with more than 1,000 Islamic dignitaries in attendance from across the Muslim world. This campaign gave official sanction to a once strictly secular Iraq. Saddam himself played a more religious-appearing role in the media, praying and building several lavish and enormous mosques, such as the Mother of All Battles (Umm al-Maarkah) Mosque in western Baghdad. Saddam ordered the words "God is Great" (Allahu Akbar) in his own handwriting integrated into the Iraqi flag. On the other hand, the Sunni campaign oversaw the widespread murder of Shiite clerics and desecration of Shiite mosques and holy sites. This substantially reduced the opposition to the regime among Sunni Islamists, building al-Douri's power within the more pious Ba'ath members. Al-Douri escaped the only assassination attempt on his life while visiting Karbala in 1998 and believed that he was blessed by Allah for his survival. Al-Douri also played a key role in strengthening the ties between Iraq and Syrian Ba'ath Parties by granting oil concessions to the Assad regime and tribes that would later owe him much. Thus, a newfound Islamic nationalism and oil formed the basis of the anti-American rejectionism that Hussein and al-Douri used to motivate the Sunni community.

While al-Douri was not technically a member of the Ba'ath Party's inner ruling circle, he was undeniably an important right-hand man to Saddam and held what has been argued to be the number two position in the regime. Most accounts also assert that he was responsible for coordinating insurgent attacks against the American occupation operating from eastern Syria. He is believed to have authorized the material-rich former regime loyalist (FRL) insurgents to give material, financial, and tactical support to most other insurgent groups, including Ansar al-Sunnah and al-Qaeda in Iraq (AQI). While there have been numerous reports of al-Douri 's capture and death during the American war and occupation in Iraq, none have been confirmed. He remained at large and number six (King of Clubs) in America's deck of most wanted criminals. Currently, the U.S. offers a $10 million reward to anyone who provides information on al-Douri's whereabouts or information confirming his death.[11] On November 12, 2005, the Ba'ath Party in exile made an unconfirmed claim that al-Douri had died, but in 2012 and 2013 a video of al-Douri surfaced, dressed in Ba'athist uniform condemning Iraqi government decisions. He is assessed to have reinspired the ex-FRLs to cooperate with the AQI/ISIS (Islamic State of Iraq and Syria) invasion of Iraq in 2014.

GODFATHERS OF THE INSURGENCY—THE PREWAR INTERNAL INTELLIGENCE APPARATUS

Clearly, the Iraq insurgency was a well-planned resistance operation, yet to understand from where the technical expertise of the insurgency comes, one must study the forces that were organized and in working order on the morning of the invasion. It was these forces that changed form in less than 1 month from seemingly frightened and incompetent irregular infantry to the deadly covert operatives of the Iraqi insurgency. Before the invasion, Iraqi intelligence and internal security agencies were comprised of approximately 57,800 men and women working in five major organizations:

SSO: Special Security Organization (Hijaz al-Amn al-Khass)
IIS: Iraqi Intelligence Service or General Intelligence Directorate (aka GID) (al-Mukhabarat)
DGS: Directorate of General Security (al-Amn al-'Amm)
DMI: Directorate of Military Intelligence (al-Estikhbarat)
DMS: Directorate of Military Security (al-Amn al-'Askari)

The purpose of these agencies was to ensure the continued survival of not only Saddam Hussein, but also the Ba'athist Party ideology and the domination of the Sunni over the Shiite. Each agency was designed to provide a redundant, overlapped system of authority in order to provide information and act as tools of intimidation in order to control the population. Special attention was paid to internal opposition, which may come from the intelligence agencies or the military itself. All intelligence agencies were principally designed to intimidate Iraqi citizens. To instill fear through arrest, murder, and torture, and neutralize all enemies of the regime. They were organized to overlap in their intelligence collection duties in an effort to check the level of power of each agency and to ensure that the president was informed of all plots from within the government as well as the populace. This continuous circular check of loyalty fostered a spirit of competition for each agency to be "purer" and more devoted to Saddam and the regime than the next.[12] Above all agencies, the SSO was the purest.

COMMANDER OF THE SECURITY APPARATUS—QUSAY HUSSEIN

The SSO/SRG was commanded by Saddam's younger son, Qusay Hussein. Qusay was also born to Saddam's first wife, Sajida, in 1966. The younger Hussein brother was often overshadowed by his older brother Uday, and during childhood was largely ignored by his father.[13] He was educated at the same school as his brother, Al Kharkh Al Namouthajiya School, and went on to study law at Baghdad University. A definitive moment in Qusay's, and perhaps more so in his brother Uday's, life was in 1979. They were taken to observe semipublic executions of Ba'athist leaders opposed to their father.[14] In 1985, Qusay married Sahar, the daughter of a military hero from the Iran-Iraq war. However, this marriage was dissolved rather quickly after two children were born.[15] Qusay had a reputation for being quiet and calculating, even from a very young age. While the horrific brutality of his older brother was well known to the public, Qusay stayed out of the public eye; nonetheless, he was a ruthless killer who knew how to get what he wanted.[16] Qusay's power base stemmed from his control of the majority of the Iraqi security forces and the merit he earned by running these organizations effectively. In 1988, he was appointed deputy director of the SSO. By 1992, he had become its director.[17] In 1991, Qusay became head of the Concealment Operations Committee, which had the job of concealing Iraq's weapons of mass destruction (WMDs) from United Nations Special Commission (UNSCOM); through this committee, Qusay also achieved joint control of the country's weapons of mass destruction from the early 1990s onward.[18]

In 1992, the dissident group the Iraqi National Accord had planned a coup against Saddam; Qusay's SSO exposed the coup. In doing so Saddam was ecstatic. His son passed a critical loyalty test. Saddam rewarded Qusay for his diligence by appointing him head of a new intelligence committee with the chiefs of the Directorate of General Security (the Mukhabarat), the SSO, and military intelligence. Thus, through his effectiveness as a security director, Qusay slowly built his power base to expand through many branches of the Ba'ath Party.[19] In 1996, Qusay increased his power further when he became chair of the National Security Council, the supreme oversight body that brought together all five of Iraq's security and intelligence organizations, as well as the president's staff. By 2002, Qusay was appointed commander of the SRG and was elected to the regional command of the Ba'ath Party. Partly as a result of his brother's physical impairments following the assassination attempt in 1996, but mostly due to his own diligence and ruthless following of orders, Qusay Hussein had become the second most powerful man in Iraq.

Following the first Gulf War, Qusay repeatedly revealed a brutality to match both his father's and brother's. Directly after the war, Qusay managed the elimination of the Shiite Muslim uprising in southern Iraq with the assistance of General al-Douri.[20] For his part, he engineered the draining of the marshes in southern Iraq, which removed the vegetation in that region, which had previously hidden insurgent refugees; "the draining of the marshes ended a centuries-old way of life for the Shi'ia Marsh Arabs."[21] Furthermore, Qusay led an attack against the al-Dulaym tribe in 1995, and again suppressed a second Shiite revolt in 1997. While his crazed older brother was more notorious for his use of personal violence, Qusay was undeniably just as dangerous and brutal. In August 2001, Qusay survived the only assassination attempt on his life. The assailants were engaged by a rocket-propelled grenade fired by the executive protection team. It destroyed the getaway car, killing all of the assassination squad.[22] Except for a wound in the arm, Qusay escaped unharmed.

Qusay spent the remaining years sharpening the skills and weapons of the Special Republican Guard. When it became apparent in the fall of 2002 that the American invasion was likely, he worked closely with his brother to see that the SRG and Fedayeen worked synergistically in combat and in the post-war insurgency. He would keep this promise to the day of his death.

SPECIAL SECURITY ORGANIZATION— SSO (HIJAZ AL-AMN AL-KHAS)

The SSO was an internal intelligence agency created during the Iran-Iraq war.[23] It became the strongest and most central of the regime intelligence apparatus because of its ability to police and enforce loyalty to Saddam Hussein throughout the intelligence community and the military forces. Its principal duties were the protection of the president through the administration of the military units, including the Republican Guard and the Special Republican Guard. The CIA reported that it was responsible for the surveillance and continued loyalty of the General

Intelligence, Military Intelligence, General Security, and Military Security Directorates. This agency, in an effort to provide security to the regime and assure quality control throughout the intelligence directorates, had the authority to carry out abduction, murder, and intimidation. All was done on direct orders from the Hussein leadership. In an ongoing effort to assure faithfulness, this agency needed to instill absolute fear and uncertainty in the Iraqi people. A small directorate of 5,000 men,[24] the SSO had disproportionate power over other intelligence agencies and the military. With the ability to root out any and all perceived enemies and to do with their bodies what they wished, a visit by the SSO was universally feared by all Iraqis.

At the end of the 2003 invasion, the majority of the predominantly Sunni SSO who were not killed in combat would reform with the remnants of the five other intelligence agencies into the insurgency's covert combat forces and intelligence collectors. Skilled in infiltration, cover stories, false identities, and fake identification while operating in a hostile environment, these SSO agents were best suited to leading and supporting the insurgent combat commanders in the newly renamed Unified Mujahideen Command. Their relatively high level of skill in understanding the complex tribal and psychological nature of Iraqi society as well as training and deploying intelligence teams to collect and analyze information about the American coalition, gave the insurgency a first-class intelligence agency. The ability of the insurgency to observe, analyze, rapidly target, and strike a range of coalition targets within a political framework showed the insurgent leadership had the SSO's touch. Some of the former SSO would go directly to work for the coalition forces and the new Iraqi government. In response to these intelligence agents joining the coalition, the FRLs started a campaign of assassination and intimidation of former SSO agents. Any agent who did not remain loyal to the regime was now marked for murder.

Within the prewar SSO were several subbureaus responsible for the collection of intelligence, personal information, and the carrying out of abduction, murder, and intimidation for the regime. These bureaus included the SSO Political Bureau (SSO-PB). This organization was responsible for keeping tabs on political enemies of the Hussein regime or loyalists who required closer scrutiny. The principal function of this office was simple: ensure absolute regime loyalty and punish or eliminate those who oppose the regime. The SSO-PB, through its operations office, was often tasked to root out perceived traitors. Iraqis would be placed under surveillance, abducted or arrested, interrogated, and executed. An estimated 100,000 Iraqis were killed since the end of the Iran-Iraq war, particularly during the Shiite uprising in 1991; they were arrested and murdered under the supervision of the political bureau's operations office.

The SSO Security Division (SSO-SD), known as Al Himayah, ran the regime's Special Protection Branch (Jihaz al-Hamayah al-Khass). This branch was directly responsible for the personal protection of Saddam Hussein, his palaces, family, and top-tier regime members in the Council of Ministers, the National Council, and Ba'ath Party.[25] This organization was the only entity allowed to provide bodyguards for the regime.[26] In its role as the personal protection of the top-tier loyalists, this bureau carried out specialized intelligence collection on locations and peoples, which came into the planning cycle of their protective duties. Countersurveillance of other regime security personnel and counterintelligence against personnel coming into contact with the senior regime members were necessary parts of their day-to-day functions. In the insurgency, these highly trained equivalents to the U.S. Secret Service would provide valuable information on how to best detect and defeat the bodyguards of the coalition and the new Iraqi government and private security company executive protection teams. Additionally, they were highly skilled in detecting surveillance and deploying countersurveillance. This skill set would allow insurgents to detect U.S.-trained agents attempting to infiltrate safe houses and strongholds.

The Special Security Organization operated an emergency military unit completely apart from the army and other internal security agencies. According to the CIA, the SSO Security Unit (SSO-SU) was a battalion-sized unit that was solely responsible for the "security of strategically important roads around Baghdad and Tikrit." The road from the presidential palace, now known as Route IRISH, was secured by this unit prior to any move by Saddam to the palace complex there.

The SSO Emergency Forces (SSO-EF) military brigade was a light infantry combat unit of approximately 1,000 men assigned as a Quick Reaction Force (QRF) for the SSO. This paramilitary organization could respond to immediate threats with a small but well-equipped QRF for any civil emergency and could directly call upon the heavier Special Republican Guard division if more firepower was necessary.

SPECIAL REPUBLICAN GUARD

The heart of the regime's loyalist military capability lay with the formation of the SSO's Special Republican Guard (SRG). The SRG was a self-contained military force assigned to an intelligence agency. It was designed to be a military force capable of taking on any other regime military force. According to *Jane's Defence*, the role of the SRG was to act as a "super-elite, well-equipped military force ... to protect the president and the regime."[27] As the SRG was fully mobilized before the war, it may have totaled between 25,000 and 26,000 men. While many battalions had specific military roles, the SRG was the true Praetorian Guard for the Hussein regime.

Operational Command of the SRG

The overall command of the SRG was given to Qusay Hussein, who was kept in balance with his brother's Saddam Fedayeen forces. The officers and men of the SRG were regime loyalists drawn from Hussein's hometown of Tikrit. Until the beginning of the war, these forces, and the intelligence apparatus, were the only ones allowed into Baghdad. The operational commander of the SRG was Gen. Barzan Abd al-Ghafur Sulayman Majid al-Tikriti. The secretary of the Republican Guard was Gen. Kamal Mustafa Abdallah Sultan al-Tikriti, a member of Saddam's inner cabinet who maintained oversight of the regular Republican Guard units and the SRG. Kamal was captured quickly after the fall of Baghdad. Barzan al-Tikriti, number 11 of the 55 most wanted men in Iraq, was captured by coalition forces on July 23, 2003, and was executed in Baghdad on January 15, 2007.

The SRG was composed of 14 battalions organized into five brigades: 1st Brigade SRG Command was the principal executive security unit of the Saddam Hussein regime apart from the personal loyalty units, such as the Mukhabarat and the Saddam Fedayeen. The 1st Brigade headquarters managed and directed four battalions. Each battalion had a specialized military function. The 1st Battalion was the executive protection force of the Saddam Hussein regime. These forces included a mobile counterassault force that provided protection to the Hussein motorcade, decoy motorcades, and anti-aircraft protection. The fleet of Hussein's 150 armored Mercedes Benz vehicles was under the direct supervision and maintenance of this unit. The 2nd Battalion was assigned protection, road security, and physical security duties of the Republican Palace and the airport palace complex. This unit worked with the security unit to secure routes in and out of sensitive locations. The 5th Battalion was the household guard of the Baghdad Republican Palace complex and the Hussein residences. Their fundamental duties were to provide security and assure authorization to access any building in the complex. This same palace would become the heart of the coalition military command and political center, called the Green Zone during the occupation. The 5th Battalion soldiers assigned to Hussein's personal residence, the "House Squad," were an elite force who alone protected Saddam Hussein's home in the Republican Palace complex. These men, next to the administrative and custodial staff who worked in this controlled district day to day, would be the most knowledgeable and valuable intelligence assets to insurgent planners for indirect rocket and direct suicide bomber attacks on the American-occupied complex. The 7th Battalion was the plainclothes unit assigned to undercover collection of intelligence in protection of the SRG-assigned residences throughout Iraq. Skilled in covert collection of intelligence and watching the populous, these men in the post-war organization would be especially skilled at collecting intelligence against coalition forces and Iraqis marked for assassination. Working with former members of the SRG Intelligence Battalion, these agents had the ability to operate comfortably in plain clothes. They would procure safe houses, conduct countersurveillance, collect radio communications, and intercept and detect coalition and the new government's own intelligence agents. This would give the insurgents a sharp advantage in urban intelligence operations within any Iraqi city.

SRG Combat Units

Although the SRG maintained well-equipped ground combat elements, the following units were heavily engaged and severely reduced during the ground combat phase of the war. Any surviving members would bring an enormous amount of experience and training capability to the insurgents. The 8th Battalion was assigned to provide the physical security of the Saddam International Airport and was destroyed in combat when the U.S. Army V Corps spearhead seized the airport. The 2nd Brigade was stationed at the Rashid military complex southeast of Baghdad where its 4th, 6th, 11th, 14th, and 15th battalions would be savaged by the U.S. Marines' advance on the south side of the city. The 3rd Brigade, stationed at Taji north of Baghdad, was responsible for defending Baghdad from the northern-most approaches. Its sister unit, the 4th Motorized Brigade, was assigned to hold the southern approaches. Organized like a regular military force, it would manage to escape and evade U.S. forces' successes. Many of its members would join the insurgency. The 4th SRG Armored Brigade, usually headquartered northwest of Baghdad near Abu Ghraib, would be ruthlessly destroyed in the war by aerial attacks. Its tanks were decimated in combat west of the international airport.[28]

IRAQI INTELLIGENCE SERVICE—IIS (AL-MUKAHBARAT)

The Iraqi Intelligence Service (IIS) was an 8,000-man agency. It was the largest of the intelligence agencies until the establishment of the SSO. From as early as 1921, Iraq maintained a national intelligence service under the monarchy. In 1966, during Saddam Hussein's tenure as the de facto leader of the Ba'ath Party, he transformed it into a far more ruthless intelligence agency staffed by personnel loyal to him. This organization was initially known as the Jihaz al-Khass, or the "Special Branch," also known to have operated under the cover name of Organization of Yearning for the Homeland (Jihaz al-Hanin). Saddam would later sarcastically rename this agency the "Public Relations Bureau."[29] The Jihaz al-Khass's role was to collect information on domestic political opposition. On Saddam's command its agents would assassinate members of other political parties and disloyal Ba'ath Party members. Composed of loyalist Bu-Nasr tribesmen, its function in intelligence and selective terrorism was critical in allowing Saddam the ability to become the leader of Iraq, particularly during the Ba'ath Party coup in 1968. In 1973 it would expand and become the IIS. Iraqi scholar Kannan Mikiya would write, "Unlike other policing agencies, the Mukhabarat was a distinctly political body, not merely a professional organ of state charged with safe-guarding national security."[30] Through its establishment, this organization would be run by various relatives of Saddam's from the al-Tikiri and al-Douri families. The IIS's state responsibilities in suppressing dissent and punishing enemies would become a bulwark duty of its former members in the stateless Sunni insurgency. Covert operations both in Iraq and abroad were hallmarks of its training. It was the IIS that secretly procured nuclear triggers or Krytons from London during the Iran-Iraq war, almost giving Iraq a nuclear capability.[31] The ability to collect intelligence on local Iraqis and pass information, money, and weapons would become a core function of many of its former members. The IIS was most likely the heart of the post-war insurgent intelligence collection system.

The preinvasion IIS was broken down into subdirectorates. Director 1 (M1) was Private Office of the Director Lt. Gen. Tahir Jalil Habbush al-Tikriti, number 14 in the Americans' 55 most wanted Iraqi regime members. During the invasion, Habbush al-Tikriti managed to escape U.S. custody. It is believed that he operated from Syria and most likely played a direct role in the day-to-day operations of the insurgency under the command of Izzat Ibrahim al-Douri or his successor. His deputy until the invasion was Khalil Ibrahim al-Sultan. Its subdirectorates had the skills that would make the insurgency one of the most lethal organizations of its day.

DIRECTOR OF FOREIGN INTELLIGENCE (M4)

M4 would arguably be one of the most important of the subdirectorates of the IIS in the insurgency. M4 was led until 2003 by Hasan Izbah Thalij al-'Ubaydi. He reported to the deputy director. According to the Duelfer Report, Hasan had been the former office director of M1.

In the prewar apparatus, M4 managed and directed covert intelligence agencies of the Iraqi government. Its members were trained to infiltrate, recruit, and manage the secret agents necessary to root out dissenters in the Ba'ath Party as well as place their own agents in other governments. These skills would be critical to infiltrating the ministries of the new government, the new Iraqi police, and army, as well as recruit and develop agents within the civilian agencies working with the American coalition. M4 had a fifth division, called M40, which operated separately from M4. M40 targeted foreign opposition groups.

DIRECTORATE OF TECHNICAL AFFAIRS (M4/4/5)

M4/4/5 was responsible for the development of special weapons and systems for use in covert agent operations. Technical affairs developed, improvised, and purpose-built bombs, silenced pistols, and concealed cameras and electronic intercept devices in conjunction with years of cooperation with the former KGB and other secret intelligence services. These skills have revealed themselves in the insurgency on a near-daily basis.

DIRECTORATE OF COUNTERINTELLIGENCE (M5)

The M5 was responsible for counterintelligence and internal security operations within its own agency and against foreign intelligence threats attempting to penetrate the IIS. Led by Muhammad 'Abd al-Wahhab Fada'am until the invasion, its forces were dedicated to detecting, monitoring, following, and if necessary, neutralizing foreign intelligence threats, including agents from the Kurdish provinces, the U.S. Central Intelligence Agency, Iran's Pasdaran/VEVAK, and the Israeli Mossad. It is said detection of Syrian penetration agents was of particular interest to this office, though that would have been a questionable target due to the aggressive operations of U.S., British, Kuwaiti, Turkish, and Iranian agents in and around Iraqi borders. They operated in parallel with M4. The M5 also operated a subdirectorate called M5/5, Section 18, or the "General Affairs Division," which operated intelligence front companies. According to the CIA, agents from this section operated more than 40 businesses, including "hotels, travel services, souvenir shops, and truck service centers, in order to collect information on foreigners routinely entering Iraq."[32] This capability in the post-war would give the insurgency a formidable ability to collect excellent intelligence of U.S. troop movements, activities of the new Iraqi government and army, and real-time data on the reconstruction efforts. Extended further, this branch's officers could be the principal covert targeting body of the insurgency. The Internal Security Directorate (M6) and its 200 men acted as the loyalty enforcement group and would behave in similar counterintelligence roles against U.S.-deployed agents in the new insurgency. The Directorate of Liberation Movements (M8) was a liaison office to Palestinian organizations and led by Khalid al-Douri. Although not an intelligence collection agency, its links to Palestinian groups such as FATAH, the Popular Front for the Liberation of Palestine, Hamas, and Palestinians working in other Arab countries would be invaluable in technical and agent support from Palestinians in Kuwait, Jordan, Syria, Lebanon, and Palestine.

DIRECTORATE OF CLANDESTINE OPERATIONS (M13)

M13 was also called the Technical Operations or Technical Monitoring Directorate; it was a special tradecraft division that performed many of the key intelligence collection roles the FRL insurgent groups use today. The operatives of the M13 conducted "black operations" support services such as "lockpicking, surveillance photography, electronic eavesdropping, and counterintelligence functions at Iraqi embassies abroad … wire taps, listening devices, and hidden cameras." The technical knowledge and skills of this division would allow the insurgents to form a cadre of skilled covert operatives who could collect video and still photography against coalition targets using simple mini-video cameras or high-technology digital cell phones now found throughout Iraq.

DIRECTORATE OF SPECIAL OPERATIONS
DEPARTMENT (M14-SOD)

M14 (SOD) was a dedicated special operations force led by Muhammad Khudayr Sabah al-Dulaymi. The principal mission of the M14-SOD was the recruitment, training, and deployment of specialty intelligence agents who performed the most sensitive special missions, including maintaining Iraq's offensive terrorism capabilities and operating an internal counterterrorism force. The M14-SOD, which operated foreign and domestic missions divisions, conducted government-directed assassinations inside and outside of Iraq.

The M14 maintained a counterterrorism (CT) division, which was tasked to stop acts of terrorism within Iraq at embassies and the airport. It allegedly took down hijackers of a Sudanese airliner at Saddam International in the 1980s. The CT unit had shoot houses and an aircraft mock-up for storming and killing hijackers. It was known to have trained Iraqi, Palestinian, Syrian, Yemeni, Lebanese, Egyptian, and Sudanese agencies in counterterrorism methods.

On the other hand, the offensive terrorism capabilities of Iraq included development, training, and supporting government-sponsored and foreign terrorist groups and their combat tactics. M14-SOD worked with other divisions to develop and deploy explosives, and train in marksmanship, tradecraft, and skills necessary for terrorism. This capability would be the basis, along with other specialized units, such as the Saddam Fedayeen, the Directorate of Military Security's Unit 999, and M14-SOD, for training the Syrian mercenaries, Arab terrorists, and other suicide car bomb volunteers just before the invasion at their facility in Salman Pak. These same capabilities have been dispersed throughout the insurgency.

The Pentagon's Joint Intelligence Task Force in Iraq found plans after the invasion that spelled out the role of M14-SOD in an insurgency. M14-SOD operatives would work alongside of the Saddam Fedayeen to arm and train the foreign and local men who would become the post-war insurgency. M14-SOD most likely continues to run as a small Mujahideen core combat group. Additionally, it developed and maintained a specialized suicide bomber division (M14-SOD-TG) prior to the war called the Tiger Group.[33] M14-SOD-TG was similar in capability to other SOD groups but was oriented to specifically develop and deploy human-guided weapons—both S-VBIEDs and pedestrian-borne improvised explosive devices (PBIEDs). A Defense Intelligence Agency report stated: "Cells of former M14 personnel are organizing and conducting a terrorist I.E.D. campaign against coalition forces throughout Iraq. The explosives section of M14 prepared for the invasion by constructing hundreds of suicide vests and belts for use by Saddam Fedayeen against coalition forces under the program 'The Challenge Project.'"[34] The capabilities of the insurgency clearly indicate that M14-SOD was one of the core pillars in the training, development, and deployment of the suicide bombers before and during the invasion, including the S-VBIED attack by Sergeant Nomani in Najaf, the women Haditha bombers, and the dozens of suicide car bombs launched at the U.S. Army and Marine Corps "thunder runs" during the assault on Baghdad.

DIRECTORATE OF SIGNALS INTELLIGENCE (M17)

Formerly known as Project 858, the IIS also maintained a branch equipped to collect voice and data communications for exploitation by the IIS. Formerly code named the Hadi Project, M17 was a 2,600-man unit responsible for the management and collection of signals intelligence (SIGINT). Led by Khalid Karim Khalifa Braish al-'Ajili, this directorate was also dedicated to wiretapping and centralized monitoring of bugging devices. A unit of this type would scan the local airwaves with specialized radio collection systems, listen to conversations on telephones or microwave systems, and provide the regime with raw intelligence and intentions of its target. Coupled with the ability to exploit and break codes and solve encryption solutions on radio systems, M17 and the Communications Directorate personnel would send communications intelligence (COMINT) intercept teams to conduct wiretaps, tap phones, and more commonly, collect radio communication in foreign languages in support of overseas intelligence operations. Various members who were fluent in English, Arabic, Kurdish, Persian, and Turkish or other languages would collect and analyze the spoken words or unique signals characteristic of their targets. Targets could be as simple as using specialized wiretap or microphone monitoring stations in the government hotels, such as the one in the basement of the government-run Babil Hotel or other hotels occupied by the United Nations during its weapons inspection regime. In the insurgency, M17 intercept operators could provide excellent warning of impending U.S. operations. Intelligence gleaned from tank, infantry, helicopter, and aircraft using clear voice radios (such as the small commercial family of radios service (FRS) systems privately purchased by soldiers at any department store) could provide the al-Hadi operator-turned-insurgent intelligence collector with ample warning of U.S. operations or intelligence from a target-rich environment.

DIRECTORATE OF SURVEILLANCE (M20)

M20 was led by Akram 'Umar Salih al-Tikriti until 2003. M20 was a division of trained human intelligence officers who maintained covert and clandestine surveillance of foreign and domestic targets. Principally aimed at the United Nations weapons inspectors, these agents would bring a unique capability necessary to train a new corps of intelligence officers in conducting covert surveillance missions against coalition targets. It learned to conduct operations with limits of 7 to 10 days on each target, principally due to limited resources.

AL GHAFIQI PROJECT DIVISION (M21)

M21 was the branch of the IIS that may have been most directly linked to creating the devastating modern IED. According to the CIA's Duelfer Report, "the Al Ghafiqi Project existed to make explosive devices for the IIS to be used in assassination and demolition operations." The name *Al*

Ghafiqi refers to a geographic area between Saudi Arabia and Kuwait. The insurgents, most likely from M21 and other special operations divisions, assisted in stockpiling artillery shells, radio-controlled triggers, car door openers, cell phones, and detonation cord. Thousands of uniform improvised detonators and preassembled triggers have been found throughout Iraq and indicate a singular development process. Insurgent bombers have used the same production train for many of their IEDs that the CIA's Duelfer Report on WMDs found to have been a trademark of M21:

> No one person constructed an entire explosive device alone. The construction process drifted through the sections of the directorate. An improvised explosive device (IED) began in the Chemistry Department which developed the explosive materials for the device, the Electronics Department prepared the timers and wiring of the IED, and the Mechanical Department produced the igniters and designed the IED. Al Ghafiqi constantly invented new designs or methods to conceal explosives; books, briefcases, belts, vests, thermoses, car seats, floor mats, and facial tissue boxes were all used to conceal PE4, C4, RDX, or TNT.[35]

The Defense Intelligence Agency (DIA) and U.S. Central Command have reported that these were the same type of materials often found in insurgent weapons caches. Examples of insurgent weapons, including thermoses, bicycle seats, and explosive vests, indicate that the technical proficiency of many of the munitions used in the insurgency had origins in M21 as well as M14-SOD.

DIRECTORATE OF OPPOSITION
GROUP ACTIVITIES (M40)

M40 was tasked with collecting intelligence of Kurdish, Shiite, and other internal opposition groups. Its individual agents bring to the insurgency a wealth of knowledge and intelligence about the cultural dynamics of the new Iraqi government. On or about April 9, 2003, the IIS as an integrated body of the Ba'athist regime of Saddam Hussein ceased to exist. According to an eyewitness on that date, a former M40 officer stated, "All M40 officers were told to burn their documents and go home. 'It was over,' the source said, 'the IIS did not exist anymore.'"[36] In fact, the IIS did not cease to exist but transformed itself from a highly compartmented series of intelligence groups into a synergistic covert intelligence force that was now operating with a purpose and mission far better suited than its Ba'athist enforcement days.

If the IIS ceased to exist on April 9, 2003, then the birth date of the neo-Ba'athist Party's Insurgent Intelligence Directorate was April 10, 2003. It gave birth to a new hybrid agency, half-intelligence agency, half special operations force—both committed to killing Americans.

DIRECTORATE OF GENERAL SECURITY— DGS (AMN AL-'AMM)

The DGS was an 8,000-man internal intelligence agency.[37] Director of the DGS was Maj. Gen. Rafi Abd al-Latif Tilfah al-Tikriti, who was number 15 on the 55 most wanted Iraqis list and who also eluded capture during the invasion. A key aide to General al-Douri, he provided information and actionable intelligence on antiregime individuals and opposition groups in each governate of Iraq, particularly Kurdish, Iranian, and Turkmen. More importantly, there was little about the culture or behaviors of individual Iraqis that Tilfah al-Tikriti and his staff did not know or could not collect. The databasing and the cultural intelligence collection skills of both himself and his former associates would allow the insurgents to target less than cooperative Iraqis with either cash or bullets as they saw fit. In a post-war Iraq, the insurgent agents who had worked in the DGS would play a similar role. Collection of intelligence against opposition groups, which are now in power as the core of the new Iraqi government, would be critical to the insurgents for evaluating their political influence or targeting them for assassination, blackmail, or bribery. The remnants of the DGS are most likely returned to Anbar after a decade operating from Syria under the direct control of General al-Douri through Tilfah al-Tikriti. Al-Douri's miraculous return to Iraq in 2014 after the al-Qaeda/ISIS offensive lends credence to this belief.

DIRECTORATE OF GENERAL MILITARY INTELLIGENCE—DGMI (MUDIRIYAH AL-ISTIKHBARAT AL-'ASKRIAH AL-'AMMAH OR ISTIKHBARAT)

The DGMI, Iraq's military intelligence service, was established in 1932 under the Iraqi monarchy. It maintained a traditional role of intelligence collection on foreign enemies and supported the military establishment. In the 1980s it transitioned from a purely military operations support unit to a government intelligence agency reporting to the presidential palace. In its military role the DGMI maintained strategic, theater, and tactical intelligence against regional military powers. Its operational analysis mission included maintaining databases and information on enemy forces, determining strategic intentions of foreign forces, and determining the readiness of Iraqi forces to defend the nation. In addition to its military information role, it was also tasked to collect information against domestic enemies, military and foreign intelligence, Kurds, and capabilities of internal enemies. It maintained a staff of 5,000 men.[38] The commander of the DGMI was Staff Lt. Gen. Zuhayr Talib 'Abd al-Sattar, number 31 of the coalition's most wanted. He was taken into custody on April 23, 2003.

DIRECTORATE OF MILITARY SECURITY— DMS (AMN AL-ASKARIA)

The DMS was a 5,000-man internal security and intelligence service of the army.[39] Unlike most other branches of Iraqi military intelligence, the DMS was loyal to Saddam Hussein and answered only to the regime. Its men and women were dedicated to collecting and operating covert deep cover agents inside Iraq and foreign countries.

The DMS political branch was tasked with recruiting and maintaining agents on a political level within other countries. It also maintained liaison at a military level with allied countries and entities. The DMS's "security branch" maintained covert intelligence collection networks and agents. Many of the trained terrorists in Iraq were sent to this organization's facilities to be trained and deployed on missions outside of Iraq.

THE DMS SPECIAL OPERATIONS UNIT 999

The DMS was responsible for maintaining a specialized covert intelligence operations group called Unit 999. Unit 999 was a highly classified, deep penetration intelligence and covert direct action unit. Unit 999 operated both clandestinely in the role of defense attachés and covertly with teams of Iraqi Special Operations personnel who could operate in the role of a terrorist direct action group or who could create, train, and liaison with terrorist groups under its control. Unit 999 was believed to have been involved in long-range reconnaissance and sabotage during the Iran-Iraq war and the alleged plots to smuggle explosives into Thailand and the Philippines, as well as planning an abduction attempt on Gen. Norman Schwarzkopf during the first Gulf War (Figure 4.2).[40]

The 999 operatives organized its agents and intelligence teams in battalions with names that designated the region of their primary target. Iranian collection and penetration was handled by the 1st Battalion, Kateeba Farsi, or Persian Battalion. The 2nd Battalion was known as

FIGURE 4.2   Soldiers from the Directorate of Military Security's Special Operations Unit 999 parade as suicide volunteers in the fall of 2002.

the Saudi Battalion and handled missions and personnel operating in the Arabian Peninsula, including Saudi Arabia, Kuwait, and other Gulf states. Areas bordering Israel, Palestine, and Jordan were handled by the 3rd Battalion, or Palestine Battalion. This unit ran agents, established contacts, and conducted liaison with Palestinian and Jordanian terrorist and political organizations, including Hamas, FATAH, al-Aqsa Martyrs Brigade, Palestinian Islamic Jihad Organization, and as the invasion became imminent, the al-Qaeda-affiliated Tawhid Wal-Jihad. The 4th Battalion, or Turkish Battalion, plied its trade in Turkey. The Internal Opposition Battalion was formed after the first Gulf War to handle special "wet" or assassination missions related to the attempted uprisings against the regime.[41] Finally, the small 5th Battalion (maritime) was designated to handle running agents through the oil smuggling routes and into other countries.

In the post-war Iraq, these agents and officers of the DMS, in addition to those of the IIS's M4 division for managing foreign agents and the IIS's M14 Special Operations division (who specialize in assassination and sabotage), would prove to be the most important agents-cum-insurgents among the entire panoply of former regime operatives. Their ability to operate within Iraq and in surrounding countries, having developed multiple identities, passports, and a network of contacts, would provide the insurgents with a highly capable intelligence agency. The DMS would provide the insurgency with a core of extremely security conscious and professional intelligence officers capable of recruiting, training, and professionalizing the Sunni terrorists to strike in the most difficult areas of Iraq. Members of this organization, though they do not have the same level of skill or training as the Saddam Fedayeen, would be among the most dangerous insurgent field leaders. The impact of this small group of men would be disproportionate to their numbers. They would be among the most effective insurgent operatives. As instructors in covert camps or safe houses, they would be able to provide thousands of recruits the skills and tradecraft necessary to conduct infiltration, sabotage, and short-duration, massed ambushes.

FORMER REGIME LOYALIST INSURGENT GROUPS

Before the political term of Anti-Iraqi Forces (AIF) became the operational description of the insurgency, U.S. intelligence had dubbed the Sunni insurgents associated with the Saddam Hussein regime as former regime loyalists (FRLs), or when they banded together to operate as insurgent units, they were called former regime elements (FREs) (Figure 4.3). As American troops continue to meet opposition in their occupation of Iraq, the former Saddam Fedayeen, Special Republican Guard, and the men of the intelligence agencies combined to create the central insurgent force in post-war Iraq. Between 80 and 85% of all attacks in the first 6 years of the insurgency have been attributed or claimed by them. This rejectionist force emerged from the ground war as the single greatest real threat to stability in the country. These relatively well-trained guerrilla fighters started out fiercely loyal to Saddam and the Ba'ath Party and promised to continue hostilities until the Ba'ath are back in power. A 2004 resistance communiqué stated:

> The Ba'ath Party characterized and predicted the predicament that the occupation would fall into, and the way that this predicament is growing deeper and accelerating, in the course of the Party's programmatic objective analysis which is being used by the armed Iraqi Resistance as political guidance. On the basis of its general directives, operational and strategic goals are set, as Resistance efforts and fighting activity are brought into confrontation with the occupation forces and their stooges.[42]

In an interview with a Jordanian newspaper, a former Ba'athist commander in the resistance said:

> It's not out of bravado or out of pretension to say that the Iraqi Resistance is the legitimate daughter of the Arab Ba'ath Socialist Party, and the principal element of this heroic Resistance is composed of Ba'ath militants and Iraqi Army elements, Republican Guards, Security

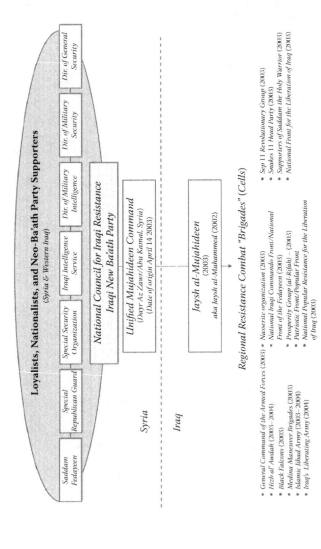

FIGURE 4.3   Former regime loyalist and neo-Ba'ath insurgent organization.

services, Saddam's Fidayyins and Alquds army. All these components as everyone knows refer to one political leadership, i.e. that of the Arab Ba'ath Socialist Party. This is what our people knows, and this what the enemy of our people knows too. And because we don't want to occupy the whole scene, let's say there are other currents and organizations, which entered the Resistance battlefield through the gateway of the Ba'ath. Yes there are national, Islamic and progressive forces, which fight with us in the great Liberation Battle. For these groups, we provide arms and training, funding, protection and data. We acted and we still do and from the very first day of the aggression to widen the circle of the popular and frontal participation in the Resistance field. A large national and unified Front exists fighting a sacred Battle for the freedom and the independence of Iraq.[43]

Until January 2004, the Ba'ath Party communiqués reported constant combat reports by Saddam Fedayeen and Al Quds army forces. Yet the association with the Ba'ath Party was having a negative effect, especially after the capture of Saddam Hussein in December 2003. To mitigate this effect and to show a more unified front, the Ba'athist resistance units adopted a series of cover names for their cells and groups, which have come and gone from the beginning of the insurgency. The leadership of the insurgency based in Syria used the two following cover names:

- **National Council of the Iraqi Resistance** (Majlis Watani al-Muqawamah al-Iraq; aka United Council for Iraqi Resistance)
- **Unified Mujahideen Command** (Qiadat al-Whidah al-Mujahideen; aka Mujahideen Central Command)

The FRLS successfully co-opted Islamic names in an effort to create a holy war-style atmosphere for support. No matter what name they operate under, these cover names were designed to identify the individual or regional operating cells, not the overall command structure.

- **Mohammed's Army** (Jaysh al-Muhammed). One of the original concept names of the planned insurgency. It is described in Ba'ath Party planning prior to the invasion in documents written in June 2002 and captured by coalition forces in April 2003.
- **Mujahideen Army** (Jaysh al-Mujahideen). A cover name for the military arm of the Unified Mujahideen Command, but in reality a cover term for the armed insurgent wing formed by the Saddam Fedayeen, SRG, and former intelligence agencies.

Numerous FRL insurgent groups have been seen in military reporting, insurgent propaganda, and media reports since December 2003. These names are examples of the FRLs' early usage of cover names to mask the actual involvement of the defeated Ba'ath Party. It is believed that they had all been brought under the umbrella name of the Unified Mujahideen Command's Mujahideen Army by the winter of 2003, though many of the smaller cells may use the cover names regionally.

- **Islamic Jihad Army.** A propaganda branch of the FRL forces formed after the April 2004 Fallujah siege; it issued an English language video statement that received widespread notoriety in its attempt to seek support in the West, and which responded to and challenged President Bush's "bring it on" statement.
- **General Command of the Armed Forces** (GCAF) (Qiadat al-Aam al-Quwat al-Askari). Led by former Iraq vice president Taha Yasin Ramadan (he was captured by the Kurdish Peshmerga militia in Mosul and executed by hanging on March 20, 2007). The GCAF is assessed to be an early iteration of the Unified Mujahideen Command. It was believed to have been headquartered in Fallujah prior to the U.S. Marine Corps Operation Phantom Fury in November 2004.
- **Black Falcons** (Sukkar al-Aswad). Prewar name of an unidentified Saddam Fedayeen group of cells preparing to operate as insurgents in the post-war.
- **Iraq's Liberating (Liberation) Army.** An FRL cell that operated in the Haditha area threatened collaborators with coalition forces and claimed to have assassinated the pro-coalition mayor of Haditha, Mohammed Nayil al-Jurayfi.
- **Medina (Division) Maneuver Brigade** (al-Madinat al-Munarawah). This name was used by a group of probable former Republican Guard Medina Division loyalists in Fallujah and Baghdad.
- **Nasserite Organization.** A group that sounds like pan-Arab nationalists but which has issued FRL-style warnings against the coalition and threatened foreigners in Iraq. They condemned the interim Iraqi governing council as "traitor" forces. They have also criticized Shiite and Kurdish participation in the government.
- **National Iraqi Commandos Front/National Front of the Fedayeen** (Jebha Watania al-Fedayeen al-Iraq). A localized name for various Saddam Fedayeen cell operations.
- **Prosperity Group** (al-Rifah). Alleged to have been a group of high-ranking FRLs in the Mosul area.

- **Patriotic Front/Popular Front** (Jebhaa Shaabi). An unidentified FRL cell.
- **National/Popular Resistance for the Liberation of Iraq** (al-Muqawamah Shaabi Lil Tahrir al-Iraq/al-Muqawamah Watani Lil Tahrir al-Iraq). An FRL front group for Saddam Fedayeen and intelligence agency-based insurgents.
- **Party of the Return/the Return** (Hizb al-'Awda/al-'Awda). Believed to have been one of the original FRL groups made up of Ba'athist political agents, intelligence, and Fedayeen personnel operating throughout Iraq, including Baghdad, Mosul, and Ramadi. First said to have been headquartered in Mosul, it was originally led by Mohammed al-Samidai, a Mosul Ba'ath Party member.
- **Resistance and Liberation in Iraq** (al-Muqawamah wah al-Tahrir fi Iraq).
- **September 11 Revolutionary Group.** A cell name for a group of local Saddam Fedayeen from the Balad area.
- **Snake's Head Party** (Harakat al-Ra's al-'Afa). A cell of FRLs that operated in the vicinity of Hawijah.
- **Supporters of Saddam the Holy Warrior** (Ansar al-Saddam al-Jihadi). This FRL cell appeared in the media on October 24, 2003, claiming resistance attacks on coalition forces.
- **National Front for the Liberation of Iraq** (Wejah Watuni lil Tahrir al-Iraq). According to the *World Peace Herald*, this front contained 10 subgroups operating independently. In truth, it was an FRL organization.

All of the above-named insurgent groups and cells carry out their operations from covert locations, networks of underground caves, or basements of buildings, and hide their weapons in similarly hard-to-find caches. Thus, it initially proved difficult for American forces to discover the insurgent forces, given the covert nature of their operations and the cell structure under which they function. By 2006 U.S. counterintelligence would identify most FRL networks.

Organization

Of all of the insurgent groups operating in Iraq, the FRLs were without question the most organized. The entire body of evidence reveals a networked command structure that managed to maintain a measure of regimentation, though it operated easily in a covert capacity.

NATIONAL COMMAND OF THE ISLAMIC RESISTANCE— UNIFIED MUJAHIDEEN COMMAND (NCIR-UMC)

NCIR-UMC Senior Command

The senior leadership of the NCIR was believed to be operating out of Damascus, Syria, until the start of the Syrian civil war in 2011, where it may have moved back into western Iraq. During the American insurgency the NCIR felt confident enough to maintain a high profile. It enjoyed overt support from the Syrian Ba'ath Party. An eyewitness reported they wore their Ba'ath Party uniforms, ranks, and attitudes on the street. These members included Izzat Ibrahim al-Douri, Rafi Abd al-Latif Tilfah al-Tikriti, Rukan Razuki, Abd al-Baqi Abd al-Karim, and Rashid Taan Kazim. The senior intelligence officer of the NCIR-UMC, unknown at this time, will most likely be an officer who had the rank of colonel or higher in the SSO. Rukan Razuki is the best candidate for this spot. His deposed staff clearly remains the most likely officers acting as liaison to the tribal chief of western Iraq and the deputy of the resistance in Anbar Province.

Regional Commands

Reports from coalition forces revealed the FRL insurgency was semi-hierarchical structure with top-down directives until the regional level; then the organization spreads into a hybrid network in semi-independent cells. Duties and roles of the cells are designed to meet the objectives of the national command. These regional commanders operate in a distinct geographic area, generally by province. It is assessed that they were divided into two areas of resistance effort. Primary resistance commands are where the operating environment, manpower, and support are the most intense. The secondary resistance commands are smaller areas where the effort is more selective and the targets are sparse but still yield good results. Cities such as Basrah, Hillah, and Kirkuk, which are not naturally supportive of the activities, still have covert cells or contacts, which could assist in intelligence collection.

Provinces with principal resistance commands are:

- Baghdad
- Anbar
- Nineveh
- Salah al-Din
- Diyala

Provinces with secondary resistance commands are:

- Babil
- Karbala
- Wasit
- Basra
- At Tamim

FRL INSURGENT ROLES AND RESPONSIBILITIES

A regional commander would be a loyal member of the former regime intelligence or party apparatus. This member would have to have extensive experience in operational and personal security as well as combat experience. It is assessed this would be a former member of the SSO or Saddam Fedayeen with the prewar rank of colonel. He would have one or more deputy officers who would facilitate his decision and take over in case of his death.

LOCAL TERROR CELLS/GROUPS (INSURGENT BRIGADES)

The local-level insurgent cells view themselves as commando squads operating in a clandestine manner. These terror cells would be the men, women, and children operating on the street. Some may be assigned a specific city to operate in, and others may work within the region. Each cell or group, often called a brigade (Kateebah), has a core group composed of a cell leader, a deputy officer, an operations officer, and a specialist in logistics who may also double as finance officer. If large enough targets present themselves, or if cooperation with other cells is needed, all cell members and even some family members join in an attack. The cells may have specialty teams of dedicated or occasional operatives who join and leave depending on their mission and skill set.

Finance and logistics cell: Several finance and logistics (FLO) officers were captured throughout the insurgency. Some were discovered distributing tens of thousands of dollars in funds as early as a week after the fall of Baghdad. A major responsibility of the FLO would be the development and distribution of special weapons; a regional car bomb preparation cell would be tasked to steal or buy vehicles, which would be hollowed and prewired for use by suicide bombers in the FRL system or given to other organizations.

Intelligence cell: The most important unit in the province would be the intelligence/liaison cell. This group of former regime intelligence officers and their assets would work with other groups and cells to collect intelligence on the coalition positions, movements, personnel, and logistics. As a covert cell they would have personnel tasked to collect against and manage collection for the American, Iraqi government/army/police, and Shiite militias. Since this would be an enormous task, this would be one of the largest cells in the province, with as many as 6 to 10 dedicated officers, working in a compartmented way, fielding reports from smaller collection teams. This group would pass on time- or politically sensitive intelligence directly to higher echelons in Syria or to a covert command center in Anbar Province. A critical group in the regional intelligence cell would be the regional IED/S-VBIED planning cell. This would be two to four persons who would integrate the information they collected from all sources and assist in the targeting of convoys for IEDs or high-value targets for car bombs (VBIEDs). Below the regional intelligence cell is the brigade's own integral and dedicated intelligence team. The cell may use intelligence collected locally or passed down from a higher echelon. The cell's role would be to collect the information on its targets from off the street, through sources it developed or direct observation. This cell also makes recommendations up the chain of command on the best targets to strike.

IED planting teams: These are the men and women who go out at night and plant the improvised explosives that kill so many soldiers and civilians. These teams are composed of dedicated terrorists as well as a person paid to drop components where the terrorists want them or to deliver a complete weapon on cash contract. The cell member is usually near the device when the target is seen and the weapon exploded.

Sniper cell: FRL snipers have proven that they can conduct competent operations by shooting individual coalition troops using the Russian, Iraqi, or Chinese versions of SVD rifle and Steyr SSG sniper rifles. They operate in teams of two, including a second man that acts as observer/videographer.

Assassination cell: In keeping with the FRL "kill-humiliate-punish" strategy, many groups have a dedicated punishment/assassination cell. These members are hard-core killers who generally assassinate perceived collaborators, unaware soldiers, and anyone who they please. Invariably, these men are ex-Ba'athists who enjoy the job.

VBIED cell: Some specialized teams have a car bomb preparation cell, which may be located at a private garage, inside a resistance, or just the occasional use of a sympathetic machine shop/repair hut. The "bomb master" of the cell fills the car bombs with artillery shells or explosives and wires them for detonation. He rarely gets involved with operations and is a highly sought after operative. The escort video trigger (EVT) cell is a team of three or four men that usually goes with the VBIED and blows it up by remote trigger, often a cell phone. They prefer to have one of the men in the vehicle videotape the detonation of the VBIED for propaganda and analysis. The video operative acts as an escort to the triggerman and generally does not drive the EVT vehicle. Interestingly, the FRLs do not appear to have embraced AQI's all-consuming lust for the suicide bomber. It is assessed that they use the intelligence cell to coordinate with suicide volunteers from other groups. In this way, FRL-based intelligence information is collated and a vehicle prepared to accept explosives as a VBIED. These assets would be passed to the FRL intelligence liaison officer, who would in turn give them to al-Qaeda in Iraq (AQI) and allow them to marry the vehicle with a suicide bomber volunteer (where it becomes an S-VBIED) and strike the target as they saw fit. In this manner, AQI gets broad operational and technical support to perform its massive S-VBIED campaigns, and the FRLs get their preferred targets struck without sacrificing their manpower.

Indirect fire support cell: The group assigned to harass the coalition with mortars and rockets is the indirect fire (IDF) cell. They move, modify, and launch rockets, mortar bombs, and guided missiles at locations that are hard to access directly. They may also accompany infantry units and support them with the small ballistic mortars as they perform ambushes. A regional battlefield mortar/rocket cell would be tasked to supply, distribute, and provide advice to the rocket and indirect fire cells in a given region. This cell could be manned by a former army artillery officer, launcher volunteers, machine tool and steel workers, chemistry teachers, and possibly even technologists from the Iraqi defense industry.

FINANCING THE INSURGENCY

The insurgency requires money to buy weapons, pay soldiers, and incentivize supporters. Insurgents and families of martyrs, those killed both in combat and in suicide bombings, would have to be paid, government agencies infiltrated by professional spies, and other weapons systems purchased. Links to the Ba'ath Party in Syria would have needed the funding to pay off not only the local tribes, but also a large part of the Syrian intelligence leadership to turn a blind eye to cross-border traffic. All of this cost an enormous quantity of cash. Where did the insurgency get its resources? The cash existed right in the middle of Baghdad at the Central Bank complex on Rashid Street. On March 15, 2003, 4 days before the invasion, the Special Republican Guard security units arrived at the Central Bank complex with tractor trailers. The bank director, Asrar al-Basri, was handed an order from Qusay Hussein to withdraw $1 billion in U.S. currency from the bank's reserves. The SRG troops and intelligence officers started to quickly move the pallets of money, including US$900 million and €100 million. The 10 tons of foreign currency, almost 25% of Iraq's entire cash currency reserve, was loaded into three tractor trailer trucks and driven off. Although much of the money was recovered by U.S. forces, more than $100 million remained unaccounted for and was most likely the financial basis for the insurgency. Soon after the fall of Baghdad, FRL insurgent financiers were caught by coalition forces distributing hundreds of thousands of dollars. The director of the new Iraqi government's intelligence, Gen. Mohamad Abdullah al-Shahwani, told *Al Hayat* newspaper that his former regime counterpart, Gen. Muhammed Yunis al-Ahmed, head of the Directorate of Military Security, worked with Saddam Hussein's half-brother Sabawi Ibrahim al-Hassan and moved back and forth across the Syria-Iraq border.[44] Hassan was captured on this very route coming into Iraq from Hasakah in northeastern Syria by Syrian forces in 2005.

ENDNOTES

1. Joe Klein, Saddam's Revenge, *Time*, September 26, 2005.
2. Ibid.
3. Reeva Spector Simon and Eleanor H. Tejirian, *The Creation of Iraq, 1914–1921*, Columbia University Press, New York, 2004, 22.
4. T.E. Lawrence, *Seven Pillars of Wisdom*, 2nd ed., Garden City Publishing Co., Garden City, NY, 1938.
5. Simon and Tejirian, 19–36; Michael Eppel, *Iraq from Monarchy to Tyranny*, University of Florida Press, Gainesville, 2004, 12–14.
6. Comprehensive Report of the Special Advisor to the DCI on Iraq's WMD, ttp://www.cia.gov/cia/reports/iraq_wmd_2004/chap1.html.
7. Scott Ritter, Facing the Enemy on the Ground, Alternet, July 9, 2004.
8. AlJazeera.net, http://english.aljazeera.net/NR/exeres/5E4030F7-A7FB-4DF9-B19A-D4F0E9C03474.htm.

9. www.globalsecurity.org/military/world/iraq/al-Duri.htm.

10. Ritter, Facing the Enemy on the Ground.

11. The Fold: The War in Iraq; Who's Caught, Who's Sought; 2 Years after the U.S.-Led Invasion, the Hunt for Saddam's Former Henchmen and Insurgents Continues, *Newsday* (New York), March 21, 2005.

12. Ibrahim al-Marashi, Iraq's Security and Intelligence Network: A Guide and Analysis, *MERIA Journal*, 6(3), 2002.

13. *Daily Telegraph*, July 24, 2003.

14. Andrew Cockburn and Patrick Cockburn, *Saddam Hussein, an American Obsession*, Verso, London, 2000, 151.

15. Con Coughlin, *Saddam, King of Terror*, Harper Collins Publishers, New York, 2002, 205.

16. After the War: the Quarry, *New York Times*, July 23, 2003.

17. Obituaries, *The Irish Times*, July 26, 2003.

18. Ibid.

19. Con Coughlin, *Saddam, King of Terror*, Harper Collins Publishers, New York, 2002, 304.

20. *Daily Telegraph*, July 24, 2003.

21. *New York Times*, July 23, 2003.

22. *Daily Telegraph*, July 24, 2003.

23. Comprehensive Report to the Special Advisor to the DCI for Iraq's WMD, Annex C, Central Intelligence Agency, September 30, 2004.

24. Iraq's Intelligence Agencies, Federation of American Scientists, http://www.fas.org.

25. Comprehensive Report to the Special Advisor to the DCI for Iraq's WMD.

26. Al-Marashi.

27. Jane's Security Sentinel, November 1999–April 2000, 184.

28. Jane's Security Sentinel, 185–187.

29. Scott Ritter, *Endgame: Solving the Iraq Problem Once and for All*, Simon & Schuster, New York, 1999.

30. Kanan Mikiya, *Republic of Fear: The Politics of Modern Iraq*, University of California Press, Berkeley, 1998.

31. Ritter, 99.

32. Ibid.

33. Thom Shanker, Hussein Agents Are Behind Attacks in Iraq: Pentagon Finds, *New York Times*, April 29, 2004.

34. Ibid.

35. Ritter, *Endgame*.

36. Ibid.

37. Sean Boyne, Inside Iraq's Security Network—Parts One and Two, *Jane's Intelligence Review*, 9(7–8), 1997.

38. Ibid.

39. Ibid.

40. Unit 999, http://www.iraqinews.com/org_unit_999.shtml.
41. Jane's Security Sentinel.
42. Ba'ath Party Communiqué, Iraqi Resistance Reports, April 26 2004, http://www.albasrah.net/moqawama/english/0404/iraqiresistan-cereport_260404.htm#b-party.
43. *AlMajid Magazine*, Iraqi Resistance Reports.
44. Iraqi Intelligence Chief Says 20,000 to 30,000 Terrorists Operating in Iraq, *Al Hayat*, January 1, 2005.

CHAPTER 5

The Insurgent's Strategy

Behind the walls of the secure Green Zone in downtown Baghdad was the headquarters convention hall of the Iraqi Ba'ath Party. For years the American army occupied the Iraqi tomb of the Syrian political philosopher Michel Aflaq, the father of the modern Ba'ath Party. The Lebanese-born, French-educated Aflaq, along with another Paris compatriot, Salah al-Din al-Bitar, co-founded the party in 1947. The party expanded in 1949 with the founding of a branch in Iraq. Throughout the 1950s, the Ba'ath Party in Iraq held little official political power, but "was deeply involved in anti-government demonstrations and other opposition activities" directed against the monarchy of King Faisal II.[1] In 1957, the Iraqi Ba'ath Party officially entered Iraq's political arena by joining forces with the Iraqi Communist Party (ICP), the National Democratic Party (NDP), and the Istiqlal Party in a national front opposing the monarchy.[2]

The centerpiece of Ba'ath ideology was Arab unity, based on a nationalism of shared language, culture, and history. Arab unity thus excluded other ethnic and linguistic groups within Iraq's borders, such as the Kurds in the north. Other tenets of Ba'ath ideology included opposition to the capitalist West, a mild form of socialism, and separation of politics from religion. However, while the Ba'athists supported this separation, the party acknowledged that Islam was the prime motivation behind pan-Arabism.[3]

When the Ba'ath Party first came into existence in Iraq, it boasted a mixed membership of both Sunni and Shiite Arabs. The party never gained the support of the Kurds due to its radical pan-Arabist ideology. Despite the appeal of pan-Arabism to both Sunnis and Shiites, "recruitment had as much to do with family and social networks as with ideology."[4] Thus, over time, the Ba'ath Party became dominated by Sunni leadership due to the personal and regional ties of those in power within the party.[5]

On July 14, 1958, Republican Army officers executed a well-planned coup d'état against the 23-year-old King Faisal II. The English-educated King Faisal, his immediate family, and loyalists were executed. In an act of barbarity, with great similarity to those experienced in post-Saddam insurgency, the monarch was beheaded by soldiers in his palace. His uncle, crown prince Abd Allah, was hacked to pieces and the remains of his body dragged through the streets, where it was hung in front of the Defense Ministry for public viewing. As the British embassy burned to the ground, the 1958 coup was the first opportunity for the Ba'ath Party to truly assert itself in Iraq's political realm. However, at the time the party played a very small role in the coup due to its limited contacts and influence within the armed forces; the only support it lent the military overthrow of the monarchy was in fueling the revolutionary atmosphere of the public. Following the coup, newly appointed president and military leader Abd al-Karim Qasim consolidated power and associated himself with the Iraq Communist Party. Qasim framed the Ba'ath Party as the opposition alongside the nationalists. Qasim wished to be associated with the ICP rather than with the pan-Arabist Ba'athists and nationalists because he did not wish to play second-in-command to Egypt's Gemal Abdul Nasser in a proposed pan-Arab federation.[6]

In March 1959, the Ba'ath Party instigated a popular revolt in Mosul, which drew upon local dissatisfaction with Qasim's regime to fuel the insurgence. The revolt failed and led ultimately to purges of Ba'athists and nationalists in Qasim's regime. This led the Ba'ath Party to formulate an assassination strategy as the only viable route to power in Iraq; "the normal method of obtaining political power in the Middle East was through the coup rather than through the ballot box."[7] Thus, the party prepared for an assassination-led coup d'état by establishing ties within the armed forces, exploiting officers' personal dissatisfaction with the way Qasim was running the country. On October 7, 1959, the Ba'ath Party attempted to assassinate Qasim, but succeeded only in killing his driver. The assassination team included a 23-year-old Ba'ath Party loyalist named Saddam Hussein; though wounded in the attempt, he and the others escaped unidentified.[8]

From 1958 to 1963, the Ba'ath Party pursued a strategy of exploiting dissatisfaction in persons within and outside of Qasim's regime in order to set the stage for a successful coup d'état. After the purges of 1959, the party regrouped in Syria, building up an "effective network with links to a number of groups opposed to the regime, including former members of the Istiqlal party, members of professional associations, and, most crucially, with a number of key military officers."[9] Since Qasim had allied himself with the ICP, many of the Ba'ath Party's actions during this period were directed against members of that party: "the nationalists and Ba'athists formed themselves into loosely coordinated underground groups and hit squads, and began to attack the Communists and their supporters in a systematic fashion."[10] By 1961, 286 party members and sympathizers had been killed, and by 1966 that number had risen to more than 400.[11]

In February 1963, the military leader Abd al-Salam Arif led a coup d'état against Qasim, which was organized by the Ba'ath Party with the aid of other nationalist army officers. At the time the Ba'ath Party of Iraq was split into several factions; though these groups cooperated to execute the coup, the Sunni–Arab faction of army generals and civilians would be the branch of the party to rise to power again in 1968. Importantly, Saddam Hussein was a blooded, middle-ranking operative of this faction in 1963.[12]

The Ba'ath Party remained in power and supported the newly installed President Arif from February to November 1963. The Ba'ath Party and Arif controlled Iraq through the militia (the Iraqi National Guard), highly organized civilian leadership, and loyal army officers. To preempt real and potential opposition to Ba'athist power, the Iraqi National Guard carried out massive numbers of arrests and executions of Communists; "many thousands were arrested, and sports grounds were turned into makeshift prisons to hold the flood of detainees. People were killed in the streets, tortured to death in prison, or executed after mock 'trials.'"[13] While this effectively destroyed the Communist opposition, the violence of the Ba'athists' activities during this period left a scar on the public's opinion of the party that persists to the present day.[14] From this point forward in Iraqi history the predominantly Sunni Ba'athists would be considered murderous thugs hungry for power.

Yet for all its power, it was factional differences within the Ba'ath Party that allowed Arif to seize complete power in November 1963. Under his military dictatorship, Ba'athists were removed from positions of power, forcing the party to go underground; "the main focus of party activity in Iraq in the period between November 1963 and July 1968 was in small, loosely interconnected conspiratorial groups of like-minded friends and kinsmen."[15] This running to ground of the party by Arif created the base of knowledge for the modern insurgency. The Ba'athists created covert political cells and established a framework for secret preparations to seize power. A key component of their secret tradecraft, despite formal disenfranchisement from the inner circles of government, was their ability to maintain access to, and foster friendly relations with, those in power throughout this period. Within the Ba'ath Party, the Sunni–Arab faction continued to consolidate its power; in 1964, Saddam Hussein, aged 27, was appointed full-time organizer of the nonmilitary wing of the party. In 1966, Hussein was assigned the figurehead position of deputy secretary general of the party. These appointments would prove a critical step in his ascension to power within the Ba'ath Party in later years.[16]

The Ba'athist coup d'état in 1968 was led by Ahmed Hassan al-Bakr (who Saddam Hussein reported to directly) and, once again, exploited dissention in the military community. The coup was bloodless, with

Abd al-Rahman Arif (brother to Abd al-Salam Arif) exiled to London in a dignified manner. The Revolutionary Command Council, manned mainly by Ba'athists and some nationalists, consolidated power through military connections that seized important facilities during the coup, including the national radio station. Al-Bakr continued to consolidate power by appointing "over one hundred Ba'athist officers to positions in the Republican Guard and other key units."[17] Following the coup and al-Bakr's consolidation of power, the Ba'ath Party oversaw widespread purges of all existing and potential opposition, determined to avoid the mistakes of 1963. Additionally, Saddam Hussein had risen to the head of the Ba'ath Party under al-Bakr's guidance and continued to gain power in Iraq's government.[18] Hussein eventually disposed of al-Bakr by exposing an elaborate "plot" that resulted in his rising to power as chairman of the Ba'ath Party, a position he would retain until March 19, 2003.

THE FRL LONG-RANGE STRATEGY

While secretly planning to overthrow the Bakr government, the influence of the party centered around building relationships with those in power, which exploited discontent with the current regime and brought new recruits to the party. Thus, membership and support for the party were based mainly on personal, tribal, and regional ties rather than ideology. Though the Ba'ath Party was small, it's excellent organization allowed for effective civilian administration once it gained power, first in 1963 and again in 1968, and allowed for the consolidation of power and the elimination of opposition groups.

Thus, during the period from 1958 to 1968, it was the long-term strategy of the Ba'ath Party to effect political change through destabilizing violence, including the liberal use of terrorism. Underground covert political and military operations, which ensured its rise to power, remains the cornerstone of its strategy. Given the clandestine nature of the Ba'ath Party's original drive for building a power base and its small membership numbers in the past, it is possible that a neo-Ba'athist movement, grounded on the past history but no longer loyal to Saddam Hussein, may be pursuing a similar strategy today. Organized more around tribal and religious loyalties, these former regime loyalists waged a destabilizing campaign to ensure the central government dominated by Shiites and Kurds is perpetually weak. Within the next decade the Ba'athist leadership of the Sunni may simply wait for an opportune moment to seize power from an incompetent or weak government. Additionally, it is logical to assume that the longer they wait, the stronger their influence and connections will become, increasing the likelihood of their success in any future attempted coup d'état.

MILITARY STRATEGY OF THE INSURGENCY

As noted earlier, the plan to inflict damage on the Americans in a second phase of the war was developed well before the invasion. Saddam Hussein was a tyrant of the highest order. He had been to war with three of his six neighbors. He had killed an estimated 200,000 of his countrymen during his 25-year reign of terror. He had developed and used weapons of mass destruction. Saddam Hussein also appeared for the first time to have exhibited traits of realism that had not been credited to him before. Even though he knew that diplomatic efforts could possibly deter American President George Bush, he also knew that there would be little time to prepare for a longer-term plan in the event of an American victory. In September 2002, Saddam secretly ordered development of Project 111—the covert plan to conduct armed resistance in an American-occupied Iraq. The mission of the tasked forces was to organize and sustain a resistance movement with the intent to keep punishing the Americans until they could take no more. The forces would operate covertly well after the occupation was in place. They would train to strike with the weapons to be buried in caches before the war. The Americans would be subject to nonstop harassment and would be bled slowly. The intended effect would be similar to that of the American experience in Somalia. Each of these strategic objectives relied on the use of specific terrorist or guerrilla tactics, to be applied selectively, in order to achieve the maximum effect of instilling fear or degrading confidence in the occupation and the follow-on government. Once the American people saw the price to pay for the occupation, they would lose their national will and push for withdrawal. Once the Americans withdrew, then the insurgents would deal with the Iraqis who had supported the invasion and seize power again. The likelihood of this happening was low but the war fighting concept of the plan was sound.

STRATEGIC PHASES OF THE INSURGENCY

Immediately following the fall of Baghdad the shadow army of Saddam's regime stepped up, recruiting, rearming, retooling, and finalizing the strategy to inflict maximum damage on the American-led coalition. The strategy for the insurgency could best be described as the KHPI strategy: kill, humiliate, punish, and inspire (Figure 5.1). The KHPI strategy would concentrate forces to perform the combat actions necessary to fulfill the following objectives:

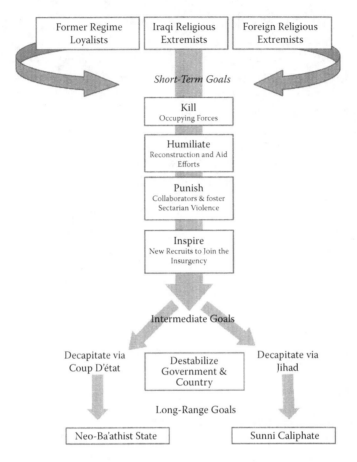

FIGURE 5.1   Comparative strategies of the Iraq insurgency.

1. **Phase 1: Kill the occupiers.** The combined insurgent forces would
   engage coalition forces and bleed them slowly through attacks on
   personnel, the bases, and supply routes. The terminal objective
   was to keep striking in pinprick fashion until the United States
   could no longer politically accept the level of casualties and would
   withdrew. On any terms, a withdrawal, voluntary or ordered
   by a new Iraqi government, would be a de facto victory for the
   insurgents. Likened to Somalia or Lebanon, it was designed to
   keep the casualty counts consistent and losses to the coalition
   high. By the time of the 2011 withdrawal of the U.S. Army, this
   would be the most successful phase of their operations.
2. **Phase 2: Humiliate neutrals.** In this phase the insurgents would
   attack the noncombatant international efforts and agencies
   involved in the reconstruction of Iraq with the goal of humiliating

the U.S. forces and their allies by demonstrating their inability to keep the country safe. Some attacks would be oriented to further antagonize the damaged relations between the United States and allied partners by striking when the heavy-handed political rhetoric of President George W. Bush would assist in the damage. This could be called the "paper tiger" strategy. The attack and its associated tactic would be carefully chosen and strategically timed to damage the American political machinery and make those tasked with the reconstruction of Iraq think twice about their safety or withdraw from projects altogether.

3. **Phase 3: Punish collaborators** (and discredit the security and political elements of the new Iraqi government). It was critical that the insurgent forces would remind those who were ever allied with the U.S. coalition that they would not forgive cooperation with the occupying army. Institutions, which were the pillars of Saddam's repression—in particular the army, the police, the national guard, the ministries, and individual members of the formerly suppressed political parties—would be subject to attack and assassination at every opportunity. Sectarian violence would be encouraged. Attacks on the Shiites would be seen as a tool to unite the Sunni community.

4. **Phase 4: Inspire new recruits.** Both the Islamic insurgents and the Ba'athists were looking at a multiyear insurgency on the scale of the Hezbollah counteroccupation war in southern Lebanon. A key to this operation would be the constant inspiration of the young men to join the jihad. The secular Ba'athists were embracing Islam and would be sincerely fighting for their tribal gains using religion more than Ba'ath Party doctrine. Heroes from Islamic history, such as Salah al-Din Ayoubi, the historical hero and warrior-poet Antar, and the image of the Islamic knight, would be called upon in propaganda to inspire young teenagers and children to dream of being a Mujahideen. Foreign and Iraqi Islamic extremists were fighting what they believed was a continuation of the battles of the Prophet Mohammed and using the images of the successful martyr and the masked Mujahideen to inspire mystery and daring. The Internet, posters, and flyers would be a key in the psychological operation to gain new recruits.

MISSION ACCOMPLISHED: THE PRIMARY
GOAL OF THE INSURGENCY WAS BREAKING
THE WILL OF THE AMERICAN PEOPLE

The art of selecting targets by a terrorist group has a name. It's called terrorist targeteering (T2). Targeteering is the act of evaluating a potential target for the best emotional, propaganda, or military impact in relation to the terrorist's objectives. Each of the terrorist's objectives depends on selecting the right tactic and delivering the right payload on the correct target. This is critical for terrorist leadership to meet their goals. It is especially true of terrorists with deep sources of accurate intelligence and decades of infiltrating entire communities, such as the Iraqi intelligence agencies. Most of the terrorist goals in Iraq come down to two simple goals: instilling maximum fear and a feeling of helplessness in the face of their attacks and degrading the confidence in the occupation forces and the Iraqi government.

Speaking before the Naval War College, then commander of the U.S. Central Command Gen. John Abazaid summarized what could be called anti-willingness operations of al-Qaeda in Iraq, but it was equally applicable to all of the insurgent groups.

> Al Qaida has no belief that they can defeat us militarily. They see our center of gravity as being the will of the American people. That is influenced by the media and they are playing to that. They don't need to win any battles. Their plan is to keep the casualties in front of the American people in the media for long enough that we will become convinced that we cannot win and leave the region. That would be tragic for our country.[19]

General Abazaid was correct in this assessment, as it has been described by Al Qaeda as the very strategy necessary to force the Americans to withdraw. The strategic goal was to bleed the willpower of America to continue the occupation. Despite the bravado of the Bush administration, Americans have proven quite sensitive to the bloodletting. Small subtle indicators gave the insurgents hope that their anti-willingness operations were scoring points. For example, the accelerated political timetable the White House established for the transition to the interim government in June 2004 showed them that the denial of the existence of the insurgency and rising death tolls of troops and civilians hurt the administration politically. To the insurgency, these internal political decisions and others like them were not the response of a well-balanced plan in the interests of the Iraqi people but had the appearance of the president wanting to toss away a political hot potato. The FRL insurgents had the political savvy to understand the moves of the White House. The terror leadership saw this as a principal desire to show forward political movement in the run-up to the 2004 U.S. elections, not a determined effort to secure democracy for the people of Iraq. Here they found the weakest link in America's willingness to stay in Iraq—internal American politics.

Insurgent target selection and strike timing plays a great role in continuing the strategic anti-willingness plan of the insurgency. Commanders selected tactical targets with broad fear values necessary to weaken and defeat America's willingness to continue the war. Therefore, the targeteering of the insurgency came down to selecting the targets that caused mass casualties on the Americans or which were ultimately blamed on the Americans. For all of the talk of "stay the course," it became clear to the insurgent leadership that the American president could be severely damaged by selectively creating televised terror campaigns at key times. The media dutifully reported it, but it was the White House itself that compounded the problem by ignoring the reality and blaming the media for activities controlled by the insurgency.

Additionally, when the 2004 and 2006 American election cycles loomed, the Iraqis learned quickly that President George W. Bush would play electoral politics above all else. The FRL leadership, with al-Qaeda in Iraq (AQI) in synch, launched suicide vehicle-borne improvised explosive device (S-VBIED) campaigns to humiliate him at every chance. With America hearing nothing but bad news (which was the on-the-ground reality of Iraq) and the White House working in a bubble of incompetence, the insurgency saw repeated chances to strike again and again and again at the American center of gravity—its willingness to sustain high numbers of casualties. The slightest reconstruction or security success announced by the Pentagon would be destroyed by a wave of S-VBIEDs and increased attacks on soldiers. The insurgents saw to it that President Bush would not be allowed to maintain credibility so long as the White House spun every attack through the prism of denial. The insurgents had the weapons to discredit him.

The insurgents did not see the military defeat against the U.S. and coalition armed forces as a strategic goal because they knew these forces could not be defeated in conventional combat. The only concession that the insurgency accepted was a limited political solution.

Additionally, the types of attacks the insurgents carried out—sniping, IED, and mortar attacks—forced the U.S. Army to maintain a high operations tempo, which takes a psychological toll on the individual soldier. However, as part of a rotating military mission, the insurgency produced a level of fatigue on equipment and manpower not thought possible. Given enough pressure, a soldier can break, overreact, and create political situations that create more damage of strategic import than any number of other tactical incidents. The insurgents not only recognized this, but they capitalized on the exploitation of each. Examples include the Abu Ghraib prison humiliations, accusations of torture, the rape/murder of a 14-year-old Iraqi girl and her family, and the massacres of innocent Iraqi men and women after an IED attack by Blackwater security guards. Each incident erased years of goodwill in the eyes of many Iraqis.

TACTICAL GOALS

At the street level, the goals of the insurgent groups combined. There was almost no difference between the goals of al-Qaeda in Iraq, the Islamic Army in Iraq, or the FRL Army of the Mujahideen. These goals included:

- **Kill Americans, coalition forces, and their contractors (2003–2011).** In the insurgent's eyes, the Americans needed to feel constant pressure. The more dead, the greater the pressure. If the intervention in Somalia in 1991 by President George H.W. Bush showed them anything, it was the limits of American tolerance for casualties. Bleeding the Americans would create pressure to withdraw. Images of dead Americans soldiers may not have arrived on American televisions screens, but the toll was relentless. Contractors and civilians were not spared. Insurgents referred to any American contractor killed, especially the armed security contractors, as members of the CIA. This was an attempt to give justification to their operations against foreign spies. The insurgents often portrayed their anticontractor missions as counterintelligence operations.
- **Kill or intimidate the new Iraqi army and police (2003–present).** The insurgents of every stripe see a force of Iraqis who know their techniques and speak their language as a powerful counterbalance to their day-to-day operations. A reinvigorated Iraqi force filled with vengeful Shiites and Kurds would need to be cautioned at every turn. Killing them as they tried to join the military or police would help, but they would also need to be killed on the job. Tactical strikes against effective checkpoints manned by cautious soldiers who would not take a bribe to allow one to pass unsearched were critical. A few well-placed drive-by shootings or beheadings and others would see that it was easier to turn a blind eye for cash than to lose one's life. The Mujahideen believed that the army needed to realize that, they would always be on the losing end. Daily suicide car bombs, IEDs, and mortar and rocket attacks would keep the

new Iraqi army dreaming of a quiet barracks and not of hunting the insurgents. The insurgents needed the new army to operate at a subsistence level. Any buildup of competence or skills would force them to operate deeper underground and expend more weapons. That would be an unacceptable state. Many attacks are designed to affect the decision of the new recruits to remain in the army after a few months. Many Iraqi recruits, the overwhelming majority of which are Shiite and Sunni Kurds, are killed to warn that they will be required to pay a price.

- **Keep the Shiite death tolls high.** The insurgents strive to make a point that local security forces and the people of Iraq who do not support the Sunni simply must suffer enough casualties to keep them in fear of the Mujahideen. For the FRLs, they believed that this pressure will allow them to gain enough representation in government to plan a reenactment of their 1963 coup d'état and regain control of the central government.
- **Kill or limit the movement/mobility of Iraqi government.** The insurgents believe that the new government must be kept in fear of its life and must not be allowed to extend its authority. This is done by simply killing government members when they are found. Exploding enough IEDs to keep the main highways militarized and limiting the ability of members of the assembly and their staffs will slow down the effectiveness of the Iraqi administration. This in turn will bring frustration to the people who will have no faith in the government and start to view it as a puppet of the U.S. or Iran.
- **Further the insurgency/jihad.** Every strike the insurgents carry out can be videotaped and used for propaganda purposes. The strikes are not portrayed as simple acts of murder. They are depicted as daring acts of military strategy led by brave men who stand up to the invaders in an occupied land. Insurgent videos emphasize their using the mystery of covert techniques to go in the face of the enemy and strike them with devastating weapons. The allure of this campaign is heightened with rousing religious music and selective justification of the attacks from quotes found in the Qu'ran.

Terrorist and guerrilla cells know the effects of their acts are quite simple but far reaching. It is in blending the day-to-day impact of these acts that each insurgent group meets their strategic plan. Some types of attacks are preferred by select groups because they wish to inflict casualties and inspire young men to join their cause. Others use limiting the movement of the army and government to meet the strategic goal of creating political pressure at the bargaining table. No matter which group is attacking, they all have one tactical goal—to do the most damage as humanly possible with the weapons they have at hand.

HOW MANY INSURGENTS WERE THERE?

Seven months before the invasion of Iraq began, the chief of British intelligence warned Prime Minister Tony Blair that the Americans were ready to go to war and had given little consideration to the aftermath. This worried the cautious British, as American military war planners gave little consideration to the likelihood of an insurgency. When the smoke cleared from the 3-week-long combat operation, many American politicians and military commanders believed that the Sunni regime loyalists would have little interest in resistance. Their assessment was that after the invasion Iraqi soldiers who continued to fight would be a few "dead-enders," soldiers who had not gotten the word that they were beaten. Saddam would be quickly captured and the invasion would herald a new day in the Middle East. This rosy assessment would prove a terrific miscalculation. Within 120 days of the fall of the regime the insurgency would outline a shadowy organization that had started its wide-ranging "kill, humiliate, punish, inspire" campaign. One of the reasons for this miscalculation of the resistance was that the coalition started with a poor estimate of the strength of the insurgency.

An Enemy without Gains or Losses

The first instance of an official estimate of the insurgent order of battle (OOB) came from the commander of coalition forces in Iraq, Gen. John Abazaid, in November 2003. From May 2003, the coalition had unofficially estimated 5,000 "dead-enders" who continued to fight. During his testimony to Congress, Abazaid stated that he believed that estimate was accurate. Within a year, this number would first triple to 15,000, then quadruple to 20,000. Officially, the insurgency suffered no loss in manpower despite large-scale combat operations, including several major offensives in Baghdad, Fallujah, Ramadi, Al Qaim, and Tel Afar. There may be a logical explanation for that, but it was inconsistent with the intensity of the fighting and the rhetoric from both the Bush administration and the new Iraqi government.

Since Vietnam, the ability of the U.S. military to accurately estimate the manpower of guerrilla and terrorist groups has been hampered by two factors that are rarely taken into account publicly:

1. The inability to accept the premise that there is, in fact, a will to resist and form an insurgency.
2. An unshakable belief in the invincibility of modern U.S. Army combat power.

Add to these the tendency of the neoconservative political class in America and Britain to completely ignore the North Vietnamese victory in the Vietnam War (with the exception of trying to control media access to the troops), and what one is left with is a form of counterinsurgency hubris. The U.S. Army and Marine Corps are arguably the most well-educated and -experienced combat force in the world; yet when the enemy struck using the tactics the U.S. Army faced for 10 years in Vietnam, it appears the entire history and lessons learned from that war were either ignored or discounted. The logic appeared to be since there was no insurgency, the lessons of Vietnam did not apply to the Sunni Triangle. The insurgency was assisted greatly because, instead of estimating its size, strength, and structure, its existence was denied at the highest levels.

When fighting a standing army, the enemy's OOB is critical in determining how to best destroy their information, logistics, and combat command structure. In a guerrilla war, the OOB estimates must always take into account the depth of support and fluidity of movement the insurgent guerrilla has in the community. According to a great historical insurgent, Mao Tse Tung, "the guerrilla must move amongst the people as a fish swims in the sea." Any misunderstanding of the depth of hatred, commitment, or fervor of the community the guerrilla operates in will inevitably lead to an underestimation of the amount of weapons, equipment, and intelligence the counterinsurgency force will encounter. If Irish grandmothers were willing to hide Provisional Irish Republican Army assassins (who might be their sons or daughters), weapons, and explosives against the British, why would the grandmothers of the Sunni Triangle be any different?

In 1967, the U. S. Army and CIA fell victim to OOB politics when estimates of the enemy forces were horribly skewed for political purposes. The U.S. Army claimed the Vietcong (VC) and People's Army of North Vietnam (PAVN) took so many losses in the previous year that they virtually had no army with which to fight. A core component of this incredulous estimate were allegations that the Military Assistance Command in Vietnam (MACV) essentially ordered that the enemy strength would not exceed 300,000 in an effort to not have to explain discrepancies to the press.

So far, our mission frustratingly unproductive since MACV stonewalling, obviously under orders.... [The] inescapable conclusion [is] that General Westmoreland (with [CORDS Chief] Komer's encouragement) has given instruction tantamount to direct order that VC total strength will not exceed 300,000 ceiling. Rationale seems to be that any higher figure would generate unacceptable level of criticism from the press. This order obviously makes it impossible for MACV to engage in serious or meaningful discussion of evidence.[20]

This politicization of estimations of enemy strength in Vietnam were a contributing factor to the near disaster during the Tet offensive when in 1968, the VC and PAVN soldiers launched a nationwide assault that took America by surprise.

Estimate of the Core Insurgency, 2003–2011

It can be argued that any analysis of the insurgency not gained from their captured documents or high-ranking insurgent leaders is a form of guesstimation. Anthony Cordesman of the Center for Strategic and International Studies sums up the exercise best:

Most experts guesstimate the number of Islamist extremist insurgents at some 5–10 percent of the total insurgents without being able to say what base number they are a percent of. U.S. experts and officers sometimes make reference to a total of 20,000 insurgents of all kinds, but such experts are among the first to state that such numbers are more nominal mid-points in a range of guesses than real estimates. Other experts guesstimate the total number of Sunni insurgents and active sympathizers; insurgents of all kinds at totals from 15,000 to 60,000, with far larger numbers of additional passive sympathizers. These guesstimates would put the Sunni Islamist extremists at anywhere from 1,500 to 6,000. Some estimates do put the total number of neo-Salafi Sunni extremists much higher. Anthony Lloyd of the *London Times* has stated that, "An intelligence summary, citing the conglomeration of insurgent groups under the al-Qa'ida banner to be the result of rebel turf wars, money, weaponry and fear, concluded that of the estimated 16,000 Sunni Muslim insurgents, 6,700 were hard-core Islamic fundamentalists who were now supplemented by a possible further 4,000 members after an amalgamation with Jaysh Muhammad, previously an insurgent group loyal to the former Ba'athist regime." Given the difficulty in distinguishing core activists from part time or fringe activists, no one can discount such estimates.[21]

However, coming up with a credible working OOB estimate is a good exercise that can provide a better understanding of how and why the insurgency is apparently gaining strength. An analysis of several pieces of evidence gives us a glimpse at the size and sophistication of the insurgency's three wings. That evidence is:

1. The rate of attacks per day and per month
2. The original number and experience of the core cadre of the insurgents
3. The base of support that the insurgents could draw from the immediate community in which they operate

Paraphrasing Mao's analogy, if an insurgency are sharks swimming in an ocean of people, we are looking for how often the sharks attack, the exact species of shark, the size and experience of the various sharks, and the size of the ocean in which a certain shark is swimming.

The Original Number and Experience of the Core Cadres

To understand the makeup of the insurgent manpower pool, the evidence pointed to the fact that the Saddam regime had a prewar plan to operate behind enemy lines and resist the American occupation. Because they knew the strength of the Americans was to strike with heavy forces and defeat their army, they were infinitely better prepared to carry out their resistance mission than the U.S. forces were prepared to defeat asymmetric warfare. In the immediate prewar period, the most reliable segments of the regime were the five major intelligence agencies, the Special Republican Guard, and the Saddam Fedayeen. The combat core of the insurgency was formed starting with the dedicated and experienced military operatives. These were the combat-experienced Saddam Fedayeen (40,000 men) and the Special Republican Guard (26,000 men). Added to that would be the 31,000 men and women of hard-core loyalists who populated the regime's five intelligence agencies, including the Special Security Organization (5,500 men), the Directorate of General Security (DGS) (5,000 men), the Iraqi Intelligence Service (8,000 men), the Directorate of Military Intelligence (5,000 men), and the Directorate of Military Security (6,000 men). These forces altogether totaled 97,000 committed men and women under arms who would suffer the most if an American occupation were to defeat the Sunni Triangle cities.

Add to this calculation the party loyalists and disenrolled soldiers who would join the professionals. A conservative approach is to gather data on the population from which the insurgency would recruit immediately after the fall of the regime, that is, the soldiers, members, and families of the former Ba'ath Party. The Iraqi Ba'ath Party was comprised of more than 1.5 million people, but apart from the 30,000 full party members, they were among the least reliable defenders of Iraq. It is assessed that for this conservative analysis, this political class would not become a significant addition to combat forces in the insurgency, but passive supporters, propagandists, and outside observers. It is well documented that many of the most active Ba'athists relocated themselves to Syria, Egypt, and the United Arab Emirates and sent support from abroad and in safety. Therefore, this analysis only includes 20% of the estimated 30,000 army officers who did show up to fight the invasion in 2003. These 6,000 recruits would also include the extremely angry and motivated Sunni senior military officers with combat experience (artillerymen, infantry officers, ex-special forces, and intelligence) who lost any chance of gaining a role in the new government with Bremer's CPA Order No. 1, the dissolution of the Iraqi army.

Few Iraqis actually lost their lives in the invasion, and their ability to return home and start the insurgency was simplified by the speed of the attack. Even though the initial invasion pounded the Iraqi army and regime with everything the Americans and British had, the losses inflicted on the Iraqi army and Ba'athist forces were relatively small.

Carl Conetta, at the Center for Defense Alternatives, conducted a thorough study of Iraqi military combat losses in Operation Iraqi Freedom Phase 1 (OIF-1) and gives what appears to be a reliable figure of 4,895 to 6,370 Iraqi military killed in action (KIA). Conetta took into account the tendency for battlefield soldiers and commanders to inflate suspected losses (like counting four dead for a tank that was empty of its crew) and an extremely low number of actual bodies found on the battlefield or in graves. He reduced the estimates between 20 and 60%, depending on the source.[22] In comparison, initial death estimates ranged wildly from 10,000 to 50,000 Iraqi KIAs. Commander of the U.S. Central Command, Gen. Tommy Franks, placed the Iraqi losses at 30,000, but proclaimed soon after that the U.S. Army did not do body counts.

When the 5,000 to 6,000 Regular Army, retirees, and Ba'athist extremists (estimated above) are added into the prewar assessment of the insurgent strength (97,000), it balances out the average figure of 5,000 KIAs the regime suffered during the war. This brings us back to the approximate 97,000 personnel from which the insurgent manpower pool would have recruited.

Other forces often mentioned are the foreign fighters seen in Iraq before the war; Ba'athist Foreign Minister Naji Sabri announced before the fighting that 5,000 volunteers had come to aid Iraqi forces, and that "most of them want to train for martyrdom attacks." Vice President Taha Yassin Ramadan claimed 6,000, saying that "more than half of them [are] martyrdom-seekers."[23] These forces were mainly Syrian mercenaries and Saudi, Palestinian, and Yemeni students. Many, especially near Salman Pak, Baghdad airport, and Basrah University, got their wish to go to paradise fulfilled. Many returned home with their $1,000 pay packet. Others may have remained and folded into the insurgency.

Doing the Math

Most OOB analysts use a general figure of 20 to 25% of active strength to estimate the combat forces on the spear tip of a military structure. That figure then generally subtracts known attrition of the enemy from combat. It was assessed at the time that the Department of Defense (DoD) used this standard to create the original 20,000-man estimate. I believe that the DoD used similar calculations and numbers (rounding to 100,000) for the hardest core forces estimate. The initial estimate of 5,000 dead-enders made in May 2003 was clearly a guesstimate of a brigade-sized scattering of men who were yet to be defeated. That assessment remained until May 2004, when the Pentagon revisited the figures. As time wore on, it was obvious that the numbers of KIAs in the war were much lower than originally thought. They may have been just a bit too optimistic when they factored between 25,000 and 30,000 Iraq loyalists were killed out of 100,000 or so that may have fought the initial invasion. The May 2004 estimate of 14,000 to 16,000 fighters reflected a change in the calculations. However, this estimate lasted only for 60 days. The Pentagon most likely revised its wartime KIA figures to fit Conetta's (5,000 KIA) and then assessed 20% of the remaining force, or approximately 19,000 to 20,000 men, would be the hardest core Ba'ath forces that continue to fight.

Terrorist Brigades or Terrorist Battalions?

Other estimates focused on the total number of terrorist groups. For example, one conducted by the International Crisis Group, claimed 50 groups existed by the end of 2005. They used a rough method of analysis: "In traditional Arab military parlance, a brigade [sic] comprises from 100 to 300 men, who would add up to a total of roughly 5,000 to 15,000 insurgents." This calculation may be in error, as they may have mistaken the Arabic word for *battalion* (100–300 men) for a brigade. Many Middle East army brigades are generally between 1,500 and 5,000 men. This confusion is easily understandable, as the insurgents of Iraq have mistranslated the Arabic word for *battalion/battalions* (*kateebah/kataieb*) as the English word *brigade/brigades* (*leewah/fowj*) in virtually all of their online communiqués, written on their battle flags and postings of videos on the Internet. The global news media did not correct this error when translating early communiqués, and the misusage of *brigade* is now the common English to describe insurgent units even when the Arabic word *battalion* (e.g., 1920 Revolution Battalion, Battalions of the Victorious Sect) sits prominently right next to it in Arabic script or transliteration. In fact, almost every Arabic language reference to insurgent forces uses the correct word, *battalions*. For the purpose of this book, the word *brigade* will continue to be used in place of *battalion* unless using a direct Arabic translation.

The use of the word is of little consequence, as the term *brigade* in terrorist and insurgent parlance is just a collective identifier of a group or cell. It has been used universally by the insurgents in Iraq for any resistance group, no matter if they had 5 men or 5,000 men. The International Crisis Group's calculation was an inexact method of assessing size, as modern, networked terrorists and guerrillas do not maintain a military OOB with such precise numbers of personnel allocated in equal strength.

SIZE AND ROLES OF THE INSURGENT CELLS

To assess the number of terrorists in Iraq, one has to go to the ground level to determine the makeup of the basic operational unit and compare this to the frequency of attacks that could be carried out by these units based on capability and intelligence. This requires determining an average size of an insurgent cell. Since there are three types of insurgent groups (FRL, IRE, and AQI/ISIS) with differing strengths and popular support, there will be different sizes.

So how many men comprised an insurgent cell? In January 2004, 7 months after the start, the CIA estimated that there were 5 to 14 insurgent cells, each consisting of 20 to 100 enemy combatants operating in Baghdad alone. Technically, any personnel over 5 to 10 men is not a cell. The CIA used this word in place of *unit*. The Ba'ath Party itself used a system of cells of three to seven people to spread party information and report disloyalty.

Early on in the insurgency the CIA figure was supposedly supported by intelligence gleaned from captives and prewar plans. That's approximately 100 to 1,400 cell members, depending on the group. That surprisingly wide range shows the nebulous characteristics of the cells in the post-war. Iraq, a cell could be 5 men or 100 men, depending on the wing of the insurgency, the group they formed under, and their day-to-day role. Many groups were small pockets of armed Ba'ath Party associates, members of sports clubs (Nadi Riadi), or just street friends who lived on the same block who organized to stop looting and went on to fight the occupation. Other groups were organized by the Saddam Fedayeen, al-Qaeda, Iraqis, or religious groups, and dedicated operational cells were established for the exact purpose to operate covertly and attack coalition soldiers.

FRL CELLS

Past estimates of insurgent strength have included figures from 5,000 to as high as 200,000.[24] The high figures may actually be correct if one includes active supporters, regime loyalists, financiers, and logisticians outside of Iraq, and family members who assist in operations, collect intelligence, engage in propaganda, etc. The aggregate could easily have extended past 200,000 for all three wings of the insurgency. For the purposes of this analysis, the insurgency will include only the active and supporting persons who assist in the day-to-day combat operations against coalition soldiers. That generally includes three levels of operative:

- Full-time insurgent combatants
- Part-time insurgent combatants/insurgent operational support personnel
- Active cell supporters (immediate family, extended family, tribe, or community)

As shown in Figure 5.2a, the FRL insurgents used a cell structure of approximately 25 men (a reduced prewar Iraqi platoon). This number was determined based on attacks carried out per weapons systems at hand per day. A certain number of men are required to transport, use, and provide security for those systems. An average FRL cell carried out the following missions:

- Sniper operations (two men)
- IED operations (three men)
- Weapons ambush operations (five men)
- Man-portable air defense (MANPAD) operations (three men)
- Indirect fire attacks on U.S. bases (five men)

Add into that five command and logistics members and a bomb master and his assistant. Despite a fair size, these cells could not operate each day, as most missions had a life cycle of intelligence collection, planning, execution, and regroup/rearm that must be done covertly to ensure they are not compromised by hasty operations. In order to ensure longevity, each phase would take 1 day at the most to accomplish. This means each cell took an average of 4 days to execute and recover from each attack per weapon system. Given that the 25-man cell could carry out the five operations listed above once every 4 days, we will use this

Commanding Officer/Cell leader

Executive Officer/Cell Logistician

Bomb Master/VBIED Assembly Team

Sniper/Observer-Videographer Team

IED Laying/Initiating Team

Mortar Battlefield Rocket Indirect Fire Team

Weapons/RPG Ambush Team

MANPADS/Anti-aircraft Team

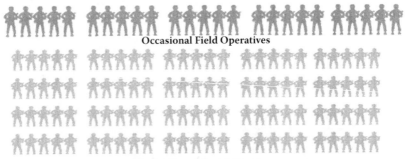

Occasional Field Operatives

Active Supporters & Family

FIGURE 5.2   (a) FRL cell structure. (Continued)

rotation to develop the general operations tempo of the cells. We can estimate there are three other cells active in the operations cycle for each one that is conducting an attack mission.

In May 2003, soon after the fall of Baghdad, the Iraqis carried out an average of 18 attacks per day (248 per month), peaking at 185 attacks per day (5,735 per month) by October 2006. Note that's a rate 23 times higher than the beginning of the war!

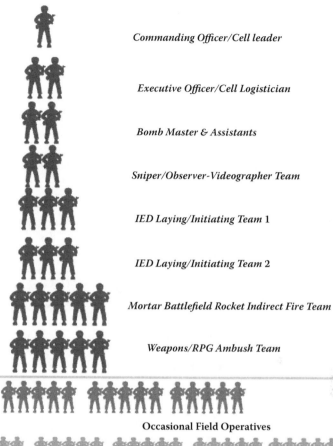

Commanding Officer/Cell leader

Executive Officer/Cell Logistician

Bomb Master & Assistants

Sniper/Observer-Videographer Team

IED Laying/Initiating Team 1

IED Laying/Initiating Team 2

Mortar Battlefield Rocket Indirect Fire Team

Weapons/RPG Ambush Team

Occasional Field Operatives

Active Supporters & Family

FIGURE 5.2   (b) Iraqi Islamic extremist group cell structure. (Continued)

Using these figures, we estimated FRL cells conducted an average of 80%, or 148, of these attacks. A three-man cell usually carried out these attacks. That means an average of 444 men are active on mission that day. Since a cell is estimated to be about 25 men, that leaves 22 other men per cell inside the planning cycle for a total of 3,256 who are off mission on that day. The total insurgents in the operations cycle is approximately 3,700. Given that there are three additional cells in the

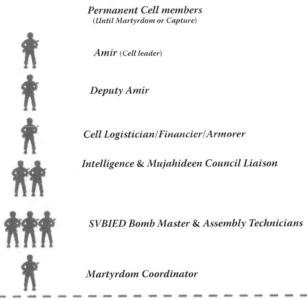

Permanent Cell members
(Until Martyrdom or Capture)

Amir *(Cell leader)*

Deputy Amir

Cell Logistician/Financier/Armorer

Intelligence & Mujahideen Council Liaison

SVBIED Bomb Master & Assembly Technicians

Martyrdom Coordinator

Fulltime Cell Members
(Until Martyrdom, Capture, or Rotation)

Security/Mobility/Ambush Teams

Temporary Cell Members
SVBIED/SPBIED Martyrdom Volunteers Awaiting Targets/Vehicles

FIGURE 5.2   (c) AQI cell structure (2004–2011).

cycle to keep up the rate of daily attacks, we can surmise there are 11,100 other insurgents inside their own attack cycle. That gives the FRL force approximately 14,800 men on full-time combat operations at their peak. It is assessed that there were a 100% active reserve of part-time operatives who are called up for surge operations, in training, or on rest/leave/family business. The total is then 29,600 active full-time and part-time combatants. That number can be divided by 25 (the average cell size) to find there were 592 FRL cells active in platoon-sized units. These cells could have been any size larger or smaller as the missions dictate. Given that each cell had approximately 100 active supporters, who carry out intelligence, money, logistics, food, and moral support, we estimate there were 59,200 men, women, and children working in rear area support or behind coalition lines. That gives the FRL insurgency an estimated tooth-to-tail strength of approximately 88,800 persons actively involved in some aspect of the war.

IRAQI RELIGIOUS EXTREMIST CELLS

For the Iraqi religious extremists (IREs), the numbers are significantly lower, as they performed 15 to 20% of combat actions. Figure 5.2b reveals their average structure is similar to that of the FRLs, but with significantly more dedicated IED and ambush assets. This would reflect that they were a force that could not perform in combat as well as the professionals in the former Saddam Fedayeen or intelligence agencies. It is assessed that they carried out only 28 attacks per day using approximately 84 men in these activities. Another 616 are engaged in their operations planning cycles, and 2,100 others are active in the operation/rest/training cycle. They are also assessed to have a 100% reserve for surges and part-time operations. That gave the IREs 112 cells of 25 men, totaling 5,600 combatants and 11,200 supporters, for a tally of 16,800 activists.

AL-QAEDA IN IRAQ AND FOREIGN FIGHTERS

Figure 5.2c reveals an extremely small force with disproportionate operational impact due to the fact they preferred the one-way suicide car bomb as their principal weapon. AQI performed 2 to 5% of attacks, which is an average nine per day, utilizing just 27 men, including 16 others per cell in the planning/operations cycle for a total of 171 members active on any given day. Given that they may utilize a 4-day operations cycle, they have a total of 684 full-time members with a 25% reserve (171). That means the estimated AQI operations force is 855 men in 45 cells of 19 men each. Additionally, AQI had a pipeline of 10 S-VBIED martyrs per cell for a total of 450 to 500 men en route to martyrdom or awaiting an opportunity to be married to an S-VBIED weapon. Between 2003 and 2011, the base of support for AQI was small, as they had no family and little community support outside of liaison with the FRL and IRE insurgents. They may have had as few as 450 active supporters in all of Iraq. These supporters, minus the one-way S-VBIED members, give AQI 1,305 men and women. This was near the peak 1,300 combatants figure that was reported by a captured senior AQI leader in 2005. In 2011 AQI acquired almost all of the Iraqi religious extremist groups and grew its cells to the size of the FRLs.

AQI CELL COMPOSITION (2003–2011)

As we have noted above, the AQI organization between 2003 and 2011 was a relatively small group in Iraq. It had been both overestimated and underestimated on a day-to-day basis. In a gross underestimation, many pro-war pundits claimed that al-Qaeda was a spent force and even predicted that Iraq was the "last stand for al-Qaeda."[25] On the other hand, in a deft piece of propaganda, al-Qaeda in Iraq's second commander, Abu Hamza al-Muhajir, gave the first estimate of how many AQI members have fought and died in Iraq. He stated, "The blood has been spilled in Iraq of more than 4,000 foreigners who came to fight."[26] Coalition spokesman Maj. Gen. William Caldwell claimed even greater success: "Since October 2004, we have now killed or captured over 7,000 al-Qaeda terrorists."[27] This is an impressive figure, but he may have considered all Iraqi dead at the time as al-Qaeda members. One captured lieutenant of Abu Musab al-Zarqawi claimed in 2005 that the peak strength of al-Qaeda in Iraq was 1,300 before the November 2004 operations in Fallujah.[28] This figure rings more true for the group to operate so covertly and successfully. Additionally, despite a steady stream of fighters and suicide bombers, it is assessed that AQI never fully recovered from its withdrawal from Fallujah, and the U.S. Army successfully whittled down the force by more than 200 members in the first few months of 2006 alone. However, AQI was extraordinarily resilient.

Some estimates of the composition of foreign fighters in al-Qaeda have generated interest. One of the first was an analysis by Dr. Reuven Paz of Israel's Global Research in International Affairs Center. His assessment of suicide bombers and jihadists in Iraq claimed that over a 6-month period (November 2004–March 2005) Saudi supporters of the jihad filled 154 names of men who martyred themselves during the Battle of Fallujah Operation Fajr/Phantom Fury to reveal that the insurgency was principally populated by Saudi Arabians.[29] Dr. Paz determined the bulk of AQI and foreign fighters at that time in history were 61% from Saudi Arabia (94 fighters), 10.4% Syrian (16), 8.4% Iraqi (13), 7.1% Kuwaiti (11), and the remainder from 10 other Arab countries. The data for these claims were jihadist websites on the Internet and open-source reporting. Dr. Paz and others, used website death claims as a major data source to estimate the number of jihadist martyrs in Iraq.[30] "We gathered data not just based on the statements and lists published on Islamist Internet forums … but also comparing this to information supplied by the American military and other allied nations and information in the mass media."[31] Though it makes for interesting analysis, it's hard not to concur with Dr. Cordesman that website-related deaths, even if the victim has died somewhere, are unreliable, as they may be fabricated to create an inspirational propaganda piece. Some of these deaths may be attributable to AQI in combat, but there is no way of knowing if a person who died on the list actually fought in Iraq unless recovered by the coalition.

A more exact estimate was conducted by the Center for Strategic and International Studies (CSIS) and Saudi intelligence. The majority of their data came from interviews of captured jihadists who were combat veterans of the Iraq conflict. The CSIS estimates reveal an inverted base of support, with Algerians leading the jihad (20%), followed by Syrians (18%), Yemenis (17%), Sudanese (15%), Egyptians (13%), Saudis (12%), and other (5%).[32] Whatever the ground truth, there is a reason people from all over the Arab world came to Iraq. "The vast majority of Saudi militants who have entered Iraq were not terrorist sympathizers before the war, and were radicalized almost exclusively by the Coalition invasion."[33]

INSURGENT CASUALTIES

The consistency of the static manpower estimates, the misperception of casualties they have allegedly incurred, and the absence of discussion of new recruits are potential errors that have given the insurgents a phantom-like quality. Despite claims of significant losses by the enemy and more than 16,000 captured or killed in 2005, alone the coalition estimate of the number of insurgents has remained steady at approximately 20,000. Joshua Green, writing for the *Atlantic* magazine, discovered that the cumulative assessment of enemy killed or captured as claimed by the DoD exceeded 47,970 combatants by December 2005.[34] Computer analyst John Robb hit the nail on the head when he asserted in his numerical analysis of the insurgency that the estimate appears to conflict with DoD assertions that they were killing an average of 1,000 to 3,000 insurgents per month. He finds that, like the Vietcong of 1967, the estimates should have destroyed the insurgency at least once over. Robb notes, "The reasons for this resilience may not be something supernatural, but rather something more mundane: bad assumptions."[35]

The methodology used by Carl Conetta to reconcile the overestimation of combat-related deaths in the initial invasion (reducing battlefield claims between 20 and 60%), particularly the effects of airpower and artillery, could explain why there had been little attrition to the original number of 20,000 insurgents, but that is assuming this number was correct in the first place. Given this consistency in active members of the enemy forces versus the claimed losses, the American success in killing large numbers of insurgents was suspect. Even in anecdotal interviews with soldiers and intelligence officers alike, the times when the coalition actually manages to capture or kill the triggerman/video teams in the act of conducting IED attacks were rare. Most IED teams got away unscathed. It appears the mortality rate among the devastating surface-to-air missile cells shooting down coalition aircraft and helicopters was virtually nil as well. The reality is the majority of insurgent cadre captures came from searches and seizures or during the occasional stand-up fights. Usually the insurgents are easily defeated in those actions.

The coalition had successes, but they may have been small in comparison to the size of the actual insurgency. It is quite possible that the large numbers of counts of enemy dead were, in fact, civilian accidental or collateral deaths. The greatest problem was that real successes were often marred by horrible overestimation and exaggerations. Hundreds of insurgents may have been killed and captured each year, but it is highly unlikely that the claimed 1,000 to 3,000 KIAs was real. Without evidence, some of the claims were just incredible. There are several examples of where the Pentagon claimed hundreds of enemy killed in a single operation without any bodies or equipment recovered. An example is the spring 2005 raid on a Secret Islamic Army in Iraq's training camp near Lake Tharthar. The coalition alleged to have killed 85 insurgents, but no bodies were found in the sweep by the U.S. forces. A spokesman called it "the single biggest one-day death toll for militants in months and the latest of a series of blows to the insurgency." European journalists visited the next day and found 30 to 40 insurgents alive and well. The insurgents were claiming only 11 dead in the raid. When confronted with the video showing this claim, the coalition spokesman said, "I would tell you that somewhere between 11 and 80 lies an accurate number ... the insurgent forces who had fled ... were able to recover their casualties and take them with them." When the question came about how could all 85 dead insurgents have dragged themselves away the spokesman said, "We could spend years going back and forth on body counts. The important thing is the effect this has on the organized insurgency."[36]

In fact, little credible data exist on the coalition's success in killing insurgents. In 2005, the U.S. Army reported that they had over 16,000 suspected insurgents and criminals in captivity, though as many as 90% of them may have been innocent Iraqis or criminals. The majority of these people were released by 2006. Except for the claim of 1,200 dead in the Second Battle of Fallujah, where the insurgents themselves have accepted that perhaps as many as 1,000 fighters may have been lost, many insurgent KIA/WIA (wounded in action) claims could have been discounted as unrealistic overestimates. Allowing that the claims in Fallujah are true, the insurgents may have been almost predominantly foreign fighters, and their deaths would have little impact on the dominant Iraqi Sunni insurgent numbers. The British forces in Basrah Province between 2003 and 2005 reveal 261 insurgents killed and 141 captured. Acknowledging that this region was far less volatile than the American sectors, it also reveals that counts can be done accurately. However, the bulk of those British kills were not part of the main Sunni insurgency, but Shiite Iraqis killed during the Mahdi Militia uprising in April, May, and August 2004.[37]

If you consider that the replacement base of the insurgents is a very conservative 10% of the active supporters, one can find that there were as many as 7,085 new recruits coming into the ranks of the insurgency each year (5,920 FRLs, 1,120 IREs, and 45 AQI). That is more than adequate to recover from major losses to coalition forces. The lack of losses in insurgent manpower estimates are most likely because Central Command intelligence analysts have made this very assessment but have not publicized it. Central Command reveals a confidence that the insurgents who are killed or captured are replaced quickly and without appreciable loss of skill because of the support pipeline.

One thing is certain. Based on the increased rates of attack between 2003 and 2007, the insurgency started out with small professional groups of ambushers and IED teams and grew in an organized fashion. It appears that the DoD's estimates of the total insurgency were flawed from the very beginning.

By the simplest of measures one could argue that the United States was easily winning the strategic battle against the insurgents just by being there to fight them whenever or wherever they decided to show up, but it was an unfair fight. On the other hand, the United States lacked the means to significantly impact the manpower and motivation pool of the enemy.

In the spring of 2005, Chairman of the Joint Chiefs of Staff Gen. Harold Meyers admitted that the insurgents' manpower numbers were not changing despite claims of large casualties inflicted on them: "I think their capacity stays about the same ... and where they are right now is about where they were a year ago."[38] An absence of a viable explanation may have impacted credibility on exactly what the U.S. Army did and did not know about the insurgent strength.

ENDNOTES

1. Amatzia Baram, *Culture, History and Ideology in the Formation of Ba'athist Iraq*, 1968–89, Macmillan, London, 1991, 11.
2. Dates and general information obtained from Baram, 9–22; confirmed by Marion Farouk-Sluglett and Peter Sluglett, *Iraq since 1958: From Revolution to Dictatorship*, I.B. Tauris Publishers, London, 2001, 87–93.

3. Information obtained from Baram, 9–10; confirmed by Farouk-Sluglett and Sluglett, 87–93.
4. Farouk-Sluglett and Sluglett, 90.
5. Information obtained from Farouk-Sluglett and Sluglett, 87–93; confirmed by Baram, 9–10.
6. Information obtained from Farouk-Sluglett and Sluglett, 49–58, and Baram, 11.
7. Farouk-Sluglett and Sluglett, 72.
8. Information obtained from Farouk-Sluglett and Sluglett, 72–73, and event confirmed in Baram, 11.
9. Farouk-Sluglett and Sluglett, 83.
10. Farouk-Sluglett and Sluglett, 65.
11. Numbers obtained from Farouk-Sluglett and Sluglett, 65; general information obtained from Baram, 11–12, and Farouk-Sluglett and Sluglett, 64–65, 83–84.
12. Information obtained from Baram, 12, and Farouk-Sluglett and Sluglett, 84.
13. Farouk-Sluglett and Sluglett, 86.
14. Information obtained from Farouk-Sluglett and Sluglett, 85–87, 92–93.
15. Farouk-Sluglett and Sluglett, 109.
16. Information obtained from Baram, 12–13, and Farouk-Sluglett and Sluglett, 108–111.
17. Farouk-Sluglett and Sluglett, 115.
18. Information obtained from Farouk-Sluglett and Sluglett, 112–123.
19. General Abazaid speech, Naval War College, November 22, 2005.
20. Harold P. Ford, CIA and the Vietnam Policy Makers: Three Episodes 1962–1968, Center for the Study of Intelligence, 1997.
21. Anthony Cordesman, The Iraqi Insurgency and the Risk of Civil War: Who Are the Players? Working Draft, Center for Strategic and International Studies, March 1, 2006.
22. Carl Conetta, The Wages of War Iraqi Combatant and Noncombatant Fatalities in the 2003 Conflict, Project on Defense Alternatives Research Monograph 8, October 20, 2003.
23. Jihad: How Many 'Volunteers' Are Coming? Washington Post, April 6, 2003.
24. Henry Schuster and Nick Robinson, Insurgency 101, CNN, October 12, 2005.
25. Rowan Scarborough, War in Iraq Looks Like Last Stand for Al Qaeda, Washington Times, May 11, 2005.
26. More Than 4,000 Insurgents Slain since 2003, Al-Qaeda in Iraq Leader Says, Associated Press, September 28, 2006.
27. 7,000 Al Qaeda 'Killed or Captured,' The Australian, November 29, 2006.

28. James A. Baker III and Lee H. Hamilton, The Iraq Study Group Report, December 2006.
29. Reuven Paz, Arab Volunteers Killed in Iraq: An Analysis, Project for Research of Islamist Movements (PRISM), Occasional Papers 1/3, Global Research in International Affairs, March 2005, 2.
30. Susan Glasser, Martyrs in Iraq Mostly Saudis, *Washington Post*, May 15, 2005; Paz.
31. Ibid.
32. Nawaf Obaid and Anthony Cordesman, Saudi Militants in Iraq: Assessment and Kingdom's Response, CSIS, September 19, 2005.
33. Tom Regan, The 'Myth' of Iraq's Foreign Fighters, *Christian Science Monitor*, September 23, 2005.
34. Joshua Green, The Numbers War, *Atlantic Monthly*, May 2006.
35. John Robb, How Big Is the Iraq Insurgency? October 14, 2005, http://globalguerrillas.typepad.com/globalguerrillas//How%20 Big%20is%20the%20Iraqi%20Insurgency.pdf.
36. Steve Fainaru, Doubts Surface on Iraq Raid Toll, *Washington Post*, March 25, 2005.
37. Handwritten Answers from Secretary of State for Defense, UK House of Commons, November 2005.
38. Transcript of Interview with General Meyers, CNN, April 27, 2005.

SECTION II

Knife Fight in a Phone Booth—Bringing On the Insurgency

CHAPTER 6

Bringing It On

THE FRLS ORGANIZE

On April 9, 2003, after 4 weeks of intense ground combat, the U.S. and British forces had won a decisive victory over the Iraqi army. Yet the victory almost immediately started to slip through the fingers of the U.S. Army. Within hours, looting of government buildings, armories, and police stations exploded. Over 2 weeks, looting, arson, sabotage, and rampant crime replaced the dictatorial orderliness of the brutal rule of Saddam. A widespread lawlessness soon reigned over Iraq.

They first went after weapons. When those were exhausted, they went after the national treasures in the great museum of Baghdad, the archeological complex at Babylon near Hillah, Basrah University library and museum, the Ziggurat of Ur in Naseriyah, and the museum of Mosul. Museums or libraries were looted for their ancient treasures and sacred texts. A collection of the oldest Qu'rans, Bibles, and Talmuds in the Middle East was stolen or burned with the national library. The massive, sloping Tomb of the Unknown Soldier was cleaned of its precious gifts and honoraria from other nations to Iraq. The residences of Saddam, Uday, Qusay, and others were stripped of their gold toilet fixtures, silver inlaid tea sets, and the dozens of gold, silver, and mother of pearl Kalashnikov machine guns. The mayhem appeared to be a surprise to U.S. Army and British units, who watched buildings gutted and set afire. The coalition forces were not prepared or equipped to stop the looting. In Basrah, the British army stood by as the Bank of Basrah was emptied. American soldiers in Baghdad did stop the robbery of the central banks in the financial district but were helpless to stop anything more. Other than the Republican Palace and the Hussein residences, one other building was seized and guarded from destruction with a company of U.S. soldiers—the Ministry of Oil.

Secretary of Defense Donald Rumsfeld seemed to take a lighthearted approach to the massive destruction. He made jokes about the mayhem by stating that the Iraqi people were just "letting off a little steam." Pro-war politicians attempted to spin the events as evidence that the military operation was so successful that a power vacuum was inevitable, manageable, and necessary to expunge the ghosts of Hussein. They saw this unpredictable period of chaos as a testament of the correctness of the entire endeavor. Bush administration officials would later refer to this period as the time of "catastrophic success." It was indeed catastrophic, but it was in no way a success.

However, like many events that would unfold in Iraq, experts at both the State Department's Office of Research and Intelligence and the CIA had predicted widespread looting as a possibility in a security vacuum. To ensure this wouldn't happen, the vacuum would have to be filled by U.S. forces almost immediately in the post-war. As almost a side note, these agencies also predicted that Iraq may have set up a preplanned guerrilla force to capitalize on post-war chaos. Unfortunately, at the time, no one at the Defense Department or the White House cared much about that possibility. Despite rumblings that the arson and destruction were increasingly systematic, Donald Rumsfeld stated, "Freedom's untidy, and free people are free to make mistakes and commit crimes and do bad things."[1]

THE FRLS DESTROY THE EVIDENCE

To all present it was clear Baghdad was being systematically set aflame. In a matter of days, hundreds of arson fires broke out across Baghdad and other cities around Iraq. Mysteriously, government buildings and their valuable files were set alight. There were no reliable forces in Iraq to stop the chaos. The American army, designed for heavy combat, was too thin to control the masses of looters. They seemed unable to shift to the police posture required to check the lawlessness. Military police units and provost martial companies in the coalition were already stretched thin controlling and protecting the long supply chain from Kuwait, which was still under attack from the remnants of the Saddam Fedayeen. There was no longer an Iraqi police force, Special Security Organization (SSO), Republican Guard divisions, or a Ba'ath political party; their absence threw the Iraqi people into a spiral of criminality and chaos that set the pace for the coming years. Was this a truly spontaneous outpouring of looting? Some evidence suggests otherwise. General al-Douri, Uday and Qusay Hussein, and other surviving officers of the intelligence and special forces apparatus may have viewed the beginning of the looting in mid-April as an opportunity to destroy evidence of the regime's crimes, paralyze the reestablishment of a new government, and wreak mayhem in the rear of the coalition. As the looting and arson erupted, the first step for the Ba'athists was to start a campaign of systematic destruction of documents, records, and buildings that could be useful to the coalition. *Newsweek* magazine reported that Ba'athist plans for the post-war included looting and burning government buildings as well as sabotaging water and electricity.[2]

The former Iraqi intelligence officers in the newly formed insurgent force saw chaos as an opportunity. The mayhem that followed the war fighting phase established a basis upon which the entire Ba'athist and Islamic fundamentalist insurgency would successfully arm and mount the second phase of their war. With U.S. forces not watching and weapons stores unguarded in a country the size of California, they took their fill of weapons and explosives from the enormous storage facilities. Islamic extremists were doing the same and took this opportunity to prepare strikes against the occupiers.

Eventually, orders to stop the public unrest were issued, and the coalition gradually reimposed security. The Iraqi people ceased looting and gave way to a self-imposed return to normalcy. However, the Americans only projected security to government facilities and the major roads. In every other part of Iraq people took security matters into their own hands. The coalition forces, switching from the role of an army of invasion to that of an army of occupation, started to exert a thin but constant dominance over the populace. On the one hand, the U.S. Army had spread out into all regions of Iraq with the intent to finish combat operations and gain the trust of the population. On the other, the regime forces were rapidly shifting from the rigidity of organized irregular combat groups to the vapor of terrorist cells.

FIRST STRIKES OF THE AFTER-WAR

On April 10, 2003, a young Arab man walked up to a U.S. Marine Corps checkpoint north of the Palestine Hotel, pushed a hidden detonator for his concealed explosives, and blew up. The explosion showered the marines with ball bearings, bone, and flesh, seriously wounding four of them. The next day the marines found another indicator of exactly what kind of war was coming. Searching for a sniper in Fallujah, they found a suicide bomb belt factory in a safe house that had been occupied by foreign fighters. One of the terrorists captured inside was wearing one of the explosive belts. The foreign terrorists, most likely of the Jordanian Tawhid Wal-Jihad (TWJ), were also found to be in possession of a store of older-style American desert uniforms. Gifts from the Iraqi Special Security Organization (SSO), they were nearly identical to those worn by the pro-American Free Iraqi Forces. A bomber wearing this uniform could walk or drive directly up to U.S. forces or enter their lines before exploding. Further evidence of prewar terrorist preparations was mounting. A few days later, a SSO bomb factory with over 310 suicide bomber vests was pointed out to the U.S. Marines by the custodian of the SSO's armory. The terrorist arsenal included 160 antipersonnel vests already filled with ball bearings. American intelligence later reported that 80 devices from a suicide bomb vest cache seized at the Salman Pak terrorist facility were missing. On a positive note, the first signs of democracy came in the form of a demonstration, but to the dismay of the Americans it was not what was expected. Tens of thousands of Iraqi Shiites poured out of mosques and into the streets the first Friday after the liberation. The protest called for an Islamic state to be established immediately.

The war had in fact not ended, but transitioned into a different form of warfare—guerrilla warfare. Throughout this period the former regime members continued to resist fervently in some sections of Baghdad. Small arms fire and sharp engagements rang out continuously with U.S. Army and Marine Corps units in the north and western sections of the city. Just a few days after the fall of the statue of Saddam Hussein, the Fedayeen terrorists struck the U.S. forces using more and more suicide weapons and guerrilla attacks. It was not without some expectation. By mid-April a U.S. Central Command intelligence report estimated that "800 to 1,000 hard-core regime supporters or non-Iraqi fighters were still operating in the Baghdad area in small two-man or three-man teams."

The looting had stopped, but another new phenomenon had started—a mass crime wave from the 100,000 prisoners Saddam and the coalition forces had let out of jail. They stole or bought Kalashnikovs and put them to good use. Home invasions skyrocketed and personal revenge murders became rule of the day. Iraqis had to take security matters into their own hands and defended their homes and streets from the criminal wave. In an effort to stop the rampant murders and home invasions by criminals, the coalition authorized one automatic rifle or pistol per household.

MISSION ACCOMPLISHED

The most successful area of the early occupation was in the Shiite-dominated southern Iraq, where British forces, headquartered in Basrah, operated with an air of ease. The British used a soft form of security where soldiers wore no helmets or body armor and patrols in local neighborhoods were friendly. In northern Iraq, Gen. David Petraeus, commander of the 101st Airborne Division, led the way in reaching out to the local Iraqi populace of Nineveh Province and the city of Mosul. His efforts to conduct an aggressive civil affairs mission of empowering the local populace and conducting peace-building missions led to civilians pointing out more than 400 arms caches hidden by the Saddam Fedayeen in the month of May 2003 alone.

On May 1, 2003, President Bush flew to San Diego, California, and landed on the deck of the aircraft carrier USS *Abraham Lincoln*. He came with a single message—that major combat operations in Iraq had ended. By this date U.S. armed forces had 138 service members killed in Operation Iraqi Freedom. The sentiment of the Bush war cabinet was that the Iraq war was best described by the banner behind him, "Mission Accomplished." He would quickly be proven wrong.

As the looting subsided toward the end of April, everyone in Iraq, most notably the Sunni leadership in the northwestern section referred to as the Sunni Triangle, waited to see what the Americans would do next. Some of the younger men had already made the choice to fight with the Saddam Fedayeen or other ad hoc groups, but most Sunnis watched the political winds. At first things looked promising; it appeared the Americans were emphasizing reconstruction and private enterprise, both acceptable to everyone. However, a singularly unfortunate political decision is universally regarded as crucial in forcing undecided Sunnis to choose the path of supporting the insurgency.

CPA ORDER NO. 1—YOU'RE FIRED

On May 12, the Coalition Provisional Authority (CPA) was formed in Baghdad. Led by Ambassador L. Paul Bremer, the CPA took operational control of the Iraq occupation from General Grainer's short-lived Organization for Reconstruction and Humanitarian Assistance (ORHA). From his office in Saddam Hussein's former seat of government, the Republican Palace, Ambassador Bremer finalized the Bush administration vision of the future of the country. On orders from the White House, it was decided that the Ba'ath Party and its members would not be welcome to participate in the new Iraq. With that, Ambassador Bremer issued CPA Order No. 1. The senior members of Saddam Hussein's political machine, the Ba'ath Party, were banned from future participation in the government or the military and were denied any opportunity to take part in reconstruction of the country. Additionally, Bremer issued CPA Order No. 2, which dissolved the army, intelligence agencies, and all organizations associated with the Ba'ath Party. This did not go over well with the former soldiers. According to Salman al-Jumaili, doctor of political science at Baghdad University, "Now you have well over a quarter of a million men who know how to use weapons sitting at home with no job and nothing to do—who are faced daily with Americans entering their homes, searching their properties, and treating them as animals."[3]

Is it popularly believed that this one act spread dissension so quickly in the Sunni Muslim community that it jump-started the armed resistance movement that became the Iraq insurgency. As with all things in Iraq, things are not necessarily as they seem. With some exceptions, most of the Iraqi Sunni population left the Ba'ath Party in the face of American combat power; the lower-ranking soldiers abandoned their positions and uniforms and walked home to await the outcome of the war. Everyone wanted to see the opportunity the new democracy would bring, or at least start a business to take advantage of this democracy. Though it is possible that many of the 250,000 Iraqi service members who lost their jobs did not have much to lose in returning home, it was the career military officers, the professional core of the Iraqi army, constituted mainly of Sunni Muslims, who saw the order as an exclusion to any future in Iraq.

Career officers were not the only ones to suffer at the hands of these orders. Civil servants who carried the bulk of the knowledge about the political, governmental, and day-to-day workings of the country's infrastructure also lost their jobs. The loss of work for these experts dropped into the hands of the insurgency expertise on oil production, power lines, canals, roads, water systems, and every other aspect of infrastructure that the insurgents would repeatedly attack. In a matter of weeks the meteoric rise of Shiite and Kurdish leaders convinced the Sunni that the best way to guarantee some future in Iraq was through armed resistance.

The catastrophic success of the war allowed many of the FRL combat elements to be bypassed by the coalition forces unscathed. The Fedayeen obligingly faded into the woodwork. Most returned to their Sunni cities and families and waited. The month of May 2003, with a few exceptions, was a period of rest for the Fedayeen and Ba'athists. Major combat had ended for the Americans, but the now covert insurgent and terrorist forces had another plan. The plan was to reorganize, rearm, and retask Iraqi FRLs and foreign fighters as quickly as possible to strike the Americans without warning using ambushes, roadside booby-traps, and suicide car bombs as their weapons of choice. Many took the opportunity at home to organize back into insurgent cells and open up the weapons caches buried before the war. Specialized teams of ex-Iraqi army men went to the military munitions storage depots and returned back to their units with large quantities of arms and explosives. Others were tasked to start looting weapons depots and recover explosive fillers from discarded bombs or bring back whole bombs. Artillery shells, rocket boosters or warheads, and even 250 kg aerial bombs could be fashioned into roadside IEDs. The Ba'ath Party started networking, and soon money handlers were bringing cash into each town's network of Saddam loyalists. On April 11, 2003, the coalition forces captured two FRL financiers who were spreading the first infusions of cash out to the recently defeated Fedayeen cadres. They were caught carrying $630,000 in $100 bills and letters offering financial rewards for killing American soldiers. Saddam himself hadn't been captured, and communiqués from him started to quietly wind their way though the Sunni Triangle. The Fedayeen, Special Republican Guard, and intelligence agencies, now working as a single body, reemerged in the post-war stronger. They now had been combat tested against the best army in the world and survived. They studied lessons learned and shared their experiences on what to do and not to do. The agents of the intelligence apparatus commenced with plying their tradecraft and spread out into Baghdad and the other major cities to see what the American forces were doing. In a period of just over 30 days, the forces led by the Saddam Fedayeen would successfully transform themselves from surviving pockets of armed irregular units into an organized ghost army in which they exchanged roles from the hunted to the hunters.

PHASE 1: THE KILL CAMPAIGN

At some point between April 19 and May 1, 2003, on Saddam's orders, the FRLs implemented Project 111 and other insurgency preparations. Large-scale military operations would be shunned. The Fedayeen and Special Republican Guard had given the Americans on the west side of the city a small taste of the suicidal terrorism they were going to deploy to win a long-term war—only this time the attacks would be far more selective and stress precision in targeting. The FRL leadership now ordered that terrorism, sabotage, and guerrilla-style attacks from a newly reorganized covert force should go forth and harass the Americans wherever they were. A second and third column of both Iraqi and foreign Islamic extremists would be given every tool and opportunity to strike the occupation forces. Initially, the main goal of each group was the same: to kill as many Americans as possible.

The Iraqis and foreign fighters would strike without warning using ambushes, roadside booby-traps, and suicide car bombs as their weapons of choice. Roving bands of Saddam Fedayeen, volunteer Ba'athist street guerrillas, intelligence groups, and contracted criminals would take the place of large combat units. The Americans would not be confronted directly in all but the smallest scale infantry attacks. The weapons of choice would not be to stand up to the Americans with tanks, but to engage them hit-and-run style with machine guns, rocket-propelled grenades (RPGs), mortars, and grenades.

In this phase the now defeated FRLs and their foreign terrorist allies would draw on their decades of internal cultural intelligence, covert combat experience, and terrorist operations capabilities to make things difficult for the Americans and any democratically elected government. The dominance shown by the Americans in major combat would be their weakness. The American hubris and apparent disregard for the determination, skill, and inventiveness of the regime would be used against them to morph large-scale military combat between nations into an intense, low-level insurgency.

The terrorist war planners of the FRL intelligence agencies and Saddam Fedayeen knew that their experience in training such terrorist groups like the Abu Nidal organization, the Mujahideen al-Khalq, and others would also pay off in an insurgency. Prior to the invasion, Iraq had given minor Palestinian splinter groups haven in Baghdad. Renowned terrorist personalities and group leaders such as Abu Nidal and Abu Abbas lived well in the posh western Baghdad neighborhood of Mansour, but without any terrorist forces or followers. Saddam offered these terrorists-past-their-prime fiery rhetoric and praise for their successful acts in the 1960s and 1970s, but as terrorists they received almost no operational support. Even Hussein's rhetorical public statements to pay the families of Palestinian martyrs killed in the intifada or suicide attacks and to mobilize a million Iraqis to assist the Palestinians appeared to have been nothing more than exciting words. Now they had to fight on their own land with more than rhetoric.

Iraq no longer possessed weapons of mass destruction (WMDs), but the Iraqis had an ace in the hole. The weapon the insurgents decided to use to harass the Americans was the artillery shell. It would be transformed into an improvised explosive device (IED), or a booby-trapped bomb that wouldn't be launched from the air, but placed on the ground to create an enormous landmine. After the rifle bullet, the IED would become the second most deadly killer in Iraq. Its invention should have been foreseen by American technical intelligence. During the Iran-Iraq war the Iraqi army had tens of thousands of pieces of artillery. Over the 10 years they had developed expert proficiency in its battlefield use. The Iraqi defense industry expanded wide enough to produce their own high-quality artillery guns, shells, and long-range battlefield rockets. No matter that artillery did not fight in the 2003 ground war because it would dominate the insurgency. The artillery shells would be tied together with a detonator and exploded next to American vehicles. The 122 or 155 mm artillery shell exploding a few meters from a lightly armored truck or armored personnel carrier would vaporize most vehicles and guarantee a few dead or wounded. IEDs would become a slow but calculated form of resistance drawing a continual flow of blood from the Americans until the American public could stand it no longer. According to former Saddam Fedayeen members, soon after mid-April the FRLs established a curriculum for training teams of personnel in how to assemble, place, and detonate simple but devastating explosive devices. Throughout May 2003, coalition reports of organized attacks started to increase. The highways were initially dangerous principally from an explosion of banditry and the risks associated with driving too closely to the trigger-happy American convoys. Now, IED attacks, occasional RPGs launched at coalition convoys, and the sporadic shooting at coalition soldiers patrolling the streets started to punctuate the devastated landscape after looting and rioting had subsided.

"This Is Not a Resistance Movement"

In the immediate aftermath of the ground war, insurgent attacks were sporadic. In the first 90 days after major combat ended the fundamental insurgent strategy was to lay low, organize, find an easy target, and then conduct a survivable hit-and-run attack. The more advanced attacks were left to the security apparatus veterans, while the remainder assisted in the secret network, logistics, and infiltration functions necessary to sustain what would become a protracted guerrilla war. Small arms, IEDs, and the odd hand grenade attack were used against the coalition. The average U.S. soldier, now moved into gendarme duties, would increasingly find himself sniped at or attacked on a small scale by rockets or roadside bombs. Though rudimentary, these introductory attacks were effective. In the period between May 1 and June 27, 2003, over 61 U.S. service members would be killed in action or incidents in Iraq. It wasn't clear to U.S. commanders who was doing the killing, but it was obviously being done with a measure of coordination. However, groupthink was back in style. Many American politicians and combat commanders didn't believe there was any movement or organization behind the attacks. The commander of V Corps, Lt. Gen. William Wallace, said, "There are a number of organized groups that are intent on attacking American soldiers.... We don't believe them to be under a central leadership and we are taking appropriate action to deal with the threat. This is not a resistance movement."[4]

In fact, resistance was organizing in the very place that would come to haunt the Americans for more than 4 years: the city of Fallujah. Even before the war the population of Fallujah was decidedly hostile. It was the center of the elite Ba'athists and a headquarters for the Saddam Fedayeen. During the invasion, British Tornado fighter bombers attempted to strike the bridge at Fallujah. Out of eight bombs dropped, three hit crowded markets in Fallujah and only one struck its target. In the devastated markets the media came upon a scene of mania and hatred for the coalition. This hatred gave al-Qaeda in Iraq a safe haven to establish their safe houses and allowed the Fedayeen to organize openly.

A significant event occurred on April 28, 2003. The U.S. Army opened fire on a crowd of 200 civilians defying a curfew and who were openly protesting the occupation. Returning from a mosque, the protesters confronted U.S. forces. The U.S. Army allegedly came under fire from the crowd. Fifteen Fallujans were killed and 75 wounded in the ensuing battle. For the Islamic fundamentalist extremists and the Saddam Fedayeen, the April massacre in Fallujah would be used as the rallying point to call openly for the population to support the insurgency. The next day crowds chanted to pledge "our blood and souls" to avenge the victims of the attacks. An unidentified insurgent stated, "Now, all preachers of Fallujah mosques and all youths ... are organizing martyr operations against the American occupiers."[5]

The post-war attacks on U.S. forces, particularly in the north and northwest regions of Iraq, were starting to gain the attention of on-the-ground commanders. On the outside, Iraq appeared to be changing for the better, especially in the south and northeast. Businesses started to boom and luxury items never allowed under Saddam flowed in. The commanders in the Sunni-dominated regions of western Iraq were having less success. The trickle effect of soldiers that continued to be killed despite the shift in the political winds was troublesome. Small pockets of resisters were found in areas near Tikrit, Baqouba, Tal Afar, and the marshes of Lake Habbaniyah. Believing these to be remnants of the Saddam Fedayeen and loyalist combat units, the commanders launched a series of "mopping up operations." Operation Peninsula Strike was launched on June 9 to roll up insurgent elements operating near Balad on the Tigris River. It led to the arrest and detention of 320 prisoners and numerous weapons. Operation Desert Scorpion was a series of raids led by elements of the 4th Infantry and 1st Armored Division. The operation detained 1,330 suspects. They also captured 497 AK-47 assault rifles, 235 hand grenades, 124 rocket-propelled grenades, 22 belt-fed machine guns, 130 pistols, 100 rifles, and 8,122 rounds of ammunition. Operation Desert Sidewinder, a series of 213 joint day patrols and 161 joint night patrols, were conducted with Iraqi police to secure dangerous areas and decrease infiltration of loyalist forces.

These operations were successful in that they kept coalition forces on guard for mopping up the "dead-enders" and criminals, but U.S. forces continued to lose an average of one dead per day. By the end of June, the feeling was that the triangular-shaped area in northern and western Iraq was settling in to resist the coalition. The new interim government was shaping up, and many believed that in a few months the new democracy would overtake their will to resist. However, for skeptics of the occupation, especially in Baghdad, there was an uneasy feeling that the Hussein regime was not completely knocked down. With Saddam and his top 50 henchmen on the run with billions of dollars and thousands of tons of weapons, the rest of the country could not fully embrace the coalition's missions.

"Bring Them On"

By mid-June 2003, Secretary of Defense Rumsfeld had to retreat on his referring to the newly born insurgents as dead-enders. In this situation they would be called guerrillas, but Rumsfeld, still resisting the idea that the regime was still fighting, refused to refer to them by any name. He started describing them in terms given to him by U.S. intelligence as "small elements" of guerrillas operating in groups of 10 to 20 men. Around June 25, two soldiers from the 3rd Infantry Division operating alone in a Humvee near Balad were reported as missing and feared abducted by extremists in the area. Their bodies were later recovered in one place and their Humvee in another. Someone had conducted the snatch operation, killed the soldiers, stole their weapons and GPS, and had dumped the bodies. It would be a tactic that led U.S. forces to patrol in units larger than one vehicle. Other tactics, including grenades thrown at tanks from speeding cars, were also spreading.

The incipient insurgency was not only slipping past the grasp of the Defense Department, but was creating open political pressure on the White House. In a July 7 news conference, the president was asked about the rising number of attacks on coalition forces. President Bush answered the question with a challenge to the insurgents: "There are some who feel like that, you know, the conditions are such that they can attack us there. My answer is bring them on. We got the force necessary to deal with the security situation."[6]

Speaking about the coordination and organization of the attacks, Secretary of Defense Rumsfeld made an amazingly tone-deaf statement to compare the increasing death rate of American soldiers to crime in a big city. Rumsfeld said, "You got to remember that if Washington, D.C. were the size of Baghdad, we would be having something like 215 murders a month. There's going to be violence in a big city." Apparently the millions of tons of automatic weapons, bombs, and rockets, which were left unguarded and were fueling the insurgency, had slipped the secretary's mind when he made this statement. The insurgency was like nothing that could be found in Washington, D.C., but closer to Mogadishu, Somalia. However, in a moment of candor, Rumsfeld also stated, "It tends not to be, at this stage, random killings.... What you're seeing instead is what we believe is purposeful attacks against Coalition forces, as opposed to simply crime and that type of thing."[7]

Denial and never-ending optimism were the principal tools the Bush administration utilized to deflect attention away from the rising casualties. Every attack and bombing event was regarded as the last breath of a dying foe. Secretary of Defense Rumsfeld would repeatedly point out how U.S. forces quickly defeated the large-scale organized Iraqi forces as justification for any future success by small insurgent forces. In one Pentagon briefing he said, "In those regions where pockets of dead enders are trying to reconstitute, General Franks and his team are rooting them out."[8] Military leaders in the coalition were supportive but still struggled against a political tide to maintain a level of realism. General Abazaid gave a more accurate answer to a question about a budding insurgency in a July 17, 2003, Pentagon briefing:

> So what is the situation in Iraq? Certainly we're fighting Ba'athist remnants throughout the country. I believe there's mid-level Ba'athist, Iraqi intelligence service people, Special Security Organization people, Special Republican Guard people that have organized at the regional level in cellular structure and are conducting what I would describe as a classical guerrilla-type campaign against us. It's low-intensity conflict, in our doctrinal terms, but it's war, however you describe it.

PHASE 2: THE HUMILIATION CAMPAIGN

On the morning of July 21, 2003, an urgent report from the United Nations security office in Baghdad was sent to all nongovernmental organizations (NGOs) supporting the Iraq reconstruction. A convoy of two Toyota Land Cruisers belonging to a UN associate agency, the International Organization for Migration (IOM), was ambushed south of Baghdad on Highway 1, or as coalition forces called it, Main Supply Route TAMPA. The IOM vehicles were en route to Hillah from Baghdad when they were approached at high speed from behind by a white Nissan 2400 pickup truck. The Nissan was manned by a two-person terrorist hit team dubbed "shark patrols" by American intelligence. White pickups were common on the streets of Iraq. It was most likely one of thousands stolen from the government ministries' fleet and dragooned into military service as a form of unarmored personnel carrier. Others were not stolen, but were part of the stock deliberately redistributed before the war to the Saddam Fedayeen guerrillas and Ba'athists tasked to fight the American invasion. The shark patrol's mission was simple: (1) to conduct surveillance and intelligence collection against coalition forces and their supporters on the main highways; (2) track, abduct, and execute Iraqis working with coalition forces; and (3) conduct hit-and-run attacks on any coalition and reconstruction-related vehicles with whatever weapons at hand.

Attacks on the United Nations International Organization of Migration and the International Committee of the Red Cross would mark the first indications that the secret post-war tactics to be used in the occupation of Iraq would affect everyone associated with the coalition's effort to rebuild the country. In mid-July 2003, some FRL forces in south-central Iraq appeared to have received orders to change from executing the kill phase and broadly expand to target reconstruction efforts. This would usher in the beginning of the second stage of the insurgency, the humiliate phase. The attacks involved targeting and attacking reconstruction projects, NGOs, the United Nations, and journalists and foreign entrepreneurs with the intent to sow doubt as to the ability of the coalition to ensure their safety.

On this day, a shark patrol from the Sunni town of Mahmudiyah was tailing two bright blue vehicles with UN-IOM written in bright orange letters across the hood and doors. The two IOM vehicles were traveling in convoy when the Iraqi hit team executed a near flawless attack profile that would become the trademark for attacks on noncoalition civilians. This attack is called a rear-hemisphere drive-by shooting, and it has a distinct profile that is easy to identify with the trained eye. However, no one in the convoy had been trained or was aware that they were about to become the first foreign civilian victims of the insurgency. The Nissan 2400 pickup truck had been shadowing the IOM convoy for several miles. It took very little time for the insurgents to assess that the chances of a successful gun attack were high, as no coalition forces were nearby to stop them. The tactics were straightforward. The insurgents would drive up behind the Land Cruiser at high speed until 10 to 15 feet away. To a witness or an untrained eye, the attacker would appear to be a tailgater trapped by blocked traffic, not a terrorist on a specific attack pattern. The gunman would keep his weapon out of sight until the victim driver was unable to maneuver or escape due to dense traffic. When all paths of escape were blocked, the gunman would load his AK-47, select full automatic fire, and prepare to execute the attack. The driver would accelerate to conduct an extremely high-speed approach until the attacking vehicle was almost touching bumpers. When ready, the insurgent shooter would pop out of the passenger window, aim, and open fire on the victim driver's head with the entire 30-round magazine. Invariably, the driver and his passengers would be killed or wounded in the shooting or the subsequent accident from attempting to avoid the fire. Observant victims could escape this form of attack by recognizing the run-up pattern. However, this day the patrol was successful against the unaware humanitarian workers.

The AK-47 Kalashnikov rifle is ubiquitous in Iraq. The heavy 7.62 × 39 mm bullet has enough energy to lift a 450-pound barrel of water an inch off the ground when it strikes. Within 200 yards it is lethal and accurate. The first burst of Kalashnikov fire struck the Iraqi driver Joel Malik and killed him instantly. His passenger, a female Australian migration protection officer, was wounded in the barrage. Driverless, the Land Cruiser careened out of control, veering left, and struck a passenger bus. The impact of the accident threw the Toyota back to the right where it left the road and rolled over and over in the desert. The shark patrol then accelerated and overtook the lead IOM vehicle by making a high-speed pass on the driver's side. The gunman leaned out again and sprayed the driver and passenger with a second magazine of high-velocity bullets. Unable to keep control in the blur of bullets, exploding metal, and glass, the driver also lost control of his Land Cruiser and flew off the highway. The attack resulted in one Iraqi staffer dead and three foreign staff wounded. The United Nations and the international humanitarian community were devastated. Never before had such a clear attack been carried out on the international reconstruction effort. It would not be the last time.

The insurgents escaped and lived to strike again 2 days later when they attacked a clearly marked ambulance vehicle belonging to the International Committee of the Red Cross. That attack, in nearly the same location and in the same manner, killed Sri Lankan technician Nadisha Yasassri Ranmuthu and wounded his Iraqi driver. It was clear that from July 20, 2003, onward, anyone associated with the international relief effort in Iraq or a coalition ally was now fair game. The stretch of Iraq's Highway 1 north of Hillah between Mahmudiyah and Iskanderiyah would become one of the three most dangerous roads in Iraq.

The clarity of thought put into killing and destroying clearly marked United Nations vehicles as well as abducting and killing armed soldiers was surprising. The United Nations IOM vehicle attack marked the beginning of a new phase of insurgent tactics against people other than the occupation army; it introduced terrorist tactics to Iraq to noncombatants, both those who supported a new Iraq and those who were innocent of being anything other than Shiite or Kurd. During this same period of time, insurgents targeted American aircraft landing at Baghdad International Airport. Within a week, two aircraft were engaged by heat-seeking surface-to-air missiles (SAMs) as they attempted to land.

On July 22, the insurgency suffered a major setback. Holed up in a Mosul residence, Qusay and Uday Hussein fought to the death with American troops. On the eve of his death, Qusay was "rated the most powerful man in Ba'athist Iraq after his father."[9] While Uday would have continued to fight for power, it is likely that had events gone differently, Qusay would have been the next ruler of Iraq. Upon hearing of their deaths, the Iraqis celebrated in high style. Hundreds of thousands of rifles fired off throughout Iraq filling the air with bright tracers and the sound of celebration. However, Gen. Izzat Din al-Douri and the other leaders of the various terrorist groups viewed this loss as anything but a defeat. Despite the death of the Hussein brothers, there was a feeling that the Iraqi insurgency was just getting started. The technical and professional challenge of waging a heated guerrilla campaign in an occupied country against a numerically and technologically superior enemy appears to have harnessed the imagination of the Sunni loyalist insurgents.

By the end of July 2003, the preferred tactics used by the Iraqi insurgents started to take form. On July 30, one in a series of IEDs killed Spc. Joel L. Bertoldie in the city of Fallujah. IED attacks were no longer unique weapons, but the pattern of their usage started to reveal a measure of planned frequency and coordination. Based on the structure of their weapons storage and skills within the ranks of the professionals and volunteers, the IED attacks were simple and easy to learn. The caches that had been laid before and after the war were designed to support the harassing attacks and slowly bleed the U.S. Army one soldier at a time. An insurgent had several weapons to choose from: the sniper rifle, the RPG-7 launcher, and the IED dominated the killing in the initial phase. Better and more devastating weapons attacks and tactics were planned. When July ended, the U.S. suffered a slight increase in casualties in RPG and sniper rifle attacks in Baghdad, Tikrit, and Mosul, but it was now clear to all that America was in an insurgency.

The insurgency in Iraq had turned to terrorism as its principal tool to harass the occupying forces, and anyone, Iraqi or foreigner, associated with them would be stalked, killed, or intimidated. The terrorist tactics applied from this point forward were marked by a certainty that there was a systematic approach to the application of the Iraqi resistance, not only inside the Sunni Triangle of northwest Iraq, but throughout all of Iraq. It was a plan oriented to disrupting all success in Iraq by all comers. In a press availability, Secretary of Defense Rumsfeld was forced to admit that a change had taken place in Iraq. He said:

> About two weeks ago, Rick Sanchez, our ground commander in Iraq—
> actually, the commander of our combined forces in Iraq—and Jerry
> Bremer and I met, and we discussed the security situation as we saw it.
> We knew that there was a period between the 14th and the 18th of July
> where we could expect a lot of activity from Ba'athist elements, and
> also, we were picking up a lot of information that indicated that there
> were significant terrorist groups and activities that we were having to
> be concerned about, as well; most of this all happening in what we call
> the Sunni Triangle, that area vaguely described by Tikrit, Ramadi, and
> Baghdad, but often stretching up into Mosul.[10]

Enter the Islamic Extremists

By August 2003, Phase 2 of the insurgency—humiliate the coalition—appeared to have been picked up by Abu Musab al-Zarqawi's al-Qaeda in Iraq. A suicide car bomb driven by a Tawhid Wal-Jihad driver rammed the Jordanian embassy, killing 19.

Within days of that attack bombing, a similar attack was carried out on the British embassy, but that suicide vehicle-borne improvised explosive device (S-VBIED) failed to explode. The errors of that account would be corrected and put into effect on August 19 when the insurgents carried out a highly successful attack against the United Nations Canal Road headquarters. Al-Zarqawi executed the attack using his suicide bomber cell called the Armed Vanguards of Mohammed's Second Army, an allusion to the Salafist belief that they are continuing the fight as contemporaries of the Prophet Mohammed. The young, clean-shaven suicide bomber maneuvered his truck against the outer wall of the United Nations Canal Road headquarters and directly under the window of the office of representative Sergio Vieira De Mello. The FBI assessment estimated that the S-VBIED's explosive payload consisted of 900 to 1,200 pounds of artillery and mortar bombs stacked and linked together. When the bomber blew up, it collapsed the front of the building, killing De Mello and 22 others.

The Iraqi Shiites were not forgotten by the terrorists. In addition to coalition and foreigners, any supporter of the Iraq invasion was now part of the targeting mix. There would be no difference to the insurgents, except that Iraqis were far easier to kill. This campaign was inaugurated with a devastating car bomb attack on the Shiite community by assassinating Ayatollah Mohammed Baqir al-Hakim and killing more than 125 others at the sacred Shrine of Imam Ali in the holy city of Najaf. It was a blatant attempt to destabilize the Iraqi Shiites and decapitate the leadership of the majority religion in Iraq. The weapon of choice was a stolen Range Rover filled with 1,000 pounds of explosive. These attacks had a sudden and intended effect. Throughout Iraq the NGOs provided the United Nations and U.S. Agency for International Development with manpower and planning for reconstruction. Many of them, particularly in the south, saw that the increasing security needs were not in line with UN requirements. It was bad enough that their UN sponsor was decapitated, but when Sheik Hakim was killed, they feared for a Shiite uprising. The aid and reconstruction process was broken, and the Americans' inability to secure the aid workers left them with a situation where contractors had to hire their own private security and not expect assistance from the U.S. Army. This was unacceptable to the international aide community, and not surprisingly, the United Nations was first to with-draw from Iraq. It was soon followed by almost every other NGO.

The Insurgency Explodes

By mid-September 2003, the expanding number of the insurgent attacks in Iraq indicated that, sidelined and now unemployed, the former Ba'athist armed forces officers and party loyalists had reestablished lines of communications with the underground networks of Saddam Fedayeen and Special Security Services and were being trained and incorporated into their ranks. Under the operational command of Saddam's deputy general, Izzat Ibrahim al-Douri, the combined FRL force had managed to create a covert operations capacity within the Sunni Triangle that could operate with near invisibility. The insurgents would continue to form their combat capability around the Saddam Fedayeen and combat experienced retired army officers, while the remnants of the Sunni-based intelligence services established the covert networks necessary to move car bombs, weapons, and money necessary to infiltrate and operate the combat cells in Fallujah, Ramadi, Mosul, Baqouba, and Baghdad.

Over 90% of attacks in Iraq against U.S. forces occurred in what is known as the Sunni Triangle, a rough, triangular piece of terrain stretch-ing from Hillah in the south, north to Baghdad, through Baqouba, northwest to Mosul, and west to the Syrian and Jordanian border. In the Sunni Triangle, anyone could become a terrorist. Dr. Salman al-Jumaili put it best when he said, "So an ex-soldier or civilian who is religious can find a movement that supports his views, a man that wants to defend his country can join, a man who wants revenge for injustice can take part, and of course even the man who simply needs money can join in—some groups can boast hundreds of members."[11]

Still failing to explain the resistance, the Bush administration attempted to apply a domestic political tactic to their view of the insur-gency. They would blame a single enemy for everything. The strategy may have come from an actual belief that it was one person or may have been a convenient foil, but it would have far-reaching consequences. The White House, if anything, was eternally optimistic. First, it denied there was an insurgency or even the slightest resistance to its adminis-tration of Iraq. Then it blamed the Kurdish group Ansar al-Islam and said Abu Musab al-Zarqawi worked for them. When the United Nations bombing highlighted the lack of security, they claimed a single terror-ist was responsible for the insurgency even after they had hunted down and killed Uday and Qusay Hussein. In fact, once the Hussein brothers had been killed, the insurgency actually gained steam. Finally, as intel-ligence came in, it was settled that Abu Musab al-Zarqawi and "foreign fighters" were to blame for the increasing number of attacks. It was true al-Zarqawi and his Tawhid Wal-Jihad groups (soon to become al-Qaeda in Iraq) were making their presence felt disproportionately to their size. A spate of several high-profile suicide car bombings, including destruction of the headquarters of the International Committee of the Red Cross in downtown Baghdad by an S-VBIED fashioned from an ambulance, horrified everyone. Hotels for American contractors became S-VBIED magnets and were starting to be struck with alarming regularity, as were police stations. Even more horrific was the insurgents' attempt to blow up Baghdad's Yarmouk Hospital. A suicide bomber was stopped by the police from entering with an orphaned baby wrapped with explosives.

PHASE 3: THE PUNISHMENT CAMPAIGN

From September 2003 onward the murder rate in Iraq seemed to expand exponentially. Crime was a major part, but political assassination came quickly on its heels. Masked by a high level of violent murders and acts of revenge in the general population, both the Islamic extremists and regime loyalists started a campaign of personal assassination against anyone associated with the coalition, the interim Iraqi government, and those related to them. The insurgents laid the ground rules about who in Iraq would suffer their wrath. The former regime loyalists would start with interim government members and members of the Iraqi police.

One of the first major assassination efforts was the attempted murder of the head of the Popular Union of Kurdistan, Jalal Talabani, by Ansar al-Islam, the enemy of the Kurdish leader. The device prepared for him was one of a wave of IEDs fashioned from large trash dumpsters. The three bombs found that day contained 2,500 pounds of explosive and metal shrapnel. He survived the attempt, but in rapid succession members of the new Iraqi government were killed or wounded. The only woman on the interim Iraqi governing council set up by Ambassador L. Paul Bremer suffered a serious assassination attempt when five men in two vehicles boxed her car and killed four relatives who were guarding her. She would die of her wounds a week later. Other members of the interim government were marked for assassination and killed, including Jala al-Din al-Sagheer, a member of the constitutional preparatory committee; Ibrahim Bahr al-Uloom, the interim Iraqi oil minister; Nabil al-Musawi, Ahmad Chalabi's deputy on the governing council; Aqil Hamed, the deputy governor of the Muaskar Saad region; Najaf's municipal council president; and many other lower-level persons. Iraqi interim Prime Minister Ayad Allawi had five assassination attempts on his life, including a suicide car bomb rammed into his residence.

It was far worse for the officers of the police and defense forces. The police chief of Khalidiya, Col. Khedeir Mekhalef Ali, who was cooperating with the Americans, was assassinated as he returned to his home in Fallujah. The chief of police of Al Amarah, Brig. Gen. Hamid Hadi Hassan al-Abe, was gunned down coming out of a mosque by gunmen. The chief of police of Erbil, Col. Tah Ahmed, was shot to death by Ansar al-Sunnah. Col. Hatem Rashid Mohammad, the chief of Balad Ruz, was killed in a machine gun ambush, and the Baghdad city deputy police chief, Col. Riyadh Abdulkrim, was shot to death on the streets. Al-Qaeda in Iraq claimed the killing Col. Abdul Karim Fahid, chief of the Balaat al-Shuhada station in Baghdad, and an IED killed Col. Moyad Bashar al-Janabi, one of the Baghdad police chiefs. The most senior member of the Iraqi forces killed to date was Gen. Salman Mohamed, commander of the Iraqi National Guard units in Basra. A shark patrol who gunned him down killed him, along with his son, while they were visiting Baghdad. A mobile assassination team also gunned down Brig. Gen. Mirza Hamza, head of the Iraqi Civil Defense Corp force in Mahmudiyah. One of the more significant murders was of Maj. Gen. Wael Rubaie, head of Special Operations at the Ministry for National Security. Killed by gunmen as he drove to work, his duties were to take command of a combined Special Operations center to help coordinate the government and American forces' fight against the insurgents. The insurgents hated these cooperating officers and sent a clear message to force others to avoid military service and limit their utility to the Americans. A Ba'ath Party communiqué detailed its intention to kill collaborators and strike the coalition:

> A new stage began in the resistance to the invader forces and in the liquidation of stooges and collaborators with the occupation. Written warnings were directed to members of the so-called governing council and letters of a different nature to foreign intelligence forces (the Mossad and Iranian intelligence) to the effect that the assassination of any Ba'athist, or scientist, or cadre of the Iraqi state would elicit an earthshaking response.... Preparations are underway for future qualitative operations, the catastrophic impact and results of which the American Administration realizes it will never be able to bear.[12]

Collecting intelligence and buying small scraps of information from locals who needed the money, the former agents of the regime created a database in each operational region for cooperating personalities. These names are then passed on to the assassination teams for murder. Some are killed by two- and three-man hit teams, and others are abducted and murdered later. The mobile shark patrol teams have also been tasked to assist in striking victims when they are on the roads ringing Baghdad and between the cities. Each team has a designated target that is known by name and face. The assassination teams generally plan their attacks based on the victim's security and preferred routes. The tactics vary, but the "step-up" hit is by far the most popular. The insurgent assassins step out from vehicles or corners, walk directly to the victims, and gun them down. They generally get away in a waiting car.

Al-Qaeda in Iraq and the Iraqi Islamic extremists took a more dramatic approach. They performed direct attacks on Iraqi army recruiting centers, police stations, and even against the lines of civilians waiting for access to the Green Zone. The most significant of these was the January 2004 Assassins' Gate suicide car bomb that drove into packed traffic waiting to enter the Republican Palace. Over 30 Iraqi workers employed by the coalition were burned to death in their cars or blasted into pieces. A Tawhid Wal-Jihad pamphlet left at the site of an execution in Baqubah read, "The flesh of those working with the Americans is more delicious than American flesh itself."

Some of the hundreds of personal assassinations were designed to foster sectarian violence. Although it would reach its peak in 2006, the first attacks in late 2003 would be the template for how it was done. The Shiite militia, the Badr brigades, and the Shiite and Kurdish members of the Iraqi police are given special treatment. The Islamic extremists often stop and take hostage large numbers of victims and execute them one by one. Numerous cases of mass assassination have been perpetrated by the insurgents, with particular emphasis on the army, national guard, and police. Examples include the abduction and murder of 11 Iraqi national guardsmen by Ansar al-Sunnah near Hillah; 11 more were found shot to death near Ramadi; 19 soldiers were lined up and shot at a soccer stadium in Haditha; 15 guardsmen were pulled off a bus and executed by Ansar al-Sunnah near Hit. A noteworthy case was the abduction and murder of 49 Iraqi army soldiers on leave from their base in Kirkush. They were stopped by insurgents, had their hands tied, and were each shot with a single bullet in the head near the town Mandali. Al-Qaeda in Iraq (AQI) claimed responsibility for the incident.

The Anti-Shiite Clerics Campaign

The anti-Shiite clerics campaign is another example of an attempt to foster civil war. The August 2003 killing of the 64-year-old sheik Ayatollah Muhammad Baqir al-Hakim with a car bomb that left a 31-foot crater and 125 people dead was just the start of the war on Shiite clerics. A week before this massacre, a relative of Sheik Hakim, Sheik Mohammed Saeed al-Hakim, was injured when a suspected Saddam Fedayeen operation was carried out in an attempt to kill him. A booby-trapped gas cylinder was placed alongside the wall of his home in Najaf. The explosion missed him but killed 3 guards and wounded 10 family members. Security for the Shiite religious leader Ayatollah Bashir al-Najafi foiled a plot on his life by a trained sniper in the Saddam Fedayeen named Mohammed Saheb. Al-Najafi was one of the four leading religious leaders of the Shiite community, and his death would have been a critical blow following the murder of Sheik al-Hakim. It was yet another in numerous attempts by Saddam to kill al-Najafi. Several failures occurred before the war by Saddam in an effort to neutralize his popularity without exposing the fingerprints of the regime intelligence agencies. Captured by the Badr militia members, Saheb confessed to being tasked to infiltrate the residence through employment in al-Najafi's home and collect intelligence on his movements. Saheb was to assassinate al-Najafi if the opportunity presented itself. Other clerics were not so lucky; Sunni assassins ambushed Shiite Islamist party member Mani Hassan and Muwaffaq Mansour outside of their homes.

In 2005, Iraqi forces in the town of Jurf al-Sakhr south of Baghdad reported they found foreign fighters from Saudi Arabia, Pakistan, and Afghanistan in possession of explosives and car bombs. An interior ministry spokesman reported that the suspects had a list of Shiite clerics targeted for assassination in Karbala and Najaf. "Some of them were tasked with attacking visitors to Karbala and Najaf with small arms fire and roadside bombs and even poisoning their food."[13] The anticleric campaign had yet to let up. Many analysts believe that the January 2006 destruction of the Golden Mosque by Ansar al-Sunnah insurgents was the breaking point for Shiite militias inside the government agencies. Soon afterwards the seeds of civil war spread. Shiite death squads started to target Sunnis on the street, and from 2006 to 2007 the daily death toll of bodies averaged 50 per night. By March 2007, even U.S. military commanders were acknowledging the success of this murderous insurgent campaign.

The FRL Anti-Human Intelligence Campaign

Coalition soldiers were usually killed on sight, but some of them were selectively targeted for their relationship to human intelligence (HUMINT) operations. In late 2003, Spanish military attaché Air Force 1st Sgt. Jose Bernal Gomez, working in the National Intelligence Center, was shot to death at his front door by three men. He had been working in Iraq at the Spanish embassy for 2 years prior to the war and was a known target for the former regime. Eight other Spanish officers attached to the coalition were killed in an ambush near Hillah when former Saddam Fedayeen insurgents shot them to death. Even the American pro-consul Ambassador Bremer, with massive security, was not spared attempts on his life. On December 6, the ambassador's security convoy of black Suburbans and U.S. Army Humvees was attacked in an IED-initiated ambush on the airport road Route IRISH. The convoy also took gunfire by AK-47 machine guns, but managed to escape to the airport without further incident. Considering that this road is one of the most heavily patrolled, the insurgents risked certain death to take a shot at him.

Beginning in the fall of 2003, the insurgents abducted and killed hundreds of Iraqis who worked in even the most minor jobs for the coalition forces, including food service workers, cleaning women at U.S. bases, sandbag fillers, and gate guards. However, the group that was one of the most punished was the Iraqi Arabic interpreters to the U.S. Army. The coalition employed more than 4,000 Iraqis and other Arabic native speakers as interpreters attached to units throughout the country. They were actually contract workers managed by American companies such as the Titan Corporation and World Wide Language Resources. The interpreters made $600 to $1,000 per month, 10 times the salary of an Iraqi army soldier or policeman. These men always wore black balaclava-type ski masks to hide their faces, but the word spread about who conducted this work. Knowing the value of these men and women, the insurgents worked carefully to identify and then kill them. The interpreters were referred to in the insurgent statements as "agents of the U.S. occupation" and universally hated by Sunni Muslims, who viewed them as the "mouthpiece" of the occupying army's arrogance. One Iraqi commando said the insurgents "think we are spies, agents, and traitors to our country because we are working with the Americans."[14] By January 2006, more than 150 would be assassinated in their homes or on the streets of Iraq.

PHASE 4: THE INSPIRE CAMPAIGN

November 2003 brought about a switch in tactics from the insurgents. Smaller groups such as the newly formed Ansar al-Islam and the Islamic Army of Iraq conducted an intense anti-air missile campaign to videotape and inspire new recruits. More than 39 soldiers were killed and 20 wounded in three incidents alone. On November 2, 2003, a team of insurgents determined the flight path of a U.S. Army CH-47 Chinook helicopter attached to the 12th Aviation Brigade and shot it down with two missiles, killing 16 soldiers and seriously wounding 20. Flying south of Fallujah with the downed helicopter, a second Chinook narrowly escaped being hit. Four days later, a UH-60 Blackhawk would be shot down near Tikrit, killing six soldiers. On

November 15, two Blackhawks flying over Mosul were downed when one was hit in the tail rotor by an RPG-7 rocket and it crashed into the other. All 17 soldiers were killed in this attack.

The war was not being limited to north and central Iraq. The next massacre took aim at the Italian contingent of the coalition forces. Their base in downtown Naseriyah was attacked one midmorning by a team from the newly formed al-Qaeda in Iraq. An Algerian immigrant butcher named Belgacem Bellil, who lived and worked in Villanova, Spain, drove the first S-VBIED. Bellil was convinced by European extremist members of al-Qaeda to come to the Iraq jihad and die attacking the Italians. He drove a fuel truck filled with explosives and fuel into the building. Immediately following the truck was a second S-VBIED that ran into the tanker and exploded both. The massive blast knocked down the building and killed 28 people, including 19 Italians.

Some tactics of the insurgents showed a remarkable level of coordination and daring. On November 30, 2003, more than 100 Saddam Fedayeen simultaneously attacked two U.S. Army tank convoys in the city of Samarra. The Fedayeen attacked the columns with numerous IEDs, waves of RPGs, and small infantry attacks in an attempt to steal billions of dollars in new Iraqi dinar. The Fedayeen were repulsed with 46 dead, but the attack stunned U.S. commanders.

The insurgents had found their stride, and winter saw a dramatic increase in insurgent attacks. Relentless use of IEDs, assassination, and infrastructure destruction inspired newer and bolder attacks. A train carrying goods for the U.S. Army on a rail line that was newly renovated was destroyed near Samarra. Oil pipelines were repeatedly blown up in both the south and north of Iraq. After the turn of the year, suicide car bombs started presenting themselves with alarming regularity in Baghdad against strategic targets such as ministries, the Green Zone checkpoints, and Iraqi army recruiting centers. Movement in Baghdad became a precarious event, and the costs of the reconstruction's security exploded.

On December 14, 2003, Saddam Hussein was captured near his hometown of Tikrit. Despite the belief that this would lessen the attacks on the coalition, it became apparent that this was not going to happen. The top of the regime and the Hussein family were dead or in custody, but the insurgents fought on. The first American Christmas in Iraq was ablaze with gun battles in the early morning hours, marauding RPG teams striking American-leased hotels and foreign embassies with potshots of explosives and pounding the American Green Zone with mortars and rockets. By spring of 2004, it would be clear that the dynamics of the occupation and the momentum built up by the three wings of the insurgency were overwhelming. The Sunni community seemed to view both the FRL and the Islamic extremist insurgency against the occupying forces as an opportunity to salvage their decimated community's esteem. Most importantly, the insurgents appeared to have taken to heart President Bush's challenge. Bush's statement was later derisively mocked in a propaganda video from the terrorist group Ansar al-Sunnah. In it, they called upon Americans to oppose the invasion and to assist the insurgents. They ended the video with this statement in English: "Mr. Bush. You said to bring it on ... and so have we, like never expected. Do you have another challenge for us?"

ENDNOTES

1. Pentagon Press Briefing, April 12, 2003.
2. Rob Noordland, Tom Masland, and Christopher Dickey, The Insurgents, *Newsweek*, February 7, 2005.
3. Lawrence Smallman, Iraqi Resistance Looks Set to Intensify, AlJazeera.net, November 21, 2003.
4. Jack Fairweather, U.S. Troops in Central Iraq Face Increasingly Sophisticated Attacks, *Irish Times*, June 11, 2003.
5. Edmund Blair, Anger Mounts after U.S. Troops Kill 13, Reuters, April 29, 2003.
6. White House Press Conference, July 2, 2003.
7. U.S. Department of Defense News Briefing, June 18, 2003.
8. U.S. Department of Defense News Briefing, July 17, 2003.
9. Obituary Qusay Hussein, *Financial Times*, London, July 23, 2003.
10. U.S. Department of Defense News Briefing, July 16, 2003.
11. Smallman.
12. Ba'ath Party Communiqué, Iraqi Resistance Reports, April 26, 2004, http://www.albasrah.net/moqawama/english/0404/iraqiresistancereport_260404.htm#b-party.
13. Naseer al-Nahr, Rebels Have a List of Clerics, Arab News, March 27, 2005.
14. Ann Scott Tyson, To the Dismay of Local Sunnis, Shi'as Arrive to Police Ramadi, *Washington Post*, May 7, 2005.

CHAPTER 7

Insurgent Weapons and Tactics

The invasion of Iraq had an unintended effect that would accelerate the calls for insurgency, fuel violent crime, and inflame sectarian violence to unimaginable levels. From the moment the Iraqi forces abandoned their positions, left military bases unguarded, and fled the battlefield, average Iraqis and the fleeing Ba'athist guerrillas would loot the entire stockpile of weapons belonging to the army and police forces. Iraqis looted what they could find in every police station, army barracks, and weapons depot. This included every type of weapon system and component in the country. Everything was for sale in Iraq, including millions of bullets, surface-to-air missiles (SAMs), rocket- propelled grenade launchers, sea mines, antiship missile warheads, and pistols and rifles from dead American soldiers. Worse yet, the suspected weapons of mass destruction (WMDs) site at the Tuwaitha nuclear research facility was looted of nearly everything, including the highly radioactive waste barrels used for rainwater storage. The facilities of the army, navy, air force, and police in a country the size of California were stripped bare, save those locations where the U.S. and British armies had garrisoned. Weapons were being sold openly on the streets—all one had to do was ask for what was needed. By July 2003, virtually any light weapons or explosives that existed in the arsenal of the 4-million-man Iraqi army could be openly found on the streets of Iraq for sale. The former regime loyalists (FRLs), the foreign jihadists, and criminal organizations were now primed to inflict a continuous flow of bloodshed from coalition forces or anyone else who attempted to support the new Iraq.

LOOTING THE ARSENALS

Where did all of these weapons come from? For a start, virtually any type of weapon that could be imagined was purchased during the 10-year

Iran-Iraq war. The Iraqi army was using tens of thousands of tons of ammunition on the Iranians daily. When peace came in 1989, Iraq was solidly armed to an amazing level of excess. Even the tremendous defeat to the U.S.-led coalition in the 1991 Gulf War did not put a dent in the stockpile. Iraq had equipped itself to keep millions of men fully armed against another invasion. It had a significant industrial capacity to build artillery shells, bullets, explosives, and battlefield rockets. According to the *Comprehensive Report of the Special Advisor to the DCI on Iraq's WMD*, the major storage facilities at Az Zubayr, Taji, Rasheed, Al Qaqaa, Al Assad, Fallujah, and others held millions of metric tons of explosives and artillery but no weapons of mass destruction. The conventional weapons found in these depots ran the gamut of basic and advanced munitions from around the globe. Three entire generations of surface-to-air missiles were from Russia and France; battlefield rockets of every size were purchased from or built in Iraq, Russia, South Africa, and Brazil; artillery shells from Jordan, the United States, South Africa, and Yugoslavia were shipped in by the tens of thousands. The explosives in these munitions, whether they were SA-2 Guideline SAMs, Silkworm antiship cruise missiles, or LGM-45 sea mines, could be removed and fashioned into a jerry-rigged bomb. Thousands upon thousands of boxes of powder bags, fuses, and unexploded projectiles littered the positions of Iraqi army units, storage depots, and weapons caches. Schools, apartments, mosques, and government buildings were filled with weapons of every type. All of it was for the taking by any civilian or terrorist in Iraq. No one was guarding them. This unguarded treasure trove of C-4, Semtex, RDX, HMX, and industrial TNT would become a leading cause of death among coalition soldiers—the improvised explosive device (IED) (Figure 7.1).

FIGURE 7.1 Typical improvised explosive device (IED). (From U.S. DoD.)

THE IMPROVISED EXPLOSIVE DEVICE (IED)

The improvised explosive device can be almost any item one wishes. Filled with explosives, this device is simply a jerry-rigged bomb with a radio-controlled detonator that is left by the side of the road. When a target nears the spot where the explosive is located, the command to explode is given. The IED is usually detonated by a trained insurgent who watches the target and a marker that identifies the location of the device. The insurgent who detonates the IED is known as the triggerman. The triggerman usually hides 200 to 500 yards away from the IED kill zone. He could be anywhere so long as he has a good view of the IED location. This could be in a passing car, a café, a window, in a concealed dugout, or on a building roof. Often triggermen hide in plain sight. Unlike booby-traps, which are explosive devices left behind and go off when handled, the IEDs in Iraq are almost exclusively command detonated. This gives the insurgents the ability to select the best target for the explosive yield of the IED. The IED in Iraq was generally fashioned from a 122 or 155 mm artillery shell. These shells were comprised of over 100 pounds of explosive filler encased in a 100 to 200-pound steel casing. When the explosive detonated, it turned the steel case into a high-velocity wall of flying twisted metal.

Artillery shells are normally fired from cannons. The Iraqi artillery corps used to be one of the finest in the world, and its experience in World War I-style trench fighting made it invaluable against the Iranian army. The Iraqi army had hundreds of thousands of these shells left over from the Iran-Iraq and Gulf wars. It was during that decade of combat that the Iraqi Special Forces learned to create IEDs out of undetonated artillery shells. This experience formed the technical basis for the pre-war Ghafiqi Project whereby the insurgents were instructed to turn the seemingly useless shells into lethal roadside bombs. During the invasion, the American M-1 Abrams tanks and Bradley infantry fighting vehicles (IFVs) proved almost impervious to rocket-propelled grenades and smaller bullets. However, in the insurgency, a nearby or direct hit from a 155 mm artillery shell IED severely damaged or destroyed an IFV or pierce the hull of the 60-ton American M-1 tank. Even the new Stryker wheeled infantry fighting vehicles suffered serious losses to IEDs. The IED threat was driven home by their early effectiveness against the standard transport, the High-Mobility Multipurpose Wheeled Vehicle (HMMWV) jeep. The standard transport vehicle of the American army, the Humvee, or Hummer as it was commercially known, suffered the most casualties. Initially used in its unarmored form, the Hummer was found to be highly vulnerable to the blast effect of roadside IEDs. If the vehicle was not hit directly, the shrapnel flew as high-speed dense masses of tiny steel particles that shredded the human body into a pulp. Many roof turret gunners or passengers were killed or injured by the IED shrapnel. Heavy armoring kits were rushed to the region and proved effective in mitigating the blast and shrapnel, but even the up-armored variants were vaporized by a direct hit from the IED. This happened all too often.

The IED was better than land mines because it did not have to be directly driven over to detonate it. No, the Iraq insurgent IED would be a man versus vehicle hunter-killer game for both sides. The IED team generally consisted of three groups of people: the builder, the layer, and the triggerman. Often a fourth person, the videographer, was added to record the devastation for propaganda. The IED cell leader assigned two men to lay an IED artillery shell or other bomb in a spot that the intelligence teams of the insurgents had determined that occupation forces were routinely operating near. Laying and priming the IED was the most dangerous part of the operation. Some shells weighed several hundred pounds, and the insurgents developed innovative methods to drop them off, including fashioning false bottoms on vans and pickup trucks to get them onto the roadside. The IEDs were deployed from or in any conveyance, including donkey carts, pushcarts, wheelbarrows, and coffins. Once in place, the IED was usually concealed in trash piles, plastic bags, dead animals, abandoned cars, molded into concrete curbs, and on several occasions in or near dead bodies, including that of a child left for the coalition to find. IEDs were also placed in spots that improved the radius of their blast or that channel the blast and shrapnel into the target. They were placed on top of walls on second-story balconies and, interestingly, hanging from high-tension power lines where they could explode in a downward shower of shrapnel.

The IED was then wired to explode using a remote detonator. Early on the IEDs were detonated using a simple electrical firing system of wires connected to car batteries or direct pressure methods such as pressure plates, switches, or toggles that required weight or direct contact to detonate it. By 2004, electric garage door openers, remote car key door openers, cell phones, walkabout personal radios, and radio-controlled airplane controller boxes were being used to allow the team to fire the device from a distance and escape. This afforded the triggerman the opportunity to act normally; he would sit nearby on a street or balcony, drinking tea, when his target came into sight. Usually a mark or pointer such as a specific spot on a parked car door, a light pole, or even a painted mark on the road would indicate the place where the triggerman would let the American vehicle get close, and then push the button and blow up the target with the IED.

DAISY CHAIN IEDS

Large-scale IEDs were developed to attempt to create wide-area death traps. Often several IEDs were strung together to provide a massive explosive killing zone. IEDs wired and detonated in this fashion to one command device were called daisy chain IEDs. On the highways and streets these daisy chain IEDs often used a vehicle to block or slightly obstruct the road so the entire force of the blast would be concentrated on a stopped or slow-moving target. Often they were used as a tactic to lure in a military unit; usually one IED was set off to damage a vehicle and lure in the rescue force. The bombers tended to sit patiently, and then when a large number of soldiers were in the blast radius of all IEDs, the daisy chains were set off simultaneously. Later, an improvisation on the daisy chain was devised: in the November 2004 fighting in Fallujah, entire buildings were rigged with daisy chain IEDs in an effort to channel the Americans into the residence and then blew it up. Called house-borne improvised explosive devices (HBIEDs) by soldiers in the field, they were a weapon with massive killing power (Figure 7.2).

SUPER IEDS

Newer, more lethal forms of IEDs came in response to better U.S. technology, especially the new up-armored Humvees and IED suppression devices that appeared to be defeating the explosive yield. In early 2005 the insurgents started creating super IEDs. These IEDs were "doubled up" by tying together two or three high-explosive artillery shells instead of the usual one and detonating them under the targets as opposed to alongside of them. This type of IED proved effective in defeating heavy armor. In August 2005 a Marine Corps amphibious assault vehicle (AAV) operating near Ramadi struck one of these super IEDs and disintegrated, killing 14 marines inside. Super IED strikes on heavy armor vehicles such as the M-1 Abrams and Bradley fighting vehicle increased, and a number of these, believed to be impervious to anything in Iraq, were completely destroyed (Figures 7.3 to 7.6).

EXPLOSIVELY FORMED PROJECTILE IEDS

A major technological advance in IEDs came in mid-2005 when the Shiite Mahdi Militia and Sunni insurgents started using a special type of advanced armor-defeating device called the explosively formed projectile

FIGURE 7.2   Insurgent daisy chain improvised explosive device in a house-borne IED configuration, Fallujah, 2004. (From U.S. DoD.)

FIGURE 7.3   U.S. Army soldier holds a factory-manufactured explosively formed projectile IED (EFP-IED). (From U.S. DoD.)

FIGURE 7.4 This explosively formed projectile IED effectively burned through the heavy armor plate on the M1114 up-armored Humvee. (From U.S. DoD.)

IED (EFP-IED). Made up of a metal alloy or copper disc behind an explosive charge, its detonation launched a molten metal projectile in a predetermined arc. This molten dart cut like a laser through extremely thick armor at incredible speeds. Superheated showers of molten metal, called spall, burned through the vehicle and spray the inside with a shower of hot flame. This caused ammunitions inside to detonate and roast the occupants. These weapons were used by the Lebanese insurgents, Hezbollah, against the Israeli army in southern Lebanon to great effect. The first sign of their arrival in Iraq was when two armored security convoys in Basra were struck by EFP-IEDs, which were often placed against walls, curbs, or in large sandbags. The coalition suspected the Iranian government of supplying these to the insurgent market through Shiite militias, but numerous homemade examples were also found.

THE WMD PROGRAM'S HIGH EXPLOSIVES

One of the depots left unguarded after the American forces passed through it was the Al Qaqaa special weapons storage facility. This facility was used by the United Nations as a monitored storage base for 380 tons of RDX and HMX plastic explosives associated with the Iraqi nuclear weapons program. These extremely sensitive high explosives were purchased in the 1980s in order to create the explosive ball that would start

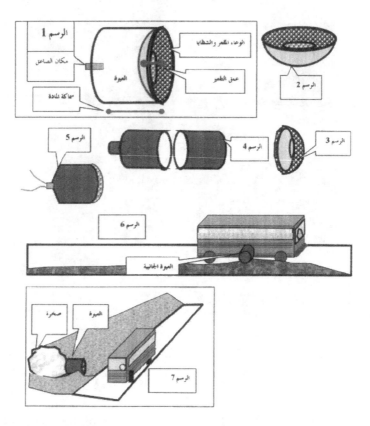

FIGURE 7.5 This graphic from an insurgent instruction manual describes the most effective placement and usage for an EFP-IED. (From U.S. DoD.)

the chain reaction in a nuclear bomb. After the nuclear program had been dismantled, the explosives were judged to be allowable for industrial use such as mining and demolition. Soon after the departure of the U.S. Army soldiers who had videotaped the bunkers and verified that the explosives were intact, the bunkers were systematically looted by an unidentified group. The International Atomic Energy Agency (IAEA) notified the U.S. government that the weapons were extant and in need of protection, but U.S. forces were not ordered to secure them. These facilities were not part of the combat plan to secure anything other than WMD sites and oil facilities. The spokesperson for the IAEA, Melissa Fleming, stated the explosives "can be used in a nuclear explosion device, for the explosion…. That's why it was under IAEA verification and monitoring." Additionally, she added that the IAEA was very concerned that the explosives may have "fallen into the wrong hands,

FIGURE 7.6 A U.S. Army M2A3 Bradley infantry fighting vehicle damaged by roadside IED. (From U.S. DoD.)

terrorists."[1] The Saddam Fedayeen and al-Qaeda in Iraq were just the kind of wrong hands the IAEA feared. It was believed that the Saddam Fedayeen and regime intelligence used the chaos of the looting to recover these explosives and move them to the Sunni Triangle. An October 2005 wave of suicide bombings in Amman, Jordan, was composed of explosive vests made of 22 pounds of RDX explosives and ball bearings. Al-Qaeda in Iraq's former leader, Abu Musab al-Zarqawi, claimed responsibility for these attacks that killed 56 Jordanians and the 3 Iraqi bombers. Though the RDX could have come from other sources in Iraq, it is more likely to have come from this enormous stockpile. Others have alleged that the Iranian government may have recovered these explosives for use in its own nuclear weapons program, though there is no unclassified evidence to support this.

THE SUICIDE BOMBER

The U.S. invasion brought a new phenomenon to Iraq—the suicide bomber. Prior to the invasion of Iraq there had never been a suicide bombing under the Hussein regime. From the middle period in the ground war, suicide bombings occurred almost daily against both the U.S.-led coalition and innocent Iraqis. Thousands of Iraqis have been killed by direct and indirect effects of suicide bombers. The suicide bombers, as they are called in common parlance, are known professionally as human-guided weapons (HGWs). A HGW is an explosive device taken and guided directly to its target by the man or woman who brings and remains with it when it detonates, killing the bearer. A way of describing its effect could be: "One man. One bomb. One target. Many kills."

In Islam, suicide in its clinical sense is not permissible and is a culturally unacceptable way to die. Suicide, or taking one's own life out of depression or other mental imbalance, is considered haram, or a sin. However, the Salafist extremist interpretation of the Qu'ran does gives bombers leave to conduct a "martyrdom" attack in defense of their people. Martyrdom is a religiously inspired attack, carried out in the name of God, in which the bomber carries out a mission to kill his enemy while sacrificing himself or herself to ensure the most damage. These operations are termed amaliyah shuheedah, or "martyrdom operations." This type of death is not considered a sin, but a form of heroism and a sign of the depth of the individual's piety and courage.

Saddam Hussein, faced with superior American forces, created squads of men committed to martyrdom using waves of S-VBIEDs. Nationalist and imperialist political groups that have used HGWs in warfare include the Tamil Tiger's Black Tigers in Sri Lanka and the Japanese army's kamikazes during World War II. The Iraqi HGWs are generally more in line with the religiously inspired precision strikes carried out by the Islamic Jihad Organization (IJO) of Lebanon and its parent group Hezbollah, "Party of God." The IJO carried out HGW attacks on American, French, and Israeli forces that killed hundreds with just the loss of a few men and women bombers. This was a historical justification the Iraqi insurgents claim. They said they were using HGWs as a form of national and religious self-defense, but also to mask its intrinsic form as a terrorist tactic.

The intensity of the post-war Iraqi S-VBIED campaign led American commanders to believe early on that only foreign fighters could conduct such attacks. It blinded even the most well-briefed and well-meaning officials. For example, despite the dozens of S-VBIEDs launched at attacking American forces during the invasion, Brig. Gen. Mark Kimmitt argued in 2004 that "any time we see a vehicle-borne bomb, any time you have a car bombing ... that gives an indicator that that's probably somebody from abroad or someone who has some training from abroad. That kind of extremism we don't typically see there in this country."[2] General Kimmitt was clearly wrong, as the history of the invasion and the capabilities of the FRLs and the Saddam Fedayeen were well known. If the phenomenon was new to Iraq, the tactics, techniques, and procedures of building the bombs extended back decades in Iraqi intelligence. However, this belief that only foreigners would use these weapons was another misperception about what the Iraqi people would or would not do.

On the other hand, American and coalition forces, subjected to relentless surprise attacks where the attackers sacrificed their lives, gave no quarter to vehicles or people that approached them suspiciously. Hundreds of Iraqi civilians were killed when they did not see the warnings from soldiers to stay clear. This lethal strategy of overreaction played into the hands of the insurgents, who used Arab media to show the Americans as heartless occupiers with little concern for the lives of the Iraqi people.

The delivery methods of the human-guided IEDs generally fell into two classes: S-VBIED and S-PBIED.

The Suicide Vehicle-Borne Improvised Explosive Device (S-VBIED)

S-VBIED is the acronym for suicide car bomb or other vehicle, such as a suicide boat. This is a vehicle specifically built as a mobile bomb and driven by the bomber. Although the S-VBIED had been used worldwide, in Iraq it was a unique feature not seen before. The Iraqi S-VBIEDs built by FRL insurgents usually used cell phone command detonators like an IED. Because the FRL insurgents used contract suicide bombers, they took control of the explosion process. A second vehicle or a fixed position near the target served as their platform to detonate the device. FRL S-VBIEDs had one rule: the bomb never came back. The FRLs detonated S-VBIEDs even if the primary target was not available. Days after being appointed Iraqi president, Ayad Allawi missed an attempted assassination as he left his compound near Zhora Park in Baghdad. As he moved en route to the Green Zone, an insurgent S-VBIED made up of a Mercedes Benz S500 sedan filled with hundreds of pounds of explosives prematurely left the target area before the U.S.-led convoy arrived. The FRL S-VBIED triggerman in another car blew the bomb up as it left the kill zone. The explosion killed eight innocent Iraqis. The FRLs also used the triggerman's vehicle to videotape the attack (Figure 7.7).

In a unique technique, S-VBIED suicide boats were used by al-Qaeda in Iraq in an attempt to destroy the main oil terminal south of Basrah in 2004. One boat was boarded by U.S. Navy sailors and blew up, killing two. Two other S-VBIED boats blew up prematurely before they could destroy Iraq's ability to export oil by sea. Islamic extremist S-VBIEDs are detonated using a combination of detonators, including triggers initiated by the bomber or a remote triggerman on a radio or cell phone command detonator. In the fervor of the Islamic extremist bombers' desperation to meet their goals, they often chained themselves to their S-VBIEDs as a sign that they did not wish to return (Figures 7.8 and 7.9).

FIGURE 7.7   Al-Qaeda in Iraq suicide vehicle-borne improvised explosive device (S-VBIED) rams and explodes in the middle of a U.S. Army truck convoy. (From U.S. DoD.)

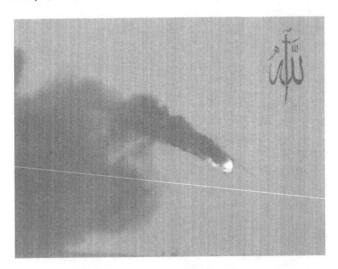

FIGURE 7.8   Burning MI-17 helicopter crashes, killing 11, in this Islamic Army of Iraq video.

Poison Gas Attacks by Chemical S-VBIEDs

In 2007, al-Qaeda in Iraq (AQI) started a new campaign using chlorine gas tankers exploded alongside of their target in an effort to kill and choke victims with the acrid gas. The first attack occurred on January 31, 2007, when a dump truck converted into an S-VBIED and enhanced with a container of chlorine gas killed 16 people in Ramadi. The vehicle

FIGURE 7.9   The remains of a former AQI suicide bomber near the doorstep of the author's office in Baghdad.

was crashed into the headquarters of the Emergency Response Unit of the Iraqi police. All of the victims were killed by the explosive blast.[3] AQI carried out a second attack on the town of Taji using a chlorine tanker filled with chlorine gas. Five people were killed when it exploded outside of a restaurant, but over 155 people in the city were sickened by the fumes. On February 19, 2007, another poisonous gas attack was carried out in Ramadi that killed 2 and wounded 16 others. A February 2007, attack in Baghdad killed 5 and gas fumes injured 55. AQI continued their campaign with a triple chlorine gas attack in the city of Fallujah on March 17, 2007, when three S-VBIEDs made from chlorine gas tankers exploded. The first struck a checkpoint in Ramadi and was quickly followed by a truck that exploded in Ameriyah south of Fallujah, 10 miles away. The S-VBIED was a dump truck rigged with chlorine gas tanks. The three same-day attacks killed 2 policemen and injured over 355 civilians and 6 U.S. soldiers from the effects of inhaling the gas.[4] Although the chlorine is used throughout Iraq industrially, al-Qaeda's usage was designed to have a psychological impact, as they know the casualties are small compared to conventional VBIEDs. Despite being described as "dirty" bombs, these were just new tactics being applied to make the Shiite public terrified. The only documented use of poisons in Iraq occurred in June 2005 when a truck full of poisoned watermelons was given to an Iraqi army unit near Mosul, where 1 soldier died and 12 others were seriously injured.[5]

The Suicide Pedestrian-Borne IED (S-PBIED)

The suicide pedestrian-borne IED (S-PBIED) is a belt or vest of explosives worn by the suicide bomber. The S-PBIED walks to the target and gains access on foot. At a point of the bombers choosing, he or she detonates the explosive device. Islamic extremist insurgents favor the use of the S-PBIED when they have the ability to infiltrate mass groups of people. The compact size of the belt or the vest, which is generally packed with ball bearings or screws and bolts, makes it a good selection for the terrorist when the target has poor gate security and the most effect would occur in a confined space. Two S-PBIED bombers from Ansar al-Islam detonated explosive vests at the headquarters of the two Kurdish political parties in 2004 during Ramadan festivities that managed to kill more than 100 victims.

SMALL ARMS—RIFLES, PISTOLS, AND MACHINE GUNS

Explosives were the least of what was stolen from Iraqi army and air force arsenals. The entire arsenal of small arms and antitank rockets was also looted and fell into the hands of the insurgents. Iraq had millions of Kalashnikov rifles, tens of thousands of PK class machine guns, thousands of SVD sniper rifles, and tens of thousands of other heavy machine guns from every country that produces them, including Russia, Egypt, China, Vietnam, Iraq, Romania, Hungary, and the former Yugoslavia. Interestingly, a trove of weapons was stolen from the Kuwaiti army, Ministry of the Interior, and police in the first Gulf War, including a massive supply of H&K MP-5N 9 mm submachine guns. These were openly for sale everywhere in Iraq. Italian M-12 submachine guns, British Sterling submachine pistols, and captured Iranian G-3 rifles were also dotting the market. Light machine guns such as the RPD squad automatic weapon and the belt-fed PKM heavy machine gun are also mainstay weapons of the insurgency. Makarov pistols from Russia, Star-Nejim 9 mm automatics from Spain, Beretta M-84 pistols from Italy, Belgian Browning Hi Powers, American-made ex-Iranian army 1911.45 caliber pistols, and the Iraqi manufactured copy of the Beretta M-9, called the Tareq, are still found on the street. The 2003 Iraqi police contract that brought in 40,000 new Glock 19 pistols quickly became available for the insurgents for less than $900 each. Captured American weapons like the M16 and M4 carbine, especially if they had the PEQ-2 laser, were regularly sold to the Lebanese mafia for a price that could buy 10 Kalashnikovs and still leave a nice profit. Hand grenades are plentiful and are sold by children at the gun market of Muraedi in Sadr City, Mosul, and Fallujah, originally for $1, but as the insurgency continued, the price skyrocketed to $5 for an old Russian F-1 or $10 for an American M-67 recovered from dead or injured coalition soldiers.

NIGHT OBSERVATION DEVICES

Of particular interest to the insurgents were the PVS-7 and PVS-14 night observation devices (NODs). With these, the insurgents watched the precise locations of American forces in early morning raids. It was by using the night vision goggles that al-Qaeda in Iraq captured an Egyptian intelligence officer carrying a covert marking strobe at night in Fallujah. He was beheaded.

SNIPER WEAPONS SYSTEMS

One particular aspect of operations in Iraq that was problematic was the emergence of skilled Iraqi snipers (al-Qanass). Using the Iraqi-built variant of the Soviet SVD sniper rifle, the Qadissiyah-built Tabouk, and a few rare Steyr SSG police sniper rifles from Saddam's intelligence agencies, these Iraqi insurgents stalked and killed American soldiers one at a time. Before the invasion the only truly skilled snipers generally belonged to the Saddam Fedayeen, the military special Unit 999, and the special operations group M14-SOD, even though the SVD rifle was used as a designated marksman weapon in regular Iraqi army units. After the invasion, many attacks attributed to snipers were actually routine shootings performed by insurgents who used a Kalashinkov rifle with commercial Chinese-manufactured scopes. They generally killed or wounded soldiers with two or more shots before fleeing. By late 2004, skilled "one shot, one kill" insurgent snipers emerged, including the infamous "Juba," a mythical figure from the Islamic Army of Iraq, who claimed to have killed more than 300 Americans in the Dora District of Baghdad alone (Figure 7.10). That figure was purely for propaganda purposes, but, in fact, there were regular skilled snipers who operated with near impunity in southern Baghdad, Fallujah, and Haditha. Two were believed to be ex-Saddam Fedayeen and Unit 999 members of the FRL Army of Mohammed. In the city of Haditha, a skilled sniper there was said to be a member of Ansar al-Sunnah. There were numerous other sniper teams operating throughout western Iraq as well. Although the number of soldiers insurgent snipers had killed was unknown, it was assessed to be well over 100. Generally, an insurgent sniper was accompanied by a videographer who acted as a spotter. In one insurgent propaganda video, the snipers shot more than 20 American soldiers, including

JUBA Rules:

1. I see nothing but my target.
2. I'm aiming to head.
3. I'm a Rock.
4. I pull the trigger !.

Res█t:

FIGURE 7.10 This propaganda photo of Juba, the nickname given by American forces to an unknown insurgent sniper operating in southern Baghdad. The Islamic Army of Iraq sniper lists rules for shooting coalition soldiers.

taking extremely difficult shots of soldiers in tanks with just their heads exposed. The insurgents also mastered the use of the sniper's mobile platform (SMP), where the shooter positioned himself in the rear window or trunk of a sedan or van and shot though a loophole at coalition soldiers. In 2006, an insurgent sniper was shot and killed by a U.S. Army sniper team in Anbar Province. The dead insurgent was in possession of a U.S. Marine Corps M-40A1 sniper rifle that had been taken from one of the bodies of a squad of marine snipers killed 2 years earlier. The loss of 24 battalions' worth of equipment in the 2014 ISIS offensive gave the insurgents many more rifles, including some of the U.S. Army's M24 Sniper weapons systems in the service of the Iraqi Special Forces.

ANTITANK ROCKET-PROPELLED GRENADES (RPGS)

The most dangerous weapon apart from the IED and S-VBIED is the RPG-7 antitank rocket launcher. Created by the Russians in the 1960s, the RPG-7 is a man-portable tube that can be fitted with a small rocket with a large explosive warhead. Made famous in the 1992 intervention in Somalia, the RPG-7 has actually been used against U.S. forces since the Vietnam War, when it replaced the older B-4 rocket launcher. Slung over the shoulder of the RPG gunner, this weapon can individually fire a quiver of rockets one at a time out to a distance 500 m with good accuracy.[6] The RPG is the queen of the light battlefield weapons, and its ability to project a highly explosive warhead quickly created problems for the American soldiers. The warhead can pierce the thin skin of the Hummers, some Marine Corps AAVs, and the unprotected skin of the U.S. Army Stryker personnel carrier.

Since Vietnam, an antidote for the RPG-7 has been sought by both the Americans and the Israelis, who often encountered them in combat. The U.S. Army developed the Bradley infantry fighting vehicle (IFV) with the capability to take and survive several hits from the RPG-7. It proved its worth in the armored invasion of Baghdad. The American main battle tank, the M-1 Abrams, and the British Challenger are also nearly impervious to RPG-7 rockets, but on occasion they are knocked out by lucky hits in the engine compartment. Some tanks took over a half dozen RPG hits and operated normally with minimal damage. The Saddam Fedayeen used RPGs by the thousands, and two-man teams roamed the battlefield with one man shooting and the other carrying 6 to 10 extra rockets. When the Stryker IFV came onto the battlefield, it had to be equipped with a steel cage around it to predetonate RPG rounds. In the insurgency the RPG also became a novel way to harass the enemy. RPGs can be launched directly at a target and destroy or damage it, or they can be launched indirectly into the air and ballistically come back down to earth to explode like mortars. Though it does not cause as many casualties as the AK-47 rifle, it is a versatile weapon and highly prized by all insurgent groups.

MORTARS—INDIRECT FIRE WEAPONS

The Iraqis needed to harass and impact the coalition's forward operating bases (FOBs) with the small infantry weapons they had at hand. Some used the rifle and RPG rocket launcher, but other weapons had the greater utility of being fired from a few kilometers away. These were called indirect fire (IDF) weapons. The IDF weapons were effective at allowing the insurgents to place a weapon within a tube, fire off projectiles that could fly 2 or 3 km, and watch them fall onto their targets and explode.

Mortars are small and their tubes can be easily transported within a few kilometers of a target. American bases were rarely spared a night without the standard salvo of three rounds striking a place predetermined by an insurgent IDF team. Most mortars require a hard-packed, level spot for the base plate of the mortar to sit in order to achieve maximum accuracy. Insurgents used prepared base plate locations regularly. A novel way of firing is to bury mortars hidden in the ground and angled precisely toward a fixed target. The tube is then hidden by covering the opening in the ground with trashcan lids or concrete blocks. An insurgent team or even children can come to a buried tube with three or four primed shells and can fire them off in a matter of 20 to 30 seconds. These mortars are a favorite harassment tool for teams without a skilled mortar gunner. The shells fall on their targets and explode, killing or injuring those within the blast radius. Mortars launch bombs in the 62, 81, and 82 mm categories with the explosive punch of several small grenades. Another popular mortar among the insurgents is the commando-style 60 mm "knee mortar." This is a small portable mortar that can be fired by one man who holds the tube in one hand and loads and fires by dropping the shell in the tube with the other hand. The Mahdi Militia used these extensively in the street fighting in Najaf and Karbala in 2004.

ARTILLERY AND GROUND-FIRED AERIAL ROCKETS

Prior to the invasion, the Iraqi army had one of the most experienced artillery rocket forces in the world. Hundreds of thousands of rockets were rained down on the Iranian army during the Iran-Iraq war. This produced a corps of competent Iraqi artillery rocket officers. Small improvised aerial rockets of 57, 76, and 100 mm, originally designed to be fired from helicopters in pods of four or more, were fired by the insurgents individually from jerry-rigged ramps. The ramps can be made to look like broken sections of metal, placed within buildings, trucks, or fields, and angled toward their targets so that a rocket can be attached and fired off rapidly (Figure 7.11). The largest are battlefield rockets designed to be fired from trucks, which are also modified to fire from improvised ramps. These rockets can strike targets as far away as 18 miles. These large rockets fired by many groups struck American bases throughout Iraq, Baghdad International Airport, and the Republican Palace. They had the ability to disrupt any gathering and send soldiers running for shelter. On occasion, they were highly successful in killing a large number of soldiers. One example of the

FIGURE 7.11 The former regime loyalist insurgent group Jaysh al-Muhammed hid a multibarrel rocket launcher in a generator cart and attacked the Rashid Hotel in the Green Zone while Deputy Secretary of Defense Paul Wolfowitz was visiting. One soldier was killed in the attack. (From U.S. DoD.)

devastating effect of IDF weapons was in 2004, when U.S. Navy Seabee sailors of Mobile Construction Battalion 14 (NMCB-14) were standing in formation awaiting a visit by an admiral to their base near Ramadi. The sailors were struck by an insurgent mortar shell that killed 5 sailors and wounded 34 others.[7] The ISIS between 2011 and 2014 learned that their rocket units could avoid major counterbattery fires and operate with speed by never changing from the use of the tube 122 mm rocket carried in a pickup truck along with three to five spare rounds. Rockets were mission specific and generally used to suppress defenders before a complex ground assault.

MANPADS—MAN-PORTABLE AIR DEFENSE SYSTEMS

There are two classes of special weapons that have come into the possession of the insurgents: anti-aircraft surface-to-air missiles launched from man-portable air defense systems (MANPADS) and the inadvertent use of Iran-Iraq war weapons of mass destruction (WMDs).

The MANPAD is a shoulder-carried surface-to-air missile designed to shoot down airplanes or helicopters on the battlefield; its limited usage by the insurgents or terrorists makes it a special weapon. The street value of these weapons on the international market could fetch as much as $10,000 per weapon. In Iraq they were found for free. Some groups such as the Ansar al-Islam, the Islamic Army of Iraq, Ansar al-Sunnah, and the FRL Army of Mohammed and Army of the Mujahideen had large inventories of these weapons and used them to shoot down American helicopters. According to the Brookings Iraq Index, between May 2003 and January 2007, 55 helicopters and aircraft were destroyed or damaged by MANPADS through machine gun fire or combat-related accidents, killing over 175 soldiers. Most were believed to be insurgent shootdowns.

The insurgents used Russian-built infrared-guided MANPADS from former Iraqi army stocks, including the SA-7 Grail (also called the Strella-2M), the SA-14 Gremlin (called the Strella-3), or the SA-16 Gimlet (called the IGLA-1). There were no reports of the American FIM-92A Stinger missile or other advanced Western weapons captured or transferred from other countries to the insurgents. Infrared MANPADS tracked the heat exhaust from aircraft and helicopters and guided themselves to a point where they exploded nearby. The shrapnel damaged the engines and fuel cells of an aircraft or destroyed the rotors of a helicopter. The SA-16 has capabilities similar to the Stinger, which gives it the ability to distinguish the true heat source from infrared countermeasures, including flares. In a technical twist, the former Saddam Fedayeen-originated Army of Mohammed claimed in 2006 to have improvised a MANPAD launcher possibly using the normal missile tubes, but mounted on hidden rails and fired remotely. These MANPADS were pre-positioned and launched against known routes of U.S. helicopters with little risk to the triggerman (Figures 7.12 and 7.13).[8]

November 2003 was the single most deadly month from insurgent MANPADs. A U.S. Army CH-47 Chinook helicopter was shot down outside of Fallujah by two SA-7s that killed 15 soldiers and wounded 21 others. Days later, two UH-60 Blackhawk helicopters operating near Mosul crashed when hit or attempting to evade a MANPAD and may have crashed into the other, which was flying in close formation. This attack killed 16 soldiers. The Army of Mohammed, the cover name for the former Saddam Fedayeen, claimed this crash. On the morning of April 22, 2005, a Bulgarian-piloted helicopter from the commercial company Skylink Corporation and contracted by Blackwater Security Consulting company was shot down while moving men and equipment from Baghdad to the U.S. Army base at Taji. The insurgents claimed to have been tracking its movements for days and shot it down with one SA-7 missile fired from behind it. The missile exploded near the engine, and the helicopter fell from an altitude of 500 feet. Ten passengers and crew were killed, but one of the pilots was thrown clear and survived. The insurgents briefly interrogated him, stood him up, and pretended to let him walk away. They then shot him in cold blood 17 times. A statement by the Islamic Army of Iraq read, "The Islamic Army in Iraq claims responsibility

FIGURE 7.12 Man-portable air defense missiles such as this SA-14 Gremlin (9K34 Strella-3) found in a cache are valuable weapon systems in the insurgency and for international terrorists. (From U.S. DoD.)

FIGURE 7.13 This U.S. Army AH-64 Apache barely survived a direct hit from a man-portable air defense missile. MANPADS can severely damage or destroy helicopters and aircraft built to withstand hits such as this. (From U.S. DoD.)

for bringing down a ... cargo aircraft and killing all those on board." The statement went on to describe the shooting of the living pilot: "One of the crew members was captured alive and killed ... to avenge Muslims killed in cold blood in Fallujah's mosques ... in front of the eyes of the world and on television screens without anyone protesting." A video of the attack and the statement were sent to Arab media.[9] In January 2004, a medical evacuation variant Blackhawk was shot down near Fallujah, killing all nine soldiers aboard. In 2005, al-Qaeda in Iraq claimed to have shot down a U.S. Marine Corps AH-1W Super Cobra near Ramadi using an SA-7 missile that killed both crewmembers. They released a statement through an intermediary that read, "Brethren in al-Qaida in Iraq's military wing downed a Super Cobra attack helicopter in Ramadi with a Strella rocket, thanks be to God."[10] Numerous other helicopters, including almost a dozen U.S. Army OH-58D Kiowa Warriors and, more surprisingly, at least six AH-64 Apache gunships, considered the toughest, most technologically advanced helicopter in the world, were shot down by ambushes from MANPADS in combination with gunfire and RPG rockets. American forces reported numerous MANPAD launches near Baghdad International Airport every week starting in June 2003.

Dozens of other near misses and hits without critically damaging the aircraft have been recorded at Iraq's air bases. Military aircraft were not the only ones targeted. In November 2003, a pair of SA-7 model MANPADs were used early on in the insurgency by the Islamic Army of Iraq to damage a DHL air cargo aircraft flying out of Baghdad. Filmed by French journalists accompanying the insurgents, this attack led to severe limitations on all air travel in Iraq at a time that the routes from Jordan and Kuwait were being opened to bring a sense of normalcy to the country.[11] The MANPAD threat also led to new flight procedures into Iraqi airports. The combat spiral or corkscrew approach is now mandatory to land in any Iraqi airport. President Bush's surprise visit to Iraq in Air Force One in November 2004 landed this way because of the serious MANPAD threat.

The insurgents have most likely found a lucrative black market for MANPADS. Al-Qaeda in Iraq may have taken courage in the effectiveness of MANPADS from their brethren al-Qaeda in East Africa (AQ-EA). In 2002, AQ-EA made a daring daylight attack with two SA-7 MANPADS on an Israeli airliner taking off from the airport in Mombasa, Kenya. Both missiles missed or failed to explode. The launchers were found near the airport painted blue like water pipes. Al-Qaeda of the Arabian Peninsula (AQ-AP) may have carried out an attack on an American E-3 Sentry AWACS aircraft a month earlier taking off out of Prince Sultan Air Base near Riyadh. In this incident, a used missile tube was found outside of the airport. Vice Chairman of the Joint Chiefs of Staff Gen. Peter Pace remarked, "That does not mean it was not fired, it simply means we do not know if that particular weapon was fired at that location or simply dropped off there. Regardless, we take very seriously the fact that that our opponents do have surface-to-air missiles, shoulder-fired surface-to-air-missiles."[12] Though these MANPADS appear to have originated from Yemeni army stocks, the Iraqi anti-aircraft missile arsenal will eventually start to seep out through Syria, Lebanon, and Saudi Arabia and present a deadly threat to global commercial airlines.

OTHER ANTI-AIR WEAPONS: HEAVY MACHINE GUNS, AERIAL IEDS, AND PIGEON CLAPPING

Heavy infantry weapons such as the PKM machine gun and the larger vehicle-mounted DsHKM 12.7 mm machine gun were used as mobile helicopter ambush platforms with some success. In a January 2005 incident, an insurgent's heavy machine gun fire struck a British C-130 Hercules transport plane as it departed Baghdad International Airport for Balad Air Base. The transport's engines caught fire, and the loss of the right wing subsequently caused it to crash. It killed all nine aircrew and one passenger.[13] In January 2007, an intense anti-helicopter campaign started using MANPADS and heavy machine guns. In an effort to re-create the same effects of the November 2003 campaign, insurgents across Iraq started engaging coalition helicopters throughout the country. A Hughes MD-500 "Little Bird" helicopter under contract to the U.S. State Department and operated by the security firm Blackwater was shot down in Baghdad by a PKM machine gun crew from the 1920 Revolution Brigades, killing all five crew. A second one was shot down near Najaf without losses. As many as five additional OH-58D and UH-50 Blackhawks were downed or damaged by heavy machine gun fire over the next 60 days. Many of these heavy machine guns (HMGs) were mounted in makeshift tripods on vehicles that were hidden in buildings along the flight path of helicopters. They engaged the helicopter quickly until it was destroyed, abandoned the vehicle at the site, and then returned to move the gun and vehicle at night.

A new anti-air weapon developed by the insurgents was an improvised explosive device that was similar to a mortar but lofted an IED into the flight path of an oncoming helicopter. The small IED then exploded and damaged the helicopter. These were called aerial IEDs and were the latest weapons to attack low-flying or hovering helicopters over dense urban areas. Using these devices from a string of rooftops could trap a helicopter in a wall of exploding shells and bring it down. Another novel form of anti-helicopter technique was called clapping pigeons. Flocks of pigeons, kept on rooftops, would be released in front of a low-flying helicopter in the hope of knocking the aircraft down by ingesting the birds into the engines or smashing against the windscreens. Discussing aerial IEDs, the U.S. commander of Army Aviation in Iraq, Brig. Gen. Edward Sinclair, noted, "The enemy is adaptive. They make changes in the way they fight, they respond to new flying tactics."[14]

DERELICT WEAPONS OF MASS DESTRUCTION (WMDS)

New production WMDs may not have existed in the arsenal of the regime of Saddam Hussein at the time of the U.S. invasion, but at one point in Iraqi history they did—and in huge quantities. The WMDs or chemical weapons factories in possession of the insurgents that were in a preponderance of reports from U.S. forces were actually explosive and car bomb laboratories that required the mixing of complex chemical compounds. However, some actual WMDs of the Iran-Iraq war vintage have been found and allegedly militarized by insurgents. In 2004, a 155 mm artillery shell filled with sarin nerve gas was discovered rigged as an IED. As it was being defused, it exploded and spread the nerve agent. Two soldiers were exposed to a low level of gas and treated successfully. Described by U.S. Central Command as an experimental binary weapon that was in Iraqi army stocks before the war, it was assessed that the insurgents were unaware of its contents. Former UN weapons inspector Hans Blix considered it part of an old munitions stockpile. Former UN weapons inspector Scott Ritter commented that in the 1980s the Iraqis had a live-fire sarin gas program being tested during the Iran-Iraq war south of Baghdad, and that this shell may have come from that stockpile. Ritter also asserted that there might be more old nerve gas shells that could be inadvertently used as IEDs. He explained:

> Iraq declared that it had produced 170 of these base-bleed Sarin artillery shells as part of a research and development program that never led to production. Ten of these shells were tested using inert fill—oil and colored water. Ten others were tested in simulated firing using the Sarin precursors. Moreover, 150 of these shells, filled with Sarin precursors, were live-fired at an artillery range south of Baghdad. A 10 percent dud rate among artillery shells is not unheard of—and even greater percentages can occur. So there's a good possibility that at least 15 of these Sarin artillery shells failed and lie forgotten in the Iraq desert, waiting to be picked up by any unsuspecting insurgent looking for raw material from which to construct an IED.[15]

That same year a mortar round found discarded in Baghdad had traces of mustard gas from the Iran-Iraq war era. It had also been claimed by two insurgent groups, Ansar al-Sunnah and al-Qaeda in Iraq, that they recovered chemical mortar and artillery shells with nerve agent or mustard gas from the scrap stockpiles of the Iraqi army and would select a proper time and place to use them where they could kill the most U.S. forces.

ENDNOTES

1. International Atomic Energy Agency, Tons of Explosives Disappeared from Iraq, Al Jazeera, October 25, 2004.
2. http://www.defenselink.mil/news/Jan2004/n01312004_2004 01311.html.
3. Emergency Response Unit Compound in Ramadi Attacked by SVBIED, Press Release 07-01-03PA, U.S. Central Command, January 31, 2007.
4. Chemical Blasts Sicken Hundreds in Iraq, Associated Press, March 17, 2007.
5. Iraqi Soldier Dies of Poison Near Mosul, Xinhuanet, June 1, 2005.
6. *Iraq Country Handbook*, U.S. Marine Corps Intelligence, February 1998.
7. Gregory Piatt, Father Talked to Seabee Son Just before Attack, *Florida Times Union*, May 6, 2004.
8. Insurgent Group Claims to Have Napalm, Nitrogen Bombs, Radio Free Europe, January 12, 2006.
9. Bulgarian Helicopter Shot Down in Iraq, Al Jazeera, April 22, 2005.
10. Iraq Militants Say They Shot Down Copter, *Boston Globe*, November 3, 2005
11. Iraq's Commercial Flights Suspended after Missile Attack, *USA Today*, November 23, 2003.
12. U.S. Department of Defense News Briefing, May 30, 2002.
13. Aircraft Accident to Royal Air Force Hercules (RAF XV197), Military Aircraft Accident Summary, Ministry of Defense, January 30, 2005.
14. Francis Harris, U.S. Helicopters in Iraq Face Menace of Aerial Bombs, *London Telegraph*, January 18, 2006.
15. Scott Ritter, Iraq Sarin Shell Is Not Part of Secret Cache, *Christian Science Monitor*, May 21, 2004.

CHAPTER 8

"Jihad Is the Only Way ..." Iraqi Islamic Extremists—Ansar al-Islam, Ansar al-Sunnah

The Islamic Army in Iraq and Others

Before the U.S.-led invasion, there were no formal Iraqi or foreign terrorist groups officially operating in Saddam's Iraq. With the exception of the Saddam-backed anti-Iranian Mujahideen al-Khalq and some minor operational support for small elements of Palestinian terrorist groups such as the Abu Abbas organization and the Arab Liberation Front, there were no active indigenous terrorist organizations in Iraq on the scale there are today. After the invasion, that changed dramatically. Terrorists of all stripes and convictions emigrated to Iraq or were spawned by the presence of American tanks in Iraq's streets. Militant specialist of *Al Hayat* newspaper Muhammad Salah notes, "All previous experiences with the activities of the underground organization is that they proved that they flourish in countries with a chaotic security situation, unchecked borders and lack of a central government—Iraq is all that.... It is the perfect environment for the fundamentalist groups to operate and grow."[1]

As noted earlier, the former regime loyalist (FRL) insurgents were the largest group, which were estimated by the CIA and DIA to number anywhere between 5,000 and 40,000 active operatives and supporters. Prewar mobilization gave them a manpower pool of more than 100,000 commandos, intelligence agents, and Ba'athist politicians from which they chose the best to harass American forces relentlessly. However, the invasion created a second wing of the insurgency never truly considered a serious threat to the coalition forces: the Iraqi Islamic extremist movement (Figure 8.1). One group, the Ansar al-Islam ("Partisans of Islam") was identified early as a terrorist threat to the coalition, but principally seen as a sponsor of foreign terrorists from al-Qaeda, not as a strong inspirational group with popular support that would constitute a long-term internal threat.

The presence of Ansar al-Islam in Kurdish northern Iraq gave the Bush administration a strong but flawed argument that al-Qaeda had an operational presence in Iraq working directly for Hussein. On the other hand, once the invasion was complete, the administration went directly past the FRLs and local Iraqis attacking U.S. forces and repeatedly emphasized those al-Qaeda-backed foreign terrorists were now the greatest threat in Iraq. In contrast, U.S. intelligence generally estimated that al-Qaeda in Iraq (AQI)-aligned foreign fighters were generally believed to have been no more than 2 to 5% of the overall resistance. In fact, it is the Iraqi Islamic extremists with varying doctrines who populated the second largest wing of resisters. That meant the insurgency was almost wholly comprised of local Iraqis fighting against the U.S. occupation for their own reason, not for Osama bin Laden. With as few as 5,500 armed guerrillas, the Iraqi Islamists represented as much as 15% of the insurgents fighting the occupation. When cooperating with the ex-Ba'athists forces, these two wings combined to make up over 95% of the insurgents in Iraq.

Until April 2004, the Iraqi Islamic extremist wing of the insurgency was comprised of almost strictly Sunni Muslims who opposed the American invasion and occupation. That changed when actions by the coalition to disarm a Shiite militia, the Jaysh al-Mahdi (Mahdi Militia), led the Shiite Muslim extremists in southern Iraq and Baghdad into an armed uprising against the Americans and British. This uprising lasted several months and killed hundreds of Iraqis and Americans in the process. From that point onward, the Iraqi religious extremist movement acting as rejectionists to the occupation was comprised of both local Sunni and Shiite Iraqis. They shared a common goal of expelling the Americans. Both sides saw the invasion as an abomination. Iraq was a Muslim country being forced to submit to occupation under a predominantly Christian nation. Many others suspected a conspiracy of the Christians being instructed by the Israelis to subjugate Arabs and take their property. One of the most successful rumors started by these rejectionists was that the coalition was buying homes with Israeli money. For months, this fueled suspicion about the origins of reconstruction money.

Still other Iraqis fought as nationalists. Many said they felt disgrace and anger when they saw the sovereignty of Iraq destroyed through force. Most of these groups, save for the Shiite militias, tended to cooperate

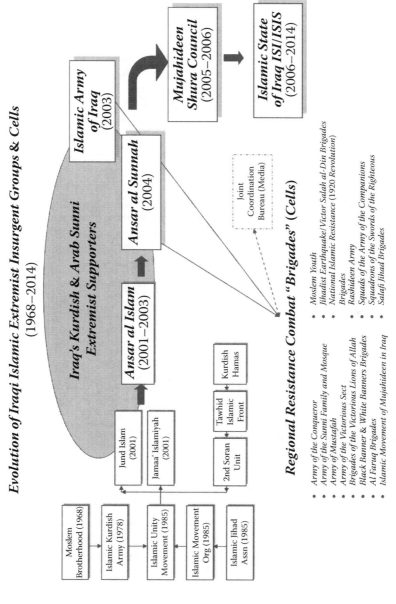

FIGURE 8.1 Iraqi Islamic extremists terror group organization chart.

with the ex-Ba'athist forces. No matter for which reason these extremists fought, one thing was clear, they needed to force political change through violence and selected terrorist tactics to do so. Naturally, many nationalists joined the ex-Ba'athist and religious insurgents and took up arms to fight the Americans and British.

The core of the Iraqi Sunni extremists are adherents to the Wahabi form of Islam. Wahabism is a 200-year-old movement founded by Muhammed Ibn Abdul al-Wahab. It is an Islamic reformation movement, which advocated purification of Islam from mysticism (such as Sufism, polytheism, saints, and pilgrimages) and other practices that were incorporated over the centuries by conquering foreigners that converted to Islam for political or economic purposes. It emphasizes the oneness of God, or Tawhid (monotheism). This form of Islam received a big boost in Iraq when Saudi government-sponsored evangelism in the 1960s and 1970s won great influence in the Iraqi community. This philosophy leads to natural enmity to Shiite Islam even though Iraq is 65% Shiite. The most hard-core Wahabi extremists are also supporters of the Salafist movement. Adopted by al-Qaeda, Salafism describes the adherents to a strictly orthodox form of Islam. Salaf literally means "predecessors" in Arabic. It generally is used by Islamic scholars to describe the first three generations of Muslims and those followers who adhere to the fundamental principles set by the Prophet Mohammed. They are strict constructionists of the Qu'ran as well.

In commemoration of their fidelity, the Islamic extremists of Iraq incorporated Wahabi and Salafi concepts into their cell names (e.g., Salafi Jihad, Tawhid Lions).

ANSAR AL-ISLAM ("PARTISANS OF ISLAM")

Just weeks before the 9/11 attacks struck the United States, a new group, Jund al-Islam, "Soldiers of Islam," came together in the American-protected northern no-fly zone. They vowed to "expel those Jews and Christians from Kurdistan and join the way of Jihad, [and] rule every piece of land with the Islamic Shar'ia rule."[2] The al-Qaeda terrorists who attacked on that fateful day were members of the largest of the global Salafist jihadist groups, but they were not unique. Like many other places in the world, there existed in northern Iraq a small group of Salafist jihadists who maintained spiritual and operational ties to al-Qaeda leadership and members throughout the Middle East. It was repeatedly alleged, but has since been proven false, by the Bush administration that Saddam Hussein supported this Islamic fundamentalist terrorist group. The Ansar al-Islam (AAI) actually drew on decades of Saudi Salafist and Wahabi inspiration that led eventually to close ties with Osama bin Laden and al-Qaeda. Islamic fundamentalism and groups associated with an extremist form of Sunni Islam have a long history in Iraq and maintained secret political structures under Saddam Hussein's regime. AAI is a group of predominantly Kurdish Sunni militants borne out of that long history. An analysis of the group and its operations reveals an organization that was openly living and operating within territory that could not be effectively reached by Saddam Hussein and protected by American airpower.

The AAI's history could be said to start with the Kurdish Muslim community's religious leaders' (ulema) rejection of the secular Western reforms taken by Mustapha Kemal Ataturk in 1924.[3] Many fought the British occupation of Iraq much in the same manner as present-day fighting. In 1952, a movement called the Muslim Brotherhood (MB) emerged in Iraq as a political mouthpiece for the fundamentalist faithful of Iraqi society. When the Ba'ath Party seized power in 1962, the MB were allowed to continue their support of religious political movements, but in 1972 were dissolved by Saddam Hussein. However, they continued to operate underground and eventually emerged within the Iraqi fundamentalist community. In the late 1960s, al-Salafiyah, an Islamic reform movement, seeped its way into the philosophies of the Iraqi Sunni religious society through missionary broadcasts from Saudi and Iraqi media, as well as proselytizing and literature distributed during the hajj of Iraqi pilgrims to Mecca. These Saudi missionaries or "theological jihadists" sought to bring Iraqi Sunnis, both Arab and Kurd, to adopt a philosophy where they maintain strict adherence to monotheism (Tawhid), reject centuries of Islamic scholarly interpretations of the Qu'ran (Kalam), and foreswear worship of Muslim shrines and saints as idolatry. Salafism emphasizes the belief that the first three generations of Muslims, the contemporaries of the Prophet Mohammed and the two generations immediately following his death, were the purest examples of a righteous Islamic society. Modern contemporary worshipers who adopt this philosophy consider themselves "companions of the prophet."

In 1978, this fundamentalist Saudi model of Salafism emerged in Iraq's Kurdish region and was distinct both politically and religiously. A year later, the Russian invasion of Afghanistan and the Iranian Islamic revolution inspired a strong jihadist trend in the Iraqi Sunni society, particularly in the Kurdish north. This trend led the Iraqis to form the first militant Islamic extremist group, the Islamic Kurdish army (Jaysh al-Islamiyah al-Akradiayh). Operating covertly and establishing themselves in the Kurdish mountains, these early jihadists made their way to Afghanistan to join the anti-Russian jihad, where some gained extensive combat experience. By 1985, two additional militant groups were formed: the Islamic Jihad Association (al-Rabitah al-Islamiyah al-Jihadiyah) and the Islamic Movement Organization (Tanzim al-Harakah al-Islamiyah), led by one Sheik Uthmar bin Abd-al-Aziz.[4] After Saddam Hussein's 1989 chemical weapons attack on the Kurdish town of Halabjah, survivors of these groups moved with the Kurdish refugees to Iranian refugee camps where they competed in proselytizing with the Iranian government's effort to create Shiite converts. After the 1991 Gulf War brought security from the Iraqi army through the establishment of the no-fly zones, most Kurdish groups returned back to northern Iraq in relative safety. In 1992, the remnants of the MB broke into two factions, one of which eventually became the Islamic Unity Movement (IUM). This group conducted large-scale evangelical activity (Dawa) in Kurdish Iraq operating two radio stations and a popular mosque. In 2001, the IUM split into two armed factions, the Islamic Group (Jama'ah Islamiyah (JI)), centered in Khormal, and the Islamic Movement (Harakat al-Islamiyah), headquartered in Halabjah.[5] A few weeks before the 9/11 attacks, the Soldiers of Islam (Jund al-Islam (JAI)) were born, including members from various smaller factions such as the Second Soran Unit and the Tawhid Islamic Front.[6] Some members of this group had experience fighting in Afghanistan with Arab Mujahideen. Based in the mountainous region of northern Iraqi Kurdistan in the village of Halabjah near Sulaimaniyah, this group quickly issued a fatwa to the surrounding villages against "the blasphemous secularist, political, social, and cultural" society of the area and carried out its promise to rule under a strict interpretation of the Shar'ia.[7] The JAI formed with its headquarters in the village of Biyarah under the religious leadership of Wirya Huliri (aka Abu Ubaydallah al-Shafi'i), a former member of the Islamic Movement in Erbil in 1994. A popular figure in the nine Kurdish villages surrounding Halabjah, he was known to al-Qaeda leadership in Afghanistan. On December 10, 2001, the Jund al-Islam and two smaller groups, the Kurdish Hamas and al-Tawhid Movement groups merged to form the Ansar al-Islam. Soon this relatively peaceful area of northern Iraq was consumed with near civil war as the group practiced its first jihad against the major political authority in the area, the Popular Union of Kurdistan (PUK).

Ansar al-Islam established itself as militant Sunni jihadists in the center of Kurdish Iraq dominated by the two dominant Kurdish political groups, the PUK and the Kurdish Democratic Party (KDP). Adhering to their Salafist beliefs, music, pictures, smoking, and drinking were all banned in regions under AAI's control. Viewing the Taliban-run Afghanistan as a perfect model of an Islamic state, the AAI subjected those who defied them to public beatings.[8] London-based Human Rights Watch accuses Ansar al-Islam of torturing its prisoners and carrying out strict Islamic punishments like amputation, flogging, and stoning for offenses like theft, the consumption of alcohol, and adultery.[9] Many were reportedly bludgeoned to death with bricks as a form of stoning. In

Biyarah, a local schoolteacher was severely beaten for having the audacity to discipline the child of an AAI fighter. Izzat Abdullah, headmaster at the time, recounts that the AAI fighter stormed into the classroom the next day. "He beat him in front of all the pupils and teachers. He punched and kicked him. He was bleeding from the mouth and nose. He wanted to kill him with a pistol."[10] A female teacher remembers that under AAI "there was no freedom," and that for simply defying the AAI's decree that boys and girls be separated, "they would punish my brothers, my father, or my headmaster."[11] AAI was no less ruthless in its relations with other groups in the area. PUK leader Jalal Talabani (now the former president of Iraq) once described Ansar al-Islam as a kind of Taliban. "They are terrorists who have declared war against all Kurdish political parties. We gave them a chance to change their ways ... and end their terrorist acts. But if we can't do it through dialogue, we are obliged to use force."[12]

AAI ORGANIZATION

The AAI is organized very similar to al-Qaeda and other Salafist groups that were inspired by al-Qaeda organizational training. Salafist organizations are usually led by an amir, "prince," who provides the spiritual and political direction for the group. The AAI was led by Mullah Najm al-Din Faraj (aka Mullah Fatih Krekar), exiled in Norway. He claims the group promotes its goal of "sacrifice in anticipation of God's reward."[13] The organization maintains two deputies who act as primary aides to the amir. One acts as an operations officer and the other as a chief administrator of the organization. Like AQI franchises, the amir has four major departments under his authority:

- Shariah committee: The Islamic law (Shariah) committee operates with a select group of religious and prominent members of the community who provide spiritual guidance within the precepts of the Qu'ran. They provide religious judgments and legal counsel.
- Military committee: The military arm of the organization is led by deputy amirs (Naieb Amir). They organize, plan, and arm the overt and covert aspects of the terrorist or guerrilla insurgent missions of the organization.
- Security committee: This committee is the internal security and covert communications management team within the organization. It provides secret pathways to communicate and dispatch weapons and equipment. It also performs internal police and

executive protection duties, including security vetting of visitors and new recruits.

- Information committee: This is the media arm of the organization, which produces press releases, arranges interviews, and processes videotapes taken in the field by the military committee of successful attacks.

Military Committee

The military arm of the AAI is led by trusted leaders who act in the role as deputy amirs. Each deputy amir is given control of forces that he will then organize and arm. Prior to the U.S. invasion, the AAI had both overt and covert structures depending on the area of operation and the mission. Until the American-led invasion, this committee operated as an openly armed militia tasked with protecting the surrounding towns near Halabjah. All operatives could come together to act as a self-defense force when threatened by the Kurdish political parties or operate covertly when infiltrating the borders of Iran, Turkey, or Syria. This was necessary for clandestine meetings or transmitting communications between agents. After the invasion, the entire organization went underground and implemented its covert operations measures. It is believed that the military committee operated as dispersed groups of commanders with autonomy to operate attacks as they saw fit. The deputy amirs are responsible for military resistance operations in the areas that are designated by the leadership as theirs to control. Each deputy does his own recruitment, logistics, and training. Groups operate in cells no bigger than 5 or 10 men and meet only with trusted agents. For precision attacks on political enemies, the AAI uses human-guided weapons (suicide bomber) attacks against persons who require immediate dispatch. The AAI security committee most likely selects the designated special mission personnel from the military committee's cells, arms them according to the wishes of the amir and desired killing effects, and then sends them out to execute their missions. Such "special tasking" is usually reserved for missions of high risk and which warrant a high degree of security to assure success. The twin suicide attacks on the PUK and KDP offices during Ramadan 2004 are an excellent example of a special mission that can only be performed by the Kurdish terrorists.

Military Operations and Tactics

The Ansar al-Islam had a rich military history from the first months of its creation. In September 2001, the group carried out its first military operation. Fighting between the AAI and the PUK broke out when the group that would become the core of AAI, the Soldiers of Islam, ambushed and killed 42 PUK fighters.[14] The Salafists were certainly not shy about using force, and operating in commanding mountainous terrain helped them when they massacred the PUK. More clashes followed that led to hundreds of dead PUK over the year and 74 AAI members killed. In April 2002, AAI is alleged to have attempted to murder PUK leader Barham Salih at his home in Sulaimaniyah. Salih was an aide to Jalal Talabani and the supposed link between the Kurdish leadership and the CIA. In a daring raid, the AAI operatives entered his home in a hail of gunfire that left five of Salih's bodyguards dead. The alleged perpetrators included one man named Qays from the Sulaimaniyah-based Islamic Jama'ah. The other would-be assassins were former members of al-Tawhid Group, Cameran Muryasi and Abd-al-Salam Abu-Bakr. These were two smaller Salafist groups that had merged with the Ansar al-Islam. Only Qays was caught. In June 2002, the AAI is alleged to have bombed a popular restaurant, injuring scores and killing a child.[15] Emboldened by these early successes, the group launched a surprise attack on the PUK during Ramadan after many Kurd soldiers went home for the holiday—they claimed to have killed 103 PUK members and wounded 117.[16] In February 2003, the AAI launched its first suicide bombing against a Kurdish checkpoint.[17] The AAI had evolved from a small constellation of local religious extremist militias to a full-fledged Mujahideen organization proficient in a broad range of terrorist operations. Soon enough its relationship with the global Salafist community would propel it into a prominent position in the pantheon of international terror targets for the Bush administration.

Links to al-Qaeda

As the American army massed its forces along the Iraq-Kuwait border in preparation for an invasion, Secretary of State Colin Powell made one last desperate attempt to convince the United Nations that Saddam Hussein's Iraq was an immediate threat to international peace. Critical to his argument was the contention that Ansar al-Islam had become affiliated with al-Qaeda through the auspices of Abu Musab al-Zarqawi. Powell asserted:

> When our coalition ousted the Taliban, the Zarqawi network helped establish another poison and explosive training center camp, and this camp is located in northeastern Iraq.... Those helping to run this camp are Zarqawi lieutenants operating in northern Kurdish areas outside

Saddam Hussein's controlled Iraq. But Baghdad has an agent in the most senior levels of the radical organization that controls this corner of Iraq. In 2000, this agent offered al-Qaeda safe haven in the region.[18]

According to Powell, not only was Ansar al-Islam associated with al-Qaeda, but it was also surreptitiously developing chemical weapons and ricin, a potent poison with no antidote. These reports were alleged by several Kurdish sources who contend that al-Qaeda fighters fleeing Afghanistan joined Ansar al-Islam and helped them build a camp for "young lions" (suicide bombers). These same sources reported that Ansar al-Islam carried out crude experiments with chemicals in an attempt to fashion a weapon for a global jihad.[19] The Bush administration believed that many of these fighters were associated with the Taliban, and some may have trained in al-Qaeda training camps in Afghanistan.[20] AAI's ranks may have been filled with foreign fighters who fled from Afghanistan to escape American forces there, perhaps crossing Iran with help of that Islamic government. However, since the invasion, it is assessed that most of these members would have joined al-Qaeda in Iraq (AQI), while the core body of AAI remained Iraqi Kurdish.

Other sources indicate that Jund al-Islam's metamorphosis into Ansar al-Islam may have been the result of seed money provided by al-Qaeda.[21] Since the war began, investigators have unearthed other incidents linking the two groups. In February 2004, the *New York Times* reported that American intelligence officials had intercepted a 17-page document detailing al-Qaeda's strategy for the Iraqi insurgency on its way to Ansar al-Islam leaders. Hassan Ghul, a Pakistani courier for al-Qaeda, was arrested in the operation. The document he carried is believed to have been written by Abu Musab al-Zarqawi, and it urged the Kurds to support sectarian violence against the majority Shiites.

U.S. leaders have been keen to emphasize these tenuous connections. U.S. proconsul Paul Bremer told reporters in February 2004 that "it's quite clear in the past three months we've seen a real step up on the part of the professional terrorists of al-Qaeda and Ansar al-Islam, conducting suicide attacks."[22] Other reports lend credence to the suggestion that Ansar al-Islam has indeed developed close ties with bin Laden's network. In May 2004, Turkish police arrested 25 militants alleged to have ties to Ansar al-Islam. The police confiscated guns, explosives, bomb-making booklets, and 4,000 CDs featuring training instructions from Osama bin Laden. The men were arrested for plotting to carry out bomb attacks on a NATO summit attended by President George W. Bush.[23] Other experts find it difficult to believe that Ansar al-Islam, a homegrown terrorist organization composed mainly of Iraqis, would have willingly subordinated themselves to al-Zarqawi, a Jordanian, in all operational matters.[24]

The American case against Iraq hinged on the assertion that not only was Ansar al-Islam directly associated with al-Qaeda, but also Saddam Hussein knew about and encouraged these connections. In essence, the White House wanted to believe that AAI was the al-Qaeda organization in Iraq and that it was funded and supported by Saddam Hussein's intelligence agencies. Kurdish commander Mustapha Saed Qada reported before the war that "we have picked up conversations on our radios between Iraqis and [Ansar] al-Islam. I believe that Iraq is also funding [Ansar] al-Islam. There are no hard facts as yet, but I believe that under the table they are supporting them because it will cause further instability for the Kurds."[25] Qassem Hussein Mohamed, a Saddam Hussein look-alike who claims to have been a part of the Mukhabarat, Hussein's secret intelligence service, reported that "Ansar and al-Qaeda groups were trained by graduates of Mukhabarat's School 999—military intelligence. My information is that the Iraqi government was directly supporting [al-Qaeda] with weapons and explosives. [Ansar] was part of al-Qaeda, and given support with training and money."[26] These are allegations, but scant evidence exists. In the days immediately following the American invasion, AAI prisoners are alleged to have pointed to Gen. Izzat Ibrahim al-Douri as a prominent leader in the resistance. Al-Douri, Saddam's number two, was suspected by the U.S. government of coordinating FRL opposition to the American occupation.[27] The prisoners may be factually correct. Many in Iraq knew that al-Douri or another like him would be fighting the Americans, and that the resistance was dominated by Sunni regime loyalists. Other reports of Hussein's involvement in the AAI chain of command have been seen. Kurds in the village of Biyarah have repeated stories about a man named Abu Wael, an Iraqi agent with an important position in Ansar al-Islam. In January, a Kurdish official stated that "the Ba'athists provide logistical support, money, weapons, transportation, [and] safehouses. Organizations like Ansar al-Islam provide people ready to commit suicide."[28] Still other Kurdish officials deny these links. For instance, Bafel Jalal Talabani (son of PUK leader and former Iraqi president Jalal Talabani) believes that links between Ba'athists and jihadists are "very negligible."[29] However, these claims have never been substantiated by American intelligence, and many have been found to have been agents of influence clearly pandering to Bush administration sentiment. The leader of the PUK, Jalal Talabani, whose forces were defeated by the AAI in two clashes, was alleged to have created the unsubstantiated story of chemical weapons testing with ricin being carried out by the AAI in an effort to get the Americans to attack. In the superheated world of the Iraqi opposition prior to the U.S. invasion, any claim against the AAI, no matter how outrageous, was given credence and encouragement if it justified an invasion. Since America was soon to own Iraq, many sources simply told the Americans what they wanted to hear. In fact, the fate of the AAI was sealed with its relationship to bin Laden. Mullah Mustapha Krekar, the leader of AAI, stated in an interview with the Kurdish newspaper *Hawlati* that bin Laden was "the crown on the head of the Islamic nation."[30] To many in Washington, that statement was as good as a death sentence.

It is clear that the AAI was one of the Salafist groups supported and encouraged by a relationship with al-Qaeda, yet it appears it was not acting as a direct al-Qaeda franchise. No matter how tenuous the connection, many fighters were inspired and believed that Ansar al-Islam had connections to al-Qaeda. Sangar Mansour, an AAI militant captured in the early fighting, stated, "Al-Qaeda was held up as the model. We looked like al-Qaeda, gave orders like al-Qaeda, trained like al-Qaeda and used their videotapes. Some non-Kurds had U.S. military uniforms, that they put on when the [U.S.] attacks started." When PUK forces captured two AAI bases they found graffiti praising bin Laden and the 9/11 attacks along with "a picture of the twin towers with a drawing of bin Laden standing on top holding a Kalashnikov rifle in one hand and a knife in the other."[31]

Ties to Iran

The United States also claimed ties between Ansar al-Islam and Iran. Donald Rumsfeld, the American Secretary of Defense, has called AAI a "foreign terrorist organization" operating in Iraq with ties to Iran. Most of these allegations came from the geographic proximity of the AAI bases with the Iranian border and its ties from the refugee period in Iran. The Kurdish head of security in the area around Halabja, Anwar Haji Othman, reports, "[Ansar fighters] go back and forth. They bring cash from Iran to Iraq across the border."[32] "They would run out of ammunition ... without the supplies they got from Iran," asserts another Kurdish official.[33] Elsewhere in Iraqi Kurdistan, officials were not so sure. Dana Ahmed Majid, the head of the Asaish, the PUK's intelligence and security arm, reports that while it might be easy to cross the border, the presence of Islamist terrorists in Iran "did not prove that Iran was sponsoring the terrorist groups."[34] Indeed, captured AAI militants report that after fleeing to Iran in the wake of the American invasion, they were fired upon by the Iranians and had to sneak in at night.[35] From 1991 to the time of the American invasion, "border dancing" from Afghanistan to Iran to Kurdish Iraq to Syria or Turkey had become a fine art for many jihadists. According to Dr. Hani al-Siba'i, this had become the preferred jihadist infiltration route into the Middle East by 1995, after U.S. pressure made transiting through Pakistan more risky. Jordanian Abu Musab al-Zarqawi, the leader of Tawhid Wal-Jihad, is alleged to have crossed Iran and

Iraq through AAI camps several times while undergoing his apprentice-ship in Afghanistan and running a TWJ camp in Herat. Iran could know many things, but in the covert world of the jihadists, it could only know so much. All of this is sparse evidence that the Iranian regime not only knew of the AAI's activities, but fostered them and those of al-Qaeda and Iraqi intelligence as well. Nawsherwan Mustapha, a PUK official, told reporters, "Iran could make a lot of problems for us if it chose to. We can draw certain conclusions from the fact that the border area [with Iran] is quiet."[36] Many experts consider it unlikely that Iran, a majority Shiite country, would support the Sunni AAI. Yet both groups are united in their opposition to the United States, but in the region's complex poli-tics, being the "enemy of my enemy" is not always enough to guarantee friendship or assistance.

OPERATION VIKING HAMMER

Ansar al-Islam went to high alert after Colin Powell's address to the United Nations where they were presented as one of the links between Saddam Hussein and al-Qaeda. In a statement on its website during the war, the AAI declared, "300 jihad martyrs renewed their pledge to Allah, the strong and the sublime, in order to be suicide bombers in the victory of Allah's religion."[37] Not surprisingly, AAI camps in northern Iraq were among the first of many targets attacked by U.S. forces in their spring 2003 invasion of Iraq. Most reports indicate that the bombing was extremely effective, at least in the short run. Gen. Tommy Franks triumphantly declared that "a massive terrorist facility in northern Iraq" was "attacked and destroyed."[38] Operation Viking Hammer was a com-bined attack, which opened with more than 30 cruise missiles striking the AAI camps and followed up with a combined ground attack made up of U.S. Special Forces and Kurdish Peshmerga soldiers. Viking Hammer killed 57 AAI guerrillas, while wounding and capturing many others. Interviews with AAI militants captured in the fighting reveal that even it's most fervent followers believed that the group had been decimated and that it was unlikely to regain its former potency.[39] It appears, how-ever, that America won this particular battle only to be outflanked in the wider war. These sentiments are captured in the eerie testimony of AAI media chief Mohammed Gharib, who was present during the ini-tial American missile strike: "I filmed the missiles falling. You wouldn't believe if I told you we were happy [to be attacked]. They gave us the sense that we were so true, so right, that even America had come to fight us."[40] A prescient captive AAI member told reporters, "I don't think the fight with Ansar will be over when American finishes its bombing."[41]

Rather than being destroyed, it seems likely that the AAI recon-
stituted itself as a more decentralized organization and folded into the
nationwide Iraqi Islamic resistance. By early 2004, Brigadier General
Abazaid, the commander of the U.S. Central Command, stated:

> Ansar al-Islam, which is a terrorist group that we hit very hard in
> the very opening stages in the war up in the area of northern Iraq
> and northeast of Sulimaniyah, is coming back. We don't know exactly
> how they're infiltrating. There's some impression that they could be
> infiltrating through Iran. There is also a possibility that there were
> people that instead of moving away from the center of Iraq after they
> were hit, moved down into Baghdad. So it's clear that Ansar al-Islam
> is reforming and is presenting a threat to us. And then it's unclear, but
> it's troubling that either al-Qaeda look-alikes or al-Qaeda people are
> making an opportunity to move against us.

It appears that many AAI teams were dispersed to safer locations
away from the Kurdish areas before the invasion occurred. These surviving groups established small, covert cells capable of acting independently.[42] "Smaller cells have spread throughout Iraq and have
concentrated in Mosul," reported Bafel Talabani. "It needs to be controlled because it has the capacity to spiral and grow.... The nature of
the threat has changed. Instead of military operations, they carry out
smaller operations."[43]

Over the course of its short existence, AAI has proven itself an
extremely flexible organization capable of staging many different types
of attacks. In its early stages, the group relied heavily on shootings and
public beatings to instill fear in the villages under its control. Very quickly
(coincidentally around the time it allegedly began receiving support from
al-Qaeda) the group expanded its terrorist repertoire to include bombings and suicide attacks. Since 2003, Kurdish officials report "Ansar has
altered its strategy and expanded its theater of operations, aiming suicide
bombers and ambushes toward cities in the interior, such as Mosul and
Kirkuk."[44] AAI has claimed credit behind some of the worst insurgent
attacks in Iraq, including the February 2002 bombing that killed more
than 100 Kurds in Erbil and the December 2004 suicide bomber attack
on an American mess hall in Mosul that killed 22 soldiers.[45] This attack
was said to have been carried out by Ahmed Said Ghamdi, a 20-year-old
Saudi who gave up his medical studies in Sudan to go to Iraq. There he
joined the Assudallah (Lions of Allah) Brigades of the Ansar al-Islam.
Wearing an Iraqi national guard uniform he infiltrated the American
base and blew up his explosive vest in the midst of a meal. This attack
was also claimed by the Ansar al-Sunnah, which AAI may have joined
by that time.

AAI Strategy

Overall, AAI's political strategy was designed to stymie American attempts to impose order by precipitating mass sectarian violence between the majority Shiites and the minority Sunnis. This strategy echoed the one used in their long-standing conflict with the major political parties in Iraqi Kurdistan, the PUK and the KDP. In the wake of the devastating Arbil bombing, Kakamin Mujar, the Erbil party boss for the KDP, speculated that the attacks were designed to prevent reconciliation between the two major Kurdish parties. "We have so many enemies that don't want us to be united—they want to keep us weak and divided."[46] The AAI's attempts to keep Iraq "weak and divided" have led it to take credit for the assassination of Sheik Mahmoud al-Madaini, an aide to Ayatollah Ali al-Sistani, the most prominent Shiite cleric in Iraq. The group claimed that the attack was part of a campaign "against mercenaries and traitors who have sold their honor."[47] The AAI military strategy was the same simple and effective KHPI strategy: kill American soldiers and their supporters and inspire new Mujahideen to come join the jihad. From 2005–2011 its members folded into AQI and formed the basis of Iraqi fighters in ISIS.

AAI in European Terrorism

Ansar al-Islam's many structural reorganizations have included a broadening of its reach in recruiting and liaison. AAI associates were found in Sweden, Germany, Spain, and Italy. In Sweden, members of Ansar al-Islam were arrested for raising funds used in terrorist activities.[48] Of interest are the conclusions of Magnus Norell, an analyst for the Swedish Defense Research Council. He told reporters that the arrests were "the first serious sign that we do have these problems. Most of what is going on you don't see. And that's the danger. This is a very good part of Europe to operate in. As long as you play it safe and cool, you're home free."[49]

Police elsewhere in Europe have been able to foil the more ambitious AAI plots. In late December 2003, Italian police arrested over a dozen suspected members of the AAI. Indictments accuse them of "sending militants to war zones to sustain terrorist activities."[50] The leader of this group, Abderrazak Mahdjoub, was known to have links with al-Qaeda. By coordinating with Mohammed Majiid, an Iraqi Kurd, the group was said to have funneled potential suicide bombers into Iraq. Transcripts of their telephone conversations released by Italian investigators feature Majiid asking Mahdjoub to send him "people who strike the ground and bring up iron," and that he was looking for "people who were in Japan" (this latter statement being a coded reference for kamikazes, or suicide bombers). Italy was long suspected as a major staging area for potential terrorists looking to make their way to the front lines in Iraq. This incident reveals that terrorist organizations like the AAI have the capability of teaming up with al-Qaeda to create sophisticated international recruiting networks—it also demonstrates that the invasion of Iraq appears to have assisted in changing Ansar al-Islam from a small local terrorist group with limited name recognition and support into a major Mujahideen organization that is receiving the largess of Muslim supporters that extends throughout the Western world.

In Germany, investigators frustrated what they believe was a possible al-Qaeda–AAI November 2004 attempt to assassinate interim Iraq Prime Minister Ayad Allawi on a state visit. Authorities in the country say that the AAI's activities included fund-raising, trafficking, and spreading propaganda (recruiting efforts).[51] The federal German prosecutor, Kai Nehm, told reporters that the cell had "close contact to the highest leadership circles" of Ansar al-Islam. The alleged mastermind behind the plot, Abu Mohammed Lubnani, had been operating in Europe for years. He had even been arrested for stealing $300,000 from an armored car in 1997. Nehm described him as the "deputy leader" of the AAI network in Iraq.[52] Though unsuccessful, the attempt on Allawi's life shows just how extensive AAI's network has become; no longer was AAI limited to the imaginary borders of an increasingly tumultuous Iraq. Dr. Günther Beckstein, the Interior Minister of Bavaria, described the AAI as having been "very good—a leading power—in terms of mobilizing its followers to fight the Americans in Iraq. They are especially brutal and they are very good at getting attention worldwide. This in turn enables them to recruit more fanatics" (Figure 8.2).[53]

FIGURE 8.2 Iraqi religious extremist insurgents street fight with U.S. Marines in city of Ramadi, 2006.

ANSAR AL-SUNNAH AND JAYSH AL-ANSAR AL-SUNNAH ("SUPPORTERS/PARTISANS OF THE SUNNI/ARMY OF THE SUPPORTERS OF THE SUNNI")

Soon after the invasion, numerous foreign volunteers flocked to Iraq and joined with groups of Iraqi Sunni who saw their Islamic beliefs (as soon to be suppressed by a rising Shiite majority) threatened. In opposition to the Mahdi Militia of the young Shiite Imam Muqtada al-Sadr, some of the cells formed a combined Sunni insurgent force capable of fighting a sectarian war as well as a guerrilla one. On September 20, 2003, several of these smaller Sunni nationalist resistance Iraqi and foreign groups merged with elements of the Ansar al-Islam to create the fourth largest insurgent group, the Ansar al-Sunnah (AAS) ("Supporters/Partisans of the Sunni").

In its first public statement, Ansar al-Sunnah described itself as "as a group of jihadists, scholars and political and military experts dedicated to creating an Islamic state in Iraq."[54] "It is known that the jihad in Iraq has become the individual duty of every Muslim after the infidel enemy fell upon the land of Islam," the group declared in its first propaganda video. "The task is great and the situation is momentous that concerns the nation's fate and the defeat of the occupation. The aim does not end with their defeat but with application of the Shar'iah of Allah and his Prophet."[55] The statements of the AAS fall in harmony with its jihadist line. They are always signed by its military committee. The leadership of the Ansar al-Islam exhorted the small local and foreign jihadist combat units in Iraq to fight together with the single goal of spoiling the occupation and driving out American forces from Iraq: "What is the point that the blood of Muslim Mujahideen is shed to resist the occupation forces if a secular Iraqi, an apostate, or a lackey of the United Sates assumes power to implement the U.S. program?"[56]

In a nutshell, Ansar al-Sunnah army is an Islamic, Salafist, Iraqi jihadist group. It had no political platform save ejecting the Americans from Iraq. When that was completed, it set about stopping Shiite dominance, and worked to form a Sunni Islamic state in cooperation with AQI/ISIS (Islamic State of Iraq and Syria). It included some Arab members who infiltrated the border from Iraq's neighboring countries, whether they were members or sympathizers with al-Qaeda, but these few operatives aside, the AAS was an almost purely Iraqi resistance group.

Abdurrahman Ali Khurshid, a captured AAI militant, and Kurdish intelligence officials assert that Ansar al-Islam merged with two Baghdad based-insurgent groups—Moahaddin and Mansour—to form Ansar al-Sunnah sometime in the spring of 2003 after the combined

PUK-American assault on the AAI base camps, Operation Viking Hammer. The name change that resulted from the merger of Ansar al-Islam to Ansar al-Sunnah reflects the organization's desire to recruit not just Kurds, but all Sunnis fighting against the American occupation.[57] In a 2007 report on foreign terrorist organizations, the State Department's Office of the Coordinator for Counterterrorism listed Ansar al-Sunnah as an alias for Ansar al-Islam.[58] James Meek, a reporter for the New York-based *Daily News*, quoted a senior U.S. counterterrorism official as saying that Ansar al-Sunnah is an "umbrella organization" set up by Ansar al-Islam.[59] Other reports confirm that this organization is simply another manifestation of Ansar al-Islam's continued metamorphosis.[60] They stated their organizational change in their first press release:

> It is known that jihad in Iraq has become an individual duty of every Muslim after the atheist enemy assailed the territory of Islam. Those who raise the banner of the blessed jihad are the Sunnis, the Ansar al-Sunnah Army, and the proponents of tawhid (Islamic concept of monotheism) and al-Salafiyah. They took action all by themselves and moved into groups, each from their own territory. They derive their jihadist program and orders from the holy Koran and the Sunni of the Prophet.[61]

AAS Military Committee

The military wing of the AAS was called the Army of the Ansar al-Sunnah (Jaysh al-Ansar al-Sunnah). This wing was formed from creating a coalition of smaller Sunni extremist and nationalist fighters, collecting and coordinating their weapons stockpiles, and consolidating their diverse combat power to strike throughout northwest Iraq. This organization harnessed the skill and intelligence collection gathering capabilities of both foreign and local Iraqi fighters into a unified combat force. The AAS uses guerrilla tactics and acts of terrorism in the exact same way as the former regime loyalists and al-Qaeda in Iraq (Figure 8.2).

The AAS (as well as the AAI) claimed to be behind some of the most deadly attacks on U.S. soldiers in Iraq, including the December 2004 suicide bomber attack on an American mess hall that killed 22 soldiers and wounded 69. Ansar al-Sunnah released a tape shortly after the attack that shows the actual explosion from the moment of the attack. "We are the Army of the Ansar al-Sunnah. We will terrorize the infidels the Americans by a crushing attack," the group announced in the video.

Other intelligence suggests that the AAI's transformation into Ansar al-Sunnah includes basic changes in its organization, but remains very similar to the original AAI model. Sarkawt Kuba, the chief Kurdish intelligence and security officer in northern Iraq, believed that "Ansar has no camps in northern Iraq anymore. So they meet with young men and prospective followers in mosques and other places in the north. They keep in contact through the Internet and e-mails. They then send recruits to Kirkuk and Mosul, where they are well organized and do have camps."[62] According to Abdurrahman Ali Khurshid, the group's operations in Kirkuk were centered on 10 to 12 guerrillas, including one bomb maker, split into three teams. These teams were led by an amir, "prince," who provided them with money, logistical support, safe houses, and munitions.[63] This model is emblematic of nearly all Iraqi insurgent groups.

Like its FRL brethren, Ansar al-Islam/Ansar al-Sunnah were adaptive and competent terrorists. They have shown time and again their ability to rebound from defeat and adapt to change—like the mythical hydra, every head cut from the Ansar body simply leaves room for two more to grow in its place. Its members were regularly killed by American forces when they confronted these forces on the battlefield dirty. On the other hand, its record of success reveals a group with reach and skill. At times, American forces made it appear that the AAS, often mischaracterized as a group of foreign terrorists, was second only to al-Qaeda in Iraq (formerly Tawhid Wal-Jihad) in committing almost every act of terrorism perpetrated in Iraq. In fact, AAS carried out far more operations than AQI over a wider geographical area, and with more capacity to inflict routine casualties against the U.S. Army and Marines. Like the AQI, the AAS carried out ritualistic beheadings of captured hostages they perceived as collaborators. One such hostage was an alleged American CIA agent named Jamal Tewefic Salman who had become an American citizen in 1980 and changed his name to Khaled Abdul Messih. He was captured by the group posing as a photojournalist. An AAS statement was accompanied by photographs and a video of the hostage being beheaded. The statement said, "We have implemented God's judgment on him and the accompanying pictures show his beheading. We call on those living off the blood of the Mujahideen to repent to God and stop what they are doing ... or else the Mujahideen's and God's hands will reach their necks one by one."

Al-Muhajirin Wa al-Ansar

In April 2004, after the battles in Fallujah, a new branch of Ansar al-Sunnah named Muhajirin Wa al-Ansar ("Emigrants and Partisans") emerged in a press statement. They claimed the same style of military operations as Ansar al-Islam. The name of the group alludes to the Arabs who accompanied Mohammed from Mecca to Medina during the historic emigration (Hegira). It also has a modern meaning as a popular name for Arabs who live abroad in Europe. They claimed to be pure-blood Iraqis fighting the occupation:

> O beloved sons of my beloved country Iraq: We are your sons, broth-ers, and fathers from the Special Forces and Frogmen units of the brave Iraqi army; young men who refuse but respond to the call of jihad for the sake of God alone. We are determined to elevate the word of Islam and to fight the band of traitors and criminals who have chosen humili-ation and living off the tables of the foreigner and killing and splitting up the one Arab nation. We have chosen to teach the occupiers who the Iraqis are.

Ansar al-Islam, Ansar al-Sunnah, and Muhajirin Wa al-Ansar are good examples of the way the American-led invasion of Iraq has cata-lyzed the growth and power of local Iraqis to join terrorist groups—a fact becoming more and more obvious to the young men and women who must endure the constant sense of fear that pervades the nebulous front lines of the war in Iraq (Figure 8.3).

FIGURE 8.3 Members of an Ansar al-Sunnah terror cell hold pieces of a U.S. Marine Corps DRAGON EYE surveillance drone they shot down over Fallujah.

THE ISLAMIC ARMY IN IRAQ

- Army of the Mujahideen
- Secret Islamic Army in Iraq

After the fall of the Hussein regime, numerous small Iraqi Islamic groups in the Sunni regions of Iraq shrugged off the mantle of the Ba'athist regime and found more solace in their religion. Although Hussein fostered a religious atmosphere in Iraq, it was tempered with the knowledge that the secular Ba'ath Party was barely allowing approved Islamic groups to exist, so long as they supported Saddam and his regime. However, pious Sunnis did remain loyal to the tenants of Islam despite Hussein's secularism. In the immediate post-war, they saw the American invasion as a gross injustice to their people and religion. Groups with true capability such as Ansar al-Islam were well prepared to fight the Americans, but the popular resistance in the Sunni Triangle was formed loosely from people with rudimentary Al Quds army training and some Iraqi army soldiers who were loyal to the imams of their neighborhood mosques above all. Unlike their foreign brethren, they did not initially desire bin Laden's dream of a new Salafist caliphate, but they did sympathize with the idea of an Islamic republic ruled by Islamic principles and laws. By July 2003, armed engagements with the U.S. Army in Sunni strongholds such as Fallujah and Baqubah led to high numbers of civilian casualties. These incidents created outrage among the Sunni population. This outrage led local Sunni clerics to form their own resistance groups from the young men who survived the war. Many of these young men were skilled soldiers from the Saddam Fedayeen, Republican Guard, and the intelligence agencies, except that they swore their allegiance to their mosque and their religion instead of returning the former regime to power. Many of the more radical joined Ansar al-Sunnah. Others formed and joined a new group, the Jaysh al-Islami al-Iraq, or the "Islamic Army in Iraq" (IAI). By the end of the summer of 2003, these groups, which fought the U.S. forces in small pockets, had begun to learn the lessons of the skilled Saddam Fedayeen and foreign fighters. They collected thousands of tons of unguarded weapons and boasted of their initial strikes on the Americans.

Writing for the French magazine *Le Figaro*, Roland Jacquard and Atmane Tazaghart assert that the IAI was founded by one Abu Abdallah Hassan Ben Mahmoud on September 29, 2003. The IAI, like most Sunni insurgent groups, operated throughout the Sunni Triangle and in the heart of Baghdad. The IAI carried out declared operations in Yusefiyah, Mahmudiyah, Baqubah, Bayji, Jarf as-Sakhr, Fallujah, Ramadi, Taji, Tal Afar, Hit, Al Latifiyah, Tikrit, Tuz Khormatu, Kirkuk, and al-Khalidiyah, just to name a few.

Until June 2005, the IAI had been an exceedingly quiet terrorist organization, but after press claims that the IAI had entered into reconciliation negotiations with the new Iraqi government, they came out in a flurry of public denials. Various spokesmen, including a Sheik Abu Khalid, denied the reports. One communiqué stated, "Between them [the U.S.-installed regime] and us there can only be fighting and expulsion from the Land of the Two Rivers.... If that is what they mean when they say they have been having a 'dialogue' [with the Resistance] then they are right, by God—we will fight them until God resolves the matter according to His wishes."[64]

Another IAI member, Ibrahim Youssef al-Shammari, was designated to announce the merger of the IAI with the largest FRL group, the Army of the Mujahideen, in an ad hoc organization called the Islamic Army Command. In fact, the Army of the Mujahideen, the IAI, and the AAS announced their joint intention to assassinate the Sunni politician who claimed to speak for the insurgency, Ayham al-Samarie. In their statement, they went on to say:

> The Islamic Army Command appoints whomever it wishes to represent it in any official activity and it is not permissible for any person to take the place of the Command and ascribe such a role to himself. Whoever does that will receive the punishment appropriate in his case.[65]

During their first year of operations, the IAI appeared to have adopted a message similar to other pro-al-Qaeda groups, but their original mission statement remains:

> The aim of the Iraqi Resistance is the expulsion of the occupation, making it an example for anyone who might dare to think in the future about occupying any Arab or Islamic state.[66]

The IAI cooperated openly with the other major resistance organizations, such as al-Qaeda in Iraq, the Ansar al-Sunnah, and until the time of their merger, the Army of the Mujahideen. After this point, the philosophical differences were ironed out, and the IAI became a wing under Ansar al-Sunnah and later al-Qaeda in Iraq (now ISIS), which was better suited philosophically than the FRLs. An instance of conflict with al-Qaeda goals occurred when the IAI rejected Abu Musab al-Zarqawi's call to strike out at and randomly kill Iraqi Shiites. In a communiqué they commented, "The Resistance would set as its aim and direct its strikes at the occupation and its stooges, and no one else. A call to kill the Shi'ah is a fire that burns all Iraqis, Sunni and Shi'i alike."[67]

IAI Tactics

From September 2003, the IAI and its subunits continued carrying out the most basic armed operations against the American and Iraqi army forces. A plethora of daily attacks waged by the IAI included planting hundreds of roadside IEDs and conducting larger bombings using car bombs (vehicle-borne improvised explosive device (VBIEDs)) parked on the side of roads and detonated near U.S. convoys. Its rocket teams shot thousands of rounds of 60 and 81 mm mortar and Tariq-improvised 122 mm rockets at American bases and carried out armed ambushes. Infantry-style ambushes sprayed vehicles and convoys with machine gun fire, RPG-7s, or improvised antipersonnel "pipe" rockets and hand grenades. The IAI carried out a wide variety of attacks, including the mortar attack on the Baghdad convention center during the first meeting of the transitional government, an attempted ambush and assassination of pro-American exile Ahmed Chalabi, the abduction and murder of Abdul Jabar Sulagh, brother of Interior Minister Bayan Baqer, and several attacks on American contractors. By the fall of 2004, the IAI started carrying out suicide car bombing attacks. A favorite IAI tactic was the suicide driver crashing his suicide VBIED (S-VBIED) directly into convoys of American soldiers. These assaults were done in the exact same manner that the Saddam Fedayeen used S-VBIEDs in Baghdad during the invasion. The S-VBIED comes from a side street or from a parked position, accelerates, and slams into the target to explode.

Following the lead of Abu Musab al-Zarqawi's Tawhid Wal-Jihad (which would later become al-Qaeda in Iraq), the IAI adopted the strategy of abducting foreigners and Iraqis as a method of punishing them for cooperating with the coalition. Some noteworthy abductees, who would be politically more valuable alive, were released unharmed, including the Iranian consul Feredion Jahani, French journalists Georges Malbrunot and Christian Chesnot, Sudanese truck drivers Mohammad Harun Hammad and Maher, and two Lebanese electrical workers, Marwan Ibrahim Kassar and Mohammed Jawdat Hussein. Some resulted in concrete concessions, such as when they captured a Filipino, Angelo dela Cruz, forcing the Philippines to withdraw its 51 troops. Some releases were designed to show the Muslim insurgents in a favorable light: the Black Banners cell abducted seven truckers from a Kuwaiti transportation company for 6 weeks but released them when they made it appear that they had become more pious and penitent Muslims. Egyptian hostage Mohammed Sanad told Arabiya TV: "They taught us religion and how to pray." In fact, the hostages were shown being released after praying and accepting Qu'rans. This group, like many others, showed videotapes of their hostages wearing the orange Guantanamo-style jumpsuits. Numerous others were not so fortunate. Again, following the al-Zarqawi lead, the IAI started beheading hostages on videotape, including the execution of three Macedonians. The IAI revealed a high measure of coordination in December 2004 when three cells ambushed and killed eight Iraqi bodyguards while abducting two others from a Western company, the Sandy Group.

However, the most notorious attack by the IAI came on April 22, 2005,[68] when an anti-aircraft missile team carrying SA-7 surface-to-air missiles had tracked the movements of a civilian Mi-8 HIP helicopter operated by Skylink Air & Logistics. Lying under the path of the low-flying aircraft, the IAI cell successfully shot it down as it transited from Baghdad to an American airbase near Taji. The crash killed nine passengers from the Blackwater USA security company, two Skylink guards, and two of the three aircrew. One of the pilots miraculously survived the crash after being ejected from the tumbling aircraft. He was able to walk away from the burning wreckage, but was brutally executed when the IAI team came to videotape the wreckage and found him lying on the ground begging for help. While being videotaped, he was forced to get up and walk and told to leave. As he tried to walk away, an IAI gunmen was instructed to deliver "Allah's justice." They then shot him 17 times.

The Islamic Army statement that followed the attack said it killed the survivor "in revenge for the Muslims who have been killed in cold blood in the mosques of tireless Fallujah before the eyes of the world and on television screens, without anyone condemning them." It was an apparent reference to the CNN videotape of a U.S. Marine shooting to death a wounded Iraqi soldier in a mosque during the fighting in Fallujah several months earlier.

IRAQI RESISTANCE BRIGADES AND BATTALIONS, TERROR CELLS, AND SUBUNITS

Like virtually every other resistance group, the IAI and its sister force, the Army of the Mujahideen, operate small cells in groups of 3 to 10 men. These cells function independently and usually adopt the name of a prominent personality or event in Islamic or Iraqi history. Cell clusters or local area commands are easily identified from actual large-scale organizations by commonly referring to themselves as brigades.

Subunits and individual cells take on the name *brigade* (*Katibah*, or battalion), *companies* (*Sariah*), or *squadrons/formations* (*Tiskhkeel*). Some units of the IAI included the Black Banners Brigade, which operated almost like the independent terrorist group it began as; Khalid ibn al-Walid Corps, Abdel Kader al-Gilani Brigades, Horror Brigades, Mutassim Bellah Brigade, Knights of the 'Ali ibn Abi Talib Brigade, Brigades of Fear, Brigades of al-Tawhid Lions, and Thi al-Nourayn

Brigades. Other smaller units included the Fourqan Company and the al-Fursan Company.

OTHER MINOR IRAQI INSURGENT GROUPS

Numerous small insurgent groups sprung up through the fall of 2003 and into the spring of 2004. These groups operated in close cooperation with the larger groups and most likely were absorbed by one of the big three insurgent groups (al-Qaeda in Iraq, Ansar al-Sunnah, or Islamic Army in Iraq) at some point.

Small independent insurgent units carried out wide-ranging tactical operations against the coalition forces, including the most common ones: placing IEDs on roads and detonating them when American convoys came by, small arms attacks on passing units, and execution and murder of Iraqis collaborating with the Americans. The insurgents were skillful in carrying out politically symbolic attacks that make them appear as a true secret army. These political seizure operations include those carried out by al-Qaeda in Iraq when they allegedly seized parts of the city of Ramadi in November 2005 while American Marines swept west of them along the Syrian border. Other examples include the November 2004 raids by Ansar al-Sunnah, the Islamic Army in Iraq, Brigades of the Army of the Mustafa, and the Army of the Conqueror in Mosul, where they seized large sections of the city from the coalition and started meting out Islamic justice to collaborators. These forces attacked U.S. Army Stryker Brigade troops and seized police stations, broke into government arsenals, and killed 18 Iraqi national guardsmen. The Army of Truth Mujahideen operating in Samarrah claimed for at least 1 day to have seized police stations and formed a free council of three religious leaders to implement law as well as conduct attacks on the coalition. Note that this list is only a partial reading of the self-proclaimed Islamic extremist groups that operated in Iraq. Many changed names after each operation or by regional assignment. During the period of intense fighting in Fallujah in 2004, these Islamic groups created an umbrella command structure for coordinating policy and operations, while each group maintained independence. The coordinating committee was called the General Command for the Islamic Resistance of Iraq (GCIRI). In early 2006, they resisted a call to unify under Abu Musab al-Zarqawi but were all brought under the same flag of AQI/ISIS by 2012.

Army of the Sunni Family and the Mosque: A new group formed in November 2005. Announced they were formed to retaliate against Iraqi police and army atrocities.

Army of Mustafa Battalions (Brigades) (Kata'ib Jaysh al-Mustafa): A small group associated with Ansar al-Sunnah. Operated in and near Mosul. Carried out light infantry weapons operations against American forces and the Iraqi army. Has carried out attacks on the U.S. Stryker Brigade with the Army of the Conqueror Brigade.

Army of the Victorious Sunni Family (Jaysh Ahel al-Sunnah al-Munasera): Operated across central and southern Iraq attacking Shiite Muslim gatherings and people. Attacks on the Shiite community included abductions and bombings at funerals.

Brigades of the Victorious Lions of Allah: Started operations around September 2004 when they announced the abduction of Fairuz Yamulky, a Canadian of Iraqi descent working for a German company. She escaped unharmed from her captors. This group also may have abducted Egyptian diplomat Mohamed Mamdouh Qutb. Only one major combat action was attributed to this cell, a barrage of rockets on a military base in Habbaniyah in 2004. This group most likely merged with another larger insurgent group such as the Ansar al-Islam or Islamic Army in Iraq.

Army of the Victorious Sect (Jaysh al-Tai'efa al-Mansoura): A group associated with the Ansar al-Sunnah that started operations in June 2003. Conducts small indirect weapons fire and light infantry operations in central Iraq, including Baghdad. Fired mortars at the palace convention center during first meeting of new Iraqi government. In late 2005, they threatened the Iraqi Sunni Party that supported participation in the election and constitution. It was led by a figure with the cover name al-Haj Uthman al-Iraqi.

Islamic Movement of Mujahideen in Iraq: A small group that performed IED and light infantry weapons attacks in western Anbar Province. Abducted and executed Italian national Salvatore Santoro (Figure 8.4) after he had run over an insurgent with his car at a roadblock near Ramadi. The group released video and photos of his execution.

Jihadist Earthquake/The Victor Salah al-Din Battalions (Kata'ib al-Zilzal al-Mujahidah): A small group that has carried out assassination operations in Ramadi. Issued threats by leaflet.

National Islamic Resistance, Battalions of the 1920 Revolution (Brigades); Islamic Resistance Movement in Iraq (Harakat al-Muqawamah al-Islamiyya fi Iraq (HAMAS-IZ)): Founded on July 12, 2003, this was one of the larger of the original nationalist resistance groups that cooperated fully and may be subordinate to the Ansar al-Sunnah. They often coordinated communications

FIGURE 8.4   Islamic Movement of Iraqi Mujahideen terrorists execute Italian hostage Salvatore Santoro.

with the Islamic Front, the Army of Mohammed, and occasionally al-Qaeda in Iraq. They carried out a wide range of operations with the exception of suicide attacks in Baghdad, Kirkuk, Bayji, Ramadi, and Khalidiyah. IED and rocket attacks are a specialty. Maintained the National Islamic Operations Center in Fallujah during the 2004 invasion. In April 2007 the group carried out a surprising change of name and called themselves Islamic Resistance Movement in Iraq, or HAMAS in Iraq. It is not known if they had any ties with the Palestinian HAMAS movement or merely feel this name better characterizes their transformation. Subordinate battalions included:

- Mohammed Sheet Khatab Battalion
- Jafar al-Tiyar Battalion (Abu Ghraieb)

- Abdullah bin Bakr Battalion (al Sharqiyah)
- Sheik Ala Salam Ibn Tamiya al-Salafiya Battalion

Squadrons of the Swords of the Righteous: A small group that claimed responsibility for the abduction of four U.S. peace activists from the Christian Peacemaker Teams off a Baghdad street in December 2005. This group had never before been seen in operations, and it may have been a cover name for the abduction cell belonging to the AAI, the Islamic Army in Iraq, or freelance cash criminal abductors.

Salafi Jihad Brigade: This cell first announced itself in a July 23, 2003 video on Al Jazeera. Allegedly run by Harbi Khudair Hamudi, a former Iraqi Air Force brigadier general. He was captured along with his deputy, Fares Younis, by Iraqi army forces in Mosul.

MEDIA AND COMMUNIQUÉS

Many of these small groups cooperated fully in training, logistics, and combat operations with the large insurgency groups of the AAS, AQI, FRL Unified Mujahideen Command's Army of Mohammed, and Islamic Army in Iraq, among others.[69] For all of the insurgents' combat skill, their best competence was in being extremely media savvy. By November 2003, the Iraqi insurgents started making videotapes and broadcasting their claims of success on sympathetic websites such as www.albasrah. net. Videos of their attacks spread like wildfire once they realized that they would receive a showing almost in their entirety by Arab media organizations such as Al Jazeera, Al Arabiyah, and MBC of Lebanon. In addition to claims of successful attacks, the insurgents even used their media platoons to deny massacres they perpetrated but which were not popular. In one unique example, al-Qaeda in Iraq and others denied attacking a bus station in Baghdad:

> We, al-Qa'idah in Iraq, the Army of Muhammad, the Army of the Ansar al-Sunnah, the Army of the Mujahideen, the Brigades of the Victor Salah ad-Din, and a group of other fighting organizations, declare that we were not responsible for the bombing attack that killed a large number of Muslims. We affirm that we had no part in it in any way whatsoever. We are continuing our jihad against the occupation wherever it might be on every inch of the land of Iraq and the land of the Muslims.[70]

On April 12, 2005, several terrorist groups, including AQI, the AAS, the main FRL group, the First Army of Muhammad, and their independent insurgent cells, the Brigades of the 1920 Revolution, the Brigades of the Victorious Salah ad-Din, the Salafist Brigades of Abu Bakr, the Salafist Brigades of ar-Rahman, and the Islamic Anger Brigades, sent out a joint communiqué demanding that U.S. forces stop an offensive on the city of Al Qa'im in western Iraq. Though their message was designed to generate sympathy for the Sunni population by demanding food and water to come in, it also bolstered their claim that they, as the Mujahideen, had concern for the Arab citizens, while U.S. forces were allegedly destroying the city. The strength of their communiqués and a fully functioning formal intergroup communications system evidence the belief that many of these groups would join AQI/ISIS over the next five years. The Mujahideen refer to themselves as Knights, Lions, Horsemen, Companions (of the Prophet), and Holy Warriors. The wide net of the groups involved in jointly agreeing to the message reveals the operational and political integration of these forces arrayed against the coalition at the time. The larger groups have consistent presence on the Internet. The AAS and Islamic Army in Iraq maintain websites that published their daily litany of attacks, manifestos, attack videos, and photographs. The IAI had a web magazine *Al Fursan* ("The Horseman"), and a multitude of communiqués and videos are hosted on sympathetic Arabic and English language websites. Almost all groups used leaflets threatening punishment on collaborators, posters espousing their position on Islamic law, and CDs with their beheading videos, and give favored journalists advanced access to special operations.

ENDNOTES

1. Neil MacFarquhar, Rising Tide of Islamic Militants See Iraq as Ultimate Battlefield, *New York Times*, August 13, 2003.
2. Jonathan Schanzer, Ansar al-Islam: Back in Iraq, *Middle East Quarterly*, Winter 2004, retrieved May 15, 2005, from http://www.meforum.org/article/579.
3. Dr. Hani al-Siba'i, Ansar al-Islam, Ansar al-Sunnah Army, Abu Musab al-Zarqawi, and Abu Hafs Brigade, Al Basrah Net, Foreign Broadcast Information Service, March 14, 2004.
4. Ibid.
5. Ibid.
6. Schanzer.
7. Catherine Taylor, Taliban-Style Group Grows in Iraq, *Christian Science Monitor*, March 15, 2002, Sec. World, 2.
8. Thanassis Cambanis, For Extremist Group in Iraq, Rise and Rapid Descent, *Boston Globe*, November 7, 2004, Sec. 1, 25.

9. Human Rights Watch, retrieved from http://www.hrw.org/back-grounder/mena/ansarbk020503.htm#Armed%20Islamist%20 groups%20in%20Iraqi%20Kurdistan.

10. Cambanis, For Extremist Group in Iraq.

11. Ibid.

12. Taylor.

13. Al-Siba'i.

14. Schanzer.

15. Ibid.

16. Ibid.

17. Ibid.

18. Colin Powell, Speech before the UN, retrieved from http://www. state.gov/secretary/former/powell/remarks/2003/17300.htm.

19. Jeffrey Fleishman, Displaced Militants Adapt, Widen Their Scope, *Los Angeles Times*, January 28, 2005, Sec. A, 5.

20. Human Rights Watch.

21. In her article, Catherine Taylor cites PUK commander Mustapha Saed Qada.

22. Retrieved from http://news.bbc.co.uk/1/hi.world/middle_east/351 5525.stm.

23. Reuters, Turks Foil NATO Summit Bomb Plot, *The Australian*, May 4, 2004, Sec. World, 8.

24. James Gordon Meek, Bush Cited Terror Group for Iraqi Invasion, *Daily News*, December 22, 2004, Sec. News, 4.

25. Taylor.

26. Scott Peterson, Iraqi Funds, Training Fuel Islamic Terror Group, *Christian Science Monitor*, April 2, 2002, Sec. World, 1.

27. Jack Fairweather, Saddam's Top Aide "Organizes Fightback," *Daily Telegraph* (London), October 31, 2003, 17.

28. Gareth Smyth, Ansar Wages War on "Heretical" Iraq, *Financial Times* (London), January 20, 2005, Sec. Middle East, 10.

29. Edward Wong, Attacks by Militant Groups Rise in Mosul, *New York Times*, February 22, 2005, Sec. A, 9.

30. Taylor.

31. Ibid.

32. Thanassis Cambanis, Along Border, Kurds Say, Iran Gives Boost to Uprising, *Boston Globe*, November 7, 2004, Sec. A, 1.

33. Ibid.

34. Ibid.

35. Scott Peterson, The Rise and Fall of Ansar al-Islam, *Christian Science Monitor*, October 16, 2003, Sec. World, 12.

36. Smyth.

37. Schanzer.

38. Peterson, The Rise and Fall of Ansar al-Islam.

39. Ibid.
40. Ibid.
41. Schanzer.
42. Some speculate that the group reorganized itself as Ansar al-Sunna. This is described in further detail below.
43. Wong.
44. Jeffrey Fleishman, The Conflict in Iraq, *Los Angeles Times*, January 28, 2005. Once again, this coincides with what some experts believe is the group's reorganization under the name Ansar al-Sunna.
45. The mess hall bombing was actually claimed by Ansar al-Sunna, an Ansar al-Islam offshoot that may or may not be the same organization under a new name.
46. Dan Murphy, "Kurdish Sept. 11" Boosts Resolve, *Christian Science Monitor*, February 5, 2004, Sec. World, 6.
47. Eric Eckholm, Sunni Group Says It Killed Cleric's Aid in Bombing, *New York Times*, January 15, 2005, Sec. 1, 6.
48. Times Wire Reports, 2 Iraqis Convicted of Raising Funds for Rebels, *Los Angeles Times*, May 13, 2005, Sec. A, 11.
49. Craig Whitlock, In Europe, New Force for Recruiting Radicals, *Washington Post Foreign Service*, February 18, 2005, Sec. A, 1.
50. Ibid.
51. Reuters, Fourth Man Arrested in Suspected Plot against Iraqi Leader, *New York Times*, December 5, 2004, Sec. 1, 22.
52. Whitlock.
53. Ibid.
54. ABC News, Iraq's Ansar al-Sunna Army Gains Clout, ABC News, December 27, 2004, online.
55. Ahmed al-Masri, Ansar al-Sunna Army's First Video, WhyWar.com, February 21, 2004.
56. Al-Siba'i.
57. Fleishman, The Conflict in Iraq.
58. Ibid.
59. James Gordon Meek, Bush Cited Terror Group for Iraq Invasion, *Daily News*, December 22, 2004, 4.
60. ABC News.
61. Iraqi Resistance Reports, November 28, 2005, http://www.albasrah.net/en_articles_2005/1105/iraqiresistancereport_281105.htm.
62. Fleishman, The Conflict in Iraq.
63. Ibid.
64. Iraqi Resistance Reports, November 28, 2005.
65. Ibid.
66. Ibid.
67. Ibid.

68. Ellen Knickmeyer, Copter Downed in Iraq; 11 killed, April 22, 2005, http://www.boston.com/news/world/middleeast/articles/   2005/04/22/copter_downed_iraq_11_killed/

69. Islamic Resistance Reports, September 7, 2005, http://www.albas-rah.net/en_articles_2005/0905/iraqiresistancereport_070905.htm.

70. Iraqi Resistance Reports, August 18, 2005, http://www.albasrah.net/en_articles_2005/0805/iraqiresistancereport_190805.htm.

CHAPTER 9

Al-Qaeda and the Foreign Terrorists in Iraq

> The confrontation that we are calling for with the
> apostate regimes does not know Socratic debates
> ... Platonic ideals ... nor Aristotelian diplomacy.
> But it knows the dialogue of bullets, the ideals of
> assassination, bombing, and destruction, and the
> diplomacy of the cannon and machine-gun.
>
> —Al-Qaeda's *Encyclopedia of the Jihad*

On March 18, 2003 Osama bin Laden received his greatest wish. America gave him a clear field of jihad with pan-Arab Islamist extremist support, numerous targets that were generally restricted to highways, and a trove of near unlimited weapons of all shapes, sizes, and explosive yield. More than that, he had highly skilled allies in the form of the Saddam Fedayeen that quickly saw the advantage of an alliance with him to drive the United States out of a historic Arab land. He named his organization al-Qaeda Fi Balad al-Rafidayn, "al-Qaeda in the Land of the Two Rivers," or what would become more commonly known as al-Qaeda in Iraq (AQI). For the United States, it would mark the beginning of a multiyear struggle with a third wing of insurgents that was not foreseen before the war and who would prove more brutal, vicious, and determined than the former regime loyalists. If the U.S. forces felt plagued by the Iraqi intelligence-supported Saddam Fedayeen, then al-Qaeda, through its original feeder organization Tawhid Wal-Jihad, was determined to strike precise political death blows to American resolve. Like most aspects of the invasion, U.S. war planners had given al-Qaeda short shrift in believing that all the few hundred members of the Ansar al-Islam (AAI) were in fact the principal al-Qaeda franchise. U.S. Central Command planners were eager to strike a decisive blow. Once the invasion was launched, AAI would be dealt with in short order. Pentagon planners believed that the AAI (which was al-Qaeda in their estimation) would be crushed in a matter of hours. Despite the exaggerated prewar rhetoric that the U.S. forces invaded Iraq to fight Iraq's direct support of al-Qaeda, it was, in fact, the invasion of Iraq that gave al-Qaeda its greatest hope. America had inadvertently given every Islamic extremist in the world a clear battleground. After the invasion of Afghanistan, even bin Laden had not predicted that he would be handed such a gift. America was committing the act of aggression against Arab lands that he had always claimed. Once the invasion appeared inevitable, bin Laden put into operation the machinery to capitalize on his greatest chance to recreate an armed resistance operation similar to the one he had helped design in the 1980s against the Soviets in Afghanistan. Al-Qaeda would run to the aid of the Iraqis, and the Mujahideen would have two missions: (1) kill Americans and (2) call the Iraqi Sunni to Allah and bring them from false Ba'athist nationalism to the Salafist interpretation of Islam. Simply put, the Iraqi insurgency has advanced al-Qaeda's global impact 10-fold, and the ramifications of this new base will resonate throughout the Middle East for years. Michael Scheuer, former head of the CIA's al-Qaeda unit and author of the book *Imperial Hubris*, has said that the greatest gift that George W. Bush could have presented to Osama bin Laden was an invasion of Iraq. With the invasion, al-Qaeda moved from the fringes of Southwest Asia and into the heart of the Arab world.

ARRIVAL OF THE "GHOST"

The shadows of Iraq's insurgency—decentralized networks, hidden weapons caches, safe houses, quick face-to-face meetings, and the wailing screams of those wounded in an indiscriminate bombing attack— were the realm of Abu Musab al-Zarqawi, the phantom menace of U.S. forces in Iraq (Figure 9.1). "The stories about him are almost likes he's a ghost," reported one U.S general.[1] So mysterious was the man that for over a year, U.S. intelligence operated on the false assumption that he had only one leg (the result of what U.S. officials called a "disinformation campaign"). Al-Zarqawi relied on face-to-face meetings and couriers to avoid America's high-tech tracking systems;[2] according to one account, he discarded the SIM card of a cell phone after only a single use.[3] "I move like a tourist in Iraq," he taunted his American pursuers after loosening his fiery arsenal in a string of bombings during the summer of 2004. "I move along the country staying with my family and brothers."[4] Al-Zarqawi and the groups he has created and nurtured, Tawhid Wal-Jihad, AQI, and the ISIS are the next evolution in terror. Before the war, al-Zarqawi was a local menace, a fringe terrorist too radical for even bin Laden, but desperate to lead an al-Qaeda region. While he lived,

FIGURE 9.1   Abu Musab al-Zarqawi (born Ahmad Fadhil al-Khalayla), commander of Tawhid Wal-Jihad and al-Qaeda in Iraq until his death in 2006. (From U.S. DoD.)

al-Zarqawi rivaled bin Laden in terms of American obsession and gave rise to its bloodiest reputation—beheading. Al-Zarqawi survived by only existing in the shadows, but his presence and, more importantly, his attacks were all too palpable.

THE FIRST COMMANDER OF AQI—ABU MUSAB AL-ZARQAWI (AKA ABU MUS'AB AL-ZARQAWI, AHMAD FADHIL AL-KHALAYLA, AHMAD FADEEL AL-NAZAL AL-KHALAYLEH)

Al-Zarqawi was born on October 20, 1966, in Zarqa, Jordan. He died on June 8, 2006, in Baqouba, Iraq.

As his name indicates, al-Zarqawi was born in the Jordanian industrial city of Zarqa, just northeast of Amman, as Ahmed Fadhil Nazzar Khalayleh. By all accounts, he had a troubled and stormy childhood, dropping out of high school and into back-alley drunken brawls. In the late 1980s, al-Zarqawi joined a mosque and was introduced to Salafism, the stringent form of Islam that seeks a return to the faith practiced in the century following the death of the Prophet Mohammed. Inspired by these new beliefs, al-Zarqawi made his way to Afghanistan eager for his first jihad against the Soviet Union. He was too late for the fighting but just in time to receive training under the tutelage of the newly created al-Qaeda. Al-Zarqawi's first attempted terrorist attack was a debacle; in 1994 he was arrested while trying to smuggle explosives into the West Bank. His first terrorist group, Jund al-Sham, was disbanded. While in prison, al-Zarqawi devoted himself to memorizing the Qu'ran and terrorizing his fellow inmates by becoming the cellblock's leading enforcer; his Jordanian prison was a microcosm of the jihad he would later wage against Americans and Shiites in Iraq. Youseff Rababa'a, a fellow inmate, recalls that "they [al-Zarqawi and his followers] were all bearded, they all wore the same Afghan clothes, and shared the same thinking. He stayed in the background, but the members of the group would do nothing without his approval.... Either you were with them or against them. There was no gray area."[5] Another fellow inmate agreed: "I was an apostate for them. They have no grey. You have to be white completely. They put very difficult conditions."[6]

Difficult conditions indeed. Al-Zarqawi emerged from prison, pardoned under a general amnesty offered by King Abdullah in 1999, more determined than ever to achieve his primary goal: the destruction of the Jordanian monarchy and the punishment of the "Jews and crusaders" who help them. Al-Zarqawi was now "a leader; he [was] strong, straight to the point, with a very strong personality."[7] He put these traits to work very quickly, reassembling his old group, Jund al-Sham, and planning to bomb the Radisson SAS hotel in Amman and several tourist sites in Jordan in what came to be called the millennium plot.[8] In late 2001 Jund al-Sham assassinated American diplomat Alex Foley in Jordan, a crime for which al-Zarqawi was subsequently convicted in absentia. Though fixated on Israel and Jordan, the 2003 invasion of Iraq gave al-Zarqawi the opportunity for a new jihad against U.S. forces and their "collaborators." Al-Zarqawi's former deputy, Abu Anas al-Shami, reported that the group's main goal in Iraq was to create a theocratic state modeled on the Taliban.[9] Still, this was primarily a tactical shift. Shadi Abdullah, an al-Zarqawi disciple arrested in Germany, told his interrogators that the organization's main goal remained the overthrow of the Jordanian monarchy, and at new recruits must be either Jordanian or Palestinian.[10] Unfortunately, for U.S. forces, the occupation of Iraq inspired al-Zarqawi to put these goals aside, at least temporarily, and to concentrate on the task of driving the American infidels out of the Middle East. He called upon the resources of al-Qaeda for this task.

In early 2003, then U.S. Secretary of State Colin Powell announced the previously unknown al-Zarqawi to the world, arguing that al-Zarqawi was the key link in the chain forging an unholy alliance between Saddam Hussein and al-Qaeda:

When our coalition ousted the Taliban, the Zarqawi network helped establish another poison and explosive training center camp, and this camp is located in northeastern Iraq.... Those helping to run this camp are Zarqawi lieutenants operating in northern Kurdish areas outside Saddam Hussein's controlled Iraq. However, Baghdad has an agent in the most senior levels of the radical organization that controls this corner of Iraq. In 2000, this agent offered al-Qaeda safe haven in the region.[11]

Powell may have overstated al-Zarqawi's influence in al-Qaeda, but he missed completely in his allegations of al-Qaeda's historical ties to Saddam Hussein. Al-Zarqawi's group did grow from Iraqi resources (but principally in the post-invasion) and did join formally with al-Qaeda, but he was never sponsored by Saddam Hussein until a few weeks before the invasion. These ties only became stronger when he joined AQI with the former regime loyalist (FRL) insurgents. In the prewar al-Zarqawi had intimate connections with Iraqis, but only with Sunni Kurds and other terrorist cadres throughout the Middle East.

For months following the invasion, al-Zarqawi and his followers operated their headquarters out of the central Iraq city of Fallujah. After several half-hearted attempts to subdue the Islamic and Fedayeen groups there in April and June 2004, the United States finally carried out Operation Phantom Fury and decisively invaded the city that November. Not surprisingly, al-Zarqawi escaped each attack. Al-Zarqawi's organization was not hurt by the loss of its headquarters in Fallujah. Senior intelligence officials told the *Washington Post* that al-Zarqawi "has an apparatus and organization that goes beyond the cells in Fallujah ... and is trying to build a network and infrastructure that is nationwide."[12] The word *trying* lends a touch of optimism that was not warranted. By June 2004, al-Zarqawi had succeeded in creating a series of regional commands that have integrated most, if not all, the foreign resistance fighters into one unified command under al-Qaeda's banner. Almost immediately after the seizure of Fallujah, al-Zarqawi launched a series of demonstration attacks against Iraqi military units across northern Iraq. His intent was to demonstrate the group's hardy constitution—if the Americans disrupted his operations in one sector, he moved to catch the Americans off guard in another. In one attack, three buses carrying 49 unarmed soldiers were ambushed by an AQI cell. Brig. Gen. Salih Sarhan, an Iraqi defense ministry official, said the soldiers were "ordered from their buses by men in police uniforms, told to lie down on the ground, and then shot in the back of the head."[13]

AQI became the most dangerous terrorists in Iraq because they were the most ideologically unfettered. Al-Zarqawi had no problem killing civilians he saw "collaborating" with the American-backed Iraqi government. Again, former prison associate in Jordan and Islamic scholar

Youssef Rababa'a remembers debating with al-Zarqawi about the meaning of the al-Anfal, a passage in the Qu'ran that is clear in its meaning
but which Salafist terrorists often corrupt as justification in allowing
attacks on civilians. Rababa'a argued that the al-Anfal meant that the
combatants should be killed, not just anyone affiliated with them.

> I used to say to him that it [the al-Anfal] meant we should kill the fight-
> ers, occupiers, and oppressors, not just anyone affiliated with them.
> So fighting the Soviets in Afghanistan was good, but killing civilians
> was unacceptable. But he [al-Zarqawi] said we should just kill anyone
> affiliated with Islam's enemies. He was simple in this way—he didn't
> want a deeper understanding.[14]

Al-Zarqawi perceived a need to convince the entire world Sunni
community to aid the Iraqi Sunni, not just in stopping the occupation,
but to impede the growth of what he saw as an apostate religion: Shiite
Islam. He openly expressed his disdain for the Shiites, though they make
up 65% of the Iraqi population. Through his ruthless attacks on the
Shiite community, he created the basis for a broader civil war. He foresaw sectarian violence as important in embroiling the Americans, but
also to tie up the military resources of the Kurds and Shiites that would
oppose a Sunni emergence. In a letter, allegedly written by al-Zarqawi
to Osama bin Laden in the summer of 2003, he called the Americans the
"biggest cowards that God has created," and then went on to say that
the way to beat the Americans was to "bring the Shia into the battle. It is
the only way to prolong the duration of the fight between the infidels and
us. If we succeed in dragging them into a sectarian war, this will awaken
the sleepy Sunnis who are fearful of destruction and death."[15]

Coupled with this religious intolerance was a profound hatred for
democracy. Al-Zarqawi espoused only the most orthodox form of religious obedience. To him political matters were settled with the Qu'ran,
and then the gun if the decision to use any authority but the Qu'ran was
offered. In a statement broadcast just before the January 2005 elections,
al-Zarqawi proclaimed, "We have declared a fierce war on this principle
of democracy and those who follow this wrong ideology. Anyone who
tried to set up this system is a part of it."[16] Additionally, the use of Iraqi
national guard troops made up of Shiite and Kurdish Peshmerga militiamen (who are Sunni Muslims) stung al-Zarqawi deeply and he declared
open war on them as well. Days before the Iraqi elections, he released
the following statement:

> The battle of Fallujah removed the ugly mask of the damned "Rafidha,"
> whose hatred (for Sunnis) was manifested in this battle.... They par-
> ticipated in the military campaign for the battle against Fallujah with
> the blessing of the imam of infidelity and apostasy. They played a big

role in the massacre, the looting, the sabotage and the spilling of innocent blood among children, women and the elderly.[17]

Al-Zarqawi delighted in referring to the Shiite as Rafidha, a derog-
atory religious term that means "apostate," or a turncoat to Islam.
Believing that Shiites are apostates, their slaughter was not only
encouraged but legal.

Al-Zarqawi's cells have staged some of the most spectacular terrorist attacks in Iraq. Suicide bombings, car bombings, and ambushes—
AQI's terrorist repertoire is as vast as its appetite for destruction.
Al-Zarqawi was also able to wage an incredibly effective media campaign alongside the larger struggle. Most infamous of all was the May
2004 videotaped beheading of American Nicholas Berg, supposedly
at al-Zarqawi's own hand. This effectiveness of such terror, however,
came at a price: many groups felt alienated by al-Zarqawi's indiscriminate murder of civilians. "Zarqawi made a lot of mistakes. When
you've got a country with ... that level of freedom—he sets off a (car
bomb) killing fellow Muslims and Iraqis in the streets, he's not helping his case. It is angering Iraqis, and that is to a degree helping us
in what we're trying to do over there," said Gen. Lance Smith. In the
competitive world of terrorism, al-Zarqawi's media savvy temporarily
backfired. According to one Iraq official, "the others are fed up with
Zarqawi. He's getting all the publicity, and their own cause has been
obscured by his fanatic cause."[18]

Al-Zarqawi had indeed obscured much of the complexities in Iraq;
his high media profile did lead American commanders and policy makers to concentrate on him at the expense of other terrorist organizations. "My message to Zarqawi," said President Bush, "is you cannot
drive us out of Iraq by your brutality."[19] Donald Rumsfeld compared
al-Zarqawi to Hitler. "They try to destroy things they could never
build and they try to kill people they could never persuade. History
teaches us that this kind of evil, over time, fails."[20] Nevertheless, turning al-Zarqawi into a bogeyman did not hurt the insurgency. In fact,
claims about what al-Zarqawi accomplished or was able to accomplish may well have been exaggerated for the sake of perpetuating an
enemy the American public could latch on to. American emphasis on
AQI has not made them any less effective, but it gave other terrorist
organizations more freedom to maneuver. "I do not think that anyone
in Europe and the Middle East honestly believes that he is responsible
for everything the United States says he has done in Iraq," argued
one European security official. "The guy is on the run. He is hiding from U.S. forces, and he is probably changing houses every night.
It would be almost impossible for him to calmly plan and execute
the operation all over Iraq that some people believe he has done."[21]

According to PUK security chief Dana Ahmed Majid, "these people like to remain anonymous. If everyone is looking for al-Zarqawi, they have more room to operate."[22] That in turn created a situation where the American coalition often turned away from effectively dealing with the Iraqi insurgents, who make up between 95 and 97% of all attackers, to pacify the political turbulence that this small band of terrorists produced.

Within the ranks of Tawhid Wal-Jihad, one member even noted in a letter to al-Zarqawi captured by the coalition, "The most important thing, Sheik, is your existence is a thorn in the mouth of the Americans as well as the traitors." Al-Zarqawi's death, when it came, was not the silver bullet the United States was hoping—the insurgency he had helped to lead was too broad, too determined, and too well-armed for that to happen. "Just like Osama," argues terrorism expert Rohan Gunaratna, "if you were to kill him [al-Zarqawi] today, it wouldn't make a difference at all to these networks he's helped create. While much of the suicide bombing in Iraq is coordinated by his network, it's being driven from the bottom up. Regional and local operational leaders plan and execute the attacks. Al-Zarqawi probably doesn't know much about them ahead of time and doesn't need to."[23] The U.S. Army realized that al-Zarqawi was but one element in a much larger insurgency, yet it was the political and military blindness to nearly everything but attacks from al-Qaeda in Iraq, now called the Islamic State of Iraq and Syria, that gave his extremely small network the respect and credibility that still make it a force believed to be all but invincible.

AQI STRATEGIC ORGANIZATION

Al-Qaeda in Iraq and its newest iteration, Islamic State of Iraq and Syria (ISIS), remain organized along the lines of traditional al-Qaeda (AQ) franchise groups, but with special compartmentation for the difficult combat environment in Iraq. Osama bin Laden, even after his death in 2011, set the ideology that still guides AQI/ISIS on a strategic level, but until fall 2003 this was not the case.

In 2003 Abu Musab al-Zarqawi was affiliated with al-Qaeda, but not run or controlled by them. During the first few months of the insurgency, al-Zarqawi used associates and intermediaries from his days in Afghanistan and managed to reestablish contact with al-Qaeda's supreme leadership hiding along the Pakistan-Afghanistan border. First, he felt he had to prove himself worthy of leading a regional jihad. Four months after the invasion, al-Zarqawi's group unleashed a series of devastating strikes against Western interests in Iraq. He had two purposes:

to humiliate the American effort and win acceptance and admiration for creating the "new jihad" in Iraq.

By July 2003, al-Zarqawi was in direct communication with bin Laden. He wrote in a letter to al-Qaeda's number two officer, Dr. Ayman al-Zawahiri, that TWJ was seeking to be officially designated al-Qaeda in Iraq. In the message he described a new terrorist force to fight the Americans directly assembled under his command. He wanted to impress bin Laden and prove that his jihad in Iraq was the real "field of jihad." With Osama's blessing, al-Zarqawi's terrorist force was poised to become the heart of a newly invigorated al-Qaeda, which could again extend global reach and strike the Americans with impunity. To ensure this, Abu Musab al-Zarqawi had done his homework. Well before the invasion of Iraq, al-Zarqawi organized TWJ into a covert commando force using the best information and techniques developed by al-Qaeda and modeled on the underground, independent command system of his new allies, the Saddam Fedayeen and the FRL intelligence agencies. For the 3 months preceding the war, TWJ prepared infiltration routes, safe houses, training bases, and ammunition caches throughout western Iraq. TWJ recruited the hundreds of foreign fighters abandoned by the regime at the fall of Baghdad.

The inaugural operation of his jihad came when TWJ carried off the first major suicide car bomb attack since the end of major combat. Delivered on the 100-day anniversary of the occupation, a suicide bomber drove his suicide vehicle-borne improvised explosive device (S-VBIED) into the Jordanian embassy gates, blowing it up and killing 19. Early speculation attempted to directly link al-Zarqawi to bin Laden, but most senior administration officials, including Ambassador L. Paul Bremer, considered the Kurdish Ansar al-Islam as the perpetrators. Al-Zarqawi was mistakenly believed to be a dangerous hanger-on to Mullah Krekar's Ansar al-Islam, which was considered to be directly run by al-Qaeda. These assessments were wildly off the mark, as al-Zarqawi had created an organization much larger than Ansar al-Islam in less than 6 months.

Never forgetting his animosity to the Jordanian monarchy that put him in prison, al-Zarqawi's attack also sent a reminder to King Abdullah that the Americans could not protect them in Iraq. His past attacks, including the murder of U.S. aid worker Lawrence Foley in Amman and the failed millennium plot to blow up the SAS Radisson Hotel in 1999 would pale in comparison to what he had planned for the American occupation.

AL-ZARQAWI VS. BIN LADEN: AQI'S
STRATEGY AND GOALS

In the August 2003 letter to the al-Qaeda second-in-command, Egyptian Dr. Ayman al-Zawahiri, al-Zarqawi directly requested al-Qaeda's strategic assistance in Iraq. Al-Qaeda's senior leadership managed to establish the flow of manpower, money, and support to the AQI.

Even al-Qaeda was stunned by the rapid rise of the insurgent movement in Iraq. "The resistance happened faster than we expected, and differently, so we were not prepared to direct it," an al-Qaeda operative is reported to have explained to the Taliban.[24] Consequently, bin Laden dispatched envoys to evaluate the situation. In most accounts, bin Laden tried to push al-Zarqawi aside to make room for a more palatable leader for the insurgency. Most reports indicate that al-Zarqawi was widely disliked during his brief sojourn to Afghanistan. CNN terrorism analyst Peter Bergen said, "It's significant that Zarqawi [in 2001] set up his own camp in Herat in western Afghanistan, because it was hundreds of miles away from bin Laden's camps in southern and eastern Afghanistan."[25] In the end, however, the envoy told bin Laden, "There is no doubt that he [al-Zarqawi] is the best man to lead foreign and Iraqi insurgents in Iraq. He deserves our support."[26] Despite reciprocal misgivings, the two terrorist leaders pledged their support for one another in October 2004: "We announce that Tawhid and Jihad, its princes and soldiers, have pledged allegiance to the leader of the mujahedin, Osama bin Laden."[27] Bin Laden's first directive was a push to broaden the organization while stimulating grassroots activism on the part of Iraqis: "My greatest wish is for you to keep the resistance alive and growing, to increase the number of local insurgents and give the Iraqis more decision making powers."[28]

In this declaration, both al-Zarqawi and bin Laden saw a greater opportunity to expand the resistance into a multiyear jihad that would work against U.S. vulnerabilities. The two forces had combined to create a closer, far more lethal enemy for the Americans than the Taliban in Afghanistan. Al-Qaeda senior leadership would provide strategic direction, media savvy, and inspiration. On an operational level, bin Laden sent word down that AQ theater commanders in Europe, the Arabian Peninsula, and North Africa should start the flow of the two critical items al-Zarqawi needed most in Iraq: manpower and talent. Cash was not a great concern. Money was to be used to facilitate the travel of men to Iraq. An informal network of Salafist mosques and fraternal groups took the men in and got them to Syria or brought them up from Saudi Arabia. Large-scale money collection was no longer a top priority for al-Qaeda, as most franchise groups transitioned after 9/11 to become self-sustaining and relied less on centralized funds transmitted from Afghanistan or the Arabian Peninsula. Large transactions of even a few thousand dollars could bring the authorities down on a group, so money was dispersed in numerous small transactions of a few hundred dollars. Most operational money was hand carried by the suicide bomber volunteers or sent through the informal Hawala banking system. Additionally, the pro-Saddam loyalists had hundreds of millions of dollars, and attacks were being paid for by their financiers. The amounts required for this jihad would be limited to moving men to the staging ground in Syria and small incidental expenses in Iraq from time to time. The financing of the Iraq operation was fed through the active supporters of the resistance and a cash flow that came in from Salafist charities, individual donors, and mosques all over the world. The individual amounts were so small that they could hardly be noticed or distinguished from the billions of other immigrant transactions, but collectively they represented a large pool of resources to sustain the combat operations against the Americans.

Al-Zarqawi's relationship with al-Qaeda seemed as amorphous as the terrorist organizations themselves. Bruce Hoffman, an analyst at the RAND Corporation, believed that "bin Laden wants to leverage off of Zarqawi's cachet and popularity amongst radical jihadists. Al-Zarqawi realizes that his association with al-Qaeda and bin Laden—perhaps not in tangible terms in the fighting in Iraq—but in terms of support and assistance can pay off vast dividends."[29] In other words, the relationship was roughly symbiotic—like two parasites feeding off one another. In another formulation, Dr. Rohan Gunaratuna believed that "Zarqawi's become the de facto operational chief of the al-Qaeda network. Osama is thinking at the strategic level, and Zarqawi is operating at the tactical level."[30] Jordanian intelligence officials were blunter: "[Al-Zarqawi] was and is the leading figure of al-Qaeda in Iraq. He is now the head of the pyramid of terrorism in Iraq, and he does have the ability and psychology to replace bin Laden."[31]

Whatever the case, there were signs that the relationship started under the strain of conflicting goals: bin Laden's principal goal was to expel the United States from the Middle East, and al-Zarqawi's was to topple the Jordanian monarchy. When al-Zarqawi was running Jordanian operations of his first terror group, the Soldiers of Islam (Jund al-Islam), he often saw AQ's goals as incompatible with his. In an account published in the *Washington Post* and based on German wiretaps, al-Zarqawi grew angry with members of his organization in the fall of 2001 for raising money for al-Qaeda. "If something should come from their side, simply do not accept it. Just forget it!" he ordered.[32] Al-Zarqawi had reportedly had a particularly icy relationship with al-Qaeda's chief ideologue, Ayman al-Zawahiri. Gen. Hamidou Laanigri, head of the Moroccan Security Service, told a French newspaper:

"Zarqawi is an operative that has never agreed with Zawahiri, the ideologue behind al-Qaeda."[33] Shadi Abdullah, an al-Zarqawi associate arrested in Germany, confirmed many of these hypotheses during his interrogation. "This is a very important document," said Bruce Hoffman, referring to a summary of the interrogations provided to the *Christian Science Monitor.* "It confirms that [al-Zarqawi] competes with Osama bin Laden and sees himself as somewhat of an emulator, or even a successor in the Muslim world."[34]

That may have been so at the time, but since the invasion of Iraq, bin Laden's goals have emerged as the strategic political plan that both agreed they must stick to in order to reach the revenge-motivated goals of al-Zarqawi. Al-Zarqawi was also far more radical—he lived jihad for the sake of jihad and was a less strategically focused terrorist than bin Laden, but a far more ruthless enemy. Al-Zarqawi viewed anyone, the innocent, the old and infirm, and children, even Shiite Muslims, as enemies to be destroyed; bin Laden, though a Sunni, was more conciliatory, yet still believes that the murder of women and children is allowed if the enemy is struck for the greater goal. These differences were less of an obstacle than most observers would hope. The thinking among many in the intelligence community was that al-Zarqawi and bin Laden, declarations to the contrary notwithstanding, worked in parallel rather than in an active partnership.[35] History of the insurgency has proven this assessment wrong in many ways. Both bin Laden and al-Zarqawi, it is now agreed, not only worked in concert, but also supported each other's goals. If there was a disagreement, the elevation of al-Zarqawi to amir of the Mujahideen in Iraq tempered those with a clearly visible leader for the entire AQ organization (Figure 9.2).

AL-QAEDA STRATEGY FOR THE USE OF TERRORISM

AQI tactical violence in Iraq has several strategic objectives:

Exact a high American or Iraqi body count: Between 2003 and 2011 the sole goal of the AQI operative on the streets of Iraq was to kill as many Americans soldiers as possible until death. Equally as important was to kill Iraqis, Sunnis, or Shiites who cooperated with Americans or the Shiite government. This tactical objective has strategic depth to it. For the first 8 years this strategy was designed to attack the consciousness of the American public. The death of an unacceptable number of Americans did shift the political center of gravity within America and created the strategic political pressure necessary to ensure the conditions necessary to force a withdrawal. In the

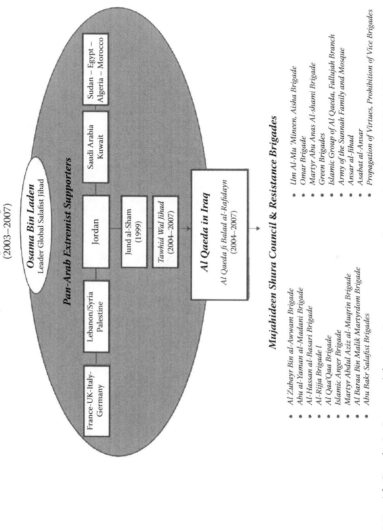

FIGURE 9.2 Al-Qaeda in Iraq and foreign insurgent group's organization, 2003–2007.

end, this in fact worked despite the loss of the Sunni insurgents. "The struggle with America has to be carefully managed, the 'Electric Shock Method' must be applied, relentless shocks that haunt the Americans all the time, everywhere, without giving them a break to regain balance or power."[36]

Seize territory and establish an Islamic caliphate: Once the American forces were withdrawn, then the religious war on the Shiites and indoctrination of the Sunni was carried out under the banner of the victorious al-Qaeda forces. A new Islamic caliphate would be established in the Sunni region, and from there they would fight to spread the Salafist brand of Islam to other countries and regions of Iraq. This strategy bore fruit only after the Syrian revolution brought new men, weapons, and inspiration to the Iraqi insurgency. Assisted by Shiite Prime Minister Nouri al-Maliki's inflaming the Sunni insurgents, ISIS launched an offensive in 2014 that seized much of the Sunni govenorates with the expressed goal of establishing a caliphate.

Inspire new jihadists: The continuation of the long war for the spread of the Salafist caliphate would require new young men inspired by the bravery of the Mujahideen who were killed in the Iraq jihad. The call went out worldwide on Islamic fundamentalist websites for men to come and join the jihad. One al-Qaeda supporter called for assistance in August 2003 in this message, which was broadcast on Al Arabiyah television: "O Muslims, wherever you are, prepare yourselves for jihad (holy war) and come to Iraq and Saudi Arabia." Even with the loss of American forces to attack, the jihadists view Shiite Muslims as Rafidha or religious apostates and make attacking them anywhere as critical to inspiring new recruits.

TACTICAL OBJECTIVES OF AQI CELLS

The tactical strategy of al-Qaeda in Iraq, that is, the street-level objectives of the terrorists in the field who are actually conducting the attack, is simple and exactly like that of the other insurgent groups, including those of the Ba'ath Party:

Strike, strike, and restrike and kill the enemy: The principal tactical goal of all al-Qaeda operatives is to kill the American soldiers and their allies, including innocent Iraqis, or die trying. This does not mean that the AQ operatives are suicidal; some are, and they are selected for that specific role, but the majority of the AQ Mujahideen are expected to fight long and hard to

further the goal of killing the enemy and achieve personal martyrdom when the time comes. The AQ Mujahideen are indoctri-
nated to believe that their time for death is selected by God and
that nothing can be done to stop that time, so unless they have
been specifically selected for a martyrdom operation, they must
live to fight another day. This fatalism allows their operatives
to practice sound tactical operations and stealthy movement,
but still violently confront their enemy with surprising ferocity,
recklessness, and courage. Of note is that when they are cor-
nered, they will fight to the death or destroy themselves and their
enemies with a suicide device or IED. Numerous operations in
Fallujah, Tel Afar, Ramadi, and Qaim have shown that the goal
of dying while killing the enemy is a mental force multiplier for
the AQ Mujahideen.

AQI attacks have the principal intent to destroy the enemies
they have designated as a threat to their way of Islam. The
American invasion gave them an opportunity to slowly destroy
the military forces of the occupation force. The attacks on the
Iraqi armed forces and infrastructure are necessary to ensure
a viable instability to meet their goal of inspiring and establishing a Sunni caliphate, even if in just northwest Iraq, in the
post-American withdrawal period. On June 24, 2004, AQI's
western, central, and northern regional commands launched a
series of wide-ranging attacks in one 24-hour period unnoticed
to all but the coalition forces. AQI intended to send a message
to the Americans that they had arrived and were ready to fully
engage in the war. No less than six major S-VBIED attacks were
launched on Iraqi and American positions in Mosul, Baqubah,
Ramadi, and Baghdad. A large-scale commando raid killed over
90 people in Baghdad. They struck hard and threw what was a
semipeaceful Iraq into turmoil, but it was just a test run.

Look for revenge and reciprocity opportunities: The Iraqi insurgents seek to carry out very distinct revenge and reciprocity
operations. Most notably, they have the ability and planning to
effect swift and spectacular operations quickly after major political and military successes of the coalition. In their claims, they
make sure that revenge is clearly spelled out for a specific slight
to Islam or in the name of the Iraqi people. The 2006 rape and
murder of an Iraqi teenager and the massacre of her family by
U.S. Army soldiers resulted in an AQI abduction of two U.S. soldiers. They were decapitated, eviscerated, and horribly mutilated
in revenge for the massacre. AQI released video of their execution
and desecration along with a statement that they had carried out
a blood-cleansing action to avenge the dead child and her family.

Seek to cause intimidation and overreaction: The attacks that the insurgents carry out on the Iraqi police and military forces are designed to show that the forces left in place after an American occupation are powerless to stop them. These attacks are "designed to transmit fear to the population through empathy with the victims of the attack so they would bend to the will of the terrorist group in the future."[37] Overreaction attacks are designed to ensure that a government overreacts and oppresses its own people. Such overreaction may be projected through curtailment of certain basic freedoms of individuals, or the limiting of basic human rights, or through action that may be seen as more horrific than those of the terrorists.

Tactical Goals of AQI Cells

- **Emphasize highly planned and effective action:** The AQI cells or teams were selected and trained to carry out *specific* combat operations with the intent to kill coalition soldiers, particularly American soldiers. The members of the cells knew that the coalition forces were large and of unmatched lethality collectively. Second chances were rarely granted to the unskilled and unprepared; therefore, precision was the hallmark of all al-Qaeda operations. Tactical attacks of the AQI cells were minutely designed to show that the terrorists were capable of carrying out the operation as planned, on time, and with concentrated firepower.
- **Video spectacular violence to inspire new recruits:** Providing the material to meet the strategic goal of inspiring new recruits to the anti-American jihad was critical to al-Qaeda operations. So successful were the videos of operations in Chechnya, the anti-Soviet Afghanistan war, and the 9/11 attacks that AQ units had dedicated teams to video document the effects of the suicide car bomb and massed infantry assaults. The objective was to draw the attention of the young men who saw their operatives as secret heroes fighting the great evil (Figure 9.3). Unfortunately, this goal was often met by beheading of hostages, indiscriminate suicide bombings in crowded areas, or dramatic acts such as the multiple bombings of a single venue. The news media or a dedicated videographer's presence was critical to this goal.
- **Die, escape, or restrike:** Although surviving an operation was not as critical to the al-Qaeda operative as assumed, it was necessary that some cadres survive to provide intelligence, lessons learned, and take best wishes and inspirational material to the other cells. Most al-Qaeda operations on the street level had

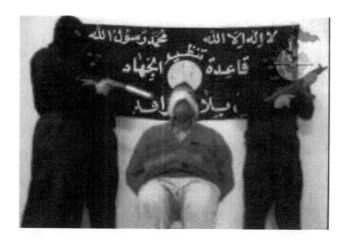

FIGURE 9.3   Al-Qaeda in Iraq executes a captured Iraqi Ministry of the Interior officer.

exact withdrawal plans, despite leaving suicidal units in place to hold down any forces chasing them. This ability for a martyrdom-driven organization to survive and redeploy for striking the enemy again and again was a sign of impressive institutional understanding of the strategic goals of the organization.

AQI IN-COUNTRY ORGANIZATION

Descriptions of the AQI organization were almost as difficult to find as the group itself. While at first this seems problematic, this might be just the point. Until November 2004, al-Qaeda in Iraq appeared to operate as an umbrella organization, a puppeteer staging a drama amidst the chaos and anger of Iraq. This drama quickly devolved into tragedy. Many smaller groups of foreign fighters, including the White Banners, Islamic Jihad Brigades, Islamic Armed Group of al-Qaeda, Fallujah branch, Muslim Youth, Black Banners, Green Brigades, and even cells of the Tawhid Wal-Jihad itself (such as the Armed Vanguards of the Second Mohammed Army), were independent agencies when they started. AQI pulled them all together into a combined foreign and Iraqi wing of the insurgency. "The bottom line," says Matthew Levitt, an analyst at the Washington Institute for Near East Policy, "is that the threat today is not so much from well-defined groups you can put in a pretty little box or flow chart. That's the nature of these things. There are connections and overlaps."[38] Others point to the fanatic loyalty of al-Zarqawi's followers as evidence of a more centralized organization in the insurgency. The foreign fighters that came into AQI showed a dedication unmatched by other groups. An Iraqi insurgent with knowledge of the organization told reporters at *Time* magazine, "There are only two ways you leave that organization. You die in battle or they kill you."[39] While it is highly unlikely that AQI kills its own personnel, their history shows that those who do wish to leave the jihad have a way out. They leave due to wounds, stress, or go home to do recruitment and organizing. Al-Qaeda has shown that they do remove wounded and the unfit from the battlefield, when they can, to fight again or go home to inspire new Mujahideen.

Like other Salafist organizations, until his death, Abu Musab al-Zarqawi was the overall prince of the holy warriors (Amir al-Mujahideen) and had several regional commanders who held the same title. His successor was Abu Hamza al-Muhajir (aka Abu Ayyub al-Masri), a former Egyptian Islamic jihad follower and student of Dr. Ayman al-Zawahiri. He was said to have been the coordinator for all jihad volunteer operations from Europe and the Middle East before assuming the executive officer position for al-Zarqawi.

When necessary, the two amirs would hold face-to-face meetings, dispatch commands through messengers and e-mails, and provide their deputies with specific directions for AQI attacks. Unlike al-Qaeda and Ansar al-Islam, AQI is believed to be a streamlined military organization with only the necessary deputies in the most critical functions. The organization maintains two deputies who act as primary aides to the amir. One acts as an operations officer, and the other as a chief administrator of the organization. The amir had four major departments under his authority (Figure 9.4).

AQI COMMAND STAFF AND LEADERSHIP GROUP (C&L)—IRAQ/SYRIA

The command and leadership group is led by a senior commander. It was led by Abu Mussab al-Zarqawi (2003–2005) and Abu Hamza al-Muhajir (aka Abbu Ayuub al-Masri) (2005–2010). Its ISIS organization can be found in Chapter 14.

The amir generally has two deputies who have operational roles within the organization. The historical al-Qaeda model is to ensure that the deputy has a series of reliable lieutenants who can assume the role of the deputy in case he is killed or captured. This has proven true in Iraq following al-Zarqawi's death, as well as those of several operational officers; they have all been killed or captured with no apparent impact on their operations. The inner circle of the C&L group is extremely loyal and was originally composed mainly of foreigners. This has led some to

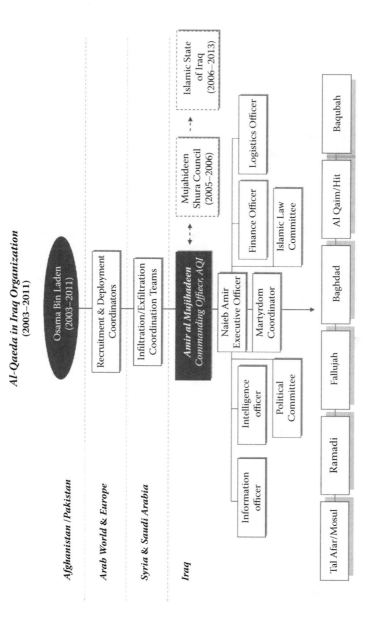

FIGURE 9.4   Al-Qaeda in Iraq theater and regional operations organization chart.

estimate that the group's numbers were quite small. An Egyptian fundamentalist leader told reporters that the organization was probably one of the smallest in Iraq, especially when compared to organizations like Ansar al-Sunnah.[40] Even when its senior leaders are killed or captured, however, the organization continues to operate effectively in Iraq. In testimony before Congress, former CIA director George Tenet reported that American attacks had "transformed the organization into a loose collection of regional networks" that "pick their own targets, they plan their own attacks."[41]

AQI logistics officer: The supply and financing of the operation was directly run under the amir. This role was fulfilled by an operative called Abu Samad before he was killed by U.S. Forces in Fallujah. Each regional organization was led by a subamir for logistics who organizes and arms the overt and covert aspects of the terrorist missions of the organization. Abu Samad, for example, was also tasked with receiving "support and guidance from Saudi Arabian extremist financiers and was believed to have been a major link for supporting terrorist activity between al-Qaeda in Iraq in Baghdad and the Western Euphrates River Valley."[42]

AQI manpower/martyrdom facilitator: The security committee was the internal security and covert communications management team within the organization. It provided pathways to communicate and dispatch weapons and equipment. It also performed internal police and executive protection duties, including security vetting visitors and new recruits.

AQI information officer: The media arm of AQI was called al-Furqan. They collected the various digital video and images from the cells operating in the field and produce high-quality propaganda videos for viral distribution over the Internet to supporters. These videos are highly popular in the jihadist movement and purport to show the real jihad and urge volunteers to come fight. Many videos reveal the tactics the AQI uses in S-VBIED attacks and the names and biographies of many of the suicide volunteers. The organization also produces press releases, arranges interviews, and processes videotapes taken in the field by the military.

Military commanders: AQI was loosely broken down into regional commands and numerous subcommands as the security situation dictates. Each regional commander is designated as an Amir al-Mujahideen ("Prince of Holy Warriors") or Amir al-Muqatilat ("Prince of the Fighters").

TACTICAL ORGANIZATION

Each amir selected deputies to conduct recruiting and personnel place-ment in the combat cells, initial and advanced combat training, and provides for the logistics. Al-Qaeda combat cells operated in groups no bigger than 10 to 20 men and, like all insurgent groups, met or com-municated only with trusted men who they knew personally or had been vouched for by the organization.

Amirs operated with complete impunity to plan and carry out activi-ties in their area of responsibility. The amir also organized his forces for the missions and intensity of security in his region. Large-scale waves of S-VBIEDs were most likely planned in the designated region, but the vehicles themselves were delivered by cooperating insurgent groups. Each amir was given control of forces that he would organize and arm. Weapons come from the large caches that AQI collected during the inva-sion, weapons captured on the battlefield, and those purchased on the open arms market.

LOGISTICS AND SAFE HOUSES

Al-Qaeda had a sophisticated covert organization of safe houses and its own personnel links established immediately before the invasion by al-Zarqawi, who worked in league with the Saddam Fedayeen, the Iraqi Intelligence Service, and Ansar al-Islam. Collecting the tools of the ter-rorist trade was critical to his mission as well. Though given weapons by the Saddam Fedayeen before the war, his terrorists spent the months after the fall of the regime culling and organizing a massive arsenal of weapons they had collected from Saddam's forces. Al-Zarqawi ordered that the Fedayeen and Al Quds army positions be stripped of thousands of AK-47 rifles, RPG launchers, mortar rounds, artillery shells, and bat-tlefield rockets. Not pausing after the invasion ended, Tawhid Wal-Jihad cadres constantly taught each terrorist operative the basics of assembling and detonating IEDs, firing mortars, and ambushing logistics convoys with AK-47 rifles and RPGs. Everyone was expected to live up to the fight. Combat drills for each type of attack were rehearsed and immedi-ately put to test on the roads of Iraq. Logistics teams met the weapons middlemen who proliferated after the war—nouveau riche arms mer-chants and former keepers of the keys to Saddam's Special Republican Guard arsenal, who sold whatever they had to anyone who wanted them. From these brokers they purchased or were directed to where they could find tons of the most lethal high explosives on the planet. TWJ managed to find even the highly volatile high explosive RDX. This explosive had been under UN control at the Al Qaqaa' weapons storage facility, but soon after the invasion, American army forces had abandoned this depot and moved on to another mission. Unguarded, it was stripped bare and sold on the terrorist market in Iraq. This RDX may have found its way into suicide attacks in both Iraq and later Jordan in 2005. Thousands of artillery shells and aerial bombs from unguarded army and air force weapons depots were taken without risk by TWJ bomb masters and trucked into secret weapons caches throughout western Iraq. TWJ set up multiple primary, secondary, and tertiary weapons storage locations. Each was given a fighting load of weapons and bombs and placed in dozens of locations capable of supporting one cell. If one was lost by American operations and treachery, as many as five or six additional ones were ready with bullets, explosives, and bombs. When TWJ transformed into AQI, all the combat logistics of smaller groups folded into this division.

AQI WEAPONS

Suicide car bomb: the al-Qaeda weapon of choice: The principal weapon of the AQI was the human-guided weapon platform, in the form of either a suicide car bomb designated as S-VBIED or a man with a bomb strapped to his body, known as a suicide pedestrian-borne improvised explosive device (S-PBIED). The AQI arsenal included the near exclusively used S-VBIEDs and S-PBIEDs in its direct attacks on American forces in Iraq. This use of precise, human-guided attacks to kill dozens or hundreds instead of the daily grind of roadside IEDs and small-scale ambushes admittedly killed less American soldiers but caught the global headlines.

Small arms and light infantry weapons: Every member of the jihad has a rifle assigned to him or her in addition to other weapons in which he or she may specialize (Figure 9.5). The standard weapon of AQI is the AK-47 assault rifle with its 30-round magazine. Heavier-volume weapons, including the RPD light machine gun, the heavy belt-fed PKM machine gun, and the near universal RPG-7 launcher, supplement each cell. The RPG-7 is a deadly weapon, as it thrusts a high explosive antitank warhead into its target accurately at ranges up to 500 ms. It is often used in combination with all of the small arms listed above and gives a wide range of deadly fire that is usually concentrated on people and light vehicles like the Humvee jeep. Al-Qaeda in Iraq often claimed small arms raids and attacks in their communiqués that begin with "O Allah! Make our shots hit their

FIGURE 9.5 Al-Qaeda used specialized silenced pistols provided by the former Regional Intelligence Agencies. The author holds a SSO Beretta M9 pistol with silencer captured from an AQI "Knights of the Silencers" assassination squad.

intended targets and fasten our feet firmly to the ground. Praise be to Allah, peace and prayer be upon our prophet, his family, and his companions."[43]

Indirect fire weapons: When fighting with more conventional weapons in dense urban areas like Fallujah and striking enemy forces at a distance, the al-Qaeda in Iraq use weapons that do not follow a direct flight path to their targets and are usually set on a ballistic arc and explode when they hit the ground or a target. The main weapons used by al-Qaeda when harassing enemies are the 60 and 82 mm mortars. These infantry weapons are fired from a tube that lofts the explosive shells great distances, up to 3 miles.

Roadside IED: The IED is a reliable killer and every insurgent group used it to strike the mobile U.S. forces on the highways and roads of Iraq. However, al-Qaeda in Iraq does not employ IEDs as the principal weapon of their fight. They use IEDs as a smaller tool in the toolbox—a stepping-stone weapon to bigger S-VBIED/S-PBIED attacks. Many operatives are introduced to combat operations by learning and engaging in IED usage. Most are triggered by a remote detonation device such as car door openers, garage door openers, cell phones, radios, and even remote control toy transmitters. These weapons are generally made up of 122 or 155 mm artillery shells, which have such explosive force that they can vaporize an unarmored vehicle, devastate a heavily armored vehicle, severely damage armored fighting vehicles, or disable a 60-ton tank. When the explosive force of one device is not considered enough, AQI is also a user of the daisy chain IED. For AQI members, this makes for good video propaganda.

AQI TACTICS IN IRAQ

Like the Ansar al-Islam, AQI had sought out many of the foreign religious extremists operating with different groups within Iraq and honed them into a highly sophisticated machine that apparently can operate in many parts of Iraq without drawing attention to themselves. AQI had manpower with expertise in a broad range of terrorist operations—but unlike the ex-Ba'athist Unified Mujahideen Command, al-Qaeda decided early on to focus on effecting singularly spectacular attacks.

Direct Martyrdom Attacks

AQI and its associated Islamic extremist supporters are masters of the direct martyrdom (suicide) attack. In this fashion, they drive a car bomb into the target and explode on impact. There are several variations of this attack that AQ has used worldwide, particularly in Saudi Arabia, where the defenses are extremely dense.

S-VBIED or S-PBIED breaching attack: The breaching attack is designed to gain access to the target behind those defenses by creating openings with a martyr-equipped bomb. They use two or more bombers or vehicles to pierce the defenses by exploding themselves against the walls, and then the second vehicle enters through the breach and crashes into the principal attack. AQI carried out this type of attack first against the Italian detachment of the coalition forces in Naseriyah, where they drove a fuel truck into the building that was then detonated by an explosives-laden sedan that then rammed the truck. Both vehicles exploded and killed 29 Carabinieri and army troops. In both 2004 and 2005 insurgent forces had three S-VBIEDs fail in breaching the gates of a military base in Qaim. The largest of them was a stolen fire truck made into a massive car bomb. In November 2005, AQI used three car bombs again for a spectacular breaching attack on the Ishtar Sheraton and Palestine Hotel complex. The first blew up near a police station a few blocks away from the Palestine Hotel to divert the attention of the U.S. forces assigned for security, and then a truck drove in at high speed and blew up against the defensive walls of the hotel. This created a large breach in the 21-foot-high "Texas barriers." Finally, a cement mixer filled with high explosive came through the hole, drove between the hotels, and exploded, killing 20 and injuring 42. Interestingly, the timing and direction of the attacks were all done so that they would be caught on the cameras of the global media lodging at the Palestine Hotel.

Kidnapping/abduction for video execution: When al-Qaeda in Iraq kidnapped and beheaded American citizen Nicholas Berg in 2004, it became the symbol of the brutality and seriousness of their mission. AQI led the way in beheading its hostages, and afterwards many other Islamic extremist groups quickly followed suit. The decapitation of its victims and holding them up in symbolism of its power is the icon of the AQI. One of the former commanders in Fallujah who returned to lead al-Qaeda on the Arabian Peninsula, Abdul Aziz al-Muqrin, published a "how to" guide on abduction in an online al-Qaeda web magazine, *Mu'askar al-Battar*, in which he defined it as "the arrest of one or more people from the opponents' side," and it is designed to:

1. Force the government or opponent to fulfill a specific set of demands.
2. Create a difficult situation for a government in its relations with the countries where the kidnapped persons come from.
3. Obtain important information from the hostages.

4. Obtain ransom money—as, for example, our brothers in the Philippines, Chechnya, and Algeria made happen and as our brothers in "Mohammed's Army" in Kashmir did when they obtained $2 million in ransom. This money can then serve as financial support for an organization.
5. To draw attention to a specific concern—as occurred at the start of the Chechnya question or in Algeria, when our brothers hijacked a French plane.[44]

Al-Muqrin also recommended organizing properly into appropriate abduction cells:

- *Early reconnaissance group.* They inform the kidnappers about the movements of the target, for example if it has already reached the requisite location.
- *Protection group.* They organize the protection of the kidnappers from all outside dangers.
- *Kidnapping group.* They transport the hostages and transfer them to the group that is responsible for security.
- *Take-down group.* Its responsibility is to take down possible pursuers or defend the kidnappings from outsiders who seek to expose them.[45]

Multidimension infantry raids. AQI, like its Saddam Fedayeen allies, occasionally carried out large-scale symbolic infantry raids designed to kill every target in the area or gain a symbolic target. In April 2005, Abu Ghraib prison was attacked by 40 to 50 members of several combined al-Qaeda terrorist cells who joined to storm the prison and free the inmates. Highly reminiscent of the Vietcong guerrillas' storming of the American embassy in Saigon, the AQI attack included terrorists storming with massed infantry, a heavy rocket, and mortar fire, as well as three suicide car bombs that slammed into the gates of the base. The attack was defeated without any penetration of the base. Ten insurgents were confirmed killed by al-Qaeda; however, more than 60 American soldiers were wounded in the attack. This attack was meant almost strictly for propaganda purposes, but it surprised U.S. forces as to the depth and intensity of the massed al-Qaeda attack. In 2005, al-Qaeda called these massed raids and simultaneous multiple light weapons attacks truthful dawn expeditions.

Close-combat martyrdom defense: AQI prefers precision offensive attacks based on highly detailed planning. Yet when combat comes to them in the form of American combat sweeps like Operation Al Fajr in Fallujah, the forces withdraw, but always leave a small suicidal combat group to cover the withdrawal.

These light infantry forces generally fight ferociously unto death. One team boarded themselves under the floor of the residence and shot U.S. Marines through the floorboards as they searched.

House razing ambush: An AQI house-borne IED (HBIED) tactic used several times in Fallujah was to rig a residence with artillery shells or explosives and tip coalition forces off to a terror "suspect." When U.S. forces would raid, the Mujahideen would blow the entire house up and raze it on the heads of the American unit. AQI reprised this tactic against Iraqi Army officers in 2011.

FOREIGN MUJAHIDEEN GROUPS IN IRAQ

By January 2005, over 325 suspected foreign fighters were captured, most of them in fighting in Fallujah, Tal Afar, and Mosul. At the time, this number may have been as little as 5% of the entire foreign force. These units had various cover names, but all fell under the main force structure of al-Qaeda in Iraq. After the withdrawal from Fallujah in December 2004, AQI and other Salafist groups formed a Mujahideen Shura Council (MSC) (Majlis al-Shura al-Mujahideen). This was formed as a consultative board to coordinate and de-conflict the cells operating under the AQI umbrella. Additionally, many AQI communiqués were issued by this council. Many small extremist groups that were on this council also announced their formation or allegiance to al-Qaeda in March or April 2005, indicating they may have taken part in a reorganization conference to reallocate AQI assets in Iraq under a new Majlis structure designed to share resources and operations areas. AQI reporting in early 2006 indicates that al-Qaeda in Iraq had formed a new Majlis al-Mujahideen, or Mujahideen advisory committee, similar to the one that was provisionally assembled after Fallujah in 2004. This council offered a one-stop coordination and consultation board for each of the cells. By 2011 virtually all of these groups would fall under the umbrella of AQI/ISI and join ISIS in 2013.

Foreign Mujahideen Groups and Cells in Iraq

Al-Zubayr bin al-Awwam Brigade: This subcell of AQI was named after one of the companions of the Prophet Mohammed's closest associates, Talhal Ibn Ubaydullah, and a second generation "companion of the prophet." Both were killed in treachery at the "Battle of the Camel" outside of Basrah in 656 AD (36 AH). This cell operated in the Abu Graib–Fallujah region and claimed to have shot down a U.S. helicopter near Abu Ghraib in August 2004. It was led by an unidentified insurgent from south-central Iraq with the name of Abu Zubaydah al-Babeli. This cell joined AQI on September 26, 2005.

Abu al-Yaman al-Madani Brigade: An AQI group that was formed in March 2005 with the announcement that they were "devoted to obedience in good times and in bad times. We won't quit, we are marching in the way of jihad and we will not stop fighting until Allah's shari'a prevails on all countries and peoples." They have claimed to have carried out numerous small arms attacks on Iraqi police and government targets. They were said to be led by Abu Mohammed al-Iraqi.[46]

Al-Hassan al-Basari Brigade: Named after the famed imam of Basra and companion of the prophet, this brigade conducted operations in the vicinity of Basra, the second largest Iraqi city. It claimed operations against Iraqi police patrols, the British army units, and the assassination of an Iraqi journalist as an apostate. It is believed to have been led by an Iraqi named Abu Huzaifah al-Iraqi. This brigade was eliminated from the nearly exclusive Shiite city with three major Shiite militias (Badr Brigade, Mahdi Army, and Hizb al-Dawa') between 2005 and 2007. This group was thought to have been operating from the Sunni community of Abu Khasib before it was ethnically cleansed by Shiites. It is possible three sophisticated explosively formed projectile IEDs (EFP-IEDs) used to attack U.S. security contractors in 2005 and 2006 were laid by this group.

Al-Rijjal Brigades: Named after the righteous "men" of distinction (al-Rijjal) who were the companions of the prophet. This may also refer to modern-day "companions," such as Sheik Azzam and Osama bin Laden. They announced their allegiance to al-Qaeda in Iraq on April 13, 2005, in a statement that read, "In response to Allah's commands to stay united and after our Shaykh Abu Musab al-Zarqawi swore an oath to our Shaykh Abu Abdullah Usama bin Laden—May Allah protect them, bless their jihad and aid them in their search for justice—those of us in the Rijjal Brigade (including the units of Al-Khattab, Zalzala, Abu Basir, Al-Qaqa, Al-Hamidoon, and Al-Farooq) have pledged allegiance to Al Qaida's Committee [in Mesopotamia]."[47] The statement was signed by Abu Abdullah al-Qurashi, commander of the cell.

Al-Qaa'Qaa Brigades (QQB): A subunit of the al-Rijjal brigades that carried out the abduction, execution, and decapitation of Turkish truck driver Ramadan Elbu in October 2004. They released a video of the execution, warning "We warn all those who cooperate with the occupying Crusaders to repent and return to the faith or else blame only themselves for their fate, which is death." They also claimed credit for the dual S-PBIED bombings of the Green Zone café and the "Haji-mart" inside the highly guarded Republican Palace complex that same month that killed five, including three American security contractors. They generally conduct small arms and mortar attacks as well in Diyala Province near Baqubah (al-Kazimiyah, al-A'zim, Baqubah, Behruz, al-Khalis). They claimed one anti-air attack on a U.S. Army Chinook, but this was never confirmed. The QQB operated the Abi Sufian al-Zaidi squad, which performed a barracks raid in 2005. The QQB merged with al-Qaeda in Iraq in the spring of 2005.

Islamic Anger Brigades: An umbrella group with several sub-cells operating throughout Iraq. Claimed to have abducted 15 Lebanese contractors working for the coalition, killing 1. The group and its subcells have performed S-VBIED attacks, abductions, and assassinations. Reportedly led by an Iraqi named Abu Jundul al-Iraqi. The group has three known associated subcells that support suicide bombing and abductions, including the abduction of American Aban Elias. All of the below named cells are believed to have been merged with al-Qaeda in Iraq:

- Khalid bin al-Walid Brigade
- Abu Bakr al-Siddiq Brigade
- Omar Ibn al-Khatab Brigade
- Abu al-Walid al-Ansari Unit

Martyr Abdul Aziz al-Muqrin Brigade: Named after the former commander of the al-Qaeda of the Arabian Peninsula (AQ-AP) and possible commander of a foreign fighter group in Fallujah. Al-Muqrin is believed to have been the executioner who decapitated American hostage Paul Johnson. The late al-Muqrin was an Afghan-Arab who fought the Soviet occupation. He was alleged to have traveled to Iraq for operational experience before returning to his native city of Riyadh. He was killed by Saudi security forces in 2004 and a cell was named in his honor.

Al-Baraa bin Malik Martyrdom Brigade: This cell is named after a companion of the Prophet Mohammed who was from a Yemeni tribe who died fighting against the Persians. They performed a number of S-VBIED attacks on coalition and Iraqi forces and may operate one of the few dedicated suicide bomber cells. Additionally, they claimed abductions of six Jordanians and Australian engineer Douglas Wood. Wood was later rescued by Iraqi forces.

Um al-Mu'mineen, Aisha Brigade: Named after Aisha, "Mother of the Faithful" and the Prophet Mohammed's second wife, this is a relatively new cell that carried out IED attacks on American convoys.

Omar Brigades: Named after Abdullah Ibn Omar, a companion of the Prophet Mohammed and a renowned scholar. They operated in Diyala Province near Baqubah and claimed its anti-Shiite assassination team, the Khalid bin al-Walid Squad, killed numerous members of the Shiite Badr Brigade and Mahdi Militia.

Martyr Abu Anas al-Shami Brigade: This is a unique organization of al-Qaeda in Iraq as it was an external support group in Saudi Arabia and Syria. Named after the al-Zarqawi deputy who was killed in action in 2004. This cell threatened operations in Saudi Arabia and Syria against Shiites for their support of the U.S. occupation. This cell also claimed credit for an attack on the American consulate in Jeddah in 2004 and may have been a feeder group for al-Qaeda of the Arabian Peninsula.

Green Brigades: A small Salafist group that folded into AQI. It operated near central Fallujah, and was responsible for the roadside checkpoint abduction of four Italian security contractors. They killed one hostage and released the rest after a ransom was paid by the Italian government.

Islamic Group of al-Qaeda, Fallujah branch: One of the earliest Salafist cells that originated in Iraq either before or just after the invasion. This group made its first claim of combat action in July 2003. They made taped statements to Al Arabiyah television asserting that it was the Islamic resistance, not the former regime loyalists, who were carrying out operations on the American forces in Fallujah. They warned, "The coming days ... will show you the strike that will break America's back. We pray to God for victory, and for him to help our brothers spread in all the Iraqi provinces and in the world, like [Osama] bin Laden and [leader of Afghanistan's former Taliban government] Mullah Omar."[48] The speaker identified himself as a possible Saudi militant called Abdur Rahman al-Najdi. U.S. officials are believed to have identified him as a propagandist for al-Qaeda whose real name was Sa'd Muhammad Mubarak al-Jubayri al-Shahri with the aliases of Abu Anas al-Tabuki, Osman, and Abu Uthman. Initially situated within Fallujah, the branch was assessed to have folded into Tawhid Wal-Jihad by September 2004. Al-Najdi accurately assessed the state of the coming insurgency when he stated, "We expected that the government in Iraq will resist for three to six months within which time mujahedeen (holy warriors) from the entire world would have reached Iraq. But the government fell earlier than our expectations."[49]

Army of the Sunni Family and the Mosque (Jaish Ahlu al-Sunnah Wal Jam'ah): Involved in fighting the Shiite Mahdi Army in late 2005 alongside al-Qaeda in Iraq. Carried out combat actions in the vicinity of Samarra. Was founded and led by Abu Bak ral-Baghdadi. In 2010 he would become the fourth and joint commander of AQI and the first amir of ISIS.[50]

Partisans of the Jihad (Ansar al-Jihad): A small group operating in the vicinity of Baghdad and Fallujah. Claimed responsibility for the abduction of the 75-year-old cousin and his daughter-in-law of interim Prime Minister Ayad Allawi. They were later released. This group also claimed to have had a French branch of followers who appear to engage in low-level vandalism and claimed the destruction of a Paris synagogue.

Asbat al-Ansar (League of the Followers/Partisans' League): A small terrorist group from Lebanon composed primarily of Palestinians associated with al-Qaeda. According to the Department of State's "Pattern of Global Terrorism" report, Asabat members "follow an extremist interpretation of Islam that justifies violence against civilian targets to achieve political ends. Some of those goals include overthrowing the Lebanese government and thwarting perceived anti-Islamic and pro-Western influences in the country." The leader of this Lebanese group headquartered out of the Ayn Hilwah refugees camp is Abu Muhjin. Muhjin communicated with Abu Musab al-Zarqawi and sent Asabat Mujahideen to Iraq in 2004. Four Asabat Mujahideen were killed by coalition forces during fighting in the city of Qaim in 2005. The cell members killed included the cell commander Saleh Shayeb (aka Abu Muaz al-Shami), Ahmed Yassin (aka Abu Haroun al-Maqdisi), the second-in-command and interim commander of the Karabila region, Nidal Mustafa, and Mohammed al-Kurdi.

Squads of the Army of the Companions (of the Prophet Mohammed) (Jama'at Jund al-Sahaba): A series of platoon-sized subcells of the Ansar al-Sunnah. Operated within Mosul and vowed vengeance against Shiite Iraqis for death squad killings. Believed to have merged with AQI.

Rashideen Army: Iraqi-based insurgent group operating in the Baghdad, Fallujah, Latifiyah, and Yusifiyah areas. They carry out basic insurgent operations, including attacking U.S. Army tank and infantry units with IEDs, weapons ambushes, as well as sniper, mortar, and improvised rocket attacks. This group claimed to have shot down an AH-64 Apache Longbow helicopter in 2006. Subunits include the Maath bin Jabal Brigade, Khalid bin Walid Brigade, and a Tabuk missile brigade (improvised battlefield rockets).

Battalions of the Army of the Conqueror (Kata'ib al-Jaysh al-Fatiheen): A group originally associated with Ansar al-Sunnah and a member of the Shura Council of the Mujahideen. A press statement claimed this unit merged with AQI in March 2005 and operated in Anbar Province with major attacks mounted near Ramadi, Samarrah, and Mosul. Carried out light infantry weapons operations against American forces and the Iraqi army. This group joined AQI in October 2006 as part of the new Islamic State of Iraq (ISI).

TRANSITING SYRIA, 2003–2011: THE EXPRESSWAY TO THE JIHAD

Within a year of the occupation, several smaller foreign fighter groups that were fighting the Americans independently came under the AQI flag. A sophisticated infiltration plan was laid down by the Syrian intelligence and former regime loyalists to ensure their flow into western Iraq. Terror volunteers came by this path from Germany, France, England, and other Western Europe countries, and Egypt, Morocco, Algeria, Saudi Arabia, and other Arab nations. Routes from France were said to cross Italy, Cyprus, and Lebanon and end in Damascus, Syria. Anyone wishing to join the jihad had only to show up with a recommendation of a known Salafist imam and pass a rigorous security screening. Critical to this mission were the jihadist way stations, residences, and safe houses of trusted agents who facilitated the step-by-step movements of the Mujahideen from collection points in Beirut, Lebanon, and Damascus, Syria. From there the jihadists would be transported to the Iraqi border near Qaim and infiltrate on foot or in small groups by car. The commander of the U.S. Central Command stated in an interview with CNN, "It seems to be pretty well established that they tend to cross over from Syria, although we know that there have been some infiltrations from the Saudi border, there have been some from the Iranian border."[51] Many of the jihadists receive their basic training in the vast Syrian-Iraq border area. Small camps appeared, designed to give a team of recruits the chance to learn how to use the AK-47 rifle, the RPG rocket launchers, and basic explosives, and IED assembly training. Operational security was stressed throughout, and once deployed over the border, they were dispersed to jihadist way stations and eventually to a group that needed the manpower. According to a *Times of London* report, "The most popular route into Iraq seems to be down the Euphrates valley from the border town of al-Qaim, through Haditha, Hit, Ramadi, Fallujah, and into Baghdad. A second supply line runs from the north through Tal Afar to Mosul."[52]

PROFILE OF AQI OPERATIVES AND FOREIGN FIGHTERS IN IRAQ

The typical jihadists from AQI were a collection of pan-Arab men and a few women who had left their homes with the specific goal of making their way to Iraq, fighting American forces, and if God wills it, losing their lives in the process. Most fighters were Arabs between 18 and 40 years old and almost exclusively male. They came from all walks of life and include many Iraqis. They believed fervently the teachings of Osama bin Laden and committed themselves to dying for the cause.

SAUDI OPERATIVES

Al-Qaeda has been operating in Saudi Arabia since near the beginning of the organization's formation in 1988. Al-Qaeda in Saudi Arabia (also known as al-Qaeda of the Arabian Peninsula (AQ-AP)) maintained a low profile and devoted themselves to working quietly within the structure of Saudi society before striking out. A few precision attacks have been suspected of being AQ-AP in origin, but scant evidence has come to be conclusive. These include the November 1995 bombings of the Saudi national guard headquarters and the VBIED bombing of the U.S. Air Force Khobar Towers in Dhahran, Saudi Arabia, in 1996. However, the invasion of Iraq gave new meaning to their mission. The jihad had moved from within their own borders to an adjacent country. It offered them an opportunity to gain combat experience and make new brothers in a very unpopular action by the Americans. The Americans seemed to recognize this unpopularity and accepted the Saudi demand to close their major operations center in Riyadh and to move to Doha, Qatar. The invasion became a magnet for young Saudis lusting for a chance to prove themselves as defenders of the faith. Saudi writer Mshari al-Thaydi said, "Those who cannot do jihad in Saudi Arabia go to Iraq.... The goals are the same, the ideology is the same and the modus operandi is the same."[53] The Saudis, who can go to Syria without a visa enter the same jihadist pipeline as other foreign fighters or attempt to cross through the barren Saudi frontier with truck convoys through Arar and Taif.[54]

Iraqis in AQI

Although the al-Qaeda organization was known to be an almost exclusive company of foreign fighters, it has always actively recruited Salafist Mujahideen from the Sunni Wahabi community. By 2013 the merger of all foreign fighters with Iraqis into one indistinguishable group was complete and the ISIS was born (see Chapter 12).

The Ansar al-Islam organization was at one time an almost exclusively Iraqi-Kurdish group. Although AAI merged with Ansar al-Sunnah in 2004, it is believed many members went over to al-Qaeda when it was still predominantly the Jordanian Tawhid Wal-Jihad. The effort to put an Iraqi face onto al-Qaeda was critical to ensure that they could infiltrate parts of the country where a foreign Arab could be recognized. Additionally, placing Iraqis forward as the new face of AQI would validate the partnership of Iraqis and their Arab brethren as a legitimate pan-Arab resistance organization. According to an Associated Press report, AQI put out the following statement on a jihadist website, announcing the mustering of an all-Iraqi cell of al-Qaeda in Iraq.

> In response to God's decree, and the heavy insistence of the (Iraqi) brothers and their longing for paradise, the Ansar platoon from the land of Iraq has been formed.... Dozens hurried to register their names to meet their God.... It told of one Iraqi youth who had rebuked his leader for failing to give him a suicide assignment, telling him he would complain to God on the Day of Judgment because "you prevented me from meeting my God."[55]

The European Jihadists

Using the al-Qaeda global network of supporters in other terror groups such as the Egyptian Islamic Jihad (EIJ), the Algerian Salafist Group for Combat, and the Call (GSPC), the AAI and al-Qaeda cells in Europe, al-Zarqawi managed to effectively stretch his influence in Europe. An alleged member of al-Qaeda-Europe, Shadi Abdullah, told German interrogators that his cell supporting the anti-U.S. jihad was composed of three members: a man named Abu Ali who directed the group's logistics, himself, and another recruit. They were tasked with getting illegal passports, illegal cell phone contracts, raising money, and in the case of an attack, planning out the relevant details.[56] In early 2004 Russian reports claimed that al-Zarqawi had sought out up to 2,000 Chechen Mujahideen to infiltrate south through Iran and to link up with AQI.[57] It is most unlikely that more than a handful took up the offer. To date, no prisoners from Russia have been found among the hundreds of foreign fighters killed or captured in Iraq. But in Syria ISIS has lost dozens of Russian and former Soviet state volunteers.

The Black Widows of Iraq—AQI Female Operatives

One startling note was the adoption of women into al-Qaeda's ranks of martyrs, though they were not the first group to use women as suicide bombers in Iraq. That distinction belonged to the former regime's Iraq Intelligence Service, the Mukhabarat. AQI was the first to use foreign women as black widow-type suicide bombers. Named after the Chechen women who lost their husbands in combat to the Russians, the black widows were women recruited to avenge their husband's deaths and sacrifice their lives in order to join them in paradise.

Al-Qaeda started using black widow-styled bombers in Iraq in 2005. One was an unidentified woman who died attacking a gathering of Iraqi army recruits near Tel Afar. A member of the al-Baraa bin Malik Martyrdom Brigade of al-Qaeda's Tel Afar regional command, she wore an explosives belt and dressed as an Arab man in a white disdasha and a checkered kuffiyah. The unknown bomber went over to the men, pressed a detonator, and blew herself up, killing 5 and wounding 30.

UNTO DEATH—MARRIED COUPLE SUICIDE BOMBERS

In addition to using women, AQI introduced a new type of bomber, the husband and wife martyrdom team. The second martyrdom bombing involving a "sister" took place as part of a husband and wife martyrdom operation when they rammed their S-VBIED into an American army convoy near Mosul. The third attack involved the first European woman and a convert to Islam. A Belgian citizen named Muriel "Myriam" Degauque was found to have blown herself up on an Iraqi police patrol in Qara Taba, near Baqubah. She killed five policemen. Degauque's death in Iraq sent a wave of anxiety through Europe. She was a Caucasian from Charleroi, who had married first a Turk and then an Algerian, and then had converted to Islam and settled with her third husband, a Belgian-Moroccan 7 years her junior named Issam Goris. He was killed after being shot during the same attack by U.S. forces. Before deciding to go with him to fight in the Iraq jihad, she had a slow-burn conversion that clashed with her parents' Western European values. Her mother recalls, "At the beginning, it was the *tchador*. More recently, Muriel accepted the veil. When one sees it, they imposed their rules. We were once in our home, but my husband had to eat in the kitchen with Issam and the women had to remain in the living room." However, this case was not the first time a Western woman had turned to Islam in such a way, but it was the first time they had been "called to jihad." The terror groups in Iraq were picking up any tool they could use, and these women suited them fine.

AQI employs a network of mixed cell structures universally used throughout the world. The men in each cell fulfill whatever role needs to be done. This Mafia-like uncompartmented structure is risky, but enhances security by ensuring unwavering loyalty among the cell members, who see each other as brothers. In Iraq, it had a greater measure of effectiveness in recruiting. The people who are called to fight in the jihad are screened extensively, and they expect not to return. As is the case with the most expert al-Qaeda operatives, AQI's liaison and recruitment officers outside of Iraq are intentionally kept out of large battles because of their important work bringing in new manpower. "Euro-jihadists" or their frontline recruiters have been seen in virtually all countries. For example, a German man is alleged to have carried out a suicide bombing in Iraq. French and Italian authorities broke several rings of jihadist facilitators as well. A 41-year-old British national from Manchester was suspected of taking part in a suicide bombing in 2005; a second Brit, named Wail al-Dhaleai, a martial arts expert from Sheffield who was born in Yemen, was killed driving a S-VBIED into an American checkpoint after infiltrating through Syria and joining an al-Qaeda-associated group. A third British Muslim from Tooting, South London, was captured in 2003 near Ramadi with traces of explosives on his hands.[58] Al-Zarqawi himself wrote that Iraq is but one front in the larger war. If they fail in Iraq, he promised, they would "pack out bags and search for another land, as is the sad, recurrent story in the arenas of jihad."[59]

ENDNOTES

1. Romesh Ratnesar, Face of Terror, *Time*, December 27, 2004, 96.
2. Mark Hosenball and Babak Dehghanpisheh, The Zarqawi Firestorm, *Newsweek*, July 5, 2004, 30.
3. Ratnesar.
4. Hosenball and Dehghanpisheh.
5. Ratnesar.
6. Leith Shubailat quoted in Suleiman Alkhalidi, War on Terror: Evolution of a Maniac, *The Advertiser*, April 9, 2005, 51.
7. Walter Pincus, Iraq Called Springboard for Insurgency Figure, *Washington Post*, October 21, 2004, Sec. A, 25.
8. Craig Whitlock, Grisly Path to Power in Iraq's Insurgency, *Washington Post*, September 27, 2004, Sec. A, 1.
9. Ratnesar.

10. Faye Bowers and Peter Grier, How Terror Groups Vied for a Player, *Christian Science Monitor*, May 11, 2004, 1.
11. Colin Powell, Speech before the UN, retrieved from http://www.state.gov/secretary/former/powell/remarks/2003/17300.htm.
12. Pincus, Iraq Called Springboard for Insurgency Figure.
13. Zarqawi's Group Admits Killing 50 Iraqi Soldiers, *The Irish Times*, October 25, 2004, Sec. World, 8.
14. Dan Murphy, Going After Iraq's Most Wanted Man, *Christian Science Monitor*, September 21, 2004, Sec. World, 1.
15. Dexter Filkins and Douglas Jehl, The Struggle for Iraq: Intelligence, *New York Times*, February 9, 2004, Sec. A, 1.
16. Jackie Spinner and Bassam Sebti, Militant Declares War on Iraqi Vote, *Washington Post*, January 24, 2005, Sec. A, 1.
17. Zarqawi says Israel, Jordon involved in Fallujah Assault, Agence France Presse, January 20, 2005, http://www.news24.com/world/news.
18. Christopher Dickey and Ron Nordland, Hunting Zarqawi, *Newsweek*, November 1, 2004, 32.
19. Barbara Starr, Who Is Abu Musab al-Zarqawi, CNN.com, retrieved May 30, 2005, from http://www.cnn.com.
20. Sharif Durhams, Rumsfeld Compares al-Zarqawi to Hitler in Ft. Bragg Speech, *Charlotte Observer*, May 26, 2005.
21. Don Van Natta, Who Is Abu Musab al-Zarqawi? *New York Times*, October 10, 2004, Sec. 4, 1.
22. Spencer Ackerman, Iraq'd, *The New Republic*, March 14, 2005, http://www.TNR.com.
23. Murphy.
24. Sami Yousafazi and Ron Moreau, How a Deadly Deal Was Made, *Newsweek*, April 11, 2005, 56.
25. Starr.
26. Yousafazi and Moreau.
27. Dickey and Nordland.
28. Yousafazi and Moreau.
29. DJ bin Laden, al-Zarqawi Would Both Benefit from Alliance, *FWN Select*, December 28, 2004.
30. Faye Bowers and Peter Grier, Rising Name on America's Most Wanted List, *Christian Science Monitor*, June 15, 2004, 3.
31. Whitlock.
32. Ibid.
33. Ibid.
34. Bowers and Grier, How Terror Groups Vied for a Player.
35. Walter Pincus, Analysts See bin Laden, Zarqawi as Independent Operators, *Washington Post*, March 5, 2005, Sec. A, 15.
36. Ibid.

37. Malcolm Nance, *The Terrorist Recognition Handbook*, Lyons Press, Guildord, CT, 2003.
38. Ratnesar.
39. Ibid.
40. Al-Zarqawi's Group Slams Elections, Pledges to Continue Hold War in Iraq, Asia-Africa Intelligence Wire, January 31, 2005.
41. Walter Pincus, Terror Suspect's Ambitions Worry U.S. Officials, *Washington Post*, March 3, 2004, Sec. A, 22.
42. Foreign Fighter Facilitator Killed, Press Release, Multinational Forces Iraq, October 8, 2005.
43. Statement from the Military Committee of Al Qaeda in the Land of the Two Rivers, Jihad Unspun, retrieved from www.jihadunspun.net.
44. Yassin Musharbash and Der Speigel, How To: The al Qaeda Guide to Kidnapping, December 1, 2005.
45. Ibid.
46. Communiqué Heralds the Arrival of a New Group of Fighters to Iraq and Their Pledge of Support to Zarqawi, SITE Institute, March 15, 2005.
47. Statement on Behalf of the Commander of the Rijjal Brigades Pledging Allegiance to al-Qaida's Committee, http://www.globalter-roralert.com/pdf/0405/zarqawi0405-17.pdf.
48. Al-Qaeda cell takes credit for string of Iraq attacks, Associated Press, July 15, 2003.
49. New Al Qaeda Tape Urges Fighters to Go to Iraq, Associated Press, August 18, 2003.
50. Abu Bakr al-Baghdadi—A Short Biography of the ISIS Sheikh, ISIS Written Statement, retrieved from http://pietervanostaeyen.word-press.com/2013/07/15/abu-bakr-al-baghdadi-a-short-biography-of-the-isis-sheikh/.
51. Interview with General Abazaid, CNN, March 27, 2005.
52. Richard Beeston, Analysis: The Syrian Route to Jihad, *Times of London*, June 21, 2005.
53. Donna Abu-Nasr, Saudis to Jihad in Iraq, Associated Press, February 24, 2005.
54. Ibid.
55. Maamoun Youssef, Al Qaeda Announces Iraqi Suicide Squad, Associated Press, June 21, 2005.
56. Bowers and Grier, How Terror Groups Vied for a Player.
57. Oleg Kiryanov and Timofey Borisov, "Wild Geese" Long for the South, *Rossiyskaya Gazeta*, February 17, 2004.
58. Ian Herbert, Jason Bennetto, and Kim Sengupta, Suicide Bomber Who Attacked Troops in Iraq "Traced to Manchester," *Independent*, June 22, 2005.
59. Ratnesar.

A New Jihad (2004–2011)
Bin Laden's Greatest Gift

CHAPTER 10

Fallujah
The Crucible of the Iraq Jihad

We really didn't see the insurgency coming.

—Ambassador L. Paul Bremer, January 2006[1]

According to the joint doctrine manual JP-1-02 and the U.S. Army field manual on counterinsurgency, FM 3-24, "An *insurgency* is organized movement aimed at the overthrow of a constituted government through use of subversion and armed conflict."[2] Insurgency is conducted in phases. Phase I, the strategic defensive phase, is the incipient or latent phase where the insurgents use subversive activities in a covert environment. Usually the victim nation has no idea there is a planned insurgency and no major outbreaks of violence are present. It capitalizes on psychological operations and propaganda. Everything appears normal and life goes on. Phase II, the move to stalemate, is the guerrilla war phase where political violence is carried out, often with external support, government agencies are infiltrated, and attempts are made to eliminate opposition groups. The government is usually strained to contain the insurgency and gets tied down protecting itself. The insurgents, on the other hand, seek to expand to additional operations areas for their acts. Phase III, the offensive, would be a war of movement, where the insurgents gain conventional forces and engage in mobile military operations like a small army. Iraq reached this phase in January 2014 when al-Qaeda in Iraq, now called Islamic State of Iraq and Syria (ISIS), launched a swift raiding operation called a Gazwah, named after the raids of the prophet Mohammed against Mecca.[3] The insurgents in phase II would conduct their covert war in the following order:

Initiation: Low-level terrorism that includes sabotage, assassinations, and low-level guerrilla action.
Insurrection: The insurgent expands his operations areas, performs larger-scale attacks, and may even proclaim a countergovernment.

Consolidation: Expands political activity as it enlarges and links forces and bases.

It is at this point that we find the three wings of the Iraq insurgency starting from January 2004. Throughout 2003, the insurgents spent an enormous amount of time performing phase I on a large scale. By April 2004, al-Qaeda in Iraq, the Islamic Army of Iraq, the Ansar al-Sunnah, and the former regime loyalist (FRL) Army of Mohammed completed the insurrection phase of the guerrilla war. A large number of suicide car bombs started to explode in Baghdad with startling precision. The al-Qaeda in Iraq struck the Assassins' Gate, the principal gateway to the Green Zone (GZ), where American and Iraqi government personnel managed the reconstruction. Named after the 3rd Infantry Division unit that took the gate (2nd Brigade, Task Force 4-64, aka the Assassins) and where they fought a major Saddam Fedayeen counterattack. Over a period of 3 months, each of the other main gates to the GZ would be struck by suicide car bombs. On January 19, 2004, 30 Iraqi staff who worked in the palace had their lives taken by an al-Qaeda suicide pedestrian-borne improvised explosive device (S-VBIED) bomber who rammed the lines of cars in an attempt to blow up a nearby Bradley infantry fighting vehicle (IFV). For the insurgents, the Green Zone and the Republican Palace were the heart of the occupation and ground zero for the most daring operations. Surrounded by hundreds of U.S. Army soldiers, backed up by Bradley IFVs and M-1 Abrams tanks, as well as thousands of armed security contractors and military police, the Green Zone was targeted with almost nonstop mortar, rocket, and suicide car bombs. Barely a day went by when the traditional three-round "We Hate America" rocket barrage didn't strike the GZ with alarming clockwork each evening between 8:00 and 10:00 p.m. The running theory in intelligence was the insurgents were delivering the attacks on their way home from work. This was more true than not.

Soon secular violence accelerated with a series of suicide bombings in Baghdad, Najaf, and Karbala that killed 181 Shiite worshippers during the annual Ashura celebrations. The insurgents were trying bolder and more daring tactics. Two attacks in early February 2004 typified the type of operations the Fallujah-based insurgents were carrying out. One almost ended in tragedy for the coalition. Gen. John P. Abizaid, the U.S. commander of Central Command, and Maj. Gen. Charles H. Swannack, the commander of the 82nd Airborne Division, were arriving for an inspection visit of an Iraqi Civil Defense Corps barracks in Fallujah when a rocket-propelled grenade (RPG) team fired three rockets in an attempt to kill them.[4] The attackers managed to escape. Soon aferwards more than 17 Iraqi police officers were massacred, shot one by

FIGURE 10.1   Propaganda photo of a Mujahideen Army (Jaysh al-Mujahideen) terror cell presenting the range of infantry weapons in their possession, including antitank rockets, sniper rifles, long-range battlefield rockets, and automatic infantry weapons.

one when Islamic extremist insurgents in Fallujah raided a police station and freed 87 prisoners (Figure 10.1).

THE APRIL 2004 REVOLUTION

By April, the Islamic extremists were essentially running the city of Fallujah, 45 miles (63 km) west of Baghdad. A city with a prewar population of about 350,000, it became the headquarters to al-Qaeda in Iraq and dozens of other groups. U.S. forces could not wrest the control of the town by the Islamic extremists. Entrenched in the city since before the occupation, all of the Islamic groups had safe houses, terror cells, and combat teams there. Fallujah is known in Iraq as the City of Mosques because of the largess bestowed upon its religious community by Saddam Hussein. He built more than 200 mosques. At one period, Fallujah also had a thriving Jewish community. In the 10 centuries before the birth of Jesus Christ, Fallujah may have been the ancient city of Pumbeditha, the center for Babylonian Talmud study. This city was considered by some scholars to have been the oldest and largest Jewish community outside of ancient Israel.[5] Nevertheless, the modern Fallujah became the hardest core of the Islamic extremist insurgency against the American occupation. Former regime loyalists of the Fedayeen and Special Security Organization had residences in Fallujah; the Tawhid Wal-Jihad (TWJ) had encamped there in March 2003 and would form al-Qaeda in Iraq there. The Ansar al-Sunnah, the Islamic Army of Iraq, and others were consolidating their local authority along with supplying any group with religious and combat support. From April 2003 to April 2004, Fallujah remained a mainstay and support base of the insurgency, but it had never been tested directly. With all of the insurgents in place, the First Battle of Fallujah was coming. The ignition source would not be the U.S. Army or Marines, but four private military contractors who were lost.

The morning of March 31, 2004, four armed contractors from Blackwater Security Consulting were conducting a simple escort mission for a food services client when they were stopped at the entrance to Fallujah by Iraqi police. U.S. Army forces were on alert after a roadside bombing that had killed five soldiers. The contractors were directed to an alternate route directly into the city. The two Suburbans, with two of the Blackwater men in each, turned and entered the town. They were escorting three tractor trailers to pick up kitchen equipment at a U.S. base on the west side of the city. Without any ability to see behind or a machine gun poised to protect their rear, the insurgents quickly ambushed them and killed all four. Videotaping their victory, the crowd in the area quickly stripped them of their weapons, set fire to the cars, and burned their corpses. The remains were dragged out of the cars and through the streets, paraded in pieces. Two of their bodies were hung from the Fallujah Bridge. Blackened limbs were carried in celebration and shown to local photographers. It was a carnival of hatred. The corpses of Scott Helvenston, Jerry Zovko, Wesley Batalona, and Michael Teague lay charred near the vehicles, being symbolically beaten with sticks or hung from a bridge. It was a carnival that would bring about the first invasion of Fallujah.

The Americans were horrified and outraged at the massacre. White House press secretary Scott McClellan, speaking for the president, said, "These are horrific attacks by people who are trying to prevent democracy from moving forward."[6] The incident also brought outrage to the coalition headquarters. In the press and on the street there was a much anticipated response in the city from the coalition forces. Ambassador L. Paul Bremer said, "Yesterday's events in Fallujah are a dramatic example of the ongoing struggle between human dignity and barbarism.... Their deaths will not go unpunished."[7] Gen. Mark Kimmet at the Republican Palace stated in a press conference, "We will be back in Fallujah. It will be at a time and a place of our choosing. We will hunt down the criminals. We will kill them or we will capture them, and we will pacify Fallujah."[8]

OPERATION VALIANT RESOLVE
AND THE TWO-FRONT WAR

Four days after the massacre at the Fallujah Bridge the U.S. Marines were ordered into the city to bring the killers of the security detail to justice. This was not the way the Marine Corps thought it should go. The marine plan under Gen. James T. Conway had been to let the situation defuse, then use soft tactics to undermine support for the insurgents in the community, then apply precision raids to destroy them when found. Water, power, and food were the tools the Marine Corps wanted to use to win over the sheiks and the population, not massive firepower. However, awesome firepower was now the order of the day.

General Conway received his orders from his immediate superior, Gen. Ricardo Sanchez, commander of U.S. forces in Iraq. He was to enter the city and carry out the orders of the president—"arrest and apprehend" the killers of the contractors. This was a mission the U.S. Marines were reluctant to carry out due to the size and strength of the numerous insurgent groups in the city, but they went as ordered.

On April 5, the U.S. Marine Corps began Operation Valiant Resolve. Marine units began to enter the city, but as they did, the fighting became intense. Running street battles with well-stocked and well-prepared insurgents quickly broke out. Over two dozen different groups and sects met the Americans with weapons that they had been caching over a year. RPGs flew at them by the hundreds. Masked terrorists roamed the streets with their PKM machine guns and RPG launchers. The foreign Mujahideen sprang from their bunkered safe houses and bragged openly to journalists about fighting the Americans. The marines fought hard, but the insurgents had the advantage of better intelligence and deeper knowledge of the terrain, and had laid elaborate IED and RPG ambushes through the line of march. The marines had the full weight of U.S. air power behind them, including the awesome AC-130U gunship. The AC-130U earned its nickname "Spooky" for its ability to operate like a vengeful, hovering ghost in the night and strike from the dark with massive firepower. Developed during the Vietnam War, this modified Hercules transport aircraft bristled with 20 mm Gatling guns and 40 mm anti-aircraft guns modified to use advanced cameras and sensors to hit minute targets on the ground. Its most devastating killing device was a computer-controlled 105 mm artillery cannon, which could lay a precision strike of massive firepower. The insurgents of Fallujah knew that buildings and mosques were their ally in this city and could offset the power of the Spooky.

The marines' fight in Fallujah rapidly became intense. With insurgents dug in, air strikes within the city were necessary. When they struck, they created a wall of fear and massive resentment from the population. The insurgents knew their ground, and the coalition knew it would not be able to continue this fight. Iraqi national guard units that were supposed to assist the marines could only control the roads the marines assigned to them outside of the city. However, those brought into the city had other ideas about facing the insurgents. They simply fled the battlefield and refused to fight. One soldier alleges U.S. forces fired on their positions to motivate them into combat. "In the beginning the Americans tried to push the Iraqi army into the fight. But when many of them declined, the Americans started to shoot at them," said Hayder al-Maliki, an Iraq army soldier wounded by American gunfire. Gen. Mark Kimmett put it mildly when he asserted, "Some Iraqi security forces showed up, some didn't. The Iraqi army battalion was mustered [for Fallujah]; it hit some improvised explosive devices and came back and decided 'maybe this is not where we want to be.'"[9] The fighting spread, and in nearby Ramadi 12 marines were killed when ambushed by a large contingent of insurgents with machine guns and RPGs.

However, the fly in the ointment of the Fallujah assault came from an unexpected place—from the American-appointed Iraqi Governing Council and its Sunni president, Ghazi al-Yawer. The marines seized sections of the northeast corner of the city and were preparing to assault even further, but before that could happen, tragedy struck. Poor American intelligence misidentified a gathering at a mosque after Friday prayer service. The mosque was designated a threat and marines identified the crowd as insurgents. U.S. forces launched missiles on the complex, killing 40 civilian worshippers. Later the Marine Corps would admit not identifying any of the casualties as insurgents before the strike.

Civilian casualties were mounting daily. News reports by the Arabic language news networks Al Jazeera and Al Arabiyah television hyped the death toll. To the U.S. intelligence community, Al Jazeera was one of the best open sources of information about insurgents and their operations. The coalition headquarters commanded Al Jazeera to leave the city. Al Jazeera camera teams, along with those of Al Arabiya, are the best in the Middle East. They have access to Iraqis that Western companies could not risk or will not support, including contacts within the insurgency. From inside Fallujah, Al Jazeera was telling the story of the fight from the insurgent's perspective, but it was even more effective at cataloging the horrific suffering of the women and children from U.S. attacks. To the politicians at the Republican Palace, it was a nuisance. In frustration, Ambassador Bremer attempted to directly control the media reporting from Fallujah. Labeled as a propaganda machine for Islamic extremists, Bremer made it clear he wanted to give the insurgents no media and limited the Qatari company's access. It only led the Iraqi people to once again wonder if the Americans were really there to give democracy and "freedom of the press," as they kept promising.

In a final blow to the operation, one of the most pro-American members of the governing council, Adnan Pachachi, denounced the entire offensive. In an interview to Al Arabiyah Pachachi said, "These (U.S.) operations were a mass punishment for the people of Fallujah.... It was not right to punish all the people of Fallujah and we consider these operations by the Americans unacceptable and illegal."[10] President al-Yawer called it collective punishment on the city for the crimes of a few. By mid-April, more than 800 people were reported dead. Somewhere between 572 and 616 of the dead were civilians, 300 of these being women and children.[11] Two hundred insurgents were also killed.

Iraqi political pressure forced the coalition to seek a solution—a fast one. Negotiations with the leaders of Fallujah started, and within a week, an internal security force was formed from ex-Iraqi army soldiers. An ex-Ba'athist, Maj. Gen. Muhammed Latif, promised he would create a unit called the Fallujah Protection Army, but referred to as the Fallujah Brigade. It had 900 men claiming to be ex-Ba'athists and ex-resistance fighters who would do battle with the foreign insurgents. General Latif was soon replaced once his association with the Saddam regime was exposed, but his replacement, Maj. Gen. Jasim Mohammed Saleh, was no better. Unfortunately, the Americans believed him and gave the brigade weapons, equipment, and training. U.S. Marine forces would withdraw and give control of the city to this security element with the assistance of the Iraqi national guard. Pro-war supporters took heart in the idea that the Iraqis were stepping forward to assist themselves with the formation of the Fallujah Brigade. The *Wall Street Journal* wrote this positive opinion about the Fallujah Brigade:

> The Marines constantly test it to make sure it is fulfilling the coalition's goals. These tests include submitting to civilian rule, taking large-caliber weapons off the streets, ensuring the rule of law is prevailing in the city, working with and positively influencing city fathers, and adhering to all the Geneva Conventions and rules of war that the Marines themselves must follow.[12]

Of course, on the surface, the Fallujah Protection Army lived up to this commitment, all the while shaking down businesses, arming their foreign and domestic insurgent brothers, and performing a brand of "reputation laundering" that even for Ba'athists was unabashedly shameless. A U.S. official told the *Washington Post*, "Many of the guys who were shooting at the marines have simply put on their old army uniforms and joined the Fallujah Brigade." No Iraqi outside of Fallujah was fooled, but the Americans seemingly were relieved and Marine Corps units withdrew to the perimeter of the city.

By May 10, the residents were in full celebration over the U.S. Marine withdrawal, and alongside them dancing in the streets were the fully armed resistance fighters of Fallujah and the Fallujah Brigade soldiers. One resident told American journalist Dahr Jamil, "Today is the first day of the war against the Americans! This is a victory for us over the Americans!"

The Mujahideen and the city's population took to the streets to declare victory over the U.S. Marines, thinking that the objective of the marines was to take control of the city and that they had failed. In another moment of defiance the Fallujah Brigade commander Major General Saleh said, "The reasons for the resistance go back to the American provocations, the raids and abolishing the army, which made Iraqis join the resistance." For this reason, he refused to hunt down or turn over the Islamic fighters in Fallujah or those responsible for the Blackwater murders.

The Fallujah bridge murders changed the way America saw the war. It was now brutal, messy, and horrific. It impacted the security for the coalition as well. What had before been a quiet, almost low-key security operation boomed into a multi-hundred-billion-dollar industry in order to protect the reconstruction effort. Andy Melville, in an interview for the documentary "Private Warriors," described the Blackwater operation as a watershed moment in the insurgency. "That incident that you refer to is a pivotal incident in security operations here in Iraq. And it was at that point that it was true to say that there was deterioration which changed the posture of all the security companies moving from soft-skin vehicles to armored vehicles. Body armor was worn. Weapons were then openly carried."[13]

The U.S. Marines were wary of the image of cutting deals with the Ba'athists, but they needed a solution to a situation they had neither sought nor desired. Orders were orders and they supported the mission until the end. By August 2004, the coalition came to the realization that they may have created a new wing of the insurgency and armed the very people they were sent to secure. The decision to officially disband the unit was ordered. The Fallujah Brigade had already disbanded in May 2004 when its members officially merged with the Army of Mohammed, the FRL insurgent group made up of ex-Saddam Fedayeen. Over the last few months of its existence, it was a hollow shell, which used its U.S.-supplied equipment on its full-time job of being the principal insurgent group in the city. It was a masterstroke of trickery on the insurgents' part. By September, the Americans would admit they were had. U.S. Marine Corps Col. Jerry L. Durrant remarked, "The whole Fallujah Brigade thing was a fiasco. Initially it worked out OK, but it wasn't a good idea for very long."[14] Nevertheless, Fallujah was always on the minds of the

American war planners. Numerous times, they claimed that an operation to take the city was pending, would be final, and would be clearly victorious. That operation, named Phantom Fury, would be delayed for 6 months, until November 2004.

COULD IT GET ANY WORSE? THE MAHDI MILITIA AND THE SHIITE UPRISING

At the same time that the Americans were preparing to attack Fallujah, they made a series of decisions that would simultaneously throw all of southern Iraq into rebellion. An extremely bad one was that they would attack the militia of an influential Shiite cleric. A small but vocal body of young Shiite men followed the spiritual teachings and the political aspirations of a young man named Sheik Muqtada al-Sadr. Al-Sadr was a Hojatoleslam, a middle-ranking religious position, but he had a distinguished lineage in the global Shiite community. He came from a long line of honored Shiite religious leaders, all of whom were considered martyrs, including his father, Sheik Mohammed Sadeq al-Sadr, who was murdered by Saddam in 1999. His uncle was the religious scholar Sheik Mohammed Bakir al-Sadr, who was tortured and executed by Saddam in 1980 and a cousin of the famous Lebanese Sheik Musa Sadr, who disappeared after a trip to Libya and is believed to have been executed. Driving around post-Saddam southern Iraq, one could find photomontages of the two senior al-Sadrs alongside that of the murdered Sheik Mohammed Bakir al-Hakim and the young Muqtada al-Sadr. Their images have replaced all of the statutes and frescos of Saddam at the entrance and exit of every village and town. Such is their regard that the northeast quarter of Baghdad, previously called Saddam City, was renamed Sadr City after the war in honor of his relatives. Thus, Muqtada al-Sadr had great influence among the disenfranchised young men of Shiite Islam in southern Iraq, particularly those poor in Sadr City. They yearned for a more active role in rejecting the Americans and resisting the occupation. The calls by the older, more patient Shiite leaders only exacerbated their anxiousness to take part in the political changes sweeping Iraq. They wanted a voice. That voice came in the name of the Sadr Movement, a political party founded by Muqtada's father, Sadeq al-Sadr. It was formed again as a political party to support the wishes of the younger, more extremist Shiite. The older Shiites tended to support the Supreme Islamic Council for the Islamic Revolution in Iraq, which had been headed by Sheik Hakim. Muqtada was its leader. At the end of July 2003, Muqtada announced he was forming a new militia, the Jaysh al-Mahdi, or the Mahdi Militia. At the time, he told Al Arabiyah television, "I am an enemy to the Americans as long as they remain in

Iraq." He claimed the Mahdi Militia would be unarmed and assigned to protect the religious shrines of Shiite Islam.

The popularity of Muqtada al-Sadr also seemed to chafe Ambassador Bremer, the U.S. proconsul of Iraq. Bremer and his commanders wanted no armed militias in Iraq and regarded the Mahdi Militia and al-Sadr as nothing but thugs. Listening to the money class of Iraqi expatriates, Bremer saw his religious inspiration as manipulation. They would quickly find that this was a grave mistake. A litany of Americans labeled al-Sadr as "inconsequential," "thug," and "criminal," all because he defied their aspirations. In one incident in July 2003, Deputy Secretary of Defense Paul Wolfowitz during a visit to Najaf had to be evacuated when Sadrists launched a massive series of protests. Ten thousand followers marched from the Holy Shrine of Imam Ali in Karbala to the U.S. headquarters there chanting, "Long live Sadr. America and the council are infidels. Muqtada, go ahead; we are your soldiers of liberation."[15] His protests were taken up in Basra and other cities. Al-Sadr's star was rising and the Americans were determined to put a stop to it.

Early on during the occupation, a U.S. Marine Corps commander of the unit occupying Najaf, Col. Christopher Woodbridge, dismissed al-Sadr and the significance of his family history. "He's an extremist and a radical, riding the coattails of his father and grandfather.... The [Shi'ite establishment] really discounts him as a poser, a little boy playing cleric."[16] Again, a horrific miscalculation. Colonel Woodbridge had been listening to the expatriate and secular merchant class of Iraq, not to the Shiite community, and he came to view al-Sadr with contempt. The actions of the Coalition Provisional Authority (CPA) in Baghdad would reflect this contempt.

First, in late March, Ambassador Bremer ordered that the Sadrist newspaper *Al Hawza* be shut down for inciting violence against the coalition. U.S. forces showed up with a massive display of firepower and chained the doors shut. Coupled with another incident, where an American Blackhawk helicopter was ordered to fly over Sadr City and remove an Islamic flag from a flagpole, these acts sparked massive protests.[17] Sadrists came out in protests that brought tens of thousands of people to the gates of the Republican Palace. One Iraqi supporter said, "What is happening now is what used to happen during the days of Saddam. No freedom of opinion. It is like the days of the Ba'ath."[18]

In April 2004, about the same time of the Fallujah bridge massacre, the coalition had formulated a strategy that would give them pretext for the arrest of al-Sadr and disband the Mahdi Militia. The three armed militias of the Shiite had been a slight nuisance to the coalition but never a military threat. The Iranian-trained Badr Brigade was tolerated, as they never appeared in public with their weapons and guarded the holy sites of Shiite Islam. The Hizb al-Da'wa was a smaller brethren, and they too hid their weapons well. It was the Jaysh al-Mahdi, or Mahdi Militia, that paraded around as a paramilitary unit and seemingly took orders from no one except al-Sadr. The protection of the holy shrines had been a thorn in the side of the coalition since the murder of Imam al-Khoei, an expatriate who returned to take control of the shrines with American and British backing. He was killed on the spot by the Shiite Iraqis who had remained and suffered under Saddam, allegedly on al-Sadr's order. However, the Americans assert it was a calculated murder with the victims having been brought before al-Sadr, and he ordered him killed. Whichever event took place, few dispute that the assassination was done by anyone other than al-Sadr's men. Al-Sadr and others believed he had earned the right to protect the shrines and not turn them over to foreign-supported Iraqis who had left the country decades earlier.

On the morning of April 5, the coalition announced that an Iraqi judge had issued an arrest warrant for Muqtada al-Sadr for the murder of the Imam al-Khoei. Brig. Gen. Mark Kimmet, director of coalition operations for Combined Joint Task Force 7, said, "Militias are inconsistent with a democratic and sovereign nation with a central government. We are particularly focused upon militias ... attacking coalition forces ... Iraqi forces ... (and) Iraqi civilians."[19] He also added, "It is a militia, an illegal militia run by an outlaw, a group of people who have attacked, first and foremost, Iraqis—Iraqi police, Iraqi army, the Iraqi civil defense force, and coalition forces and Americans.... And we will deal with them."[20]

Sensing an opportunity, the Sunni insurgents and community started to support the uprising. In the Sunni Azamiyah District, attacks on American soldiers skyrocketed not just by insurgents, but locals with guns. Throughout the week, each night was peppered with gunfire and ambushes on U.S. patrols. Baghdad from northwest to northeast had become a shooting gallery for U.S. troops. This informal alliance of the Sunni, who were angry over the U.S. assault on Fallujah, and the Shiites, who were angry over the assault on Muqtada al-Sadr, was a dangerous one for the Americans. It appeared that most of Iraq, from Basrah to Mosul to Ramadi, was rising in rebellion against the coalition, and the insurgents would gain from it in the end.

The first day after the announcement of the arrest warrant, Shiite militiamen opened fire on American forces throughout Baghdad, Najaf, and Karbala. The first day, 54 Iraqis and 9 coalition soldiers were killed. Eight Americans were killed in a massive ambush in Sadr City where the Mahdi supporters fought from roofs and streets. In Najaf, one El Salvadorian army soldier was killed. The Mahdi Militia seized control of the access roads into Sadr City, setting the stage for a showdown with U.S. forces. Al-Sadr seized the city of Najaf and called all Shiites in Iraq to arms. "America has shown its evil intentions, and the proud Iraqi people cannot accept it. They must defend their rights by any means they see fit.... I'm prepared to have my own blood shed for what is holy to me."[21] Al-Sadr also pledged loyalty to the head of the largest Shiite party, Supreme Council for the Islamic Republic in Iraq, Sheik al-Sistani, successor to the dead Sheik al-Hakim. "I proclaim my solidarity with Ali Sistani and he should know that I am his military wing in Iraq."

The Americans arrested two of al-Sadr's Baghdad representatives, Amr Husseini and Amjad Saedi. This further antagonized the militia members and sparked a spate of RPG and machine gun ambushes in Sadr City. In Kufa, U.S. armored calvary engaged in battles that left 34 dead. Surprisingly, the moderate middle-class Shiite neighborhood of Khadimiyah in Baghdad became the location for an ambush that killed three U.S. soldiers. The rebellion was spreading. Within days, the Mahdi was fighting in Karbala, Naseriyah, Al Kut, Samawa, Najaf, Al Amarah, and Hillah. U.S. forces in Najaf used heavy armor and helicopter gunships to carry out offensive operations. The Mahdi Militia had none of the skills of the Sunni insurgents, and their tactics led them to early graves. Hundreds of militiamen were killed, but U.S. forces too took many casualties. The Americans fought the Mahdi Militia furiously through Najaf and Karbala. The Mahdi Militia was pushed by the Americans from the city toward a corner of the Najaf cemetery. The Shiites fell back directly to the holy shrine at the heart of the city, the Mosque of Imam Ali. Baghdad's Sadr City became a deadly area to patrol, as the militia started to adopt insurgent tactics of IEDs and RPG ambushes to counterbalance American firepower. Al-Zarqawi's group, AQI, and the other Sunni insurgents took full advantage of this chaos. As the Americans fought the militia, suicide bombers struck them where they assembled and on the highways to their patrol areas. The American forces in Iraq were getting hit everywhere, by everyone, with everything, and there was nothing to do about it but fight on contact and prevail (Figure 10.2).

Again, denial of the direness and intensity of the situation and its future political impact was the word of the day. Ambassador Bremer ruled out negotiation. Brig. Gen. Mark Kimmett said, "If he [al-Sadr] wants to calm the situation, he can turn himself in to an Iraqi police station and face justice."[22] However, the prospect of a Shiite-Sunni alliance, such as had occurred in the British revolt of 1920, was in the offing, and the coalition commanders had to head it off. U.S. forces fought and retook the Shrines of Ali in Najaf and Hussein in Karbala. Then just as quickly, the arrest warrant against al-Sadr was lifted. Muqtada subsequently called off his militia on April 26. In Al Kut and Naseriyah, sieges of the coalition governor's centers dissipated after days of nonstop fighting. The tenuous cease-fire would last, but only until August 2004. Al-Sadr had lost his militia, but in the end had won his right to represent

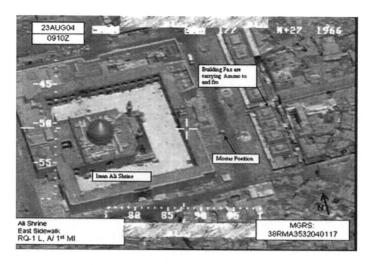

FIGURE 10.2   During the August 2004 fighting with the U.S. Army, the Shiite Mahdi Militia (Jaysh al-Mahdi) set up 82 mm mortar firing positions directly on the grounds of the Shrine of the Imam Ali in Najaf. (From U.S. DoD.)

the Sadrists movement in Iraq. While the south was restabilized, things were only worsening for the coalition in the west and north.

LOSING ANBAR

The Americans antagonized any remaining support in Anbar Province not only by attacking Fallujah, but also by losing the support of the largest tribe in Iraq at the same time. On April 11, 2004 the Americans made the next horrific miscalculation—they killed Sheik Malik al-Kharbit, leader of one of the largest tribes in Iraq, and 21 of his immediate family as they slept. Sheik of the 2-million-strong al-Dulaym tribe, Sheik Malik al-Kharbit and his brother Mudher had been in communication with the Americans throughout the reign of Hussein. Al-Kharbit collaborated with the CIA to find subtle ways to remove the strongman. The Dulaym included the towns of Qaim, Fallujah, Rutbah, and Ramadi—a large majority of the Sunni Triangle. Yet on this evening, U.S. intelligence thought they had isolated a wanted Ba'athist in the al-Kharbit home. According to Mudher al-Kharbit, the prominent Ba'athist was Rukan Razuki (also called Rokan Abd al-Ghafur Suleiman al-Majid). Razuki had come to al-Kharbit under the flag of truce and a request for shelter. Depending on this tribal tradition among Arabs, he was given sanctuary and hospitality by al-Kharbit, but only for dinner. Razuki left soon afterwards. As Saddam's Minister of Tribal Affairs, he came to ask al-Kharbit to join the anti-American alliance, or perhaps it was a real request for sanctuary; the Americans never found out. The coalition apparently either decided that Rukan was too important to the insurgency to let live or believed that al-Kharbit was actively collaborating with the FRLs. They determined both men needed to die. A strategic reconnaissance team was dispatched to the location, observed the activity, and reported back their findings. The house was full of civilians. Apparently, the coalition determined that the numerous innocent people in the house would just have to die with Razuki and al-Kharbit. They would be collateral damage.

On the night of April 11, American bombers dropped six joint direct attack munitions (JDAMs), 2,000-pound precision-guided bombs, on the al-Kharbit residence, killing him and obliterating his large family.[23] His brother Mudfeh would recall it this way: "History will remember that the Al-Kharbits sacrificed 22 family members for the sake of a guest. It's the tribal way." The Americans had alienated the most important tribe in western Iraq and created a bloodlust to avenge the family.

The death of the al-Kharbit family and the Ba'athists trick in giving Fallujah back to the former regime's own agents were but two of the litany of failures and miscalculations that were attributable to an ignorance of culture. Journalist Paul McGeogh noted the observation of a Jordanian analyst about the dilemma the Americans had placed themselves in with their ignorance or dismissal of the cost of the lives of this family.

> The Americans should be trying to win the tribes over. Instead, they kill half of this man's family and they arrest the other half; and when he comes to talk to them, they demand that he take a polygraph test. If you don't know how to live in this part of the world, the Bedouin and the tribes will teach you a very expensive lesson.[24]

With the loss of Anbar's Sunni community, Fallujah once again became a center for the foreign fighters, Islamic extremists, and FRL terrorists to rest, reload, and restrike the Americans at their leisure. It became a safe haven for the insurgency, and the Americans, by doing nothing, were providing the security.

THE HOSTAGE WAR AND THE TRANSITION TO SOVEREIGNTY

Nick Berg was an American adrift in Iraq. He had come to find work in the wild world of government contracting but had little respect for the dangers. The Jewish American telecommunications worker, who was a supporter of the war, ended up in a rundown Baghdad hotel. On a few occasions, he visited an Iraqi ex-husband of his aunt who lived in Mosul. For a time he had been picked up by coalition authorities and held for either his own good or suspicion of being an insurgent sympathizer. He was let go from detention with an offer of assistance to leave the country, but he turned it down. On or about April 10, 2004, he was abducted by members of al-Qaeda in Iraq. He was still missing and incommunicado when the photos of the prisoner abuse at Abu Ghraib broke. The outcry of horror from the world that America was abusing prisoners in the same prison and in similar ways as Saddam Hussein would have fatal consequences for him. The images of the prisoners being humiliated would be the starting point on the road to death for Westerners taken hostage by the insurgents from that time onward.

Berg is believed to have been moved from the Mosul area and held at an AQI hostage prison in Fallujah. A month after his abduction a video was released with the title "Abu Musa'b al-Zarqawi Slaughters an American." In it was Nicholas Berg wearing an orange jumpsuit, similar to the ones the prisoners of Guantanamo wore, seated before the black-hooded Abu Musab al-Zarqawi and his lieutenants. Berg made a statement confirming his identity. When he finished, al-Zarqawi came behind him with a sword, grasped his hair, cut his throat, and severed his head from his body. Al-Zarqawi held Berg's decapitated head up before the video camera and pledged it in revenge for the alleged American murders at Abu Ghraib. The calmness of the beheading and the wide distribution of the video via the Internet made the act even more horrific. The world condemned the killing, but the execution had made its point. Americans were on the menu—all of them (Figure 10.3).

The American offensive on Fallujah had emboldened the resistance. Abduction became the order of the day and a way to make money. A wave of abductions of Westerners started. Numerous other contractors and civilians were kidnapped, including Italian bodyguard Fabrizio Quatrocchi and three other security subcontractors, who were abducted on their way to Jordan after their weapons had been seized by American forces at a checkpoint outside Fallujah. Quatrocchi had been forced to dig his own grave. In a last moment of defiance he removed his hood and told the insurgents, "Now you will see how an Italian man dies." They then shot him in the head.

The killings in Iraq escalated. Daily multiple suicide bombings in Baghdad rocked the city. The Americans worked hard to effect the transition to an independent interim government, but the insurgents saw this transition as an opportunity to play their long-range strategy. The economy would be crippled. Oil pipelines near Kirkuk, Mosul, and Basrah were constantly blown up to damage the economy. Instead

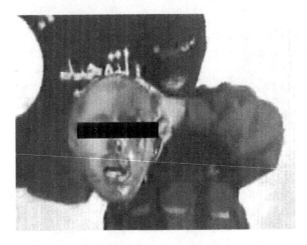

FIGURE 10.3 Masked figure, believed to be Abu Hamza al-Muhajir (aka Abu Ayyub al-Masri), holds up head of slain hostage.

of destabilizing a government with little real power, they would continue to assassinate the potential future leaders and prepare for a larger nationwide offense. Using precision S-VBIEDs, al-Qaeda in Iraq killed the Shiite president of Iraq's governing council, Izzedin Salim, and his bodyguards. His motorcade was vaporized by a TWJ suicide bomber waiting for him near the gates to the Green Zone. New insurgent groups were springing up from the remnants of the small fractious cells that had defended Fallujah. There was strength in numbers, and both TWJ and Ansar al-Sunni were benefiting from the Islamic call to arms that Fallujah had highlighted. While the FRL insurgents and their Iraqi Islamic extremists continued their attacks on the coalition for an average of 50 to 60 per day, the foreign fighters of Iraq had an entirely different plan. They had contributed to the defense of Fallujah, but they were about to demonstrate on a large scale that they were a force to be reckoned with.

BLACK THURSDAY—THE ONE-DAY SALAFIST MINI-JIHAD

The forces of Abu Musab al-Zarqawi had been watching with interest the events of April by the Mahdi Militia. They planned to replicate the same style of uprising throughout the Sunni Triangle. On June 24, 2004, 4 days before American-appointed proconsul L. Paul Bremer handed over control of Iraq to an interim Iraqi government, the combined forces of the foreign jihadists, led by al-Zarqawi, launched an offensive in virtually every major city of the Sunni Triangle. The principal target was the Iraqi police and American forces. Baghdad, Baqubah, Fallujah, Ramadi, and Mosul were struck with over a dozen car bombs. In Mosul alone, 62 people were killed when numerous police stations and a hospital were attacked by suicide car bombs. Police stations throughout the Sunni Triangle were attacked or seized by gunmen. At the end of the day, 92 people were dead and 285 were wounded. The police commissioner of Ramadi was assassinated in a drive-by shooting. In Baqubah, insurgents seized the city hall and police stations. According to *Al Hayat* newspaper, the TWJ fighters wore black uniforms and yellow headbands with "Monotheism and Holy War Battalions" written across them. From this day, Abu Musab al-Zarqawi's group, TWJ, would combine all the foreign fighters in Iraq to become al-Qaeda in Iraq (AQI). They claimed Islamic control of the city of Baqouba and roamed the streets openly waiting to confront U.S. forces. The Americans responded by calling in air strikes on their positions. After the intense 6-hour period of combat, these terrorist forces quickly melted back into the deserts and safe houses, but their attacks continued on the highways. The foreign Islamic insurgents had thrown a punch with a level of coordination that had never been expected. The attacks killed 103 Iraqis and 3 U.S. soldiers. One U.S. Marine helicopter was shot down, but the crew survived. Over 321 soldiers and civilians were wounded in the fighting. Although the fighting had been occurring throughout the week around Baqubah and Ramadi, the level of coordination by the new AQI was amazing. They carried out an ambitious plan to explode numerous simultaneous car bombs and armed raids on multiple sets of targets in 1 day and then disappear. This was the first example of multiple terrorist cells from among the foreign fighters conducting what could be best described as a swarm attack. The number of targets struck and the instantaneous spike of casualties must have pleased al-Zarqawi immensely, and history would show he would use this concentrated attack strategy again and again in the coming year. To keep up the pressure, AQI immediately followed up the raids with a devastating S-VBIED attack in Fallujah on a truck carrying female marines. That attack killed 4 marines, 3 of whom were women, and wounded 13, including 2 men. The use of women marines to search female residents going in and out of Fallujah was well known, and al-Zarqawi knew the propaganda power of striking them in the Muslim world. Therefore, he tasked a suicide team to attack. Al-Zarqawi used every weapon at his disposal, but with precision. By August, the FRL insurgents had started openly cooperating with AQI and foreign Islamic extremists. Al-Zarqawi no longer wasted statements belittling the FRL insurgent groups. He and his regional cell commanders would coordinate their attacks with them.

In the south, a second Mahdi uprising in August 2004 ended with the same disastrous results as the first, but the level of respect for al-Sadr had been exacted. He was offered a place in the new government in exchange for peace. He accepted, but his militia kept its weapons. One could imagine he would never know when another political concession would need to be forced out of the Americans, so better to maintain the leash on the tiger. However, day to day amidst this carnage the former regime insurgents were killing on average one to two American soldiers with IEDs, mortar, and RPG attacks. The drip, drip, drip of low-intensity strikes would bring America to the mark of 1,000 soldiers, sailors, airmen, and marines dead.

Nevertheless, the mergers of the Islamist groups had accelerated throughout the year. After much speculation about the nature of who was supporting Tawhid Wal-Jihad, a message from Abu Musab al-Zarqawi to Osama bin Laden was published in its online magazine *Mu'askar al-Battar.* In it came the official announcement that bin Laden had designated Tawhid Wal-Jihad as al-Qaeda in Mesopotamia (aka AQI). Al-Zarqawi wrote:

> By God, O sheikh of the Mujahideen, if you bid us plunge into the ocean, we would follow you. If you ordered it so, we would obey. If you forbade us something, we would abide by your wishes. For what a fine commander you are to the armies of Islam, against the inveterate infidels and apostates! Now then, people of Islam, come rally to the flag of the leader of the Mujahideen, which we raise together, and let us cry ["there is no God but the one God"], as the flag waves, raised by our newest heroes. Let us cleanse all Muslim lands of every infidel and wicked apostate until Islam enters the home of every city-dweller and nomad.[25]

As late as the fall of 2004, American war planners remained in denial about the insurgency. One report quoted a U.S. official in Baghdad as saying, "We're not at the forefront of a Jihadist war here." Mullah Mustapha Krekar, founder and spiritual leader of Ansar al-Islam, begged to differ. In an interview he said, "There is no difference between this occupation and the Soviet occupation of Afghanistan in 1979."[26]

ENDNOTES

1. Bremer on Iraq: We Really Didn't See the Insurgency Coming, NBC Dateline, January 6, 2006.
2. Counterinsurgency, U.S. Army FM 3-54, December 15, 2006.
3. Ibid.

4. Donna Miles, Abazaid, Swannick Escape Injury in Fallujah Attack, Armed Forces Information Services, February 12, 2004.
5. Alexandra J. Wall, Center of Iraq Insurgency May Have Ancient Jewish Ties, *Jewish News Weekly of Northern California*, December 10, 2004.
6. Grim Images of Fallujah Ambush Fill U.S. Airwaves, Middle East Online, April 1, 2005.
7. Ibid.
8. Sewell Chan and Karl Vick, U.S. Vows to Find Civilians Killers, *Washington Post*, April 1, 2004.
9. Sarmand S. Ali and Melinda Liu, Mutiny in the Ranks, *Newsweek*, April 16, 2004.
10. Anger Grows on Iraq Governing Council, Associated Press, April 9, 2004.
11. No Longer Unknowable: Falluja's April Civilian Toll Is 600, Iraq Body Count, October 26, 2004.
12. Brendan Miniter, The Fallujah Brigade, *Wall Street Journal*, June 1, 2004.
13. Private Warriors, PBS Frontline, April 21, 2005.
14. Kevin Drum, Political Animal-Fiasco in Fallujah, *Washington Monthly*, September 11, 2004.
15. Juan Cole, Will Sunnis Fight Shiites in Iraq? *Daily Star*, July 22, 2003.
16. Thanassis Cambanis, Cleric's Message Stirs Fears, *Boston Globe*, September 9, 2003.
17. Robert Fisk, Bremer Closes *Hardline* Newspaper and Iraqis Ask: Is This Democracy US-Style? *Independent*, March 30, 2004.
18. Closure of al-Sadr *Daily* Stirs Protests, Al Jazeera, March 29, 2004.
19. Arrest Warrant Issued for Iraqi Shi'ite Cleric al-Sadr, U.S. State Department.
20. Ibid.
21. Jeffery Gettleman and Douglas Jehl, Marines Were Killed in the Stronghold of Ramadi, *New York Times*, April 6, 2004.
22. Patrick Cockburn, A Guided Missile, a Misguided War, *Independent*, April 8, 2004.
23. Who Are the Insurgents? U.S. Institute of Peace Special Report.
24. Paul McGeogh, Share Power or Lose Control, *Sydney Morning Herald*, July 22, 2004.
25. Jeffrey Pool, Zarqawi's Pledge of Allegiance to Al Qaeda, Jamestown Foundation, December 16, 2004.
26. Interview with Mullah Krekar, LBC Broadcasting, August 10, 2003.

CHAPTER **11**

Stepping on Mercury

NOVEMBER 2004—SHOWDOWN AT FALLUJAH

The Americans had not forgotten their humiliation with the first Fallujah offensive, and intelligence had shown that the insurgents had created a base of operations in Fallujah that was unparalleled in Iraq. It needed to be cleared out, and the Sunni Triangle was going to be made safe for the upcoming elections in January 2005. The insurgents knew the attack was coming. Egyptian and Iraqi army intelligence agents had been captured carrying infrared strobes. All were executed by shots to the head or decapitated as spies. Fallujah was occupied by virtually every resistance group in Iraq, including the Army of Mohammed, the Army of the Mujahideen, the Secret Islamic Army of Iraq, the Islamic Army of Iraq, Ansar al-Sunnah, and al-Qaeda in Iraq. Three groups had their nationwide headquarters in Fallujah, including the Islamic Army of Iraq, the National Islamic Army (1920 brigades), and al-Qaeda in Iraq. The Americans were facing what they estimated were 2,000 Iraqi insurgents from the Army of Mohammed (the ex-Saddam Fedayeen), the Ansar al-Sunnah, and various smaller Iraqi groups. The American intelligence estimated there were only 200 foreign fighters in the city. With what was believed to be a small force, Mujahideen fighters in Fallujah and the Americans were going to have it out once and for all.

The Americans gave the insurgents an ultimatum to hand over their heavy weapons, which in this case was anything larger than a pistol, by midnight, November 8, 2004. The deadline came and went and the Mujahideen girded for battle. The insurgents had made Fallujah a warren of bunkered safe houses, arms caches, and pathways that led to every part of the Sunni Triangle. After the fighting in April, most road traffic from Jordan was under constant fire or hijacking. Fallujah wasn't just a warren for terrorists; it cut the rest of Iraq off from Jordan and Syria.

The Mujahideen leadership knew that it was a place to tie the Americans down. Wisely, its leaders left the city in advance so they could continue their terror campaign and wage the propaganda war.

Fallujah is divided in half by Highway 10, the main east-west highway in the city. The bottom half of the city center is referred to as the Old City. It is comprised of several neighborhoods as well as the industrial area. These areas showed the most resistance, as most of the fighting in the north drove the insurgents to the southern parts of the city. On the northwest side of the city was the Jolan District; it supported smaller insurgent groups and criminal gangs. The Mujahideen organized a unified command, called the National Islamic Command, that was centered in two parts of the city. Insurgents waited in fixed defensive positions or sent reconnaissance teams into the city's streets to see where the Americans would come in first. Some small contacts with U.S. Marine and Army Special Forces units occurred when their snipers opened up on roving patrols. Each resistance group dug caves and spider holes to hide weapons caches and filled schools, houses, and other sensitive cultural locations. In hard-core neighborhoods, the buildings were rigged with daisy-chained improvised explosive devices (IEDs), booby-trapped houses, and hundreds of roadside IEDs and sustained with dozens of bomb factories.

Out of 100 mosques in Fallujah, 60 were used in violation of the laws of war as sniper posts, observation towers and rocket-propelled grenade (RPG) strong points. The rules of war did not apply to the terrorist Mujahideen. Many were used as weapons storage caches where the squads of terrorists could run from location to location to get the ammunition, RPG rockets, and grenades that they needed. Intelligence reported tunnels connecting one mosque to the other. As each mosque fell, there would be a backup. With mosques like the Shaki Mahmud Mosque, the Hadhrah al-Muhammdaiyah Mosque, the Fallujah mosque, and Bediyah al-Samawat, weapons storage and resupply were always plentiful.

OPERATION PHANTOM FURY

On November 8, 2004, the U.S. forces, led by the Marine Corps, thrust into Fallujah directly and quickly. Six thousand marines supported by U.S. Army Special Forces and infantry as well as 1,300 Iraqi army and national guard troops blitzed the city. On the first day's march, over 70% of the city was seized, but it was the downtown and the Jolan District that housed the toughest nuts, and no force would be spared to break them.

The U.S. Army and Marine Corps struck hard. In the northwest sector along the river in the Jolan District, Mujahideen were quickly overrun. These were the smaller terror groups who lacked the professionalism and discipline of the hard-core Islamists. The strongest defensive locations of the Mujahideen lay downtown in the area of the Old City. In the Old City the insurgents set up their command post, called the National Islamic Resistance Operations Center (NIROC). It was a focal point for the Mujahideen from several groups. These groups formed a provisional command called Consultative Council of the Mujahideen of al-Fallujah (CCMF). The CCMF had a press spokesman who during the fighting was tasked to keep the Arab world up to date through interviews with Al Arabiya and Al Jazeera television. Calling from Fallujah, an insurgent who named himself Abu Sa'd ad-Daylami would brief the press on the locations of American advances and make claims about their successes and martyrs. Inadvertently, ad-Daylami gave lots of good intelligence about the insurgent tactics, including verifying rocket launches from three neighborhoods.

In the old city, fighting was intense as well as slow. The insurgents exacted blood at each step. Six marines were killed in the previous 3 days and more than 120 were wounded. Only 10% of the objective area had been taken even though now 80% of the city was controlled. The insurgents played ambush and targeted the M-1 tanks and marine amphibious assault vehicles (AAVs). The successful lessons learned by the Saddam Fedayeen in Naseriyah in the invasion and the First Battle of Fallujah were being played out. The marines quickly noted there were two types of insurgents in the fighting: guerrillas who fought and fell back and "martyrs" who fought and fought and fought until they died.[1] That same day the martyrs declared their intent to do just that style of fighting; in a statement read on Al Jazeera, the Islamic Mujahideen wrote, "Al-Fallujah Resistance pledged to die for their faith and city."

Fighting positions included cemeteries, fighting pits dug into the ground, and basements. The insurgents fell back on position after position and kept up the fire on the Americans at every turn. They resorted to desperate tactics, including rigging a suicide bomber with explosive vests and having him play dead until marines surrounded him only to blow up. Fear of this tactic caused an American marine to shoot a wounded insurgent in a mosque in front of a television camera crew.

The Mujahideen fought from every structure they could find. The laws of war did not apply to them, and they ignored any shred of human decency. People who did not assist them were summarily shot. They went to the three hospitals where they had casualties and fought from them when they needed to. They had more than 354 weapons caches hidden throughout the city full of mortar rounds, RPGs, and explosives. IED factories and garages for making suicide vehicle-borne improvised explosive devices (S-VBIEDs) were found in more than 26 locations. One human corpse was rigged as a roadside IED waiting for marines to pass by and detonate. Another corpse was rigged with grenades with the primer pins removed, so when the corpse was moved it would release the grenades. The body of an Iraqi woman, tortured and mutilated, was found in another location. The insurgents engaged U.S. Marine helicopter gunships when they could. The marines were flying at near rooftop levels and two AH-1W Sea Cobras were shot down without casualties.[2]

The NIROC was controlled by the National Islamic Resistance 1920 Revolution Brigades. When captured, many were surprised at its size and sophistication. It had communications, an Internet café, and weapons storage that indicated it was used by many jihadists as a central point to share intelligence and coordinate attacks before Phantom Fury. It was also found to be a training center filled with training manuals, videos of hostages being beheaded, and films of American forces being attacked. Exploited after the operation, the NIROC maintained a torture chamber with bloodstained walls and numerous sandbags filled with bloodied sand. The flags of the 1920 Revolution Brigades, several computers in a command and control room, defensive positions maps of the city, and a huge cache of weapons were recovered. On November 11, the Americans found a different sort of surprise. They discovered a human slaughterhouse and a hostage in one group's headquarters in Jolan District. Tawhid Wal-Jihad lost two explosives manufacturing safe houses for their suicide bombs full of chemicals. Another group, most likely the Saddam Fedayeen, had a safe house that manufactured passports and other documents from the interim government.

Insurgents would tie or "daisy chain" five or six 155 mm artillery shells together to create a huge IED and detonate them as squads entered the residence. In one incident, 3 solders were killed and 13 wounded when the building they were searching blew up and collapsed on them. It was the first of the "house-borne" IEDs. The resistance claimed 60 U.S. Marines dead, according to propaganda reports. The insurgents learned quickly to shoot the first man in the door when the marines stormed a room. They found this would bottle the soldiers up and distract the next men. Another group found that lying under the floorboards of a room allowed the terrorists to shoot up and through the wood floor. Basements became dug-in positions and the martyr insurgents, screaming "Allahu Akbar!" would fight until the Americans burned them out with white phosphorous or rockets. By November 16, the intensity of the fighting led to 30 more marines killed and 275 U.S. troops wounded. However, the U.S. Marines reported the city was at last secure. Sporadic fighting continued as insurgents withdrew to flee the city or stumbled into marine positions. But in the end, for all of their courage and toughness, the U.S. Marines had only stepped on a puddle of mercury. The insurgents evacuated and spread out into pockets of two and three fighters and engaged the Marine Corps at every chance over the following month. In the first week of December, the marines lost 71 men with more than 300 wounded. Fallujah became a ghost town. To secure it required it be cordoned off and no one allowed in the city without being approved by the coalition.

Though they had retreated, the Mujahideen were closely watching. The coalition removed many of the men involved in the fighting soon after the resistance was broken. In observing the supporting forces leave the city as well, one CCMF report from mid-December noted:

> The Consultative Council of the Mujahideen of al-Fallujah announces that the U.S. forces have withdrawn along all the four axes along which they were attacking the south of al-Fallujah—from the north, east, west, and south. This occurred after the defeat of the assault begun by the American forces at about 2pm Thursday, which lasted until about 11pm.... By the grace of God the Exalted, that attack was repulsed and significant losses were inflicted on the American forces which will be detailed tomorrow. According to preliminary estimates six of our fighters were martyred, one in a guerrilla operation that he carried out. Two rocket launchers belonging to our men were destroyed. U.S. forces also destroyed 17 houses of citizens in various places in the an-Nazal neighborhood and the ash-Shuhada' neighborhood.[3]

The final tally in Operation Phantom Fury was reportedly 1,200 insurgents killed and more than 1,000 captured, but no one seemed able to say where the remains were. Dr. Ali Fadhil in the movie *Fallujah, City of Ghosts* claimed most Mujahideen were Fallujan Iraqis and that the foreign Mujahideen had mostly left the city. The Americans claimed to have stored the bodies of hundreds of dead insurgents at the Hajji Dahham Ice Factory in the industrial zone. Marine patrols, accompanied by embedded journalists throughout the city, came up with little in the way of dead insurgents, so there was a terrific discrepancy between the estimated 1,200 to 1,600 enemy dead and the actual number of bodies recovered. The insurgents themselves, through the CCMF spokesman, claimed only 100 dead, but their accounts also had them denying the Americans took the city, so they would be less than forthcoming about casualties. Yet in the end, even the insurgents would accept the 1,000 dead figure for propaganda purposes. The most concrete count came from a visit to the Fallujah Martyrs' Cemetery by Dr. Ali Fadhil. At the gate is a sign that reads, "This cemetery is being given by the people of Fallujah to the heroic martyrs of the battle against the Americans and to the martyrs of the Jihadi operations against the Americans, assigned and approved by the Mujahideen Shura council in Fallujah." Meeting the keeper of the cemetery, he buried just 76 bodies of fighters.[4] The civilians suffered the worst of it. More than 2,000 people who did not leave the city were killed. One Fallujan, Sheik Mehdea Salah Jassam, told a journalist, "Fallouja did something bad and God sent the terrorists to punish us.... Then he sent the Americans to punish us some more."[5]

FIGURE 11.1   U.S. Army Humvee destroyed by roadside IED in Anbar Province. (From U.S. DoD.)

The insurgency did not stop while the fighting in Fallujah continued. A new series of tactics were being tried in the north of Iraq. The small-scale ambush attacks that had been carried out by the various insurgent groups never used more than 5 or 10 Mujahideen and 2 or 3 IEDs. In Mosul, the newly arrived American Stryker Brigade, using the Stryker armored personnel carrier, came under the largest attack to date when an estimated 70 insurgents ambushed them. The insurgents engaged the Americans with numerous RPGs and machine guns after setting over 10 daisy-chained IEDs. The patrol fought a massive battle out of the 2 km long kill zone and reassembled for a successful counter-attack (Figure 11.1).[6]

In Mosul, the single greatest loss of life in the war to date was inflicted in a noncombat setting. A suicide bomber from Ansar al-Sunnah, dressed as an Iraqi army soldier, managed to infiltrate the mess hall at the U.S. Army base camp, Camp Marez, and blow himself up. He killed 24 American and Iraqi soldiers and wounded 64 others.

RESISTANCE IN FALLUJAH WITHDRAWS

The balls of mercury that were the resistance forces in Fallujah were now gravitating to other cities and friendly groups. When Fallujah at last seemed peaceful, several attacks started to occur in Habbaniyah, Ramadi, Mosul, Tel Afar, and Qaim. The insurgents had withdrawn those whom they could and continued to keep up the pressure. Around

Fallujah, attacks occurred as well. Some resistance reports reflected real attacks, which were confirmed by the Americans, and others that were completely fabricated. However, some details of the foreign fighters in Anbar Province were coming out. The Americans had captured Moroccans, Saudis, and Syrians during the fighting. The CCMF, which had moved its headquarters to Qaim, reported that others, including Algerians, Egyptians, and a small contingent of Sudanese, had been martyred in the combat actions after withdrawal.[7] The National Islamic Resistance and the former regime insurgents had taken a brutal beating. In the Arab world, such a defeat is a badge of honor. They had stood up to the U.S. forces and been slaughtered. For the insurgents this meant they died for their nation, God, and each other, so they were martyred.

The Consultative Council of Mujahideen announcements ended and soon gave way to the more military-sounding General Command of the Islamic Resistance of Iraq (GCIRI). This organization may have been a regional support structure led by the Ansar al-Sunnah and which collectively supported smaller brigades. The first report came from the GCIRI-Mosul in December 2004, and another was followed by the GCIRI-al-Anbar. Whatever the moniker, it was clear that soon after, Fallujah groups were joining forces for ease of operations and revenge. In January 2005, the surviving leadership from Fallujah issued a communiqué to explain why they had withdrawn:

> The Declaration of Victory of the General Command of the Iraqi Islamic Resistance in the Battle of al-Fallujah, the second Battle of Badr.
>
> More than 1,000 of your brothers have died martyrs fighting devotedly in the path of God. But you harvested seven times that number of them [the enemy], and God is the witness of that, as are you, and some of the written news media testify to that as well, such as your brother the correspondent of Mafkarat al-Islam, may God reward them. They have striven with their tongues and their hearts in the best jihad.
>
> You know that God has supported us in the past and present battle of al-Fallujah. We are a small number, yet against us the Jews, Christians, and apostates from God's religion have massed. We have nothing but God, but He is the Best of supporters.
>
> As you know, you were able to repel, parry, and break the strongest army in the world, because God is stronger than it. With His help you were able to destroy that army. You killed them by the thousands and wounded them by the thousands. You destroyed more than thousands of pieces of their equipment.... You fought them and you were a match for that army. You established that you are the sons of the Community of Muhammad, and you showed that you are the stronger, by the grace of God.
>
> Therefore the General Command of the Iraqi Islamic Resistance, represented by all the fighting detachments and all the jihadi armies has resolved to pull out of al-Fallujah, the city of pride and glory, the

graveyard of the Americans, in order to preserve their noble lions and to take the battle to every inch of the wounded territory of Iraq, with all the fighters ... with their deadly weapons that have not and will not be exhausted, by the grace of God for many long years, until the infidel occupation leaves the free land of Iraq. We will begin the battle anew, calling it the Second Battle of the Clans.

On Fallujah—Observers noted that the events in al-Fallujah had resembled the Battle of Mu'tah [in the eighth year of the hijrah] in which 3,000 Muslims fought 200,000 Byzantines, and at which the new convert but seasoned military commander Khalid ibn al-Walid took over the Muslim leadership after three other commanders had been martyred. Khalid regrouped the Muslim fighters, reorganized their battle tactics so as to limit the Byzantines' ability to take advantage of their numbers. After nightfall he arranged a trick that fooled the Byzantines into thinking that a huge army was coming to reinforce the Muslims, who despite their small numbers had inflicted heavy losses on the Byzantines. The Byzantines, accordingly, withdrew and the Muslim army returned to al-Madinah. Upon its return when news spread that so many of their commanders had been killed, the army was accused of having fled. But the Prophet Muhammad announced that they had not fled but withdrawn in order so that, with God's will, they would advance again.[8]

The loss of Fallujah was a serious logistical blow to the insurgency and its ability to dominate the road access from Jordan to Baghdad, but psychologically it was not serious. The men who came for martyrdom got it, and the others received a rallying point to launch new offensives. In fact, it was a boon to recruitment, especially for men from Anbar Province and European Arabs.

SHOCK AND AWE JIHADIST STYLE—THE S-VBIED WAR

Fallujah was horrific, but it was not the end of the insurgency by any stretch of the imagination. In the run-up to the election at the end of January 2005, a new phase of the jihadists' war was starting. They would launch a jihadist variant of the American "shock and awe" strategy. To do it would take careful planning and husbanding of men and resources, but once it hit the coalition, they would appear helpless. The Mujahideen did not have cruise missiles or 2,000-pound laser-guided bombs, but they did have one ace in the hole: the human-guided weapon. The insurgents would launch a nationwide campaign of suicide bombs that would eclipse anything done before. Everything of value to the Americans or the new Iraqi government would be hit. Ministries, camps, recruiting centers, police stations, and American convoys would be specially targeted. The foreign Islamic extremists would also be allowed to strike their favorite targets, Shiite holy sites, funerals, and Husseinyahs, or Shiite prayer centers.

The plan was clearly a product of the imagination of the former regime intelligence and its insurgent group, Army of Mohammed (AOM). The AOM had announced its leadership of the General Command of the Islamic Resistance of Iraq (GCIRI) in a statement during the December attacks in Mosul. It was another convenient cover for the AOM, who were previously known as the Saddam Fedayeen. Since the Islamic extremists had expended much effort and manpower fighting in Fallujah, the AOM and its GCIRI had been working their daily IED war all over Iraq with nary a loss. During this time, the insurgents had been stealing and prepping a wide variety of cars to be converted into S-VBIEDs and infiltrating them into Baghdad. The vehicles were cut open and prewired for an explosive payload, which would be added just before they were assigned to a target. This meant the S-VBIEDs were just empty cars with special hollow points for explosives when they arrived in Baghdad. Filling them up was easy, as explosives and bombs were plentiful for all the groups involved. The former regime loyalists (FRLs) in the AOM were masters of infiltration to any Iraqi city, and this campaign could be easily done. The Islamic insurgents had large numbers of men who missed the Fallujah action and desired martyrdom; the FRLs and al-Qaeda in Iraq (AQI) had a large number of S-VBIEDs and a very long target list. The two would work together to ensure both of their goals would be met. The Tawhid Wal-Jihad, now formally transformed into al-Qaeda in Iraq, had been besting the FRLs in S-VBIED attacks for the previous 2 years. Al-Qaeda preferred the spectacular martyrdom attacks. For the jihadist shock and awe campaign, all of the insurgents would need to cooperate.

The coalition had been hit by S-VBIEDs before, but not the way they were going to be hit over the next few months. Al-Qaeda had not forgotten about keeping up the pressure on the coalition during the Fallujah campaign. Moreover, al-Zarqawi definitely had not forgotten about his hatred for the Jordanian government. On Christmas 2004, Saudi suicide bomber Ahmed Abdullah al-Shayea left his safe house to drive his S-VBIED, a fuel tanker full of explosives, into the Jordanian embassy. The tanker was rigged with a command detonator that would be ignited by a team leader and recorded by a videographer. The device exploded on target, killing 10 innocent victims, but miraculously al-Shayea, the driver, was not immediately vaporized. Somehow, the blast overpressure of the igniting fuel shot him through the windshield. He was thrown hundreds of feet away and mistaken for a victim. However, after he was being treated in the hospital for third-degree burns over 70% of his body the Iraqi police came to a realization that he was a foreigner—and no pieces of the bomber were found.[9] Based on information provided to the coalition from al-Shayea, two of al-Qaeda in Iraq's senior staff were arrested, including the central Iraq bomb master, Sami Muhammed Saeed al-Jafi. Al-Jafi was proud of his work, and once captured, he bragged openly about his bombs being used against the Jordanian embassy, the United Nations, and the murder of 125 Iraqis in Najaf when Sheik Hakim was killed. All in all, he claimed to have personally built 32 car bombs. He did not let on to what was to come.

The first clue of a change in operations came with the wave of attacks leading up to the elections. What was happening was hinted at in a January 26 communiqué by the GCIRI. They issued a statement that a campaign was beginning called Operations of the Children of Muhammad the Messenger of God to Break the Back of God's Enemies:

> Today, Wednesday, 16 Dhu al-Hijjah 1425H, the equivalent of 26 January 2005 represents the beginning of the end of the occupation and its ultimate collapse.... [GCIRI promised to] turn Iraq into a graveyard for the occupiers.... We have prepared weapons, ammunition and men sufficient to shake the earth under the feet of the occupiers. Leading us in this army of ours is Muhammad ibn 'Abdallah the trustworthy Messenger of God, may God's peace and blessings be upon him. Leading them is Bush, the infidel denier.[10]

From the beginning of the war to January 1, 2005, the coalition had been struck with 181 suicide bombings. In preparing for attacks leading up to the elections, U.S. Air Force Brig. Gen. Erv Lessel, deputy chief of staff for strategic communications in Iraq, said, "I think a worst case is where they have a series of horrific attacks that cause mass casualties in some spectacular fashion in the days leading up to the elections.... If you look over the last six months, they have steadily escalated the barbaric nature of the attacks they have been committing. A year ago, you didn't see these kinds of horrific things."[11] Perhaps General Lessel had not read the history of the suicide bombers in western Baghdad during the invasion; nevertheless, the coalition was about to get a new lesson.

Starting January 2, 2005, the suicide bomb wave rolled across Iraq, killing 22 Iraqi national guardsmen when an S-VBIED rammed their bus near Balad. The next day the Iraqi National Accord offices were struck by an S-VBIED. Another killed four Westerners returning from the airport to the Green Zone, and yet another hit a national guard recruiting office in Dujail. Then the Iraqi Special Forces compound was struck by a fuel truck bomb, killing 10. The next day it was S-VBIEDs in Baqubah, western Baghdad, against a U.S. convoy, then another convoy in Ameriyah. Later, on January 5, a pedestrian-borne improvised explosive device (PBIED) bomber joined a crowd of men waiting for jobs with the police in Ramadi; 80 were killed. Another PBIED blew up in

Karbala, killing 45 on the same day. Virtually every police station was a target. Political party offices from the Shiite SCIRI headquarters, passport offices in Tikrit, gates to the Green Zone, and to the Ministry of the Interior—all were being struck by suicide car bombs. On election day suicide bombers struck polling places in Baghdad. The elections were a success, but disrupting the polls was not the principal goal of the insurgents. Their principal goal was to show that the loss in Fallujah did not matter because the rest of the insurgency was alive, active, and capable of more terror than ever before.

The intensity of the campaign continued through February with multiple attacks in Baghdad, Iskanderiyah, Mosul, Baqubah, Abu Dishr, Mahmudiyah, Haweijah, Kirkuk, Latifiyah, Tikrit, and Mussaieb. The only difference that month was that in two bombings on the same day in Baghdad and Baya, a small town south of Baghdad, the bombers were wearing explosive vests and riding bicycles. One of them was from Sudan or sub-Saharan Africa. The month ended with a final massacre of 114 people killed and 129 wounded in Hillah at a medical center. Throughout the months of March to August, dozens of S-VBIEDs and S-PBIEDs would strike Iraq, bringing the total since 2003 to more than 400 suicide attacks, the most recorded and sustained suicide bomb campaign since the Japanese Kamikaze in World War II.

The litany of the attacks is far too large and graphic to detail here, but the trend shifted to a wider spread of targets and a deepening hatred toward the Shiites. Whatever advantage the offensive in Fallujah had done to deny the insurgents the capacity to strike had been lost in a wall of mushroom clouds. Perhaps it was al-Zarqawi's attempt to move Iraq from a guerrilla war against America to a civil and religious war against all of Shiite Islam. It would not be unbelievable. By 2006, Iraq would teeter on the brink of civil war. The new Iraqi army was predominantly made up of Kurds and Shiite soldiers, and when they operated in the Sunni Triangle, it bred hatred and discontent. Capt. Bart Nagle, an intelligence officer with the 1st Battalion, 5th Marine Regiment in Ramadi, once told journalists, "You get a Shi'a outsider shooting a local policeman, and with a big incident like that, you can see the whole city rising up."[12]

By May 2005, over 250 car bombs had struck throughout Iraq, killing 938 people and wounding 1,771.[13] The U.S. military was so concerned about the claims from al-Zarqawi that AQI was conducting the majority of the bombings that the U.S. commanders were seriously considering shifting their 2-year-long emphasis from going after the Ba'athist insurgents, who were killing two U.S. soldiers per day, to almost exclusively going after foreign groups. This created a firestorm of controversy between traditional intelligence officers, who saw the insurgency for what it was, an orchestrated amalgam of groups being supported by the former regime loyalists, and those who needed to get al-Zarqawi for propaganda purposes.[14] Collectively, the S-VBIED war was not where America was taking the most casualties. The most dangerous mission in Iraq was driving down a road—any road. Removing intelligence assets from the main force of the insurgency and focusing on al-Zarqawi and the foreign fighters would prove terribly fatal for the U.S. Army. In the end, there was a split, and some of the resources were shifted to the foreign fighters.

THE JIHAD REACHES OUT—AQI ATTACKS IN JORDAN

Al-Zarqawi may have been running one of the smaller insurgency groups, but he never forgot that the global Salafist revolution he foresaw from the womb of Iraq was really a campaign to inspire the same events across the Middle East. Tawhid Wal-Jihad, his original group of operatives, had converted officially to al-Qaeda in Iraq, but it still had good capability to extend his reach to American interests in Jordan.

On August 19, 2005, three members of al-Qaeda in Iraq laid the finishing touches on improvised rocket launchers they had built in their warehouse on the north side of Aqaba, Jordan. Most likely, the rockets were Chinese 107 mm type 63 artillery rockets with high explosive fragmentation warheads. Although not very accurate, they are used everywhere by the Mujahideen in Lebanon, Palestine, Iraq, Syria, and Afghanistan; they are also easy to smuggle, perhaps in pipes or as scrap metal. Sitting on the hills of Aqaba, the insurgents had a beautiful down-valley view of the Jordanian port of Aqaba and the Israeli city of Eliat's airport. The geometric calculations had been done, and the rails had been aligned at the precise angle and bearing for the rocket to fly to its intended targets: two U.S. warships—one of them an amphibious assault ship, the USS *Kearsarge* covered with U.S. Marines Corps helicopters, and another amphibious ship, the USS *Ashland*—and the Israeli airport. With this attack, al-Qaeda would be able to claim having struck both America and Israel, all done in the face of their "puppet," the government of Jordan. The rocket attack cell was a wing of al-Qaeda's Martyr Abdullah al-Azzam Brigades, named after the famous Palestinian friend of Osama bin Laden who created the Azzam Brigades, an organization that would become al-Qaeda. Although Abdullah Azzam may have become a martyr at the hands of bin Laden himself, he was revered among Mujahideen. This same group, which claimed the suicide bomb attack on Western tourists at the Egyptian city of Sharm al-Sheik, was suspected of "border dancing" between Egypt, Jordan, Palestine, Syria, and Iraq. In Egypt, they had killed more than 100 innocent people. They had access to weapons, equipment, and manpower from Islamic extremists in each country. On August 19, 2005, at 8:22 a.m., the first of the Katyusha rockets flew off the rails and narrowly missed the USS *Ashland*. It hit a nearby Jordanian army warehouse and killed a soldier. The second rocket missed entirely and exploded near a hospital. The third, aimed at Israel, struck an empty street near Eliat's international airport. Although ultimately unsuccessful, the attacks raised the specter of a spreading conflict.

Al-Zarqawi did not wait long to again demonstrate his newfound professionalism and power back to his enemies in Jordan. On November 9, 2005, he dispatched four suicide bombers, including one husband and wife team, to Amman, Jordan. They struck three large hotels popular with Westerners, including the Days Inn, the Hyatt, and the Radisson SAS. The attacks killed 57 and wounded 117 people. The Radisson SAS was a logical target. Al-Qaeda tends to have a long institutional memory and prefers to strike a target that has been missed in previous attacks. Al-Zarqawi himself had been implicated in a plot to blow this hotel up on New Year's during the year 2000 millennium celebrations. Each of the AQI suicide bombers was wearing PBIED explosive vests. Each had entered when the waiting areas were the most crowded, and then detonated within minutes of each other. A fourth bomber, the woman in the husband and wife team, failed to detonate her belt and was arrested. She had a PBIED belt made of RDX explosive and packed with industrial ball bearings. Note that RDX was the same type of explosive stolen from the Iraqi nuclear weapons program storage lockers at Al Qaqaa in 2003. She confessed she was a member of al-Qaeda in Iraq and she had been dispatched by Abu Mussab al-Zarqawi.

ENDING AL-ZARQAWI

By September 2005, al-Zarqawi's precision attacks had become enough of a nuisance that even the chief of army intelligence in Iraq, Army Maj. Gen. Richard Zahner, seemed to throw in the towel on the Ba'athists and wanted to focus solely on al-Zarqawi. Zahner said, "I think what you really have here is an insurgency that's been hijacked by a terrorist campaign.... In part, by Zarqawi becoming the face of this thing, he has certainly gotten the funding, the media and, frankly, has allowed other folks to work along in his draft.... You'll see some of the old regime elements on there, mainly just to maintain pressure and, frankly, accountability.... But when you look at those individuals central to the inflicting of huge amounts of violence, it really is not those folks. The Saddamists, the former regime guys, they're riding this."[15]

Zahner was absolutely correct; the FRLs were riding the al-Zarqawi wave, and that is how they had made 2004, 2005, and 2006 more deadly than each previous year. Others saw the picture as it truly has been since the start. Anthony Cordesman from the Center for Strategic and International Studies, speaking to the *Washington Post*, stated:

> Both Iraqis and coalition people often exaggerate the role of foreign infiltrators and downplay the role of Iraqi resentment in the insurgency.... It makes the government's counterinsurgency efforts seem more legitimate, and it links what's going on in Iraq to the war on terrorism. When people go out into battle, they often characterize enemies in the most negative way possible. Obviously there are all kinds of interacting political prejudices they can bring out by blaming outsiders.

In the end, Pentagon officials saw al-Zarqawi as public enemy number one, which meant al-Zarqawi's strategy of the spectacular attack worked to the benefit of the former regime insurgents. After 3 years of searching, the manhunt for al-Zarqawi also revealed the true limits of what 160,000 men can do in a country of 25 million.

By late fall 2005, the U.S. forces went on the offensive again to find al-Zarqawi and destroy his forces by carrying out operations almost simultaneously in Mosul, Tel Afar, and a large sweep through Qaim near the Syrian border. In fact, from January 2006, al-Qaeda in Iraq had suffered grievous losses. More than 200 members had been killed, captured, or wounded, yet the attacks increased throughout the summer. However, al-Zarqawi's time ran out on June 8, 2006. By tracking his followers through the use of American and Iraqi counterintelligence, al-Zarqawi was positively identified entering a safe house near Baqubah. With Special Forces soldiers observing, an F-16 fighter-bomber dropped 2,000-pound laser-guided bombs onto the house. Al-Zarqawi died in the strike, and with him the Americans hoped they had broken the back of the insurgency. Al-Zarqawi's death had not lessened the al-Qaeda insurgency. Suicide bombers and partisan attacks increased. The lesson the Americans seemed to not learn was that it is easier to kill a single man than to stop his dreams.

ENDNOTES

1. Sgt. E.J. Catagnus Jr., Cpl. B.Z. Edison, LCpl. J.D. Keeling, and LCpl. D.A. Moon, Lessons Learned: Infantry Squad Tactics in Military Operations in Urban Terrain during Operation Phantom Fury in Fallujah, Iraq, Unclassified After Action Report, March 15, 2005.
2. Operation Al-Fajr, Operation Phantom Fury, Global Security, http://www.globalsecurity.org/military/ops/oif-phantom-fury-fallujah.htm.

3. Iraqi Resistance Reports, December 16, 2004.
4. Ali Fadhil, Fallujah, City of Ghosts, *The Guardian*, January 11, 2005.
5. Tony Parry, After Leveling City, U.S. Tries to Build Trust, *LA Times*, January 7, 2005.
6. Iraqi Police, Multi-National Forces Foil Insurgent Attacks, U.S. Central Command Press Release, December 4, 2004.
7. Iraqi Resistance Reports, December 31, 2004.
8. Iraqi Resistance Reports, January 23, 2005, http://www.albasrah. net/moqawama/english/0105/iraqiresistancereport_230105.htm.
9. Rod Nordland, Tom Masland, and Christopher Dickey, The Insurgents, *Newsweek*, February 7, 2005.
10. Iraqi Resistance Reports, Communique from the GC of the Iraqi Islamic Resistance.
11. Dusan Stojanovic, General Warns of "Spectacular" Attacks in Iraq, Associated Press, January 8, 2005.
12. Ann Scott Tyson, To the Dismay of Local Sunnis, Shiites Arrive to Police Ramadi, *Washington Post*, May 7, 2005.
13. The Iraq Index, Brookings Institution, June 23, 2005.
14. U.S. Iraq Officers Shift Focus on Insurgents, *Washington Post*, May 9, 2005.
15. Bradley Graham, Zarqawi Hijacked Insurgency, *Washington Post*, September 28, 2005.

SECTION IV

No Longer a Wounded Lion

AQI to ISIS (2006–2014)

CHAPTER 12

Al-Qaeda's Lonely Road to Recovery

THE METAMORPHOSIS FROM AQI TO THE ISLAMIC STATE OF IRAQ (2006–2011)

As early as 2005 al-Qaeda in Iraq (AQI) had sought to carve out a national entity within Iraq. They went so far as to declare an Islamic Emirate of Iraq. At the time they only occupied a few dozen safe houses in the Western governorates, some in Baghdad and a neighborhood in Anbar Province. The Jolan District in Fallujah had been dominated by AQI members and sympathizers starting in the months after the invasion. It was quickly lost along with more than 1,000 jihadist fighters to the U.S. Marines, who rooted them out in intense house-to-house combat. Even without occupying any land, they understood that the concept of appearing to be a virtual entity was a psychological multiplier for their fighters. Better to be considered heroes of a nation instead of operatives in a terrorist group. Under the protection of the Iraqi Sunni community, they wanted to carve out a piece of secure terrain that would allow foreign fighters to abandon their homes and families, come via Syria to the "state" in their jihadist version of the Prophet Mohammed's Hijra (emigration), and start a new life toward an eventual place in paradise. They could take on local wives, train, brag, and fight alongside other men like themselves. They needed a place of their own where they could be involved in something bigger than themselves—they could fight like the companions of the prophet Mohammed in a real, live jihad against the "crusaders" and "apostates." The best of them would volunteer to die in martyrdom bombings and go straight to heaven! So it was decided that even itinerant "knights" needed a base of operations to call home.

Fostering this romantic image was extremely important to AQI for recruitment. Osama bin Laden wanted Iraq to become the central battlefield in the Middle East. As Abu Musab al-Zarqawi and his men achieved success, they would ultimately convert or betray their Iraqi sponsors by any means necessary to start the formation of a religious nation in the mold of the Taliban's Afghanistan. Iraq would become a safe harbor from which to spread their fighters, weapons, and ideology to destabilize other nations of the Muslim world, including Saudi Arabia and Syria.

In early 2005, with the al-Qaeda chief's blessing, they declared an Islamic Emirate of Iraq. This rebranding never really caught on, but it was more important internally to establish a change in mindset for the fighters. Then again, previous name changes by AQI were overshadowed by al-Zarqawi's brutality. Tenzim al-Qa'ida fi Balad al-Rafidayn, or al-Qaeda in Iraq, remained the battlefield name for its fighters. Besides, the news and social media loved this name.

One year later al-Zarqawi was dead and the Americans were starting to discover that some Sunni tribes did not want al-Qaeda's brand of Islam. Abu Ayyub al-Masri, a former Egyptian Army officer who operated under the nickname Abu Hamza al-Muhajir, took over AQI after al-Zarqawi's death (Figure 12.1). Unlike al-Zarqawi, he listened to the leadership of al-Qaeda and sought to create a more inclusive group where all jihadists could operate together to create the only legitimate Islamic nation-state on earth. This effort at reaching out was necessary. In some of the frontline zones Iraqi religious extremist (IRE) groups were finding that logistics and manpower were becoming difficult. Some groups were not getting supplies or fighters while taking on a large share of the day-to-day combat. Due to al-Zarqawi's notoriety, AQI was reaping the lion's share of foreign fighters and was accused of ignoring Iraqi Islamic groups. The operational difficulties also increased. Many of the Sunni tribes in Anbar governorate under the influence of Sheikh Abdul Sattar Abu Risha al-Dulaimi, chief of the biggest tribe in Anbar, formed the Sawahat al-Anbar (the Anbar Awakening) to reject AQI's operations.

FIGURE 12.1 Al-Qaeda commanders Abu Ayyub al-Masri (Egyptian) and Abu Umar al-Baghdadi (Iraqi) take command in 2005 after the death of Abu Mussab al-Zarqawi.

Abu Risha's turning on AQI led to a series of tribal defections to the central government. That started the withdrawal of the major Sunni former regime loyalist combat forces away from the armed insurgency. At the same time, the Americans started to produce results in intelligence collection that led to the killing or capturing of senior members of many groups.

AQI and its advisory council decided that to counteract the Awakening, it would need to form its own alliance of tribes and fighters. On October 9, 2006, the Mujahideen Shura Council announced the formation of the Mutayibeen Coalition.[1] Al-Masri knew he would need to bring all fighters and Sunni tribes loyal to jihad together to counteract the effect of losing the largest insurgent groups in Iraq. The Ansar al-Sunnah and jaysh al-Mohammed, the former regime loyalist terrorists, were joining the government supporting "Sons of Iraq" as part of the Awakening. As ex-terrorists, they were becoming lethally effective enemies. The key to doing anything in the Sunni regions relies on the direct cooperation of the tribal chiefs. Without their permission, nothing was possible—no operation was safe. Al-Zarqawi could not stand negotiation and preferred elimination of tribal chiefs who opposed him. He would kidnap their relatives and force their daughters to marry his jihadists—after they had been raped, of course. Al-Zarqawi wanted coalition by rule of the gun. He was scolded by harsh letters from al-Qaeda's advisory council members, such as Aymen al-Zawahiri and Attiya al-Jaza'eri. They told him to work with the tribes, stop the beheadings, and rein in the foreign attacks on Jordan and Israel by AQI cells. Al-Masri understood what al-Zarqawi could not. Tribal politics trump everything and combat success was job number one—territorial expansion could come at a later date.

Khalf al-Mutayibeen, which is Arabic for "Coalition of the Nobility," proclaimed it would act as an umbrella organization for all Sunni jihadist groups and tribes that shared its vision of warfare and nation building. For the first time, Iraqi operatives and commanders would be allowed to take over leadership roles and directly supervise foreign fighters as equals. Al-Qaeda Central (AQC), the favored name for the original senior leadership of the group, remained hidden in Pakistan. They were wisely encouraging integration of all Iraqi groups. Al-Zawahiri dispatched a liaison officer to al-Masri, an Iraqi named Khaled Abdul-Fattah Dawoud Mahmoud al-Mashhadani (Figure 12.2). Al-Mashdani was better known as Abu Shaheed. Abu Shaheed was the highest ranking of the Iraqis in AQC's senior management team and would be vital to meeting bin Laden's vision of bringing all groups onboard for a unified jihad structure. With his help, al-Masri created a truly integrated force comprised of an international jihadist collective that gave Iraqi locals a lead role since they knew the terrain and where to pressure the Shiite

FIGURE 12.2   Khaled al-Mashadani (aka Abu Shaheed) was bin Laden's senior liaison to ISI before his capture in 2007. He attempted to mislead by telling U.S. intelligence that ISI and its leaders were fictitious entities and statements were given by actors.

government. Operationally, they would all be called the Islamic State of Iraq (ISI).

The Mutayibeen declaration stated that the jihadists had established a free Sunni "Islamic state" composed of the eight northwest and western governorates in Iraq, as well as Baghdad. In their first collective statement, they said:

> These are the glad tidings coming out from the Land of the Two Rivers, the land of the Caliphates, and from Baghdad, the home of the Khilafa, may Allah free it from the Crusaders [Americans] and Saffavids [Iranians], in the blessed month of Ramadan. The fruits of the tree of Tawheed [monotheism] that the martyrs watered with their blood, have ripened and their time for harvest has come.
>
>   The truthful Mujahideen in the land of the two rivers have unified and reinforced one another and announce to the Muslims everywhere and Ahl-as-Sunni in Iraq especially, the glad tiding of the establishment of the State of Truth, the State of Islam that will implement Allah's Shariah for the people in the land, that will protect Islam and be a strong shield for Ahl-as-Sunni in the land of the two rivers.[2]
>
>   It is the pleasure of the Media Committee to present to all Muslims the official spokesman of the Islamic State of Iraq, the spokesman of the Ministry of Information, to bring you the good news. And we call Upon all Muslims in the world, to support this state with money, men and Du'a, and Allah has full power and control over His affairs, but most of the men know not, and to Allah belongs all thanks and favour.[3]

The communiqué also delineated the boundaries of the Islamic State:

> Your brothers announce the establishment of the Islamic State in Baghdad, Anbar, Diyala, Kirkuk, Salah al-Din, Ninawa, and in other

parts of the governorate of Babel, in order to protect our religion and our people. Further, the Mujahid delivers a special call to the tribal heads in Iraq, and to all Sunni Muslims in that country, to pledge loyalty to the Emir of the Believers, Abu Umar al-Baghdadi, by their adherence and obedience.[4]

On July 18, 2007, Abu Shaheed was arrested by U.S. and Iraqi forces. In a brilliant display of counterintelligence, al-Mashadani soon had some U.S. interrogators convinced that there was no commander of AQI after al-Zarqawi. He claimed that Abu Ayyub al-Masri did not even exist. He also claimed that that ISI was not a real organization, but just a front for al-Qaeda.

Al-Mashadani was clever enough to give up enough information that was real and verifiable in order to spread his disinformation. He even stated that ISI media recordings of Ayyub al-Masri were an actor reading lines created by committee. U.S. force commanders questioned the veracity of the claim but gave it some credibility to the news media, maybe to smoke out al-Masri or to see which group would actually claim leadership. In the end, the ruse didn't work. Intelligence indicated that there was a real person named al-Masri and that he was working with a senior Iraqi commander, Abu Umar al-Baghdadi. They were coordinating missions hand in hand. During this period al-Masri oversaw major terror operations in Iraq that included hundreds of improvised explosive device (IED) attacks and massive suicide bombings. He and Abu Umar even managed to place an IED at the house of Abdul Sattar Abu Risha for his treachery in creating the Anbar Awakening. It killed him instantly. However, it was the joint pragmatism of al-Masri and Abu Umar that made ISIS flourish. They decided to allow the Iraqis to take the lead of ISI in the insurgency that would have longer-lasting consequences.

The 2009 inauguration of a new American president didn't change the outlook of ISI toward the Americans. Whether the American President was George W. Bush or Barack H. Obama mattered little. They had a caliphate to establish and the crusaders were still in Iraq so the killings would continue.

Now that both Iraqi and foreign fighters were vertically integrated, the ISI suicide tactics decidedly improved. The ISI kept up a sustained suicide bombing campaign. Deploying people in trucks to blow up was safer than complex small infantry attacks. For now, they would capitalize on the Iraqi groups' expertise at covert infiltration of men, weapons, and explosive trucks into the cities. One of the largest bombings in Iraq's history occurred in August 2009, when the Iraqi Foreign Ministry and Finance Ministry in Baghdad were attacked simultaneously, resulting in over 250 dead. More importantly, they targeted the hotel of the Awakening councils during a national meeting of all the tribal sheiks.

The suicide truck bomb managed to killed dozens of "traitors" meeting with the Iraqi government.

AQI/ISI had been using IED and individual suicide bombs for years, but al-Masri and Abu Umar decided using multiple suicide car bomb attacks in a spectacular fashion was sure to get more satellite TV airtime, particularly if the TV crews were the target. Deliberately attacking the media would give anyone reporting in or on Iraq a message—we will not be ignored. On the morning of February 16, 2010, no less than four suicide vehicle-borne improvised explosive devices (S-VBIEDs) struck at the four hotels that supported the foreign news media. The attack started when a bomb was set off near a police station in central Baghdad. It brought the journalists and TV crews to their balconies to see what was happening across the traffic circle at Firdos Square. This attack was strategically selected, as it was in direct line of sight to the mezzanine balcony in the Palestine Hotel. Virtually all television satellite crews in the world used this location as a backdrop for reporting on Iraq from the safety of the Palestine and adjacent Ishtar Sheraton Hotels. When the journalists rushed to the windows, balconies, and the roof to see the attack, a second car bomb rammed the Texas barriers that protected the building—Texas barriers are 12- to 20-foot-high interlocking concrete walls. The massive explosion breached the wall. Moments later a third human-guided truck bomb, this one a 20-ton cement mixer filled with high explosives, crawled into the opening between the two hotels. It was stuck momentarily on the concrete debris, and that was the chance the Americans needed to stop the attack. The snipers and machine gunners on the top of the Sheraton opened fire and raked the giant truck with hundreds of direct hits. An American army sniper managed to place the killing shot through the head of the driver and the vehicle ground to a halt halfway through the walls. But ISI prepared for that possibility too; a backup "trigger" team detonated the truck with a remote cell phone detonator attached to the cement mixer. The explosion devastated the two hotels. Fortunately for the journalists, it had not completely entered the breach; if it had, it would have most likely collapsed both buildings (Figure 12.3).

On the other side of downtown, a S-VBIED raced up the ramp to the formidable Babylon Hotel and exploded in the entrance. The Babil was a massive concrete monstrosity on the south side of the Euphrates River situated directly across from the new American embassy in the Green Zone. It was a former guest hotel where Saddam would spy on his guests with listening devices built in to each room.

The S-VBIED onslaught was not complete. A fourth S-VBIED in a stolen ambulance raced into the perimeter of the Hamra Hotel. This hotel was favored by freelance journalists not associated with big media outfits. Located near the Australian embassy, the Hamra's location gave it security advantages: a narrow street blocked by armed guards and

FIGURE 12.3 A massive cement mixer S-VBIED prepares to devastate the Palestine and Sheraton Hotels in Baghdad.

a security barrier cut it off from Karada Street, and it had a T-barrier wall that surrounded it. Previous attempts to hit it had failed, so it was believed to be relatively safe. However, because the hotel let its guard down, an ISI car bomb in the guise of an ambulance managed to get past the security barrier and explode inside of the perimeter. The day's tally was 36 dead and hundreds wounded, but the value of such a high-profile antimedia attack was priceless.

However, the Americans were now operating at their best in counterintelligence. Having eschewed ruthless interrogation, they used effective methods of gleaning information. Intense professional interviews and cash incentives got them actionable tips. They were also working with the former Iraqi insurgents and had a good track record on helping break ISI cells. One such tip led them to carry out a combined U.S.-Iraqi Special Forces raid on a house in Tikrit. On the night of April 17, 2010, the residence under surveillance was confirmed by Iraqi and U.S. intelligence assets to have one or two high-value targets (HVTs) present. The mission was handed off to the combined Iraqi-U.S. Special Forces. The mission was to capture the targets, but if resistance was met, they were to use any and all force necessary to neutralize them. As the task force attempted to take the residence, they were fired upon by the occupants. The Iraqis and Americans called in aerial missile support. Between the Hellfire missile bombardment, rockets, and gunfire, Abu Ayyub al-Masri and Abu Umar al-Baghdadi were killed. Al-Qaeda was again decapitated. One American Army Ranger was killed when a supporting UH-60 helicopter crashed returning from the mission.

The deaths of the two ISI commanders finally put to rest the notion that Abu Umar was a fictional character. A full dossier was released, including confirmation of his DNA. Quite a bit was known about Abu Umar al-Baghdadi. He was an Iraqi-born Hamid Dawud Mohamed Khalil al-Zawi. He was the senior Iraqi member of the Mujihdeen Shura Council (MSC), along with Abu Musab al-Zarqawi, spiritual advisor Sheik Abd al-Rahman, and operations officer Abu Ayyub al-Masri and Abu Shaheed, the Iraqi who was the AQC's liaison to ISI.[5] Abu Umar was highly successful at staying out of the line of fire even though the entirety of U.S. forces was searching for him. Unlike al-Zarqawi, he led operations from the rear, maintained a high level of operational security, and managed the ISI like a CEO. He directed subordinate commanders to carry out missions and report back results, and fine-tuned the campaigns despite enormous pressure from the Americans and Iraqi government. Operating in Anbar and other Sunni areas was increasingly difficult as well, though under Abu Umar attacks were sustained, devastating, and professional. Although he was named as al-Zarqawi's successor in 2005, he actually would not lead combined operations until 2007. For a fictional character, Abu Umar was alleged to have been captured or killed no less than three times between 2007 and 2010.

Fortunately for the insurgency, the winding down of U.S. combat operations required the closing of Camp Bucca in 2009. Camp Bucca was the principal detention facility for the bulk of the Iraqi extremist insurgents captured in the five previous years. Despite the best efforts of American security forces, the detention of so many suspected and real insurgents at Camp Bucca had inadvertently created a concentrated ideas and team building environment. This location allowed the guilty, the innocent, and the unlucky to convalesce, strengthen relationships, and hobnob among the terror elite. Camp Bucca allowed the lowest key insurgents to meet, share lessons and knowledge, and conduct terror practicums on what each different group had learned from dealing with a large-scale professional force such as the Americans. The detainees knew they would eventually be released and that the Iraqi army would just be a hollow, well-equipped shell the U.S. Army designed.

One of those low-key Iraqi detainees was nicknamed Abu Bakr al-Baghdadi, an Iraqi held captive for 4 years in Camp Bucca. With the death of the top two commanders, he would be tapped to be leader of al-Qaeda in Iraq's next generation, the Islamic State of Iraq and Syria (ISIS).[6]

FORMATION OF THE REAL ISLAMIC STATE OF IRAQ (ISI)

Abu Ayyub al-Masri and Abu Umar al-Baghdadi were dead. It was a low point for the organization and a blow to jihadist cooperative efforts.

Militarily they were being damaged. Politically the situation was improving. Iraqi Prime Minister Nouri al-Maliki was behaving like a pure partisan Shiite. His decision to cut out the Sunni tribes from ruling or gaining favor was isolating the Western governorates. The former insurgents who had joined the pro-government Awakening councils found themselves shut out of work; salaries were cut and their weapons often confiscated. The *New York Times* reported that by October 2010 men in the Sunni regions could only find work for their peculiar skills with the one company that was hiring—the Islamic State of Iraq.[7] The rosters of ISI's cells started growing, and news of the American withdrawal in the next year stoked their motivation.

The new ISI commander, Abu Bakr al-Baghdadi (Figure 12.4), appreciated his predecessor's efforts of bringing all jihadists together, but he was cut from the al-Zarqawi brand of stone. Abu Bakr wanted to sustain the pressure and continue the high-profile strategic terror attacks, but with a touch more ruthlessness. He decided that the Christians of Iraq had been sorely overlooked and needed his special brand of attention.

On October 31, 2010, an eight-man team of ISI terrorists penetrated Baghdad's Karada District and attacked the Assyriac Catholic church, As-Sayadat al-Najat ("Our Lady of Salvation"). They struck first by killing guards and throwing explosives at the Iraqi stock exchange across the street, but their real objective was to conduct a suicide hostage-barricade at the church. They would seize the Christian worshipers, make wild media-grabbing demands, and then kill themselves and all of the hostages at the moment they were opposed. It would be a textbook attack.

After killing the guards at the stock exchange, the ISI terrorists entered the church and started shooting. They killed 2 priests and took

Wanted
Information leading to the location of
Abu Du'a
Up to $10 Million Reward

Place of Birth : Samarra, Iraq
Date of Birth : 1971
Sex : Male
Hair : Black
Eyes : Brown
Complexion : Olive
Aliases : Dr. Ibrahim 'Awwad Ibrahim 'Ali al-Badri al-Samarrai', Ibrahim 'Awad Ibrahim al-Badri al Samarrai, Abu Duaa', Dr. Ibrahim, Abu Bakr al-Baghdadi

FIGURE 12.4 A U.S. Justice of Department rewards poster for Abu Musab al-Bagdadi, the leader of AQI/ISI/ISIL. He planned the 2010 massacre at the Church of Our Lady of Salvation in Baghdad. (From U.S. Department of Justice.)

100 worshippers hostage. Knowing that the church was directly located between two major U.S. and Iraqi bases, they waited for a response. During the lull they carried out typical al-Qaeda hostage barricade activities seen in Saudi Arabia, Yemen, and Pakistan. First, they rigged the building with IEDs and booby traps. Then the terrorist cell leader called the Arab news media. Al Baghdadiya television received a call from the church demanding the release of al-Qaeda sympathizers in Egypt and Iraq. The terrorist cell leader spoke about their complaints about Muslim women's treatment in Egypt by Coptic Christians. ISI also released a statement that read:

> The Ministry of War of the Islamic State of Iraq announces that all Christian centers, organizations, and committees, whether their leaders or their workers, are legitimate targets for the Mujahideen wherever they may be. Let these idolaters know, especially the senile Vatican Taghoot, that the sword of death will not rise from the necks of their followers until they announce their disassociation from the doings of the dog of the Egyptian Church, and they show the Mujahideen true efforts that they are pressurizing this war waging Church to free the female prisoners of their Church. Let them stay to their monasteries after this, and stop their attacks against Islam, His Book, and His Prophet (s), and its followers.[8]

Knowing the demands were unsupportable, the attacks intended to draw coalition forces into a bloodbath. It was more than 2 hours before the Iraqi Special Forces stormed the church. In the ensuing melee 41 hostages, 2 priests, and 7 policemen were killed along with all of the ISI terrorists. The ISI team detonated suicide vests and IEDs they had placed as the assault began.

In classic al-Qaeda fashion, they succeeded in staging an attack that the pope himself had to address and which mortified most of the world. This attack may also have been a final salute to the Egyptian members of al-Qaeda in honor of the Egyptian Abu Ayyub al-Masri killed earlier in the year.

The December 2011 withdrawal of American forces went without one shot fired at them. A parting gift from ISI, but even with the Americans gone there were dangers. Now the Iraqi Special Forces and special police continued the night raids exactly like the Americans, but the level of counterintelligence pressure lowered. Five years of attacks and a lack of support by the Sunni tribes in western and northern Iraq, coupled with an Iraqi army that demonstrated rudimentary combat capability, managed to reduce some ISI units into skeleton forces, but in 2011 and 2012 their ranks swelled; 2011 was the most successful recruitment year for al-Qaeda in Iraq since 2006, especially if one adds the return of many Sunni insurgents to the fight in ISI's trademark black jerseys.

In 2012 Abu Bakr decided to once again work on undermining the confidence of the government and the security forces' ability to protect prominent individuals and facilities. He launched a campaign called Destroying the Walls.[9] The strategic goal was to build confidence in the Sunni communities that the Islamic State of Iraq and Syria (ISIS) was attacking on their behalf against hated al-Maliki locations such as the judiciary and the intelligence agencies. Al-Baghdadi said in a statement that this campaign was to release prisoners and kill judges and prosecutors throughout Iraq. One area of Iraq received bombs with almost boring regularity. They launched IED attacks almost weekly in the Shiite Sadr City and Kazamiya Districts of Baghdad. However, the attack strategy of large lots of daily suicide bombings was to give way to more precise and coordinated nationwide bombing attacks that would have measurable impact. No suicide bombers would be wasted.

In mid-July ISIS launched the first wave of suicide bombings that killed over 112 people. It was also the first time ISI stated that it would start to take terrain from the Iraqi government toward its goal of an Islamic state. In September 2012, Abu Bakr al-Baghdadi released a statement saying that ISI would be shifting its targets more toward killing soldiers and security forces that propped up the al-Maliki government. This campaign was called Harvesting the Soldiers. It was identical to the 2003 FRL "punishment campaign."

Some groups still operated separately from ISI, including the Islamic Army of Iraq (IAI) and smaller former regime loyalist (FRL) organizations, such as the Army of the Men of the Naqishbandi (Jaish al-Rijal al-Naqishbandi (JRTN)). The Ansar al-Sunnah (AAS), who were the largest of the former regime loyalist insurgents, remained disbanded. However, some former AAS rebels had started returning to ISI. The FRL still had cells operating in Sunni governorates where they collected intelligence, weapons, and maintained ties to al-Qaeda. One Awakening member put their reasons for cooperating with ISI to the *New York Times*: "At this point, Awakening members have two options: Stay with the government, which would be a threat to their lives, or help Al Qaeda by being a double agent.... The Awakening is like a database for Al Qaeda that can be used to target places that had been out of reach before."[10]

For the Sunni tribes in the Awakening council, being ready to turn traitor against al-Maliki was an insurance policy. In case the predominantly Shiite government was to isolate or attack them, they would just rejoin the ISI and go back to insurgency. By 2013 that is precisely what would happen, and they would cash in that policy in exchange for the ISIS black banner.

THE SYRIA CIVIL WAR—AN OPPORTUNITY
FOR A SAFE HAVEN AND A NATION

The death of Osama bin Laden in April 2011 at the hands of U.S. Navy SEALs did not impact the Iraq organization as much as one would like to imagine. ISI had already embraced and exported the ideology of al-Qaeda-ism. They were not invested in the health and welfare of the man himself. To ISI, bin Laden had been called to God as a reward for all of those he killed in God's name. However, the words and vision of the dead man still lived. The absence of bin Laden meant that there was an opportunity for a new leader.

In 2011, when the Syrian civil war started, it presented the ambitious al-Baghdadi with yet another opportunity to rise. AQI/ISI had been looking to branch out beyond the borders of Iraq for some time. Within ISI the foreign fighters from Syria and the jihadists from Saudi Arabia demanded that they be allowed to cross into Syria and attack the remotely located forces of Bashar al-Assad. Many members did not feel they were being well used while Syria slid into civil war. Lobbing suicide bombs against the overwhelming sea of Iraqi Shiites was not as sexy as major armed raids on Syrian army bases. They wanted action, and Syria's civil war was a chance for death and glory.

As early as 2003 Syria had allowed al-Qaeda's foreign fighters to transit east from Damascus and infiltrate the deserts of western Iraq where they would fight. Additionally, they had stores of weapons and supplies available that were given to them by Syrian intelligence for use against the Americans. Eight years later, this facilitation of terror would come to bite Syria literally in its rear end. All ISI had to do was move west instead of east directly along its logistic lines and seize terrain and weapons from Bashar al-Assad. The terrorists had good relations with the tribes of eastern Syria, who now wished to overthrow the al-Assad regime. Syria was no longer a nation sponsoring al-Qaeda and pointing it toward Iraq. Al-Baghdadi imagined that Syria could be overthrown, its weapons seized, and it could become a Sunni-dominated Islamic state—that bordered Israel. Even bin Laden had not been able to get close to this goal.

Al-Baghdadi knew that the Syrian civil war and rising Sunni disillusion with Iraqi Prime Minister Nouri al-Maliki could provide him twin levers to bring his fighters back to the forefront of the global Islamic jihad. According to internal discussions revealed to Arabic media, ISI deployed a force of Syrian and Gulf state jihadists to seize the lead in the Syrian civil war. They were allowed to enter Syria from their Iraqi infiltration lines and establish a foothold in the city of Aleppo. This force would be named the Jebhat al-Nusra ("the Victory Front"). The commander was Abu Mohammed al-Joulani (Figure 12.5).

FIGURE 12.5   Al-Nusra Front fighters in Syria.

The civil war in Syria created a source of wealth, weapons, and equipment for ISI. Where resources or manpower were scarce, both al-Nusra and ISI would shift back and forth across the Syria-Iraq borders from one country's battlefront to the other. Because of their discipline and combat skills learned in Iraq, al-Nusra Front (ANF) quickly became the "shock troops" of the Syrian civil war. They taught other groups how to infiltrate enemy lines and deploy suicide truck bombs against key enemy command centers, particularly intelligence offices and communications posts. In the siege of Aleppo, when all would seem lost, the al-Nusra jihadists would swoop in to contested battles and throw themselves at Syrian army soldiers and save the day through sheer courage and fanaticism. By 2012 the ANF had made a name for themselves in Syria and internationally. From this point, al-Joulani got ahead of himself. Believing he had exceeded ISI's command, he simply started ignoring orders from al-Baghdadi in Iraq.

The rise of the Nusra Front within the Syrian opposition forces quickly led to a schism with ISI. Al-Baghdadi decided it was time to get rid of al-Nusra and take over its operations in both Syria and Iraq. Al-Baghdadi is said to have deliberately created a rift between the members in ANF by ordering the most hard-core foreign fighters to contravene an ANF prohibition on the issue of Takfir. Takfir is a principal al-Qaeda doctrine that authorizes its fighters to determine exactly who is and who is not a Muslim and kill them according to their whim. Within Islam it is a serious transgression and considered an un-Islamic, cult-like behavior.[11] Al-Nusra's al-Joulani knew that AQ doctrine needed to be tempered to cooperate with non-AQ militias in Syria, so he ordered this practice suspended. That was the opening al-Baghdadi needed to turn the most devoted fighters back to his side and abandon al-Nusra. It is quite possible that the international media attention to ANF as "the next great al-Qaeda" movement motivated Abu Bakr to critically damage al-Joulani.

In April 2013 al-Baghdadi announced that all foreign and Iraqi forces of ISI and some loyal units of the al-Nusra Front in Syria were combining to create ad-Dawla al-Islāmiyya fi al-'Iraq wa-sh-Sham, "The Islamic State of Iraq and al-Sham [Syria]." In Arabic they used the acronym that was pronounced *al-Da'esh*. Intelligence agencies referred to them with the more accurate ISIL, but the Western media used the easily consumed ISIS.

ENDNOTES

1. Stephen Negus, Call for Sunni State in Iraq, *Financial Times*, October 15, 2006, retrieved from http://www.ft.com/cms/s/0/e239159e-5c6a-11db-9e7e-0000779e2340.html#axzz35lDqWFpp.
2. Anonymous, Statement from the Islamic State of Iraq, retrieved from http://www.kavkazcenter.com/eng/content/2006/10/16/5985.shtml.
3. Ibid.
4. Ibid.
5. John Burns and Dexter Filkins, A Jihadist Web Site Says Zarqawi's Group in Iraq Has a New Leader in Place, *New York Times*, June 13, 2006, http://www.nytimes.com/2006/06/13/world/middleeast/13iraq.html?_r=0.
6. Michael Daly, ISIS Leader, "See You in New York," *The Daily Beast*, June 14, 2014, http://www.thedailybeast.com/articles/2014/06/14/isis-leader-see-you-in-new-york.html.
7. Timothy Williams and Duraid Adnan, Sunnis in Iraq Allied with U.S. Rejoin Rebels, *New York Times*, October 7, 2010, retrieved from http://www.nytimes.com/2010/10/17/world/middleeast/17awakening.html?pagewanted=all&_r=0.
8. Statement from the Ministry of War of the Islamic State of Iraq, Al Fajr Amedia Center, November 3, 2010, retrieved from http://forum.arrahmah.com/forum/ar-rahmah-english-section/mujahedeen-press-releases/351-statement-from-the-ministry-of-war-of-the-islamic-state-of-iraq-11-02-2010.
9. Al-Qaeda Claims Deadly Iraq Attacks as Part of "Destroying the Walls" Campaign, Al Arabiya, July 25, 2012, retrieved from http://www.alarabiya.net/articles/2012/07/25/228270.html.
10. Williams and Adnan.
11. Malcolm W. Nance, *An End to al-Qaeda: Destroying bin Laden's Jihad and Restoring America's Honor*, St. Martin's Press, New York, 2010, 78.

CHAPTER 13

Lions of God
ISIS and the Islamic Caliphate (2013–2014)

THE AL-BAGHDADI-ZAWAHIRI CLASH

Despite adding *Syria* (*ash Sham* is Arabic for the Levant, Syria, Lebanon, and Palestine) to their name, the Islamic State of Iraq and Syria (ISIS) is al-Qaeda in Iraq with Syrian bases. It is the same organization operated by Abu Mussab al-Zarqawi. They also had the same frictions with al-Qaeda Central's (AQC) senior leadership, who were holed up in the remote tribal areas of Pakistan.

Like al-Zarqawi, Abu Bakr al-Baghdadi loved displaying his men's ability to generate terror shock value (TSV) in social media. On Twitter, Facebook, and their own web forums, they once again started to reveal what they would do when they were victorious in villages and towns throughout Iraq. ISI enjoyed exercising absolute compliance and did not spare the brutality of al-Zarqawi's old beheading days. And like al-Zarqawi, ISIS was ordered by bin Laden's successor, Dr. Ayman al-Zawahiri, to once again temper their lust for dispersing videos of their hostage beheadings and crucifixions, as it was creating revulsion on a strategic scale. They complied grudgingly so long as the beheadings of Shiites could continue and videos were distributed only among the jihadist network. Under Abu Bakr ISIS became a fiercely jealous organization, particularly with regards to media attention. It did not help matters in Iraq that AQC in Pakistan was giving all of its public blessings and resources to al-Qaeda of the Arabian Peninsula (AQAP) in Yemen, the al-Shaabab in Somalia, and the North African al-Qaeda in the Islamic Maghreb (AQIM). Al-Baghdadi resented the years they spent sweating out a campaign of night raids by Iraqi Special Forces. He apparently also deeply resented having to obey the orders of old men who could not fight. When al-Zawahiri started to complain about his al-Zarqawi-like behavior,

Abu Bakr simply ignored him. This did not go over well in Pakistan. In early June 2013, Al Jazeera television learned of a significant rift in the relationship between al-Qaeda's branches that would bring al-Qaeda to an existential crisis.[1]

Abu Bakr was not slacking off on his combat operations. He constantly ordered major terror operations to give him leverage in his leadership troubles with al-Zawahiri and al-Nusra. He decided that the best option was to find more hard-core fighters who would give him the support he needed.

The largest collection of underutilized terrorists in Iraq was sitting in Abu Ghraib prison wasting away under harsh Iraqi army treatment. Virtually all of the surviving cell members of al-Qaeda and other insurgent groups who were too dangerous to release from Camp Bucca were transferred to Abu Ghraib and Taji prisons. This lot included Abdul Rahman al-Bilawi, ISI's former Minister of War.[2] Abu Bakr decided to change their status from prisoners to ISIS employees. On July 22, 2013, he attacked both prisons with a large-scale task force numbering more than 100 men. He used the same tactics that had failed when AQI tried it in April 2005 against the U.S. Army forces stationed there. The assault started with rockets bombarding the site, followed up by suicide bomber trucks that breached holes in the gates. Toyota trucks with anti-aircraft guns mounted on the rear would provide suppressive fire against the guard towers until they finished the attack with a direct infantry assault. As predicted, the Iraqi police and army abandoned the facility as the attackers pressed on. Abu Ghraib was breeched and more than 500 members of AQI, ISI, and other terrorist groups and criminals were released. At Taji, located near the largest Army base in Iraq, the assault failed and no prisoners escaped. It mattered little because the news of the fall of Abu Ghraib prison was a stunning blow to the al-Maliki government. Iraqis started to accuse him of indifference to the terrorists and more concerned about consolidating Shiite power. Charges of the army's incompetence or collusion were leveled daily in the Arabic media. It was a canary in the coal mine moment. Every person in Iraq knew the army and police did not seem to be able to stand up to a direct attack. People held their breath about where the next blow would land. It seemed even the water sellers in the souks knew ISIS would take on the army and who would win.

THE WINTER OFFENSIVE OF 2013–2014: ISIS DECAPITATION ATTACK ON SYRIAN RESISTANCE

In the September 2013 al-Baghdadi indicated to his staff that he wanted to eliminate all Syrian rebel groups fighting al-Assad. They would first plan to destroy the Western-backed and independent Syrian rebel forces of the Free Syrian Army (FSA). The FSA was an amalgam of former Syrian army units of multiple faiths, but made up predominantly of non-Salafist Sunni Muslims. Al-Baghdadi decided this plan would also give him a chance to give al-Nusra's commander al-Joulani a loyalty test. According to Wikibaghdady, a blog that detailed the internal discussions of the group, Abu Bakr ordered al-Joulani to send suicide bombers to the next commander's meeting of the FSA, whether in Turkey or in Syria. He expected al-Nusra to kill all of the FSA commanders in one fell swoop. When al-Joulani balked, Abu Bakr ordered him to carry out these orders or al-Nusra would be disbanded. At the same time, he decided that ISIS would take over combat operations from al-Nusra Front.

True to its reputation, ISIS's military committee planned a campaign of scorched total elimination of other rebel forces from the battlefield as well. While ISIS fought the FSA,[3] it was time to take on the Islamic groups. In early December 2013, ISIS launched an offensive designed to overrun, kidnap, or kill all major Syrian Islamic and rebel opposition forces and their commanders in the western Aleppo villages. ISIS started on December 7 with an operation that removed and seized the Free Syrian Army forces at the Bab al-Hawa border crossing. The Bab al-Hawa is a principal crossing between Turkey and Syria and access to the Turkish refugee camp at Reyhanli. ISIS fighters assassinated and mutilated the body of a popular young commander in the Ahrar al-Sham militia, medical doctor Hussein al-Sulayman. The photo of the mutilated body spread throughout social media.[4] Anger exploded at ISIS from both rebels and civilians over his death. Throughout the month ISIS kidnapped no less than six senior commanders of the Islamic Front and other militias, executing and mutilating two of them. They also continued operations that kidnapped and killed local opposition commanders, took over bases and camps, and raised their black flag in villages that had already been cleared of Syrian government forces.[5] Seven major militias quickly turned on ISIS and attacked their forces in a series of vicious clashes.[6] In the words of Hassan Aboud of the Islamic Front:

> All this fighting [between rebel forces] will only weaken the revolution and help the regime. We, in the Islamic Front, did not take the decision to fight ISIS, but whoever did it had his reasons because of the way ISIS treats other groups. ISIS denies reality, refusing to recognize that it is simply another group. It refuses to go to independent courts; it attacked many other groups, stole their weapons, occupied their headquarters, and arbitrarily apprehended numerous activists, journalists and rebels. It has been torturing its prisoners. These transgressions accumulated, and people got fed up with ISIS. Some of those people have attacked ISIS's positions, but ISIS was first to attack in other places, bringing this on itself.[7]

On January 3, 2014, no less than seven opposition groups counter-attacked ISIS positions. These groups rejected ISIS' heavy-handedness and brutality. They intended to hand down a punishment until the perpetrators were handed over. Fierce clashes broke out between ISIS and the Islamic Front, the newly formed Army of the Mujadhideen, and the Front of Syrian Revolutionaries around Aleppo. These firefights were carried out right in front of the astonished al-Assad army forces. These forces gave ISIS an ultimatum to surrender the unit responsible for the murder of Dr. Sulayman and other fighters kidnapped by their forces in Aleppo. According to the *New York Times*, the Army of the Mujahideen released a statement declaring ISIS an enemy equal to the al-Assad regime: "We, the Mujahedeen Army, declare that we will defend ourselves, our honor, properties and land and we declare the fight against the ISIS organization, the unjust to God's law, until it dissolves its formation and its members join other military formations or abandon their arms and leave Syria."[8]

In an effort to take over control of the Aleppo insurgency, ISIS damaged the resistance in a way that the al-Assad regime could not. ISIS works from fear of its strength, which is discipline and terror shock value of its operations. Its doctrine of religious-based dictatorial terror was starting to be seen as a bad sign of what an ISIS-led country could become. This led the local antigovernment populations to turn on ISIS. According to Agence France Presse, one local fighter described ISIS's activities within the Syrian opposition thusly: "I'd say about 90 percent of people in the opposition areas are against ISIS.... They use violence and abuses to crush dissent. They are only Islamic in name. All they want is power."[9]

Another Syrian commander, Mohamad Rafei al-Raya of the Free Syrian Army, described ISIS's terror shock value operations and inter-rebel fighting as a strategic operation in which Syrian government opponents will eventually fall into a regional religious war.

> I swear by Allah, Even if you were in Germany and I told you what they've been doing, you would have come here to fight them, they're assaulting Christians and Ismailis, they went to Latakia countryside and killed the people and kidnapped women and children.... I carried arms and I rose up to fight the armed man that wants to kill me and my family, I did not rise up to kill children and innocent people and its like they're scaring the world about this revolution so that the world forsakes it and sees it as a sectarian struggle.[10]

THE INTER-AL-QAEDA CIVIL WAR STARTS

The next leg of their plan was to eliminate one of the oldest al-Qaeda commanders in the world. On February 24, 2014, two ISIS suicide bombers entered the compound of the Syrian resistance group Ahrar al-Sham and blew themselves up, killing Abu Khaled al-Suri, commander of Ahrar al-Sham and a former confidant of Osama bin Laden and Dr. Ayman al-Zawahiri (Figure 13.1). The attack was attributed to ISIS in its effort to decapitate the major resistance groups. Now it appeared it was out to kill al-Qaeda Central's personally anointed senior commanders.[11]

Abu Khaled was born Mohammed al-Bahaiya in the city of Aleppo. His decades' long fight in the jihad made him a natural commander, though he shunned the limelight. He joined the global jihad to fight the Soviet Union in Afghanistan with Abudullah Azzam and Osama bin Laden in the 1980s. He was a close companion with the al-Qaeda strategist Abu Musab al-Suri and was jailed with him when al-Suri was turned over to the Syrian government by the United States after the two were captured in Afghanistan. Somehow Abu Khaled was released while Abu Musab disappeared into the Syrian torture system. Abu Khaled was the hardest surviving of the hard-core neo-Salafists. However, the two Syrians never truly directly associated themselves with AQ senior leadership, though they enjoyed a close working relationship with bin Laden, al-Zawahiri, and Mullah Omar of the Taliban.

When the Syrian civil war started, Abu Khaled returned from his imprisonment and started his own jihadist group, Ahrar al-Sham. Abu

FIGURE 13.1   Abu Khaled al-Suri commander of Ahrar al-Sham group in Syria. Killed at the orders of Abu Bakr al-Baghdadi in 2014.

Khaled was asked by Dr. Ayman al-Zawahiri to act as his representative in Syria. This declaration effectively made Abu Khaled and the Ahrar-al Sham group the official and sanctioned AQ-backed resistance group. This also dropped him directly between the ISIS–al-Nusra clash, and it cost him his life. Ahrar al-Sham was supposed to join the al-Nusra group, which would make Abu Khaled al-Suri the shadow commander of resistance forces in Syria.[12] Al-Baghdadi would have none if it, and suicide bombers were deployed to send Abu Khaled al-Suri into the next life.

On February 26, 2014, al-Jolani issued an ultimatum for the end to fighting; withdrawal of the mandatory Takfir order that allowed ISIS fighters to declare anyone a non-Muslim, and to turn over the responsible parties that killed al-Souri.[13] Abu Qatadah, a reknowned Jordanian jihadist cleric, condemned ISIS powerfully in statements made before his own terrorism trial, furthering the split between the methods of implementing bid Laden's vision. He said:

> I am very sad about the killing of the Mujahid Abu Khaled.... I never expected that he would die at the hands of these criminals who adopt a deviant ideology.... [Souri's] killing resembled the murder of the Caliph Ali, may God bless him, who was killed by the criminal [Abdel Rahman] Ibn Muljam ... [the death] of Abu Khaled was a great loss for us. I knew him well and met with him in London. His loss is like the loss of the Mujahid Sheikh Osama bin Laden.[14]

OPERATION LION OF GOD AL-BILAWI PHASE 1: THE CAMPAIGN TO SEIZE WESTERN IRAQ

By 2014 ISIS and other groups were able to finally conceptualize and execute a broad Sunni-supported military operation in Iraq in order to secure the eastern borders of a jihadist-led Islamic state that has been the dreams of neo-Salafists since the 19th century.

At the same time ISIS forces were attempting to seize control of the Syrian insurgency, their forces in Iraq were flush with money, experienced fighters, and found that the Iraqi army was not all it seemed. ISIS started consolidating small gains against the Iraqi government and capitalizing on increasing support by the tribes of the Anbar governorates. The political difficulties between the Shiite-led al-Maliki government and the Sunni tribes was evolving into a full-blown political clash. ISIS had maintained covert presence in sympathetic neighborhoods in Fallujah, Ramadi, and other al-Anbar villages. During 2012 and 2013 they upped their presence and made plans to go to what the U.S. counterinsurgency manual calls a phase III insurgency: the war of movement.

Phase III is when a terrorist group has moved from static insurgency or terror operations and then creates an army that moves to seize terrain. Only groups that have the capacity to sustain the logistics and manpower necessary to seize and hold terrain can successfully move into this phase. Normally groups that do this prematurely are destroyed by larger forces, as they spread themselves too thin and their mobility and resupply become too limited.

In July 2013 ISIS announced a new campaign that would help them validate their assessment of the Iraqi security forces called the Soldier's Harvest Campaign.[15] They would attack key Iraqi army forces and individuals in order to prepare the battlefield for a war of movement. Their campaign to liberate Anbar started with a well-planned mission to eliminate the single most significant obstacle to their military success, the commanding officer of the Iraqi army's 7th Division, Brigadier General Mohammed al-Karawi. On December 21, 2013, he and 23 of his senior staff and security personnel were conducting an inspection of a captured ISIS safe house in the town of al-Rutba in the western reaches of Anbar. The ISI had booby-trapped it with a house-borne improvised explosive device (HBIED) configuration and detonated it when the inspection team entered the site.[16] Everyone was killed. The HBIED was a tactic they had been using successfully since 2004. With the 7th Division completely headless, the ISIS could progress to seizing the Anbar governorate.

On January 2, 2014, ISIS forces came out of their safe houses and launched operations to seize government buildings in the cities of Ramadi and Fallujah (Figure 13.2). These two cities have had an ISIS presence for over 11 years and were distant enough from the central government

FIGURE 13.2   ISIS fighters seize Fallujah and Ramadi in January 2014.

to take quickly. First, they attacked the Fallujah city hall and the central police headquarters. The Iraqi army fought sporadically, and military units outside of the city used heavy artillery to shell positions of ISIS fighters. After a day of fighting the Iraqi army and police withdrew. ISIS fighters paraded triumphantly through the cities, and according to the *New York Times*, one shouted "We are here to defend you from the army of Maliki and the Iranian Safavids!"[17] The fighters declared their liberation and announced the establishment of "a new Islamic state." Although the government tried to claim that the Awakening forces where holding ISIS from completely taking the cities, little did they know that most of the Awakening had joined ISIS.

The minimal opposition that the al-Maliki government had thrown up and the indifference of the Awakening forces proved to al-Bakr that the Iraqi army was a paper tiger ready to be burned in the fire of his attacks. Iraqi security forces operated defensively and without the capacity that the Americans had to accept casualties and take ISIS head on. The Iraqi air force and army did have some ability to strike from above, but the ground forces were proving to be worthless. In Fallujah and Ramadi the Iraqi police ran, as did the government administrators. It was an indication that led ISIS commanders to assess the capacity of the Iraqi army to resist a larger operation. Shifting forces from Syria and Anbar, ISIS decided it was going to make a move on Mosul, the second largest city in Iraq. If Mosul fell, it would be easy to move down Highway 1 to Tikrit and Samarra, turn east to Baqubah, and pressure Baghdad. If the Iraqi army fought, then al-Baghdadi's forces would fall back and liberate smaller cities. The high-mobility mission using pickup truck task forces would be named the northern gazwa (a historic term for a desert raid). But soon after fighting killed the deputy commander of ISIS, whose *nom de guerre* was Abu Abdul Rahman al-Bilawi, it was renamed Operation Lion of God al-Bilawi (Figure 13.3).

ISIS FINAL DECLARATION OF INDEPENDENCE FROM AL-QAEDA'S CORPORATE MANAGEMENT TEAM

Success in Iraq or not, Abu Bakr had to deal with Dr. Ayman al-Zawahiri, the titular head of al-Qaeda. Before any strategic move to change the borders of Iraq and Syria could be effected, al-Baghdadi needed to resolve the issue of al-Qaeda Central's senior leadership. In May 2014 ISIS issued a statement in online forums declaring that the AQC had strayed away from the bin Laden vision and declared their emancipation from them. ISIS's spokesman, Abu Mohammed al-Adnani, released a statement that read:

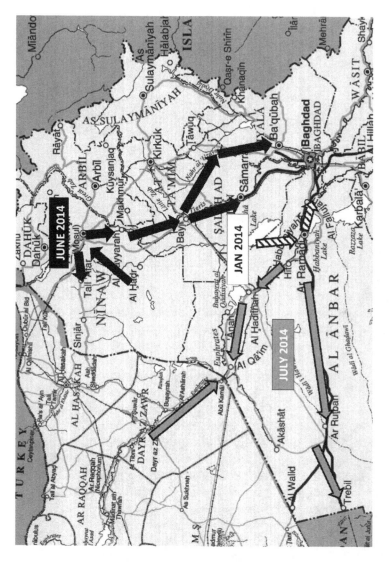

FIGURE 13.3 Map of Lion of God Abdul Rahman al-Bilawi offensives.

Al-Qaeda today is no longer a base of jihad. Its leadership has become a hammer to break the project of the Islamic State ... the leaders of al-Qaeda have deviated from the correct path.... They have divided the ranks of the mujahideen (holy warriors) in every place.[18]

Al-Zawahiri responded by making an official proclamation that ordered al-Baghdadi keep al-Nusra separate from ISIS and withdraw Iraqi fighters from Syria.[19] Al-Baghdadi was having none of it and essentially decided that he no longer had to answer to old men in Pakistan.

OPERATION LION OF GOD AL-BILAWI PHASE 2: TAKING MOSUL, ANBAR, AND CENTRAL IRAQ

On June 9–11 ISIS forces stormed the city of Mosul with an estimated 800- to 1,000-man task force. Mosul was the second largest city in Iraq, and the concept was a bold stroke. It was far enough north to be relatively isolated from the central government, deep inside the Sunni community, and dotted with towns that would quickly join them to push for the approaches to Baghdad. If done correctly, the entirety of western, northern, and a fair part of central Iraq would become the Islamic State of Iraq and Syria. One thing was sure; if done with speed, violence, and shock of surprise, the Iraqi army would blow away like sand in the wind. Other benefits of a blitzkrieg were that the central bank of Mosul would be al-Baghdadi's for the taking, and all of the weapons, equipment, and supplies of the 2nd Division would give him the resources of a full-scale army with which to march south toward Baghdad (Figure 13.4).

FIGURE 13.4 ISIS fighters in Operation Lion of God al-Bilawi storm Mosul, Tikrit, and Baqubah.

ISIS insurgents had infiltrated into Mosul over weeks, and others arrived from out of the western desert in Toyota pickup trucks with rockets and machine guns mounted. These are called Toyota task forces (TTFs). Just as rapidly as ISIS arrived, the Iraqi police folded. Iraqi army and police checkpoints along the major roads were attacked and suppressed while the main forces ran into the city. Most of these Hesco sandbagged sites were formerly American combat observation posts. Once inside, the soldiers had to fight, die, or run. Most Iraqis ran from the fight. The city's checkpoints would not be the first. The headquarters of one of the largest military bases in Iraq was Camp Kindi, former home of the Multinational Force North. It was now home of the Iraqi army 2nd Division with its five combat brigades. ISIS struck the base with a wave of direct frontal attacks and suicide bomber assaults. The security force around the perimeter fought, but the front gate was hit with suicide bombers and the guard towers raked with machine guns and RPG-7 rockets. The perimeter's quick reaction force with its Polish-made Dzik armored cars responded to the assault on the front gate, but lost their vehicles in the rocket-propelled grenade (RPG) attacks. After the unit's security force was overwhelmed, the men in the 2nd Division Combat Operations Center for the Nineveh Operations Command—the headquarters for all combined combat operations in northern Iraq—could not figure out what was happening, despite the fact that this had happened a few months before in both Fallujah and Ramadi. Once they realized they were under a sustained and organized attack, they abandoned the headquarters, took off their uniforms, and ran. Iraqi army soldiers in the barracks who were Shiite knew that this would not end well for them. They too took off their gear and uniforms and headed south in taxis and commandeered military trucks. Those who did not run or fight were captured within a day.

ISIS's own videos, Twitter feeds, and press releases would testify to the lesson they give the Iraqi army in what happens when paper tigers meet the heat of a fanatic's flame. Over the course of a week they executed over 1,700 captives from the police and army and hunted down any civil administrators who worked for the Maliki government (Figure 13.5).

The ISIS media team was ready to exploit the global media's hunger for news, so they released a statement on how they managed to capture Mosul:

> By guidance from our leadership, the leadership of the ISIS, favored by Allah, the brothers in the ISIS camps began drawing up precise plans to conquer the entire Wilaya and purge it of apostates. This blessed battle began by intelligence jihad by the special detachments whereby the apostates' weak areas were studied and then the military force entered the city of Mosul from several directions and by the grace of Allah took complete control of their headquarters, including the Ghazlani

FIGURE 13.5   Photo of mass executions of Iraqi army soldiers by ISIS in Mosul, June 2014.

> HQ, the operations command, the second division HQ, Badush and Tasfirat prisons, and the headquarters of the battalions and brigades. Thousands of prisoners were also released as well as some female prisoners, and the praise and grace is to Allah. And now there is complete control over all internal and external access points to the Wilaya and with Allah's permission this series of blessed incursions that delight the eyes of the monotheists shall not cease either till Allah fulfills his promise or we shall perish.[20]

The capture of Mosul was just a sample of what was to befall the local population, the Iraqi army, and anyone who stood in the way of ISIS. Immediately after the reports of executions came news that hundreds of hostages were being taken. People were disappearing from Mosul. The foreigners were not spared. The Turkish consulate in Mosul was stormed; 48 diplomats and their families as well as 31 Turk truck drivers vanished and were feared dead or hostages.

Following in the footsteps of the Taliban's destruction of the giant Buddhas of Bamiyan, ISIS's cultural cleansing of Iraq started immediately. Any and all non-Sunni shrines, Shiite mosques (called Husseiniyas), were being declared as idolatry. The giant statutes of Abu Tamam, the famed Abbasid Arabic poet, and Othman al-Mosuli, a 19th-century musician, were toppled. The blue-domed tomb of Ibn al-Athir, a philosopher and wazir for Salah al-Din al-Ayyubi, was razed. The Mosque of the Biblical Jonah was torn down with a bulldozer. The third-century ancient city of Hatra, a UNESCO World Heritage site, was threatened. ISIS promised to eliminate all Iraqi heritage it viewed as un-Islamic and return Iraq back to the seventh century.[21]

The ISIS offensive had never planned to stop in Mosul. The objective of the mission was to take all Sunni regions of Iraq. A blitzkrieg would create a psychological panic in the Iraq and police forces, and they would run away. ISIS had fighters who had seen this happen in Syria, and they knew from intelligence and the January operations in Anbar that this would repeat itself.

Their spearhead force pushed outside of Mosul to the south and quickly took possession of the Qayyarah West army base and the oil fields in Nineveh. As they moved on, they found that the Iraqi police and army were running away from all posts. The path was clear straight down to Tikrit. The ISIS pickup truck army entered the Salah al-Din governorate and split into mission-specific forces. One group broke off to seize and surrounded Bayji oil refinery. The refinery was being protected by the Iraqi Oil Field Protection Force (OPF) called the oil field police. The oil field police were the laziest of all Iraqi security forces. The flimsiest of groups, they were only known for their corruption. If the Iraqi army was a paper tiger, the OPF was a paper donkey. Like clockwork, they immediately abandoned the facility and begged to join ISIS or fled. Elements of the Iraqi 12th Division's 46th and 48th Infantry Brigades and a company-sized task force from the Iraqi Special Forces dispatched from Baghdad held the facility and fought fiercely. During the fighting, 17 oil storage tanks were set aflame. Within a day ISIS raised its black flag over the facility (Figure 13.6).

Bayji is the largest facility of its kind in Iraq and a crown jewel for either side. After a day of intense fighting, the local tribes intervened. One of the most interesting aspects of Iraqi tribal society is their capacity to turn any issue into a negotiation that will enrich them all or spare

FIGURE 13.6   ISIS fighters seize oil field police and army vehicles at the Bayji oil refinery.

them pain from a more powerful force. The tribes of Iraq are willing to raise the Qu'ran at any time to call a powwow to determine who is right, who is wrong, and lessen the impact of decisions against them. In this instance they went directly to ISIS and negotiated a cease-fire that allowed the oil field workers from the local Sunni community to leave and gave the Iraqi task force a safe passage out of the oil field. Of course, they did not publicly pledge loyalty to ISIS, but the face-saving fix was in. Bayji belonged to ISIS, and so did the Sunni tribal chiefs.

A second column of ISIS fighters moved south to Tikrit. Many covert cells from ISIS and other allied Iraqi Sunni terror groups had already come from the shadows and were engaging elements of the Iraqi police in the center of the city. It was a small column that reached the outskirts of Camp Speicher, the former U.S. base and headquarters of six infantry brigades of the 12th Division. After ignoring calls for assistance from the Iraqi SWAT and special police in the city center, the 12th Division decided that the 10 to 20 pickup trucks of ISIS were just the start of a much bigger force. After sporadic fighting, these army units abandoned their base and thus surrendered the city. The 12th Division was equipped with tanks, armored fighting vehicles, and artillery. Had any of the combat units given even the most cursory fight, the ISIS columns would have been destroyed in a matter of minutes.

An ISIS TTF was dispatched to move toward the Kurdish border crossings near the oil city of Kirkuk, but the Kurdish Peshmerga were faster and had seized the city. The next objective was to liberate the Diyala governorate and the city of Baqubah. This city was a strong point of AQI in the insurgency and was the tip of the eastern part of ISIS's Sunni Crescent. They always had deep-rooted support from the local Sunni community. As one Iraqi Special Forces officer once told me, "Baqubah is where al-Qaeda goes to vacation when they need a rest from fighting in Baghdad and Fallujah."

The Baqubah Toyota Task Force moved southeast from Tikrit into the Diyala countryside. Their forces, even if they were just a few trucks with black banners, touched as far east as Sadiya, where they fought with Kurdish forces. The real prize was to cut off the lines of control around Baqubah and link up with the fighters within the city. Fighting in Baqubah started when ISIS and Sunni insurgent's covert cells that had been pre-positioned there started fighting with the Iraqi police and army in the city. They too were trying to link up with the ISIS TTF and fought for control of the city. In the end, ISIS did not take control, and by June Shiite militias of the rearmed Jaysh al-Mahdi (JAM) militia and the Iraqi army stopped the advance of ISIS.[17]

MISSION ACCOMPLISHED: ISIS STYLE

Why did 30,000 of the American-trained Iraqi army literally throw down their weapons and flee or submit to be slaughtered by less than 1,000 ISIS fighters? Why did they run and turn over $2 billion of equipment to the most ruthless terrorists in the Middle East? Fear. Fear of the ISIS terror shock value (TSV). Through social and news media the Iraqi army soldiers understood ISIS's capacity for bloodletting, and they knew that the terrorists didn't just like their jobs—they loved slaughter with a passion. ISIS's brutal retaliation methods created a flight reaction in the Iraqi army. This gave ISIS a force multiplier more valuable than weapons or numbers.

ISIS had used its well-groomed social media savvy to create TSV disproportionate to its actual combat capacity. Its sudden execution and brutality armed with little more than rifles and RPGs essentially scared two divisions of more than 30,000 Iraqi army soldiers, with hundreds of tanks and armored vehicles to flee or surrender, although they had enough combat capacity to obliterate the ISIS force many times over.

ISIS immediately capitalized on its TSV by broadcasting internationally videos, photos, and statements where it proudly mass murdered hundreds of Shiite soldiers, civil workers, or anyone on the street who did not comply immediately. It promised more where that came from to anyone who resisted its further incursions. This brutal media braggadocio gave ISIS an asymmetric ability to project fear across the globe that this regional terror group could become a marauding jihadist army that could cross oceans on an international scale.

On June 25, 2014, the London-based Syrian Observatory for Human Rights reported that the local Egyptian al-Nusra Front commander at the Syrian-Iraqi border swore a loyalty oath to ISIS.[22] Although it may have been agreements between local commanders, it may have been the chink in the armor for the remaining ANF fighters to come over to ISIS. If it were to go organization-wide, it would effectively end the 2-year-old blood feud between the organizations. Al-Baghdadi's decapitation of al-Qaeda-backed opposition placed him at the top of the heap of the best equipped and wealthiest of terrorists in the world, as well as occupier of the heart of the Middle East.

BREAKING BAD: ISIS FINALLY BREAKS FROM AL-QAEDA CENTRAL

Granted, al-Qaeda's senior commander in Pakistan had ordered al-Baghdadi to keep the two wings of ISIS as separate and independent commands, but the success of ISIS's Anbar and Mosul campaigns left him feeling emboldened. The moment had arrived to do what he had wanted to do for a long time. Abu Bakr al-Baghdadi had decided that al-Qaeda's senior leaders were worthless. He would no longer obey their commands.[23] On June 15, 2014, al-Baghdadi made an audio record of his desires so there would be no mistaking what he wanted to say. In his message he flatly rejected al-Zawahiri's order given to him the month before. Abu Bakr said that ISIS was the center for the start of a new Islamic caliphate:

> The Islamic State of Iraq and the Levant will remain, as long as we have a vein pumping or an eye blinking. It remains and we will not compromise nor give it up.... It remains, and we will not compromise; we will not give up ... until we die.

THE NEW ISLAMIC CALIPHATE

In one last act of defiance and what will forever be a seminal moment for al-Qaeda as an organization, Abu Bakr al-Baghdadi took one step that none of his predecessors dared. He let pride, a sense of self-aggrandizement, and a temporary victory over the Iraqi security forces go to straight to his head.

On the first day of the Islamic holy month of Ramadan in the Islamic year 1435 (Sunday, June 29, 2014 AD on the Christian calendar), an official statement was released by Abu Bakr al-Baghdadi through his spokesman. He declared that the organization called ISIS was dissolved, and its name would be removed from the rolls of al-Qaeda terrorist groups. He declared that ISIS was no longer just a combat group of unified Iraqi and foreign terrorists—it was now the first Islamic caliphate since March 3, 1924. The communiqué demanded that all Muslims will now refer to them as "the Islamic State." Abu Bakr said that as the only legitimate Islamic nation-state in the world, he was the caliph of all Islam. He renamed himself Caliph Ibrahim (Figure 13.7) and ordered that as ruler of Islam, all Muslims worldwide fall under his authority. His first act was to call upon all al-Qaeda-inspired terrorists in all regions of the world to pledge full allegiance to the caliph and to ignore all other rulers of Muslims on earth:

> ... announce the establishment of the Islamic khilāfah, the appointment of a khalīfah for the Muslims, and the pledge of allegiance to the shaykh (sheikh), the mujāhid, the scholar who practices what he preaches, the worshipper, the leader, the warrior, the reviver, descendent from the family of the Prophet, the slave of Allah, Ibrāhīm Ibn 'Awwād Ibn Ibrāhīm Ibn 'Alī Ibn Muhammad al-Badrī al-Hāshimī

FIGURE 13.7 Abu Bakr al-Baghdadi renamed himself Caliph Ibrahim and declared an Islamic caliphate from the captured regions of Iraq and Syria.

> al-Husaynī al-Qurashī by lineage, as-Sāmurrā'ī by birth and upbringing, al-Baghdādī by residence and scholarship. And he has accepted the bay'ah (pledge of allegiance). Thus, he is the imam and khalīfah for the Muslims everywhere. Accordingly, the "Iraq and Shām" in the name of the Islamic State is henceforth removed from all official deliberations and communications, and the official name is the Islamic State from the date of this declaration.[24]

This was a bold step. One that is as certifiably grandiose as to be called insane. It may also be among the shortest caliphates in the history of Islam. To Muslims this was not a laughing matter. To proclaim oneself as spiritual leader on par with the pope and above all national rulers and next only to God is as close to blasphemy as one could come short of desecrating the grave of the prophet.

A few days before the announcement of the caliphate, al-Baghdadi informed Dr. Ayman al-Zawahiri that he can no longer give him orders now that Osama bin Laden is dead. Al-Baghdadi was going to be caliph of all Muslims, and ISIS, now the Islamic State, would only respond to a higher authority: God.

ENDNOTES

1. Basma Atassi, Qaeda Chief Annuls Syrian-Iraqi Jihad Merger, Al Jazeera, June 2, 2013, http://www.aljazeera.com/news/middle-east/2013/06/2013699425657882.html.

2. Musheq Abbas, Al-Qaeda Militants Raid Iraq's Abu Ghraib, Taji Prisons, Al Monitor, http://www.al-monitor.com/pulse/originals/2013/07/iraq-al-qaeda-prison-raid-abu-ghraib.html##ixzz35nSwZfCt.

3. Dan Layman, Extremist Group Islamic State of Iraq and al-Sham Declares Combat Operations against Moderate FSA Groups, September 13, 2013, http://www.syriansupportgroup.org/wp-content/uploads/2013/08/Release-ISIS-Declaration-of-War-on-FSA-9162013.pdf.

4. Twitter post, Body of Dr. Hussein Sulayman, https://twitter.com/HadiAlabdallah/status/418137853990682625/photo/1.

5. Alexander Dziadosz and Dasha Afanasieva, Syrian Islamists Seize Western-Backed Rebel Bases: Monitoring Group, December 7, 2013, http://www.reuters.com/article/2013/12/07/us-syria-crisis-fsa-idUSBRE9B607S20131207.

6. Marlin Dick, ISIS Condemned for Brutal Murder of Fellow Jihadist, *Daily Star*, March 1, 2014, http://www.dailystar.com.lb/News/Middle-East/2014/Jan-03/242966-isis-condemned-for-brutal-murder-of-fellow-jihadist.ashx#axzz2pLg4RPrP.

7. Joshua Landis, Battle between ISIS and Syrian Rebel Militias, http://www.joshualandis.com/blog/battle-isis-syrias-rebel-militias/.

8. Hawa Saad and Rick Gladstone, Qaeda-Linked Insurgents Clash with Other Rebels in Syria, as Schism Grows, *New York Times*, March 1, 2014, http://www.nytimes.com/2014/01/04/world/middleeast/qaeda-insurgents-in-syria.html?_r=1.

9. Syrian Rebels Demand Surrender of al-Qaeda Brigade, Al Jazeera, April 1, 2014, http://www.aljazeera.com/news/middle-east/2014/01/syria-rebels-demand-al-qaeda-group-surrender-20141413149507176.html.

10. Joshua Landis.

11. Diaa Hadid, Abu Khaled al-Suri Dead: Syrian Rebels Say Senior al-Qaeda Fighter Killed by Suicide Bombers, Associated Press, February 24, 2014, http://www.huffingtonpost.com/2014/02/24/abu-khaled-al-suri-dead_n_4846371.html.

12. Biography of Abu Khaled al-Suri, *Kulna Shuurka*, http://www.all-4syria.info/.

13. Radwan Mortada, Syria: al-Nusra Front Declares War on ISIS, February 26, 2014, http://english.al-akhbar.com/content/syria-al-nusra-front-declares-war-isis.

14. Abu Qatada Denounces ISIS "Gold" Tax on Syrian Christians, Ammon, February 26, 2014, http://en.ammonnews.net/article.aspx?articleno=24470#.U6sN3GYg99A.

15. Jessica D. Lewis, AQI's "Soldier's Harvest" Campaign, October 9, 2013, http://www.understandingwar.org/sites/default/files/Backgrounder_SoldiersHarvest.pdf.

16. Hawar Berwani, 24 Iraqi Military Officers Killed in Karawi Bombing, Iraq News, December 21, 2013, http://www.iraqinews.com/iraq-war/death-toll-of-karawi-bombing-reach-death-of-military-officers/.

17. Yasir Ghazi and Tim Arango, Iraq Fighters, Qaeda Allies, Claim Falluja as New State, March 1, 2014, http://www.nytimes.com/2014/01/04/world/middleeast/fighting-in-falluja-and-ramadi.html?_r=0.

18. ISIS Accuses al-Qaeda of Betrayal, Agence France Presse, April 18, 2014, http://english.al-akhbar.com/content/isis-accuses-al-qaeda-betrayal.

19. Basma Atassi.

20. Orden Adaki, ISIS Statement Details Gains in Mosul, December 6, 2014, http://www.longwarjournal.org/threat-matrix/archives/2014/06/isis_statement_details_gains_i.php.

21. Colin Freeman, Iraq's "Exorcist" Temple Falls into ISIS Jihadist Hands, June 25, 2014, http://www.telegraph.co.uk/news/world-news/middleeast/iraq/10925751/Iraqs-Exorcist-temple-falls-into-Isis-jihadist-hands.html.

22. Qaida Merges with ISIS at Syrian-Iraq Bordertown: NGO, AFP, June 25, 2014, http://timesofindia.indiatimes.com/world/middle-east/Qaida-merges-with-ISIS-at-Syria-Iraq-border-town-NGO/articleshow/37191544.cms.

23. 23. Iraqi Al-Qaeda Chief rejects Zawahiri orders. Al Jazeera, June 15, 2013. http://www.aljazeera.com/news/middle-east/2013/06/2013615172217827810.html

24. This Is the Promise of Allah, English translation of statement by Abu Bakr al-Baghdadi, June 29, 2014, retrieved from https://ia902505.us.archive.org/28/items/poa_25984/EN.pdf.

CHAPTER **14**

Internal Organization of the ISIS

ISLAMIC STATE OF IRAQ AND SYRIA (THE LEVANT) (ISIS/ISIL (AL-DAWLA AL-ISLAMIYA FI AL-IRAQ WA AL-SHAM)) AND THE ISLAMIC STATE CALIPHATE (ISC)

The Arabic acronym is al-Daash, Daesh, Dae'esh.

ISIS maintains a clandestine top-down military command organization. At the national level it operates with covert cells of subcommanders who are known only to those within the military and Shura councils. Commands were regionally divided, usually in a compartmented fashion. Under the ISIS operations in 2014, this system has come aboveground and operates an overt political machine that carries out the day-to-day military and civil functions of the Islamic caliphate (Figure 14.1).

COMMAND AND LEADERSHIP APPARATUS

Regional combat commands: The governorates of Syria and Iraq that fall under ISIS's control are divided into 16 Wiliyat, "states," as delineated by the governornates maps. They are each commanded and managed by a prince or Amir al-Muijahideen. Each amir has subamirs who are commanders of combat zones in specific cities, towns, or subregions. This system may change under the ISIS caliphate fashioned in 2014.

Northern Iraq Operations Command:

- Nineveh State (Wiliya Nineveh)
- Salah al-Din State (Wiliya Salah'al-deen)
- Kirkuk State (Wiliya Kirkuk)

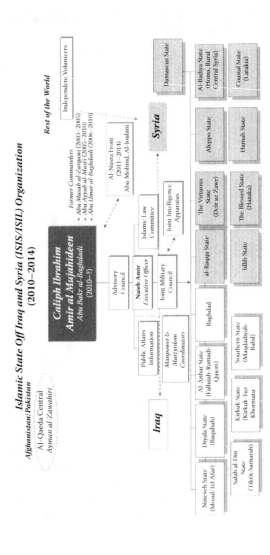

FIGURE 14.1 Organization chart of ISIS, 2010–2014.

Central Iraq Operations Command:
- Diyala State (Wiliya Deeyala)
- Baghdad (al-Baghdad)

Southern Iraq Operations Command:
- Southern (Babil) State (Wiliya al-Janoub)

Western Iraq Command:
- Anbar State (Wiliya al-Anbar)

Eastern Syria Command:
- The Virtuous State (Wiliya al-Khair—Deir az Zawr, Syria)
- The Blessed State (Wiliya al-Baraka—Hasaka, Syria)
- Ar-Raqqa State (Wiliya ar'Raqqah—Raqqah, Syria; this is the titular capital of the Islamic State)

Western Syria Command:
- Aleppo State (Wiliya al-Halab)
- Idlib State (Wiliya Idlib)
- Hamah State (Wiliya Hamah)
- The Coastal State (Wiliya al-Sahl)

Central Syria Operations Command:
- Al-Badia State (Wiliya al-Badiya—Homs, Syria, and rural Damascus)
- Damascus State (Wiliya al-Dameshq)

Battalions: The operating subunit of the ISIS organization is the battalion (Katiba, Kitaieb (plural)). Like all irregular forces, this is more of an organizational designation and does not have a set number of personnel or function. A battalion could be 5 men or 500 and is expected to perform all of its own operational actions, logistics, and administration.

LEADERSHIP ORGANIZATION

Caliph of the Islamic State Caliphate and Amir
al-Mujahideen ("Prince of the Holy Warriors")

This is Ibrahim Awwad Ibrahim Bou Badri bin Armoush (aka Abu Bakr al-Baghdadi, Caliph Ibrahim). Former commanders are:

- Abu Mussab al-Zarqawi, killed in 2005
- Abu Ayyub al-Masri, killed in 2010
- Abu Umar al-Baghdadi, killed in 2010

Deputy Amir (Naieb al-Amir al-Mujahideen)

This was Adnan Isma'il Najm (aka Abu Abdul Rahman al-Bilawi al-Anbari). He is the master planner for the ISIS operations in Anbar and Mosul. He was a former Iraqi insurgent from the town of al-Khalidiyah in Anbar governorate near Habbaniyah, and a former Iraqi army soldier under Saddam Hussein who became a close associate of Abu Musab al-Zarqawi. He was captured by U.S. forces on January 27, 2005, and sent to Camp Bucca prison. He was released by the Iraqis in 2007, where he rose in the ranks of the ISI and subsequently became one of the members of the ISIS military council. ISIS reports he was killed in fighting on June 11, 2014.[1]

POLITICAL/RELIGIOUS ORGANIZATION

State of Iraq Advisory Council (Shura al-Dawlat al-Iraq)

According to the Wikibaghdady leaks, this council is almost identical to the model established by Osama bin Laden in Afghanistan/Pakistan and used by al-Qaeda in all of its past iterations (AQI, IEI, MSC, ISI). It is comprised of three to seven members (depending on operational tempo, counterintelligence, and survival capacity) who give advice and direct political master planning for the organization. Al-Baghdadi, in fear of infiltration by foreign intelligence, ensured that it was made up of only Iraqi jihadists:

> Abu Bakr Omar al-Qahtani: A former fighter from al-Qaeda in Iraq (AQI) who joined the al-Nusra Front in Syria and was expelled for propagating al-Qaeda Takfir ideology.
>
> Abdallah al-Muhysini: Saudi religious preacher in Syria who runs the Twitter feed "Preachers of Jihad." Negotiates and represents the ISIS.[2]
>
> Abu Muhammad al-'Adnani: Media spokesman for ISIS.

ISIS MILITARY COUNCIL

Commander ISIS Military Council (Majlis al-Askari; formerly Minister of War—Wazir al-Harb): Operational commander of all ISIS combat forces. Answers only to the Emir al-Mujahideen or the caliph. After the death of Nasser al-Din Sulayaman (see below), ISIS moved away from the model of a single man in command of all fighters, called a

War Minister (Wazir al-Harb), to an advisory council-type organization made up of regional commanders.

PAST COMMANDERS

Samir Mohammed Abdul Alkhlafawi (aka Haji Bakr): According to an ISIS biography, he was a former Ba'athist and a staff colonel in charge of army weapons development. He may have been a previous commander in Ansar al-Sunnah, the largest Iraqi insurgent group. Captured twice by coalition forces, he was held in Camp Bucca for four years and later released. He was killed in Syria on January 24, 2014, while coordinating attacks on other resistance groups.[3]

Mazen Nahir: Special advisor to the council. He acted as a trusted intelligence operative who was handled covertly by Hajji Bakr. A spy and infiltrator into Iraqi government operations, Nahir may have replaced Hajji Bakr as leader of the military council.[4]

Neaman Salman Mansour al-Zaidi (aka Nasser al-Din Allah Abu Suleiman): ISI War Minister for 13 months. Killed in 2011 when Iraqi forces engaged his vehicle in the city of Hit when a suicide car bomb at his safe house exploded.[5]

MILITARY COUNCIL MEMBERS

These participants offer guidance to the military council commander and Shura council and legislate by majority vote.[6] Most members are senior commanders in ISIS.

Abu Muhannad Suedawi (aka Abu Ayman al-Iraqi): Born in Iraq in 1965. According to Al Arabiya news Abu Ayman was a lieutenant colonel in the air defense intelligence apparatus of the Iraqi army under Saddam Hussein. He was arrested by Iraqi police in 2007 and held in Abu Ghraib prison until 2010. He was sent to command forces in Syria's Deir ez-Zour governorate in 2011. He is said to be have assumed command of ISIS forces in Idlib, Latakia, and Allepo governorates in Syria.

Waleed Jassim al-Alwani (Abu Ahmed al-Alwani): Former Iraqi army officer under Saddam.[7]

Nehme Abdul Nayef al-Jubouri (Abu Fatima Algehiche): An Algerian national who Al Jazeera television identified as leading operations for ISIS in southern Iraq and after the 2014 invasion took over command in Kirkuk and Mosul.

INTERNAL SECURITY APPARATUS
(JEHAZ AL-AMN AL-DAKILI)

Safwan Rifai is commander of internal security. The Internal Security Apparatus (ISF) carried out internal investigations, abductions, and assassinations to meet the dual goals of imposing loyalty to ISIS and eliminating suspected intelligence agents or infiltrators. The Wikibaghdady reports that ISIS created a four-man Saudi communications intelligence team tasked to carry out secret recording of their own members and rival commanders' telephones and radio communications. ISIS would then mark them for assassination or discredit them by playing the recordings.[8]

MANPOWER POOL

ISIS inherited all of the manpower of the previous iterations of AQI/ISI and broke off a large portion of its fighters in 2011 to go to Syria. That brought its manpower down from a conservative 5,000 in 2011 to what U.S. intelligence officials believe is 3,000 in Iraq today. The overwhelming number of ISIS manpower, perhaps as high as 7,000, is in Syria on the front lines against the al-Assad regime. There are as many as 20% of fighters in both branches who are foreign born (Figure 14.2).

The manpower pool of the ISIS has always been pan-Islamic. Even though ISIS is dominated by Iraqis, it still utilizes foreign volunteers as the basis of its suicide bomber pool. ISIS reports and videos in social media detail the biographies of its suicide bombers and fighters as being British, American, Australian, German, French, Russian, Egyptian,

FIGURE 14.2 British, American, and Australians fought in Syria and Iraq, like this one named Abu Muhammed al-Amriki. He joined the battalion of Chechen terrorist Abu Omar Shishani. According to his video, he "emigrated from America to Syria for joining the jihad."

Afghani, Norwegian, Pakistani, Moroccan, Algerian, Tunisian, Azeri, Chechen, Iraqi, Emirati, Saudi, and even an Uzbek from Denmark. Turkey claims that it has stopped 50,000 people trying to enter its borders to head to Syria to participate in the civil war. Most of those who do get through end up joining groups such as ISIS. European passport holders claim they are heading to tourist spots on the Aegean Sea coast, but go by smaller conveyance to Iskenderun and then by bus or taxi to the town of Rayhanli, where groups recruit at UN refugee camps.

Americans: Individual dual-passport holders have been known to have participated in the insurgency for years. There have been reports that in 2014 as many as 15 Somali Americans left Minnesota to join ISIS operations in Syria and Iraq.[9] Director of National Intelligence (DNI) James Clapper assesses there are more than 50 Americans fighting in Iraq and Syria for ISIS.

Australians: The largest numbers of foreign fighters per capita in ISIS are believed to be Australian citizens and dual-passport holders. Australian intelligence believes that there are as many as 300 Australian nationals fighting in ISIS.[10] Two Australian citizens were identified in a 2013 English language ISIS recruitment video.[11]

British: According to British intelligence, as many as 400 to 500 British are members of ISIS.[12] The former Chief of Mi6, Richard Barrett, told BBC that hundreds of former fighters from Syria and Iraq have returned home to the UK and were impossible to track.[13]

Central Asians (Tajiks, Afghans, Kazhaks): Large contingents of fighters that could not otherwise head to Afghanistan have found it easier to travel through Iran to Turkey and enter into Syria to perform their jihad. Many of these fighters bring their entire families with them, some with reportedly disastrous results. Reportedly the Syrian government targeted ISIS families for elimination while the fighters were off attacking government facilities.[14]

Egyptians: Egyptians have figured highly in the Iraq insurgency since 2003. In 2004 Abu Ayyub al-Masri, an Egyptian, took over command of AQI from Abu Mussab al-Zarqawi, a Jordanian. Egyptians in ISIS number in the hundreds according to Iraqi intelligence.

French, German, and Belgian: French journalists who embedded with ISIS and al-Nusra fighters found that there were as many as 500 French- and Belgian-speaking fighters who could not speak Arabic who took part in operations. They refer to themselves as l'Escuadron Franco-belge ("the French Belgian Squadron"). A unit of only German-speaking jihadists was also identified.

Some were present and posted to social media their participation in the ethnic cleansing and murder of civilians.[15]

Gulf Staters (Khalijis): Saudis, Emiratis, Qataris, Bahrainis, and Kuwaitis make up a sizable number of ISIS members. However, according to the Wikibaghdady Twitter leaks, the Saudis are not trusted and are generally tasked to die in suicide bomb attacks in order to ensure they do not defect to other groups or go home. An Emirati commander of an al-Nusra Front battalion was killed in Deir Az Zawr in 2013.

North Africans: The governments of Algeria, Libya, and Morocco know that ISIS has senior commanders from each of those countries. Libya, particularly the town of Deraa in eastern Libya, was a major contributor of fighters when ISIS was AQI. One of the top ISIS leadership is an Algerian named Abu Fatima Agehiche.

Russians (Caucasians): Groups of Azerbaijanis, Chechens, Daghestani, and Russian fighters have been documented as fighting and dying in Syria and Iraq under the ISIS flag since 2011. A group of 12 Azeris were killed in Syria fighting in 2013–2014.[16]

Scandinavians: Norway, Denmark, and Sweden have citizens who have left to participate in ISIS operations. According to terrorism expert Magnus Ransdorp, as many as 75 Swedes may be fighting in Syria. One Norwegian of Albanian birth was killed in Syria in 2014.

Tunisians: The government of Tunisia claims that it has stopped more than 6,000 men from going to Syria and Iraq. According to comments made in ISIS's annual report, there are entire units of Tunisian fighters in Syria and a significant number of commanders. The Wikibaghdady leaks claimed that Tunisians are the most loyal of foreign fighters to ISIS.

WOMEN OPERATIVES

Women had been generally relegated to family duties in ISIS, which was a direct change from the AQI model of using women in intelligence collection and suicide bombings. ISIS, being a more traditional group, only started using women in Syria to support its operations through the collection of charity and food, making meals, and attending to the medical needs of the fighters. Some ISIS-related groups such as the Ahrar al-Sham used women in intelligence collections and secure communications relay.

SEX JIHAD

In a practice never before seen in Islam, ISIS was quietly announcing to its members that women should be encouraged to come to Iraq and Syria for what is termed the Jihad al-Nikah, "sex jihad" (Figure 14.3). This bizarre assertion perplexed Middle East religious experts, as there is nothing in the Q'uran or Islamic texts such as the Hadiths where single unmarried women are encouraged to travel to a jihad zone and have sexual relations with multiple partners. ISIS documents state that it is designed to strengthen the Aqeeda, or deeply held spirit of Islamic faith of the fighters. It is also a way for women to participate in their jihad since they cannot fight. Tunisian Interior Minister Lotfi ben Jeddou announced that they had been intercepting women who were returning from Syria and claiming that had been performing the Jihad al-Nikah. The minister detailed the process:

> They have sexual relations with 20, 30, 100 militants.... After the sexual liaisons they have there in the name of 'jihad al-nikah'—(sexual holy war, in Arabic)—they come home pregnant.[17]

The sexual jihad was at the center of much discussion and propaganda. The Syrian government released television interviews of a girl who had

FIGURE 14.3 At the end of the al-Baghdadi invasion of northern Iraq this ISIS memorandum was distributed throughout Mosul demanding that "unmarried women offer themselves for Sex Jihad." It also warned of consequences under Sharia law for those who resisted.

allegedly been given by her father for Jihad al-Nikah. Documentation of the sex jihad blossomed again in 2014, after leaflets were spread throughout Mosul demanding that young, unmarried women should surrender themselves for sexual jihad duty to ISIS fighters. Forced and voluntary marriage is often a result of the Jihad al-Nikah. Women in Raqqa, Syria were forced to marry ISIS fighters. The weddings were closer to the Shiite-styled Muta marriages, or temporary marriages (a sort of legal short-termed prostitution), as they were expected to last only 2 months.[18] The King's College London's International Centre for the Study of Radicalization claims to have tracked four British women from London, Portsmouth, and Surrey who have already heeded this call and married fighters in ISIS.[19]

Most likely in response to the explosive charges that ISIS was using volunteer women as sex slaves and comfort women, ISIS announced in 2014 that two battalions of women would take part in combat operations in Syria. These were called the al-Khansaa and Umm al-Rayan Battalions (Figure 14.4).[20]

CHILD SOLDIERS

Like the Taliban in Afghanistan/Pakistan, al-Shabaab in Somalia, al-Qaeda in the Islamic Maghreb, al-Qaeda in the Arabian Peninsula, and

FIGURE 14.4 In response to charges that ISIS encourages foreign women to emigrate to Syria and Iraq for the purpose of engaging in sex jihad, it formed battalions of women jihadists. American, British, and European women serve in these units or collect intelligence for ISIS and its allies.

Boko Haram in Nigeria, neo-Salafist groups adhere to a bin Laden-inspired policy of self-isolation called Hijra. This is supposed to reflect the emigration away from the un-Islamic world, to live with like-minded individuals. These groups create families through marriage to local tribes or women who come to be part of the group. They are considered the future of the jihad and integral parts of the military operations once they are old enough to tote ammunition or handle a gun. Jihadists who have sons of fighting age bring them into the group as apprentices. Often young soldiers are recruited to learn the ways of jihad from the ground up and become future leaders. ISIS has used preteen and teen soldiers as intelligence collectors, communications signalers/message runners, ammunition mules, tea boys, and suicide bombers.

ISIS, during its invasion of Mosul, was seen with its fighters carrying into battle their sons as young as 5 and child soldiers aged 10, witnessing the execution of hundreds of Iraqi army soldiers (Figure 14.5).

FIGURE 14.5 The ISIS media arm distributed this photograph of a 13-year-old ISIS fighter carrying a Kalasnikov and allegedly wounded in battle. Although most likely propaganda, these images have a dramatic effect on recruitment of younger men.

PROPAGANDA AND SOCIAL MEDIA
AS ASYMMETRIC WEAPONS

The expansion of technology has changed how ISIS uses the Internet compared to its predecessors in AQI and other al-Qaeda affiliates. Not unlike the news media's facilitation of the Arab Spring, or the explosive protests over the film *Innocence of Muslims*, ISIS relies upon interconnecting the new generation of followers with easy-to-find media and communication tools. With quickly assembled pages on Twitter, YouTube, and Facebook, the modern extremist merely needs a cell phone with enough applications power to freely communicate widely. The jihadist no longer needs an office and desktop computer or thousand dollar digital cameras. The most remotely located individual with a cellular telephone signal can become a key communications node, a media reporting center, or an intelligence collector.

Most of the online graphics, videos, and memes used in ISIS were produced for no money outside the purchase of an app. They only needed access to a laptop or high-capacity cell phone. With pirated video software, the modern takfiri fighter can also produce nice presentations to convince the world that they are preceding the arrival of the perfect Islamic state. Free tutorials exist all over the Internet on how to master special effects for both Photoshop work and any number of popular video programs. Many phones now have apps that will do most of the work.

This evolution from previous propaganda work by al-Qaeda in Iraq and its sister organizations worldwide demonstrates the necessity to maintain information dominance in Internet messaging. Previously, AQI gained ground by using books, pamphlets, letters, and videos of lectures. They've moved from cassette tapes and Internet forums in the 1990s through fringe World Wide Web sites located on pop-up servers to today's capriciously used social media tools like Twitter, YouTube, and Facebook, and mobile phone-based apps via Google.

ISIS had a social media app developed called the Dawn of Glad Tidings that was listed in the Google store for Android phones. The app would allow users to sign in and allow their Twitter channels to be reused by ISIS to propagate their message. The app was eventually pulled from public distribution.[21]

When ISIS launched its campaign in Iraq in June 2014, it led the way with hundreds of tweets, photos, and a feature-length movie, *Clanging of the Swords IV*.[22] Locked solely to the images given to them, the TV media began to cover the videos from ISIS as "most brutal" ever seen. The coverage was often focused on videos of victims being murdered by ISIS or photos of beheadings or mass executions. ISIS uses Twitter to control the narrative when it wants to be seen as populist or to refute accusations that would undermine its efforts, not unlike past videos, where battle tales always emphasized the victories and dismissed losses. If a bombing like that in Baghdad station in August 2005 was unpopular, AQI would deny any involvement. Today ISIS parades a claim one day, until it becomes unpopular, and then comes the voice of reason.

The jovial nature of most posts indicates the core messengers often feel blissful about their gains, and that they are keenly aware of how the world follows trends via the Internet. They post the most horrifically graphic images of decapitations, eviscerations, crucifixions, strangulations, and rapes that shock. Each disgusting image is punctuated with thousands of supportive postings, written in the euphoric tones lauding the detail and mercilessness of the acts (Figure 14.6).

Internet providers did apply some limits. Individual ISIS members and supporters were kicked off of social media such as Twitter only to be mourned by their followers as if they themselves had been martyred.

FIGURE 14.6   ISIS is an extremely results-oriented terror group. Since 2010 it has put out an annual report with the details of its attacks to inspire new donors.

When they popped back up in another guise or username they were celebrated. Twitter was forced to delete accounts of users like @nnewsi that were streaming live coverage of the invasion of June 2014.[23] The postings of general followers often reflect extreme bitterness, less upon the United States or non-Muslims than to Nouri al-Malaki and their Shiite opponents. They generally assumed everyone in Mosul, Tikrit, and other conquered towns were happy and free to enjoy the new rule of ISIS. These perceptions have power when retweeted or redistributed via social media. They reinforce the internal perceptions no matter how wrong.

Many posts are directed under a series of hashtags (Twitter categories that place all posts into one stream of information) that are far harder to erase than a single account. The most prominent being #AllEyesonISIS, first created by user @ansaar999. Other hashtags were either local or fleeting. Minute by minute coverage of the expansion of their reach into Iraq is provided by these conversations, which also include feedback from Syria, Egypt, and other areas of the Arab-speaking world.

Perhaps most interesting about the coverage and the Twitter campaign itself was the coincidence of the World Cup being in the news on a daily level. ISIS took to using the World Cup in its campaign, including beheading an Iraqi police chief and posting: "This is our ball. It is made of skin. #WorldCup."[24]

When ISIS performs a shocking act, the media struggles to characterize it (Figure 14.7). ISIS seems very adept at lending a hand. The group itself handed out custom media packages. They showed a deep media savvy in projecting fear, power, and respect. Failing to understand how the tactics of the guerrilla marketer works, the major news media fumbles over the continual evolution of ISIS. Investigative journalists are more likely to follow the battles with each posting on Twitter as they search for clues behind the screen. ISIS's media organization is the careful development of propaganda honed over 20 years from other al-Qaeda affiliates. Their user base and operators are getting younger and more technically savvy, and this makes the ability to limit their propaganda more and more difficult.

It would need social media to sell its new caliphate to the Muslim world, and the hungry news media would assist them at every step. So instead of sending a fax or an e-mail, ISIS tweeted out its announcement of its goals on #caliphaterestored.

POPULIST WARFARE TOOLS

To pacify worried Muslims, ISIS engages in what could be termed populism warfare. That is, it brings services and traditional Islamic values and actions to chaotic environments they themselves may have created. First implemented by Hezbollah in Lebanon and the Taliban in

FIGURE 14.7   In August of 2014 ISIS started a campaign of beheading American and British citizens captured in Syria and posting the videos on social media. This strategy of spectacular beheadings was used successfully by al-Qaeda to incite rash and emotional responses by foreign governments from as early as 2002.

Afghanistan, ISIS in Syria and Iraq has brought in religious and social engineering support infrastructures to displace and act like a local government. Some components include:

Eliminating profiteering. ISIS units immediately enter into areas and restructure the ability of merchants and individuals to profit from or gouge clients in relation to the chaos that is visited upon them. ISIS establishes social safety nets such as free bread distribution, removes profiteering, and occasionally executes those who are trying to make money from ISIS actions. Cloaked in Islamic rhetoric, this has a positive effect on simple people who want violence to end and to live life simply.

Distributing food and charity to the poor. ISIS uses the Taliban model of the righteous itinerant knight who sacrifices and bestows goodness to the needy as a form of Zakat or charity. Usually these activities are considered equal in jihad to engaging in armed combat and lend a mythical Robin Hood status to their actions.

Offering letters of repentance and reconciliation councils. After removing opponents, ISIS commanders have the authority to establish truth and repentance courts. This is a system that allows those who have transgressed or supported transgressors to admit they were an opponent, promise to never get in the way of ISIS units again, and swear a blood oath of loyalty. In the Mosul offensive of 2014 this was necessary to ensure Sunni loyalist and community leaders did not betray their limited numbers. Given as a form of religious *carnet de passage*, each Bayan ("oath") to accept ISIS blessing is kept in a registry. This also acts to record and document those who could later be found and executed should they betray the community.

Run Sharia courts: Islamic guidance, jurisprudence, and negotiations—most operational areas will use commanders as a Qadi, or an appointed Islamic judge with which to execute Sharia law. Oftentimes commanders will co-opt or bring in with them a respected local imam to act in this role but according to the commander's wishes. The Qadi will negotiate disputes, pass judgment, and validate complaints or negate them according to ISIS's variation of Islamic law.

DOLING OUT ISLAMIC ACCEPTED PUNISHMENTS (HUDUD)

Punishments are outlined in the Sharia law as written in the Holy Qu'ran. It stipulates the acceptable and unacceptable limits (Hudud) on serious crimes. The three major categories of punishment are:

Capital punishments, such as beheading by sword for murder and crucifixion for only the most aggravated and heinous homicides. ISIS has been running a systematic campaign of murderous punishments all across Syria and Iraq, including crucifixion, beheading, strangling, and shooting captives through the head (Figure 14.8).

Adultery is punished in Sharia law by stoning to death, but under the neo-Salafist method, execution by gunfire is an acceptable substitute.

Theft is to be punished by amputation followed by medical care.

Human rights groups have frequently reported that ISIS views almost any offense as a capital offense, and most are subject to death by execution (Figure 14.9).

FIGURE 14.8   Crucifixion was a very popular ISIS execution technique. ISIS killed and displayed the bodies of its own fighters, its enemies, or civilians who displeased the commanders.

FIGURE 14.9   ISIS is believed to have executed this Syrian Christian woman for the crime of drinking beer, although it is allowed in her religion and protected by Islam.

ISIS also aggressively enforces among its fighters the policy of Takfir. They or their commanders may declare any Muslim who opposes them an infidel and treat them according to Sharia law. That allows any of their men to act as a judge, jury, and executioner to anyone they feel enmity toward. ISIS applies the literal reading of Surat al-Ma'idah, Qu'ran 5:33, as justification to kill anyone who gets in its path. This Sura reads:

> Indeed, the penalty for those who wage war against Allah and His Messenger and strive upon earth [to cause] corruption is none but that they be killed or crucified or that their hands and feet be cut off from opposite sides or that they be exiled from the land. That is for them a disgrace in this world; and for them in the Hereafter is a great punishment.[25]

FINANCE MECHANISMS

After they had looted approximately $450 million in cash and gold from the central bank of Mosul, ISIS is now considered the most well-financed terrorist group in the world. ISIS created many financial mechanisms to fund its operations over the last decade, but it has capitalized on its ability to gain funding from street-level activities in which each cell member can participate.

Infrastructure seizure: Al-Baghdadi believed that all infrastructures within the Syrian and Iraqi oil regions under Sunni control were the property of ISIS and a future source of oil revenue. Operation Lion of God Bilawi has the goal of seizing all of the major infrastructure in Sunni Iraq, including the Bayji oil refinery, Qayyarah oil field, and Haditha Dam.

Cash confiscation: ISIS soldiers and commanders, when given an area of operations, can elect to confiscate the money of any Christians, Kurds, Druze, Shiites, Assyrians, or anyone designated. This would be justified by calling it a donation to ISIS. Roadside shakedowns are where cash is stolen from all truckers entering into their areas of control. Abu Bakr al-Baghdadi bragged about the $200 per truck that his units were making.

Extortion and protection rackets: This is a routine criminal activity AQI/ISIS mastered early on in the insurgency. All business owners in ISIS-controlled areas were threatened with death or seizure of all their property if protection taxes were not paid monthly. In Sunni areas this was less than in areas of others, but the result of not paying was the same: swift execution of punishment through shooting, blowing up one's house with the family in it, or the rape and murder of family members. Any individual or group associated or doing business with the Iraqi central government resulted in the seizure of all resources or assassination.

Islamic taxes (Jizya) on non-Muslims: The Qu'ran specified that non-Muslims who live in the community are exempt from military service and paying mandatory charity (zakat). They are to be allowed to worship without fear. Since Muslims lived without taxes, in its place was a tax for non-Muslims called the Jizya. It was essentially eliminated by the 20th century, but ISIS saw it as a way to generate revenue in Syria and Iraq from the Christian, Assyrian, Druze, and Shiite communities under their control to fund terror operations. In Syria, ISIS went so far as to impose that the Jizya for Christians could only be paid in gold. It was so far out of line that even a hard-core Salafist theologian rejected it and called ISIS's actions un-Islamic.[26]

ENDNOTES

1. Al Arabiya Identifies the Leadership of ISIS Militant Group, retrieved from http://yalibnan.com/2014/02/14/al-arabiya-identifies-the-leadership-of-isis-militant-group/.

2. Preachers of Jihad, https://twitter.com/Mmmkadee.

3. Bassem Maroue, Key al-Qaida Militant Reported Killed in Syria, *Daily Star of Lebanon*, January 27, 2014, retrieved from http://www.dailystar.com.lb/News/Middle-East/2014/Jan-27/245450-activists-key-al-qaeda-militant-killed-in-syria.ashx#ixzz2ri0a5SxK.

4. Matthew Barber, New ISIS Leaks Reveal Particulars of al-Qaida Strategy, January 12, 2014, retrieved from http://www.joshualandis.com/blog/new-isis-leaks-reveal-particulars-of-al-qaida-strategy/.

5. Mazin Yayah, Iraq Forces Kill "War Minister" in Raid, Associated Press, November 25, 2011, retrieved from http://www.washington-post.com/wp-dyn/content/article/2011/02/25/AR2011022501803.html.

6. Al Arabiya Identifies the Leadership of ISIS Militant Group, retrieved from http://yalibnan.com/2014/02/14/al-arabiya-identifies-the-leadership-of-isis-militant-group/.

7. Al Arabiya Identifies the Leadership of ISIS Militant Group, retrieved from http://yalibnan.com/2014/02/14/al-arabiya-identifies-the-leadership-of-isis-militant-group/.

8. Yousef bin Tashfin, English Translations of the Wikibaghdady Twitter Feed, downloaded June 27, 2014, from http://justpaste.it/e90q.

9. http://www.dailymail.co.uk/news/article-2661727/Jihad-Cool-The-young-Americans-lured-fight-ISIS-militants-rap-videos-adventurism-hand-accounts-fun-guerrilla-war.html#ixzz356cztmVS.

10. Chris Uhlmann and James Glenday, Australian Jihadists Prompt Government to Consider New Security Rethink, ABC TV, June 23, 2014, http://www.abc.net.au/news/2014-06-23/australian-jihadists-prompt-government-to-consider-new-security/5542738.

11. Peter Lloyd, Australian Militants Abu Yahya ash Shami and Abu Nour al-Iraqi Identified in ISIS Recruitment Video, http://www.abc.net.au/news/2014-06-20/isis-fighter-identfied-as-an-australian-in-recruitment-video/5540116.

12. John Bew and Shiraz Maher, Blowback: Who Are Isis and Why Are Young Brits Fighting with Them? June 23, 2014, retrieved from http://www.newstatesman.com/uk-politics/2014/06/blowback-who-are-isis-and-why-are-young-brits-fighting-them.

13. Jonathan Owen, Syria Civil War: Hundreds of Radicalised Fighters Are Already Back in the UK, Warns Former MI6 chief, retrieved from http://www.independent.co.uk/news/uk/home-news/syria-civil-war-mi6-fears-the-jihadist-enemy-within-9554429.html.

14. ISIS: Syrian Brigade Massacred Families from Kazakhstan and Azerbijian. June 18, 2014, retrieved from: www.chechensinsyria.com/?P=22184

15. John Rosenthal, European Jihadists Form ISIS Brigades in Syria, retrieved from http://www.al-monitor.com/pulse/originals/2014/04/europe-jihadist-isis-syria-qaeda-terror-france-germany.html#.

16. Report: 12 Azeri ISIS Fighters Killed in Syria Last Week, retrieved from http://www.chechensinsyria.com/?p=21484.

17. Sex Jihad Raging in Syria, Claims Minister, Agence France Presse, retrieved from http://www.telegraph.co.uk/news/worldnews/middleeast/syria/10322578/Sex-Jihad-raging-in-Syria-claims-minister.html.

18. ISIS Forcing Raqqa Women to Wed Its Fighters, Say Activists, February 17, 2014, retrieved from http://www.aawsat.net/2014/02/article55329041.

19. British Women Headed to Syria for Jihad al-Nikah: Report, retrieved from http://en.alalam.ir/news/1567279.

20. Al-Qaeda in Syria Forms Female Brigades, February 2, 2014, retrieved from http://english.alarabiya.net/en/News/middle-east/2014/02/02/Syria-jihadist-group-ISIS-forms-women-only-battalions.html.

21. Paul Marks, How ISIS Is Winning the Online War for Iraq, June 25, 2014, retrieved from http://www.newscientist.com/article/dn25788-how-isis-is-winning-the-online-war-for-iraq.html#.U7HKVPldV8E.

22. Patrick Kingsley, Who Is Behind Isis's Terrifying Online Propaganda Operation? The Guardian, June 23, 2014, retrieved from http://www.theguardian.com/world/2014/jun/23/who-behind-isis-propaganda-operation-iraq.

23. Miriam Berger, Twitter Has Suspended an ISIS Account That Live-Tweeted Its Advance in Iraq, retrieved from http://www.buzzfeed.com/miriamberger/twitter-has-suspended-an-isis-account-that-live-tweeted-its.

24. How Isis Used Twitter and the World Cup to Spread Its Terror, AFP, retrieved from http://www.telegraph.co.uk/news/worldnews/middleeast/iraq/10923046/How-Isis-used-Twitter-and-the-World-Cup-to-spread-its-terror.html.

25. Holy Qu'ran, Surat Ma'idah 5:33, retrieved from http://quran.com/5/33.

26. Abu Qatada Denounces ISIS "Gold" Tax on Syrian Christians, Ammon, retrieved February 26, 2014, http://en.ammonnews.net/article.aspx?articleno=24470#.U6sN3GYg99A.

CHAPTER 15

Welcome to the Jihadist Crescent

[We] have been led in Mesopotamia into a trap from
which it will be hard to escape with dignity and
honour. [We] have been tricked into it by a steady
withholding of information. The Baghdad communiqués
are belated, insincere, incomplete. Things have been
far worse than we have been told, our administration
more bloody and inefficient than the public knows....
Our unfortunate troops, ... under hard conditions
of climate and supply, are policing an immense area,
paying dearly every day in lives for the willfully wrong
policy of the civil administration in Baghdad.

—T.E. Lawrence, *Sunday Times of London,* August 22, 1920

THE ISLAMIC CALIPHATE HAS ALREADY BECOME THE HEART OF AL-QAEDA

What is to be learned from studying the strategy and tactics of the Iraq terror insurgency? We have seen that they were not the paper targets depicted both before and after the invasion of Iraq. The 2014 Islamic State of Iraq and Syria (ISIS) iteration of the 2003 Iraqi insurgent now has a deep international corporate knowledge base and a vetting process that creates a terror careerist. These terror professionals are steeped in the al-Qaeda ideology of the "itinerant knight" who pilgrimages from battlefield to battlefield to fight the crusader here, or the apostate or the Jew in order to right the wrongs against their cultist version of Islam. Should they die trying, they reap the reward of God for their efforts. The fighting capacity of ISIS was only enriched by a decade of liaising with the men, strategy, and tactics from not one, but five former regime loy-alist intelligence agencies and the Saddam Fedayeen, one of the largest

Middle East commando forces. That joint insurgent marriage of convenience ended in 2009 with the Iraq Awakening due to al-Qaeda's own
brutal excesses against the Sunni tribes. However, after withdrawal of
U.S. forces from Iraq in 2011 and the decisions of Shiite Prime Minister
Nouri al-Maliki to shut the Sunni tribes out of the predominantly Shiite
government, the terror relationship reformed. The newly emboldened
and manned al-Qaeda joined by the other Iraqi groups and awakening
tribes, are now called ISIS. The winter 2014 offensive that seized large
parts of Sunni Iraq, including the cities of Fallujah, Ramadi, Mosul,
Tal Afar, Tikrit, Bayji, and Baqubah, and threatened the approaches to
Baghdad (Figure 15.1) is their Declaration of Independence.

The blood of many men and women has been shed to learn these and
many other lessons in the second Iraq war. These lessons should guide
us to understand what the risks are in future combat with a seemingly
easy-to-defeat enemy. A commitment must be made to avoid the painful
litany of mistakes made by both the Bush administration and the Iraqis
in underestimating the capacity of the terrorist neo-Salafists in fighting
for their goals multigenerationally.

Iraq from 2003 to 2014 proved to be a catalyst to radicalized young
men from around the world, who, had America and Britain not invaded,
would have skirted around the fringes of extremism but may not have

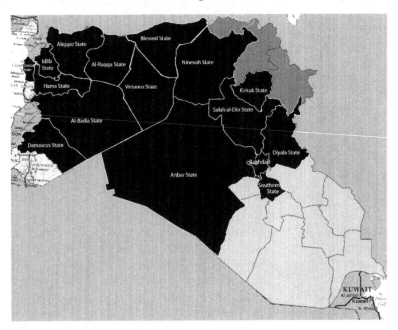

FIGURE 15.1   Map of the ISIS caliphate and its 16 subordinate states.

joined the al-Qaeda global jihad. Eleven years of continuous opportunity to strive for the heroism of war and the opportunity to die doing something greater than themselves has given the potential jihadist recruit a cause to strive toward, an opportunity for greatness and honor that would never have come otherwise. None of this had to be. The Middle East is in far more danger from destabilizing collapse of states due to the effects of the American invasion today than it has ever been.

As early as 2005, the CIA's National Intelligence Council (NIC) reported, "Iraq has now replaced Afghanistan as the training ground for the next generation of 'professionalized' terrorists" "providing a recruitment ground and the opportunity for enhancing technical skills."[1] The NIC also asserted that Iraq was a more effective training ground than Afghanistan: "The urban nature of the war in Iraq was helping combatants learn how to carry out assassinations, kidnappings, car bombings, and other kinds of attacks that were never the staple of the fighting in Afghanistan during the anti-Soviet campaigns of the 1980s."[1]

On the other hand, the same neoconservative politicians and media pundits that took America into Iraq in 2003 insisted in 2014 that the al-Qaeda terrorists were just paper targets that only need to stand still to be mowed down by superior American firepower. These same people who created the Iraq war on the basis of false claims of weapons of mass destruction completely ignored the fact that 8 years of American combat supremacy with an occupation army of 150,000 men and nearly unlimited firepower could not defeat the insurgents. All the while they blissfully ignored the fact that the best way to defeat the terrorists is the traditional method: remove popular support from the men and women who embrace a rejectionist ideology that has fringe appeal throughout many parts of the Muslim world.

Neither al-Qaeda in Iraq (AQI) in its day nor ISIS today is an invincible super army. They should not be made out as such. Each leader of the al-Qaeda terrorists, from Abu Musab al-Zarqawi to Abu Ayyub al-Masri to Abu Umar al-Baghdadi to Osama bin Laden himself, learned that being the supreme leader of al-Qaeda will eventually cost them their lives. Abu Bakr al-Baghdadi is but a mortal man and may find his delusions of a global caliphate most likely will burn as quickly as his body in a hailstorm of Hellfire missiles.

ISIS MAY TRY TO STRIKE AMERICA DIRECTLY

Another of the unfortunate habits of the U.S. government during its occupation of Iraq was the constant promotion of each Iraqi or foreign terrorist leader or terror groups as the next great direct threat to American national security (Figure 15.2). With regards to Iraq, this may

We will conquer Jerusalem, o Jews.
We will conquer Rome,

FIGURE 15.2   ISIS fighters in Mosul rant on how they will start operations outside of Iraq, including in the Gulf states, Israel, Europe, and the United States.

finally be true. After the June 2014 ISIS offensive on Mosul, Senator Lindsey Graham stated somewhat hyperbolically that he thought the tactical victories of ISIS would immediately bring about the next 9/11:

> I think it's inevitable. The seeds of 9/11 are being planted all over Iraq and Syria. You don't have to believe me, this is what they're telling you they're gonna do. They're not hiding their agenda. They want an Islamic caliphate.... They plan to drive us out of the Mideast by attacking us here at home.[2]

In some respects Senator Graham is far more correct in 2014 than the same breathless prognostications of 2003–2005.

As early as 2004, the Iraqi terrorist group Muhajirin wal Ansar threatened:

> Prepare yourselves, O' mean, terrorist, and lying Americans! For we will teach you lessons that you will not forget as long as you live about sacrifice and martyrdom for the sake of the homelands and the defense of honor, principles, and values ... you will see blacker days than the 11 September incidents.[3]

However, striking the American homeland remains the strategic goal of almost every al-Qaeda-inspired group, from Yemen to Somalia and to Nigeria to Mali. Any successful attack on America, inspired or planned regionally, brings notoriety and fame within the jihadist ranks. For a time it was al-Qaeda of the Arabian Peninsula (AQ-AP) in Yemen, after their leader Anwar al-Awlaki inspired the pistol attack in Fort Hood by

U.S. Army Maj. Nidal Hassan, or when they dispatched bombs in printers on a UPS airliner, or when they sent the Nigerian underwear bomber to blow up a plane over Detroit. Any al-Qaeda group that claims capacity to strike the United States or Europe and can succeed reaps a coup in terror shock value (TSV), which in turn brings more recruits, money, and the desired effect of being the target of America's wrath.

Many potential terrorists could slip past the safety net of American security. The Americans, British, Europeans, and Australians on "vacation" in Turkey (in other words, having infiltrated to Iraq and Syria and fighting for ISIS) could be the next wave of returnees. They could bring with them the seeds of ISIS's ideology and the skills of hard-core Islamic extremists who seek to do true harm to our interests or people or they could be human guided weapons. Some of them will return and may determine that one well-placed strike would send a chilling message to their home country greater than all the combat in Iraq over a decade.

For ISIS's Iraqi terrorists, they too have opportunity to infiltrate agents into the west. Iraq is a sovereign nation with relatively open access to the rest of the world. Émigrés and businessmen from Iraq are now traveling all over the world. Families are moving from Iraq to the West. For all of the systems put into place, the invasion facilitated a much simpler and more difficult counterintelligence nether world of easily forged and purchased passports and documents. In 2004, during the second assault on Fallujah, an entire passport and document manufacturing safe house was found filled with forged new Iraqi government documents, including digital passports. In Sadr City's Umm' Raidi market, former government passport officials can copy or forge birth certificates and other documents. Ten years later, in 2014, with the loss of the northern Iraqi cities of Mosul, Tikrit, Tel Afar, and Ramadi, thousands of valid Iraqi passports, documents, and millions of dollars were taken by ISIS from government offices. Government officials can be bribed to provide a real Iraqi passport if the money is right, and ISIS may utilize this windfall to get some resources into place quickly while the West struggles with responding to its activities in Iraq.

Even though America has long left Iraq, the motivation for Iraqi-Syrian-based terrorists to carry out a revenge attack on the American homeland is not just tempting—they view it as a holy obligation. A successful attack by an ISIS martyr in the United States would strike a serious blow to the will of the American people as a whole to remain engaged in the Middle East. Then again, it could galvanize America to engage in a global campaign for the absolute elimination of ISIS and al-Qaeda. The only benefit for ISIS is that the perception generated is the wrath of the United States would come down on all Muslims, not just terrorists. This in turn would enhance recruiting and prove once again to the skeptical that all Muslims are America's enemy. No matter what is done, the jihadists will approve.

Striking at the United States and Europe has a complex matrix of risks. Although Abu Bakr al-Baghdadi, now Caliph Ibrahim the First, thinks he has defeated the West and cowed them from the risk of combating him directly, the capacity to strike Iraq remotely and relentlessly through the use of multiple classes of drones has expanded exponentially since 2003. A dedicated drone campaign would risk no American lives and bring about the same intensity of aerial bombardment that existed when America was actually in Iraq. ISIS may be enjoying its moment under the sun, but with American power, if coupled with Iraqi, Iranian, and possibly Saudi and European assets and even rudimentary Iraqi army offensives, the ISIS jihadists could find themselves back on the deserts of eastern Syria dreaming of that time when they ruled Islam.

DRINKING ANTIFREEZE: THE IRAQI SUNNI'S MASS SUICIDE PACT OF 2014

In the 2007 edition of this book I made the prediction that AQI would seek to merge all insurgent groups into a terrorist supergroup capable of seizing terrain. The al-Qaeda super group would declare a caliphate and move on to a traditional phase III of the insurgency where they gain tanks and military units and roll into Baghdad. It was an easy prediction, as virtually all of their ideological rhetoric and actions aimed toward this eventuality. Little did I know they would also seize half of Syria in the bargain. However, the only way that any of these goals could be achieved was to have the complicity and cooperation of the Sunni tribes of Iraq.

The Sunni tribes that allowed for the 2014 incursion to happen thought they were being clever. Angry with their lack of political opportunity, they supposed that ISIS would come in and terrorize the al-Maliki regime. That much was true. They also supposed that their tribal chiefs would eventually negotiate a favorable agreement with the government, which would benefit them greatly. Their biggest error may have been in believing that they held the cards against ISIS's continued existence in Anbar and northern Iraq. It is a surety that the chiefs believed that once they extract concessions out of the al-Maliki or a follow-on government, they could force ISIS's departure by threatening or starting another Sunni Awakening. If this version of the triple double-cross was in their planning, then it was akin to drinking antifreeze. The Sunni tribes of Iraq do not realize that they not only cooperated with ISIS, but also surrendered to them. ISIS, and its brutal corruption of Islam, is the leading power in the Sunni provinces. It is their women that ISIS will force their families to marry. It is their declared caliphate. In the mind of Abu Brak al-Baghdadi, now Caliph Ibrahim, there is no longer a Sunni tribal system or Iraqi governorates, just subordinate regions of his neo-Salafist never-never land.

With the announcement of the establishment of the ISIS caliphate added to the fact that they have a half billion dollars in cash and gold and are recruiting thousands of foreign fighters to return to Iraq, the Iraqi Sunni will no longer control their own destinies. Apart from land and manpower, ISIS needs nothing from these sheikhs except unwavering obedience. This time the Iraqi Sunni leadership have signed their own death warrants in the form of willful pledges to a terrorist leader who would rather kill them than negotiate with them.

In my past interviews with Sunni Muslims in both Iraq and Syria, they saw the al-Qaeda/al-Nusra Front and ISIS members as a sort of special forces necessary to make the point that pain could be brought to the government of Iraq if they did not behave well. The Sunni saw ISIS as fellow insurgents, but not as rulers. As horrible as the beheadings of hostages were during the 2004–2009 reign of terror, the TSV perpetrated by AQI during its time was almost always successful. As lead terror group, they brought enormous international pressure on the new Iraqi government and the Americans to make the political concessions necessary to create the Iraq Awakening in 2009. Removing the Sunni insurgents from the equation in turn led to the U.S. withdrawal in 2011 and the near destruction of al-Qaeda.

The circumstances that led to the Anbar Awakening may never happen again the way they did in 2007–2009. At that time the Sunni community and its insurgent group, the Ansar al-Sunnah, were the heart of the insurgency. They had 25,000 active combatants and as many as 88,000 part-time and supporting insurgents. When they came over to the Awakening councils, they brought with them all of the necessary manpower and weapons to fight off AQI. At that time they could easily push AQI out of the major cities and into the Iraqi outback. Iraqi terror groups that remain, such as the Naqishbandi, are far too small to make a difference except in the area of Mosul and Tikrit.

It should be noted that the Americans biometrically and photographically documented all of them by name: family name, names of distant relatives on mother's and father's side. These data bases are in the hands of ISIS (Figure 15.3). It will allow them to root out and kill or blackmail the entirety of all Awakening participants. When Anbar and Mosul fell to ISIS, the world witnessed the capitulation of a 5-million-strong Sunni community to a terrorist group.

The 11 years of al-Qaeda in Mesopotamia has seen the small al-Zarqawi-led Jordanian group Tawhid Wal-Jihad (TWJ) open its arms to foreign-born suicide fighters and transform into al-Qaeda fi Bilad

FIGURE 15.3   Like the FARC terrorists in Colombia, ISIS learned early that detailed cloud-based computer data were critical to identifying its enemies. After the fall of Mosul, ISIS used captured Iraq/U.S. biometric databases of Iraqi government and military personnel records to capture soldiers, intelligence officers, and government employees at city checkpoints.

al-Rafidayn (AQI). The almost exclusively foreign fighters of AQI then morphed into the closely cooperating Mujahideen Shura Council (MSC) that allowed Iraqis to make decisions in the terror strategy. The MSC declared the Islamic Emirate of Iraq (IEI) and, with guidance from bin Laden, subsequently renamed itself the Islamic State of Iraq (ISI) and took on Iraqi leaders. Finally, the ISI finally merged the best of all Iraqi Islamic resistance groups with the loyal al-Nusra Front fighters of Syria to become the more combat experienced ISIS. They have many more foreign jihadists than they did at their peak of 2006, and many more will emigrate to take their place and establish a home within the Iraqi-led caliphate. ISIS lost thousands of fighters and killed tens of thousands more Iraqis, Syrians, and Americans to become the new rulers of the Syrian and Iraqi Sunni communities. They will not let this go without a fight to the death.

ISIS has already started making the occupied communities swear loyalty to their leadership—or else. Although ISIS is now the "Islamic caliphate," its men will show no interest in ruling municipalities or restoring water, power, and sewage. After a few months of dealing with the day-to-day corruption and spitefulness of Iraq's byzantine internal politics, they will start to lose their battle edge, but not their ruthlessness. What ISIS commanders will do is enjoy their newfound power. They will exact an extremely painful level of control over the Sunni population that will make them regret the very moment they fooled themselves into believing Maliki was worse than Saddam, and that ISIS could relieve the pressure of political indecision.

ISIS has metamorphosed into what both bin Laden and al-Zarqawi wanted AQI to be—an uncontrolled group of itinerant knights and full of what the Pakistanis call "Jusbah E Jihad," the "intoxication of jihad," ready to establish a Taliban-like country in the heart of the Middle East and branch out to take Lebanon, Palestine, and take on Israel.

What will happen inside the future ISIS caliphate is simple. Opposition will mean death. Will the Sunni tire of this again and revolt? Recall that when AQI started killing the Sunni leadership of Anbar and other governorates, the Sunni community revolted and came over to the Awakening. There is no coming over to the Americans or the Shiites now. The Iraqi Sunni has opened Pandora's box.

ISIS's most likely course of action is enforcement of religious and political purity. It will conduct an ethnic cleansing of the northern cities of anyone who does not embrace its neo-Salafist ideology. Anyone with a history of collaboration with the Shiites, the Iraqi government, or who worked for the Americans will swear loyalty by blood oath or die. Merchants doing commerce with the Turks, Iranians, Assyriacs, or Kurds, and religious groups such as Christians, Shebaks, Yazidis, Yarsani, and perhaps even the Sufi Muslims or other Iraqis, and who seek to hide ISIS's cut of their income, may be ruled an infidel or apostate and killed. That means even the tribal leaders. After some measure of purity is attained, they would start to hunt the ex-Ba'athists in their midst. Since most Iraqi ex-Ba'athist insurgent groups worked with Syria's Bashar al-Assad and headquartered their command in Damascus, they will be fair game. After the ex-Ba'athists are terminated, the time will come for anyone who participated in the Awakening. No Iraqi Sunni Muslim, unless they swear their undying loyalty to ISIS, will pass the purity test for the new caliphate. Anyone from the newly occupied caliphate will be welcome to start at the bottom and show their dedication to the cause by driving a suicide vehicle-borne improvised explosive device (S-VBIED) into an enemy target. Those who stick their heads up might have them literally cut off.

Unless ISIS is engaged militarily, its lines of communication and resupply cut off, and its most loyal fighters killed off, it will grow into a mortal threat far beyond the borders of Iraq and Syria. In Iraq, ISIS may eventually make the Iraqi-Syrian nether region look like Phnom Penh after Pol Pot's Year Zero. There won't be a general genocide, but the impure leaders and past collaborators will have to be culled. The entire concept of Jihadist Hijra (emigration away from the impure, including abandoning all past family ties) is to create a community that is white and unblemished, where al-Wala wal Bara (swearing loyalty to God and rejecting un-Islamic things, such as Coca-Cola, Persian tea, or discussions of the World Cup) is the way life, where the only person one can trust is another jihadist. ISIS will want everyone to reject the Iraqi traditions and old ways, all old ways, and to stay away from anyone or anything they cannot completely dominate. This is the cult of al-Qaedaism.

The strategic vision of ISIS is to make the caliphate reflect a "Sunni crescent"—from Jerusalem to Baghdad and eventually to Mecca and Medina. It is a strategic game playing out that may take another decade or two. Its shock-and-awe campaigns worked because of their inherent terror shock value (TSV), and its social media campaign scared everyone. So it will be forced to scare the entire globe to achieve its goals and limit actions taken against it as it incrementally crawls toward a cultic victory.

I fear ISIS will have no intention of going back to being a small insurgent group. It will attempt to consolidate captured terrain. It will offer the Sunni a chance to rule under it at the technocrat level, but that's when the pogroms will start.

In the end, the Islamic caliphate will attempt and fail at creating a popular Iraqi-Syrian nation out of stolen governorates. But unless confronted quickly and forcefully, it may become an isolated jihadistan from which no end of terror will spawn.

ENDNOTES

1. Dana Priest, Iraq New Terror Breeding Ground, *Washington Post*, January 14, 2005.
2. Graham: Next 9/11 Attack Could Come from Iraq, Syria, http://www.cbsnews.com/news/sen-lindsey-graham-next-911-attack-could-come-from-iraq-and-syria/.
3. Statement No. 1 Issued by the Muhajirin wa al-Anser, Baghdad Branch, Foreign Broadcast Information Service, April 4, 2004.

Index